"*The 21st-Century Intranet* is a triumph, as Gonz insightful framework for successful Intranet deployme... lively and pragmatic road map full of examples on how to (and how not to) build and manage these machines of the knowledge economy. In spite of the dramatic potential benefits of Intranet computing, to date there have been more Intranet failures than successes, so too many have underestimated the challenges of Intranet deployment. Gonzalez provides an approach which is both holistic and pragmatic, outlining not only the technical but also the human and behavioral issues that must be addressed to harness the remarkable power of Intranet computing. This book is required reading for any "intranet champion" who wants not only to make sense of the recent dramatic changes in technology, but to capitalize on them."

—Malcolm Frank
Vice President, Cambridge Technology Partners

"*The 21st-Century Intranet* is chock full of pragmatic advice for sucessfully designing and implementing your company's intranet."

—Dick Baumbusch
President, The Knowledge Advantage Group

"Dr. Gonzalez has added a valuable contribution to our understanding of a critical new business communications technology. In particular, she adds depth to the analysis of the critical interplay between Intranet deployment and corporate culture and communications which will outlive rapidly evolving technologies."

—Keven Han
Chief Information Architect, Just in Time Solutions, Inc.

"Gonzalez's book is a very useful guide for technological change agents. It's practical, well-researched, and filled with stories about real-life implementation experiences.

—Mary E. BoonePresident, Boone Associates
Author of *Leadership and the Computer*

"Jennifer Stone Gonzalez has created an outstanding analysis of the benefits and challenges of developing Intranets. *The 21st-Century Intranet* reveals a deep understanding of the cultural and organizational issues underlying the Intranet phenomenon and should be required reading for developers, consultants, and managers alike. As someone who lives and breathes corporate Intranet development on a daily basis, I find the *The 21st Century Intranet* transcends the trivia of speeds and feeds and instead delivers a higher vision of the value Intranets can bring to any organization."

—Richard S. Gaston, Jr.
Business Development Manager, Sage Solutions, Inc.

"A key learning from this book is to balance people and technology during Intranet development. I enjoyed the "cultural" and ethnographic stories in this book which convey a powerful message to all Intranet developers—'build the tool, but to be real cool, add folk to the pool.' *The 21st Century Intranet* extends beyond a promise of easy publishing, flash graphics and interactive scripts to the core values of knowledge creation, innovation through idea recombination, trust and community."

—Denham Grey
President, GreyMatter Inc.

"Jennifer Stone Gonzalez has written the definitive handbook for IT professionals pondering the bewildering array of technologies relentlessly coming down the pike. The good news is that you don't have to replace your computer systems. It's about alignment, not replacement."

—Alan Chamberlain
Strategic Planning Analyst, Bay Networks

"An indispensable guide for getting the most from technology investments. Jennifer Stone Gonzalez demystifies the confusion for the technologist and business manager alike."

—Maynard Webb
Vice President and CIO, Bay Networks

"This book is clearly for leaders, key decision makers and strategic planners. Jennifer Stone Gonzalez has taken the mysticism of the Internet and made it practical for the layperson and daily business use. I suggest [this book] for all leaders who want their organizations to be vital and competitive in the knowledge economy. More than likely your customers and competitors have a copy."

—Charles L. Fred
President, International Learning Systems
Author of *The Race to Proficieny*

"*The 21st-Century Intranet* is a powerful guide for the worker of the future. This book will help us all understand and adapt to the profound realities of intranet communication. Don't be left behind in the world of the past—read this book and move into the future."

—Bruce Tulgan
President, Ranmaker, Inc.
Author of *Managing Generation X*

The 21st-Century Intranet

ISBN 0-13-842337-7

The 21st-Century Intranet

Jennifer Stone Gonzalez

To join a Prentice Hall PTR Internet mailing list, point to
http://www.prenhall.com/mail_lists/

Prentice Hall PTR, Upper Saddle River, NJ   07458

Library of Congress Cataloging-in-Publication Date

Gonzalez, Jennifer Stone
      The 21st-Century Intranet/Jennifer S. Gonzalez.
            p.   cm.
      Includes index.
      ISBN 0-13-842337-7
      1. Intranets (Computer networks) I. Title.
TK5105.875.I6G66   1997   97-29162
658'.0546--DC21   CIP

Editorial/Production Supervision: Nicholas Radhuber
Acquisitions Editor: Mark Taub
Editorial Assistant: Tara Ruggiero
Marketing Manager: Dan Rush
Buyer: Alexis Heydt
Cover Design: Jeannette Jacobs
Cover Design Direction: Jerry Votta
Interior Design: Gail Cocker-Bogusz

Prentice Hall books are widely used by corporations and government agencies
for training, marketing, and resale.

The publisher offers discounts on this book when ordered in bulk quantities.
For more information, contact: phone: 800-382-3419; fax: 201-236-7141;
e-mail: corpsales@prenhall.com, or write:
Corporate Sales Department
Prentice Hall PTR
One Lake Street
Upper Saddle River, NJ 07458

Printed in the United States of America

10 9 8 7 6 5 4

ISBN 0-13-842337-7

Prentice-Hall International (UK) Limited, London
Prentice-Hall of Australia Pty. Limited, Sydney
Prentice-Hall Canada Inc., Toronto
Prentice-Hall Hispanoamericana, S.A., Mexico
Prentice-Hall of India Private Limited, New Delhi
Prentice-Hall of Japan, Inc., Tokyo
Pearson Education Asia Pte. Ltd., Singapore
Editora Prentice-Hall do Brasil, Ltda., Rio de Janeiro

"Given the right circumstances, from no more than dreams, determination, and liberty to try, quite ordinary people consistently do extraordinary things."

—Dee Hock, Founder,
The Chaordic Alliance

Contents

SECTION THREE
Future Proof Design   145

Chapter   7
Contexts for Intranet Communication 145

Chapter   8
A "Preferred Product". 167

Chapter 9
The Value Triad 189

Chapter 10
The Case for Dialog as a Design Premise 213

SECTION FOUR
Intranet Development Methodologies   227

Chapter   16
Designing the Open Network 343

Chapter   17
Communicating with Management 359

SECTION SIX
Resources   **375**

Chapter   18
Cybrarians and Other Secrets of Cyberspace 375

Chapter   19
Tool Kit 381

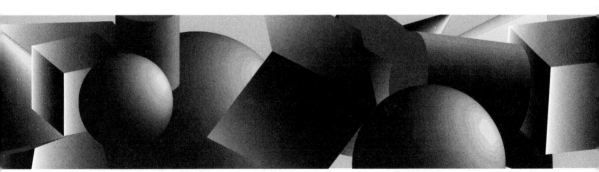

Preface

Jim Collins, co-author of *Built to Last: Successful Habits of Visionary Companies,* has argued that "the next wave of enduring great companies will be built not by technical or product visionaries but by social visionaries—those who see their company and how it operates as their ultimate creation and who invent entirely new ways of organizing human effort and creativity."

This book was written with those visionaries in mind. I wanted to write a book for people within organizations who have a genuine desire to improve communication within their companies, educational institutions, consulting firms and nonprofit organizations, and who also wish to use web-based technologies as one of their tools. The materials in this book are based on my experiences developing internal web sites, intranets and knowledge-sharing systems for a half-dozen large corporations. More importantly, the materials are also based on the experiences of my colleagues who very generously shared their knowledge about intranet development with me, and gave me permission to include their work here. I owe many debts of gratitude for, as the "Acknowledgments" points out in some detail, I could not have begun to write this book alone.

The book reflects two of my core beliefs about technology and communication. I believe first that technology can be beneficial when it is used to amplify human intelligence which is abundant but squandered. Second, the key to greater productivity and wealth is not more control or measurement, but rather better communication so that knowledge can surface, become visible and can be put to use.

As I was writing the book, a serendipitous event occurred. I was introduced via the web to Douglas C. Engelbart by Howard Rheingold. A Silicon Valley legend, Engelbart invented the mouse, conceived the use of multiple windows on computer screens, invented groupware and hypertext (the system of nodes and links that is the basis of the World Wide Web), and was the first to augment electronic mail with files and graphics. He was among first to receive information over the ARPANET, the foundation for the Internet, when Vinton Cerf sent the first packets of data from UCLA to the Stanford Research Institute. Recently, Englebart at 72 was awarded the enormously prestigious Lemelson-MIT prize for his technology inventions.

Several years ago, Englebart founded the Bootstrap Institute with the belief that organizations need to build the capacity to get better at getting better. Every organization, he argues has a *"capability infrastructure"*—what we use to do our jobs. There is also an *"improvement infrastructure"*—things we do to get better at getting better.

Englebart says that we typically spend a great deal of time, energy and resources on the capability infrastructure. We try to improve the "human system" by designing new organizational structures, by devoting resources to employee training and development, by creating policies and procedures, and by restructuring manufacturing processes. Organizations also devote plenty of resources to augmenting the human system with a "tool system" comprised of computers, office facilities, vehicles and other equipment. We tend to focus on these things, Englebart says, because they are tied to sales and to profits.

Englebart argues, however, that the correct way to become resilient and able to increase wealth is to pay more attention to the "improvement infrastructure"—things that improve an organization's ability to improve. In the past decade, various improvement strategies have moved across the horizon from reengineering to aggressive use of new information technologies to "knowledge management." The gains expected from such activities have been slow to materialize. Why? Englebart argues that while technological change has raced ahead, the human system lags. We are still focused around projects and task forces with short-term expectations and short-term lifecycles, and have been too much in love with chasing after the latest tools and technologies.

The most important activity we can do to develop the improvement infrastructure, Engelbart says, is to encourage and fund cross-functional "improvement communities" whose members work on common challenges to explicitly improve improvement. Such communities have an existence that is at once dependent upon yet separate from each member's independent existence. Although people may circulate in and out of the organization, the community retains a life of its own, and the community itself becomes a knowledge accelerator.

In essence, the human network, supported with a stable, sound technology network, is the way to get better at getting better. It is my hope that this book will help to advance the concept of the network as not only the starting place for organizational change, but as the desired end state. We are all in this together.

I look forward to hearing from you.

Jennifer Stone Gonzalez
www.luminella.com

Executive Summary

Developing an intranet is one of the most rewarding things you can do for your company or organization. Being an intranet champion is an opportunity to

- Participate in a media revolution that is profoundly affecting the way we think about and use information.

- Significantly improve the ways in which people in your organization communicate.

- Extend your skill set and add greater value to your organization.

Intranet champions have a window to the future, and the opportunities are tremendous.

Fueled by media attention, interest in intranets is growing at a phenomenal rate. Forrester Research reported that the majority of U.S. companies either have an intranet, plan to get it or are studying it. Intranets have made the cover of *Business Week* and other major publications. *Fortune* magazine spotlighted intranets in its top ten list of technology trends ("The Next Big Thing," they wrote).[1] Intranets can be found in corporations, small businesses, government organizations, schools and universities, hospitals, consulting firms, advertising agencies, and nonprofit organizations.

■ Intranet Definitions

An intranet is any private transmission control protocol/Internet protocol (TCP/IP) network that supports internet applications—primarily web (hypertext transfer protocol [HTTP]), but also other applications such as file transfer protocol (FTP). Intranet web servers and browsers work the same way they do on the World Wide Web (the Web), except that information on an intranet is protected by a firewall which secures the network from external use.

You may have heard the term *web-centric intranet*. It refers to a development environment based on web technologies with other systems radiating from it. The term *web-centric* is meant to distinguish a web-based intranet from other forms of internal network communication systems, such as those comprised of an e-mail system, a database system and a groupware system, all accessed over a common local area network (LAN) or wide area network (WAN). Throughout this book, the term *intranet* means "web-based." To use an organization's intranet, an employee or member of the organization uses a web browser to tap into the organization's own universe of network-accessible information, in the same way they would use a web browser to access the World Wide Web and other parts of the Internet (the Net).

> The premise of the book is that a successful intranet provides long-term value to an organization. It enhances job performance and extends an organization's capabilities. An intranet can be used to build organizational capacity and to facilitate learning. *A successful intranet is one that becomes essential to the way a company does business.*

Creating an intranet would seem easy. Compared with the information technologies that were available previously, intranets have some obvious advantages, such as lower costs, ease of use, shorter development cycles, and the ability to use existing hardware and network infrastructures.

■ The Computer Industry's Rush Toward Intranets

In the history of computing and data processing, this is the first time that a new technology has gained this level of acceptance so quickly. The consequences for Silicon Valley have been profound. The race to develop new internet and intranet technologies is intense and extraordinarily competitive. Sun, Netscape, Compaq, Digital Equipment, Hewlett-Packard, IBM, and Silicon Graphics see huge markets for work stations, server computers, and network-management software. Netscape, Microsoft, Apple, and many other companies are competing to develop the best web authoring and editing tools. Millions of dollars are literally at stake in what has been described as the cyber equivalent of the Western gold rush. The hype and exaggerations about intranets are hardly surprising.

■ Unexpected Challenges "Behind the Scenes"

For people who want to develop intranets, the amount of energy being focused on intranet product development has both benefits and drawbacks. When you stand inside your organization and look outward, it seems as though everyone "out there" understands the value of intranet technologies and how to put them in place. Other companies and organizations seem to be racing confidently toward the future of intranet-based computing. "This is so fantastic," you think. "This is what I want to do for my organization." Then you look inward and find a different reality. Developing and implementing intranets turns out to be more difficult than the media or trade shows would suggest.

Intranet proponents typically meet unanticipated barriers and roadblocks, including "turf battles," skepticism from upper management, and difficulty securing employees' ongoing participation. Many groups launch internal web sites, enthusiastic about the promise of the technology, only to see their budgets and staffs cut later, when employee use wanes and management no longer believes that the web development costs are justified.

Other intranet developers find the opposite situation to be the case: success brings added responsibility and headache, but insufficient recognition or reward. Often, the work of intranet champions is most appreciated by front-line employees whose jobs are made easier over time by improved communication and access to information. Senior management doesn't seem to recognize how the evolution of the organization's intranet has affected revenue streams, profits, cost of goods sold, or even employee job satisfaction.

■ The Purpose of the Book

This book is written to help intranet champions increase the value of their intranet to the organization, thereby ensuring the long-term success of the project. The focus is on strategies to overcome barriers and roadblocks to that success. It's a roadmap of sorts and provides useful guidelines for people who are just starting to work on intranet development, as well as for those who are further ahead on the journey. The project plans and flowcharts were developed to enable intranet champions to work efficiently and systematically. The stories and tips come from intranet webmasters who have developed intranets in a variety of organizational settings. They've already faced many hurdles and roadblocks, and they offer valuable insights.

■ Three Main Challenges of Intranet Work and How This Book Can Help

Typically, people who want to implement intranets will face three issues: a) identity of the intranet proponents; b) measurement of results; and c) intranet ownership structure (centralization versus decentralization).

This book addresses basic "What and Why" questions, such as:

- What is an intranet?
- Why is it a unique communication medium?
- What are the advantages of an intranet over groupware such as Lotus Notes?

The book also provides guidance on:

- Discovering which features add value to the intranet.

- Involving senior management.
- Creating order out of chaos when dozens of groups decide to create their own sites.
- Motivating employees to migrate to the intranet as their preferred communication medium.
- Assuaging anxieties about how the intranet changes the way people work.

The book also addresses issues that are at the heart of intranet aspirations:

- Measuring your success and knowing whether your intranet is truly adding value.
- Making your success visible to senior management.
- Turning a "labor of love" into a career opportunity.

Clearly, successful intranet development requires a lot of work and a lot of coordination. Because there are so many issues involved with intranet development – both technical and non-technical issues—this book offers a five-phase macro plan that can be used as an overarching template. The steps include establishing a network of people who can make contributions to the project, developing a convincing narrative about why an intranet is important to the organization, creating test sites or pilot projects, and gradually transforming the organization's use of web technology. The plan is laid out in the review part of this section.

NOTE: Throughout this book, there are many references to articles, essays, and other things located on the Web. These are underlined, and their URLs are listed by chapter at the end of the book in the section entitled "Hyperlinks."

■ Communication and Persuasion Are the Focus of This Book

One of the reasons to read this book is to discover ways to convince upper management to invest in the creation or extension of a reliable networking environment that is secure and scalable. The technology infrastructure is absolutely essential. It is crucial to ensure that your network exists, that it can be accessed by local and remote staff, and that it can support the increased traffic that the web creates.

It is not always the case that MIS alone can determine the quality and reach of the networking infrastructure. A convincing business plan, a communication needs analysis, and/or an intranet project plan can strengthen the argument for why an organization should develop a better network or should add resources such as additional technical staff.

The technological network by itself is not enough. One of the main points in this book is that if you approach intranets from a solely technical perspective, the returns on your investment in time, energy, and money will be slow to materialize. Applying a new technology to old-fashioned work designs is like "paving the cowpaths," so to speak. All of glitter and hype in the media about intranets won't make the path any easier to travel. A multitiered, interdisciplinary approach, on the other hand, views the intranet not simply as a fantastic technology, but as something galvanizing and stimulating—a significant *event* to be leveraged as a way to help people in the organization work differently and more effectively. If intranet development in your organization seems easy and uncomplicated, this book outlines ways to have greater impact. If it seems difficult, this book illumines why it's difficult and gives strategies for turning counterforces into advantages.

Part of an intranet champion's job is to understand how web technology works, what it costs, and what is required to maintain it. That kind of knowledge is important, and this book addresses such issues. However, the technical side of intranet development is not the primary emphasis. There are many other sources of information about web page design and web site construction and many good books on TCP/IP, UNIX, SGML (Standard Generalized Markup Language), HTML, Java, firewalls and so on.

For people who are new to intranets, especially those without a background in computers, a good place to begin to learn about technical issues is _Intranet Design_ magazine's "Intranet FAQ." A terrific guide to using visual design to communicate information and engage audiences is <u>David Siegel's</u> <u>_Creating Killer Web Sites_ and the up-to-date companion web site</u>. It's good to be familiar with the Web's features as unique visual communication medium and as an information technology. Working knowledge facilitates dialog with other intranet champions. It also makes it easier to envision what type of intranet would be most useful to your organization. You'll also have a better idea about what is required to build in the kind of sites you envision.

■ Setting the Stage: Stepping "Back In Time"

In the next chapter, we begin with some background on how the Internet and the Web came into being. The history highlights the fact that intranets are actually not a later development. The media often gives the impression that in the chain of events, intranets followed the explosive growth of the World Wide Web as a commercial medium and the advent of groupware as an internal platform for communication. However, the people who created the computer networks and the programming languages—the founders of the Net and the Web—were actually motivated by a desire to improve communication within and among _organizations_. They wanted to improve the kinds of computer-based communication systems that had been available since the 1960s.

Chapter One reveals how a number of people in the 60s, 70s and 80s developed new technologies as ways to overcome organizational communication barriers, and how that work surprisingly resulted in a technology that would begin to profoundly affect marketing economics and popular culture in the 90s. "Social change results in the purposive behavior of people acting from individual and often idiosyncratic motives in pursuit of real goals," James Beniger notes.[2] This is how several brilliant but otherwise ordinary individuals got things started.

■ References

¹ David Kirpatrick, "Riding the Real Trends in Technology." *Fortune*, February 19, 1996.

² James Beringer, *The Control Revolution: Technical and Economic Origins of the Information Society* (Cambridge: Harvard University Press), 1986, p. 11.

Acknowledgments

This is a rather long "Acknowledgments" section because, although there is one name listed as the author of this book, *The 21ˢᵗ-Century Intranet* represents the contributions of a great many people. I am very grateful to those who contributed ideas and who helped make this book a reality.

I appreciate the help and encouragement given to me by my editor, Mark Taub, Executive Editor at <u>Prentice Hall</u>. Mark guided the development of the book and helped me to appreciate the realities of the publishing world. Dave Churbuck gave me Mark's e-mail address, setting the whole thing in motion. <u>Charles Goldfarb</u>, one of the proposal reviewers, pinpointed the primary value of the book relative to all other intranet books on the market, and provided comments that shaped some of my central arguments.

When the merits of including intranet demos on a CD-ROM became obvious, several people responded immediately to my requests for information: Rick Faulk at <u>IntraNetics</u>, Ken Volpe and Jay Seaton at <u>RadNet</u>, and Jennifer Penunuri and Suzanne Anthony at <u>Netscape</u> Communications Corporation Publishing Relations. We were linked though e-mail and everyone turned around requests within hours. This type of responsiveness, I believe, portends the future of e-commerce.

Two authors were very kind to correspond with me so that I could secure permission to include the full text of their magazine articles, <u>Tom Stewart</u> and <u>Chris Locke</u>. Several people helped me to secure permission to use materials authored by other people. I very much appreciate the assistance of Lisa Romero at <u>Business Design Associates</u> and Susan Rossi at <u>Excel, Inc</u>.

Marti B. Jones, this book's copyeditor, cleaned up all of the things I overlooked and she made the copy sparkle. Nicholas Radhuber, the production editor, played a very important role in the creation of the final product. I'd like to thank Nick for his collegiality and hard work.

Several people reviewed advance copies of the manuscript (typos and all) and were kind enough to provide feedback on a very tight deadline. They include Malcolm Frank, Kevin Han, Elliott Masie, Jessica Lipnack, Richard S. Gaston Jr. and Bruce Tulgan. Thank you so very much.

Many of the arguments in the book were first tested in conversation with Dave Carlson, president of <u>Ontogenics </u>in Boulder, Colorado. Dave is a serious scholar, a man of many talents and has an incredible grasp of the potential of technologies to transform organizations. Dave provided me with research material from his own collection, including valuable papers by Wanda Orlikowski and Patricia Sachs. Every time we met, Dave had another article to share with me, and he made time to listen to my concerns and ideas. Dave not only talked about knowledge sharing, he modeled it in its finest form.

A few years ago, I had the pleasure of working with Dick Baumbusch and Brian Thomson on the first electronic Knowledge Sharing System at <u>U S WEST</u>. Dick, an Executive Director, and Brian, a Manager with an MBA and J.D., taught me a lot about the business world along the way: I had arrived directly out of academe with an outsider's naiveté about the corporate world. From working with Dick and Brian, I came to appreciate the need to use tools, terms and techniques from the world of business to launch a knowledge-sharing system that made sense to managers and executives in the corporate environment. Many of the tools in The ToolKit in Chapter 19 began to take form when Brian and I worked together. Brian, for example, was the chief architect of our business plan which has been modified for publication here. Dick continues to be a trusted and valued sounding board. He is now president of the Knowledge Advantage Group in Denver. Brian now is the V.P. of Sales and Marketing for <u>The Trip.com</u>, a one-stop shopping web site for harried business travelers.

This book would not have been written if not for Kristina Jonell Yarrington, who was instrumental in creating The Link at U S WEST, and who is now Director of Marketing Communications/Advertising for New Products. Kristina was involved with web development long before others in the company had begun to glimpse its potential. Kristina introduced me to two other gearheads at U S WEST, Ryan Martens and Mike Vaughan. Together the four of us founded the U S WEST Web Developers Coalition and developed a number of key learnings about the pleasures and difficulties of self-organized networks. Ryan, then a consultant for BDM Technologies, was instrumental in the Global Village's development as well. Ryan is a pro and he helped me to appreciate the value of a well-connected, enthusiastic, knowledgeable external consultant. Ryan could do things we could not do for ourselves and was terrific at keeping things in perspective. Ryan is now a V.P. at Avitech in Boulder, Colorado.

After co-founding the Web Developers Coalition, Mike Vaughan and I then founded the WisdomLink Group at <u>International Learning Systems</u>. Mike is an exceptionally talented programmer and team leader. He created the model for the U S WEST Web Developer's Coalition, discussed in Chapters 3 and 15. Mike is also the programming genius who designed and developed ILS's WisdomLink™ software. I admire Mike's programming skills as well as his project management skills. Working with Mike on projects proved to me without question that technical and nontechnical specialists can work together cooperatively with a great deal of positive mutual regard.

Charles "Chuck" Fred, former president of ILS, believed in the importance of computer-based knowledge sharing, and in this book. An engineer by training, a leader by choice, Chuck is also the author of the forthcoming book *The Race to Proficiency*, which discusses a pattern of traits unfolding in successful companies that learn fast.

Dan Guenther, former V.P. of New Business and Technologies at ILS was my link back to ILS new business while I telecommuted from my home in Rhinebeck, New York. A published author of both fiction and poetry, Dan provided tremendous moral support and helped me to believe that writing this book was part of my calling in life. Fred Pope and I worked on a very interesting consulting project while I wrote this book. We had some wonderful conversations in Milwaukee and Denver which stimulated my thinking about the nature of organization change. Mark Brandow, who ran MIS single-handedly at ILS, somehow always found time to help me at my most desperate computing moments. He rescued my files when my laptop, sweating from too much obese software, crashed and died. The word "technician" impoverishes his actual contribution to the organization.

Tom Athenour, Vice President of Marketing at ILS, gave me an opportunity to present material from the book in front of current and potential clients as the book was being written. I very much appreciated the opportunity to get reaction and feedback from such varied audiences. Often, the audience members' questions and comments signaled the need for me to develop clearer lines of reasoning or to provide more detail in the examples and case studies in the book. Peggy Steele, founder of ILS, has been an inspiration since we first met. As the owner of the third largest woman-owned business in the state of Colorado, Peggy has seen the company through dozens of business cycles. As the winds of change rock ILS, Peggy remains steadfast to a core set of values, including customer focus.

Besides the ILS community, I was supported by a virtual community of colleagues. For this, I owe <u>Howard Rheingold</u> a tremendous debt of gratitude. First, although Howard was extremely busy with the creation and management of <u>Electric Minds</u>, he reviewed portions of the book. Howard e-mailed words of encouragement that fueled my writing for months. Electric Minds and this book ran parallel for a while as Howard struggled to find the right economic model to fit the concept of web-based discussions about technology and the future. As I was finishing the book, the E Minds community members were forming a coalition to ensure the survival of the community after the venture capitalists tripped.

Electric Minds community was essential in the development of this book. In addition to Howard, the regular participants on the Knowledge Sharing topic on Electric Minds' "Fundamentals" became virtual companions: Alan Chamberlain, Denham Grey, Craig Maudlin, Elizabeth Lewis, Neil Krey, Joe Katzman, Bob Watson, Gene Davis, Jeff Beddow and Heather Duggan. All shared ideas unselfishly and talked as peers; their only motive to help each other learn. I tested my "public voice" with these folks. They provided feedback that fueled the writing project. My identity as an "online thinker" and community member blossomed in the midst of this small community. The Knowledge Sharing topic in Electric Minds's "Fundamentals" was safe harbor. It kept my spirit alive. Our discussion from late November '96 to early June '97 ran to nearly 500 posts (or over 275 printed pages). That conversation alone could be a book unto itself.

My family has always provided tremendous support. My sister, Debra Stone, shared her insights into the computer industry and connected me to a couple of people at <u>Cambridge Technology Partners</u> with whom I tested some of my ideas. Deb is an example of what it means to be dedicated to excellence in your work and to be loyal to the people who support your ambitions. My brother <u>Chris Stone</u>, a multimedia web developer and consultant, was a contributor to this book. His examples and ideas are integrated into several chapters. While I was writing, Chris also sent me e-mail with ideas and suggestions, always trying to help me to stay on the cutting edge of web development.

Doug Stone, the youngest brother in our family and president of <u>Figure One, Inc</u>. (formerly Stone Interactive) advised me about computer purchases and all sorts of technology-related things. While I was writing this book, Doug was profiled as a leading-edge CD-ROM multimedia developer by a Chicago paper. Some sibling rivalry was injected into the writing project as a result, but more importantly, the article reminded me how much influence our dad, Alexander Stone, had on all of our lives before his death. Our Dad was the first American president of a Japanese-owned company in the U.S (Quasar, owned by Matsushita), and we saw the globalization of the American economy through Dad's eyes. Back in the 1980s, Dad was giving speeches about the convergence of communication technologies, long before others in the industry caught the wave. Dad looked to the future and was optimistic about the promise of technology even though his position as an executive in the consumer electronics business was extraordinarily demanding. I became interested in technology and communication because of my dad. His influence is woven throughout every page I've ever written on the topic.

Carole Stone, our mom, provided support that made possible the writing of this book. Thank you for lighting the candles, Mom.

My thinking about the power of visual metaphors was strengthened through my relationship with Eric and Todd Siler, of <u>PsiPhi Communications</u> in Denver. In 1996, the Silers conducted a workshop with Dick and me at U S WEST, and then we stayed in touch. Todd's book *Think Like A Genius* stimulated my own creative process on many occasions. Conversations with Todd in Arizona when we worked together, and then regularly with Eric on the phone, were like shots of pure adrenaline. The Siler's optimism and expressive enthusiasm for life is incredibly contagious.

For a too brief time, I worked with Janet Logothetti at ILS. Our conversations helped me to gain clarity about many things, including the importance of storytelling in organizations. Janet has launched her own company, <u>Terra Firma Design</u>, one that combines web-technologies with storytelling principles. Mary E. Boone, author of *Leadership and the Computer* and president of <u>Boone & Associates,</u> shared ideas and provided inspiration. Judith Weiss, scholar and research wizard, shared many of her on-line research discoveries and e-mailed dozens of very valuable hyperlinks.

I wish to also thank ILS clients with whom I have had the pleasure to work. Some of the my clients have included Johnson Controls, Amoco, Gates Rubber and USAA. I cherish my experiences with the people at those companies. Thank you for your professionalism, for your openness to new ideas and for your "real world" perspective.

Peggy Tumey, a Vice President at U S WEST, was the management visionary behind U S WEST's Global Village, which is described in several chapters in this book. Peggy helped to establish and fund the Global Village, thereby stimulating web development initiatives within the company. To Peggy, I owe great debt, first, for her leadership within the company, and then for her responding so quickly to my series of requests for permission to write about web development at U S WEST.

Other people I wish to thank are Peggy Holman, with whom I worked briefly on the development of a web site for the U S WEST Quality community, and who introduced me to Open Space Technologies. Peggy also graciously permitted me to include her Organizational Environment Survey in the book. (The survey is in the Tool Kit). I thank Gloria Farler, Ellen Campos, Meredith Ceh, Dave Dutcher, Peter Horst, Maria Kernen, Hunt Lambert, John McCaffrey and Angela Stewart, all who were former members of U S WEST's Market Strategy Development group. I thank Sherman Woo, Barbara Bauer and Patricia Hursh, who were all part of U S WEST's IT group. Suzanne Mullison, at U S WEST's Global Village, shared her living memory of how the GV came into existence and what it has meant for her personally to be able to be involved. I owe a debt of gratitude to Tom Smith and to all of the frontline people at U S WEST with whom I worked during 1995–1996. You all taught me more about the business world than I can ever begin to document. I regret that I never had a chance to finish our work together. Perhaps in some way, this book represents a form of continuity.

Three professors with whom I once studied, Michael Hyde, Lee Tractman and Willard "Wick" Rowland have been very instrumental in the development of my thinking about science, technology, society, culture and communication. Professors Hyde, Tractman and Rowland, each corresponded with me during the writing of this book. They, as well as Profs. Stephen Presser and Steve Vibbert, have remained a powerful presence in my life even though many years have passed since our days together at the university. Knowledge lives.

I relied on a number of technology-based support services through the course of writing this book: Electric Library, Epix (an ISP) and Amazon.com

— each a *very* good value for the money. A huge portion of my book advance went towards the purchase of books at Amazon. Amazon.com had the books I needed when I needed them, and provided impeccable service. Writing from a small town in the countryside, a trip to a large bookstore would have cost me a half day of travel time. Thanks, Amazon, for making it possible to get good books delivered anywhere one makes their home! I could not have made my publication deadline if Amazon.com did not come into existence *before* I signed my book contract.

I wish to acknowledge the encouragement and support provided by the fairly large and extended Gonzalez family, and especially by my long-time friends, Liz McCarter, Wendy Redal, and Ginny Conners.

Finally, I wish to acknowledge with love, gratitude and admiration my husband, Dr. Luis F. Gonzalez, III. No words could express my heartfelt appreciation. My husband is my rock and my foundation. M. Scott Peck compares marriage to a base camp for mountain climbing. Writes Joseph Jaworski, "If you want to make a peak climb, you've got to have a good base camp, a place where there is shelter and where provision are kept, where one may receive nurture and rest before one ventures forth again to seek another summit." While I was writing this book, the small community hospital where Luis heads the radiology department underwent a tumultuous change as a consequence of the new economics of health care. Still, Luis kept the base camp going. An exceptional father, Luis also created out-of-town adventures for our boys on several weekends so that their mom could write uninterrupted.

This book is dedicated to Luis and to our twin sons, Christian Birk Gonzalez and Cody Alexander Gonzalez. Hand in hand, we look toward the future.

The 21st-Century Intranet

C H A P T E R

The Network
and the Language

Eager to get things moving along, we tend to plunge right into the work and develop our key learning through trial and error along the way. The purpose of this book is to provide some guidance so that the peaks and valleys of intranet development are not so extreme. The majority of the pages in this book contain "just-in-time" tools. But, by stepping back in time, we can also actually avoid costly mistakes and wasted effort.

Instructions for creating road maps for the future are found in stories about the past. The stories in this chapter about the challenges faced by the developers of the Internet and the Web give us a lot of information about how to make our lives and our jobs easier. What history teaches is actually the foundation for the Five Phase Plan laid out at the end of Section One. Fernando Flores, in a notable address[1], stated:

> In my experience, every good entrepreneur that I know, every innovator that I know, is an amateur historian. Because without looking at history, we don't know our nature. A great part of what we do are practices that are in the background for us, that we don't think about, and which come to us from the past. . . . The first thing

we need to do is to discover who we are. We need to discover what our relationship is to the past, where our relations are going, where the industry is going, where other industries are going.

■ Creating Common Ground for Technical and Nontechnical Members of an Intranet Team

This chapter focuses on the creation of the Internet and on the protocols and languages that enabled computers to connect. One of the challenges that nontechnical professionals face is understanding terms like *packet-switching, nodes, protocols, SGML, HTML, Java, client-server, hypertext, hyperlink,* and so forth.

It is difficult to engage imaginatively with these kinds of technical terms when you are learning them simply as terms. Stories, however, help to provide a context of meaning. Recall when you were a new employee in the organization, trying to learn something new. It was helpful when someone sat down with you and gave you some background and some context for understanding. Having a way to anchor your new knowledge in "the big picture" makes learning easier. That's one reason this chapter is here.

People who are already fluent in the technical terms may be particularly drawn to this section of the book since these are not just stories about the evolution of the Internet and the Web. They are stories about people with technical skills who brought something valuable into the world, using technology as a way to solve problems as well as a way to express themselves. The technology happened to become their medium for self-expression. The work combined both the art of seeing and the science of construction.

■ Your Story Will Become Part of This Unfolding History

Whether you are a technical or a nontechnical professional, as an intranet champion you will be writing your own story into the history of your organization and the history of your career. It's good to know that some of the same roadblocks you face as an intranet champion have been faced by the founders of the Internet and the Web, and by other intranet champions. Knowing about these challenges and the ways in which people turned adversity into opportunity will help you to see the road ahead.

As an intranet champion, you will be joining a journey that is truly remarkable—one that could not have occurred in any other time in history. We begin.

■ Phase One, the Network

Tim Berners-Lee created the first web browser/editor and is credited for the creation of the World Wide Web. Incredibly, if Berners-Lee had been born only a decade earlier, he would not have been able to change history with his innovation. Berners-Lee's unique contribution required two foundational elements to be in place before the World Wide Web could come into being: the network and a language. Creating a network was the first major phase.

Communication over computer networks first occurred in the 1960s with electronic mail on time-sharing computers. People communicated by sending messages using the same mainframe computers through dumb terminals connected to the mainframe or through dial-up telephone lines. The reasons for turning to computers as a communication tool were fairly obvious. People working on similar issues or problems were physically separated from each other—by floors in large office buildings, by cities, or by states. Often, people who wished to communicate with each other were also separated by organizational structures, which meant that they did not report to the same groups or bosses. Like the telephone, networked computers enabled people to bridge the distances and to connect with each other. Computers enabled the transfer of digital data—both text and computer code.

Kick-Starting the Process: The Request for Quotation

One of the challenges was to enable the exchange of data from one mainframe to another. In 1968, the Advanced Research Projects Agency (ARPA) developed and released a *Request for Quotation* (RFQ) for a communication system based on a set of small, interconnected computers it called Interface Message Processors (IMPs). The competition was won by Bolt Beranek and Newman (BBN), a research firm in Cambridge, Massachusetts. A small, select group of engineers at BBN linked several university-based computer sites to establish the initial electronic network. By September 1969, BBN had developed and delivered the first IMP to the Network Measurement Center located at UCLA. In 1969, the Advanced Research Projects Agency Network (ARPANET), a U.S. government experiment in multisite package switching, was launched, initially to link researchers with remote computer centers for sharing of hardware and software resources. This was the genesis of the Internet, the massive global network of interconnected *packet-switched* computer networks.

An Essential First Step: Packet-Switching Data to Nodes

Vinton Cerf, one of the people central to the development of the intranet, explains the importance of the innovation called packet switching[2]:

> Packet-switching technology is fundamentally different from the technology that was then employed by the telephone system (which was based on "circuit switching") or by the military messaging system (which was based on "message switching"). In a packet-switching system, data to be communicated is broken into small chunks that are labeled to show where they come from and where they are to go, rather like postcards in the postal system. Like postcards, packets have a maximum length and are not necessarily reliable. Packets are forwarded from one computer to another until they arrive at their destination. If any are lost, they are re-sent by the originator. The recipient acknowledges receipt of packets to eliminate unnecessary re-transmissions.

Packet switching, therefore, is basically a way to manage the flow of data. Packets of data do not simply float around the network. They are routed to "nodes." A node is computer that serves as a point of connection in a network. Seen as a group, the nodes make up the network's backbone.

The Drivers Were Aspirations and Dreams

Today, we take packet switching and the existence of the Internet for granted. However, there were struggles all along the way. Cerf recounts[2] that

> ARPA set a crucial tone for this work by making the research entirely unclassified and by engaging some of the most creative members of the computer science community who tackled this communication problem without the benefit of the experience (and hence bias) of traditional telephony groups. Even within the computer science community, though, the technical approach was not uniformly well-received, and it is to ARPA's credit that it persevered despite much advice to the contrary.

The participants' perseverance was fueled by passion and commitment. As recounted in a wonderful book by Katie Hafner and Matthew Lyons, _Where Wizards Stay Up Late: The Origins of the Internet_, the brilliant people at BBN, ARPANET, and the Network Working Group who developed the network were motivated by deeply philosophical and personal reasons to improve computer systems.

For example, one of the major contributors was J.C.R. Licklider, a director at ARPA, who brought a rich academic background in psychology to computing. Licklider believed that a close coupling of computers and humans would eventually lead to better decision making. Computers would be used for what they did best, rote work. This would free humans to devote energy to making better decisions and to developing clearer insights than they would be capable of alone. In 1960, he wrote, "The hope is that in not too many years, human brains and computing machines will be coupled ... tightly, and the resulting partnership will think as no human brain has ever thought and process data in a way not approached by the information-handling machines we know today." Licklider's dream was that improved decision-making would lead to more intelligent policy, better use of resources, and a higher level of participation in policy-making by ordinary people.

Each person who contributed to the creation of the Internet brought feelings and opinions about why it was important to improve technology as a way to improve communication among people. As Hafner and Lyon[3] recount in _Where Wizards Stay Up Late_, this particular piece of history, the creation of the Internet, would not have been written had it not been for the qualities each contributor brought to the table.

Step Two: Creating Protocols and Getting the Computers to Talk Like Peers

After the problem of getting information to move across the network was solved, a new problem emerged. The next challenge was to find ways to get computers to "talk" to each other. Hafner and Lyon[3] eloquently explain the problem:

> The computers themselves were extremely egocentric devices. The typical mainframe of the period behaved as if it were the only computer in the universe. There was no obvious or easy way to engage two diverse machines in even the most minimal communication needed to move bits back and forth. You could connect machines, but once they were connected, what would they say to each other?
>
> In those days, a computer interacted with the devices that were attached to it, like a monarch communicating with his subjects. Everything connected to the main computer performed a specific task, and each peripheral device was presumed to be ready at all times for a "fetch-my-slippers" type of command. (In computer parlance, this is known as *master–slave communication*.) Computers were designed for this kind of interaction; they send instructions to subordinate card readers, terminals, and tape units, and they initiate all dialogues. But if another device in effect tapped the computer on the shoulder with a signal that said, "Hi, I'm a computer, too," the receiving machine would be stumped.
>
> The goal in devising the host-to-host protocol was to get the mainframe machines talking as peers, so that either side could initiate a simple dialogue and the other would be ready to respond with at least an acknowledgment of the other machine's existence.

With this communication challenge in hand—the challenge of designing protocols—people who were attracted to the problem and able to make contributions to its solution found each other through human nodes in their network of personal and organizational relationships. *They also sent signals out to the community that they were looking for others to help solve certain technical problems.* For example, an ad hoc group comprised primarily of graduate students in California were working on the problem of how to develop the basic "handshake" between two computers.

Inviting Others to the Party: Request for Comment Leads to the "Handshake"

One of the graduate students who helped to lead the initiative, Steve Crocker, captured the problem in a note he sent out to other groups of graduate students and labeled it *Request for Comments*, which came to be known as an *RFC*. Crocker's invitation reflected the graduate student ethos and helped to set the tone for work of creating the Internet. Hafner and Lyon[4]:

> When you read RFC 1, you walked away with a sense of "Oh, this is a club that I can play in too," recalled Brian Reid, later a graduate student at Carnegie-Mellon. "It has rules, but it welcomes other members so long as the members are aware of those rules." The language of the RFC was warm and welcoming. The idea was to promote cooperation, not ego. The fact that Crocker kept his ego out of the first RFC set the style and inspired others to follow suit in the hundreds of friendly and cooperative RFCs that followed. "It is impossible to underestimate the importance of that," Reid asserted. "I did not feel excluded by a little core of protocol kings. I felt included by a friendly group of people who recognized that the purpose of networking was to bring everybody in."
>
> For years afterward (and to this day), RFCs have been the principal means of open expression in the computer networking community, the accepted way of recommending, reviewing, and adopting new technical standards.

The computer network that came to be known as the Internet *was thus a result of people developing their own open networks of like-minded colleagues who could help solve a problem.* In 1972, the Department of Defense Advanced Research Projects Agency (DARPA) adopted the research for military purposes. Its main characteristic was the automatic routing of information packets, circumventing the problem of network vulnerability through failure of single transmission nodes. By mid-1975, ARPA had concluded that the ARPANET was stable and should be turned over to a separate agency for operational management. Therefore, responsibility was transferred to the Defense Communications Agency (now known as the Defense Information Systems Agency).

A Critical Success Factor: Vertical and Horizontal Distribution of Resources

Other countries had computers and computer scientists working in government and industry. Why did the Internet emerge from the U.S? Why were these talented individuals able to find each other and the resources required to go forward? America's leadership in this area is the result of extraordinarily complex and fruitful long-term partnership among government, industry, and academia that had its origins in World War II. At the close of the war, Vannevar Bush, a former Massachusetts Institute of Technology president and Director of the Wartime Office of Scientific Research and Development, wrote a visionary manifesto titled *Science, the Endless Frontier*, which laid the foundation for this three-way partnership.

There were many advantages from the three-way partnership: the space program, the atomic energy and nuclear weapons programs, as well as the Internet. Fundamental research in computing and communications—particularly that sponsored by DARPA through its Computing Systems Technology Office, Electronic Systems Technology Office, and Software and Intelligent Systems Technology Office, and by the National Science Foundation through its Directorate for Computer and Information Science and Engineering—and that carried out at universities and at companies like BBN was critical to the development of intranet technologies. *Those partnerships and the vertical and horizontal distribution of resources to sustain innovation were critical success factors.*

Using the Network to Enable Person-to-Person Communication: E-Mail and Distribution Lists

The people who worked to build the network were motivated by a desire to improve communication. As the computer networks came into being, users quickly realized that they wanted to use them to send messages to each other about the status of their projects. In the early 1970s, an e-mail function was added, and it became the most used service on the network. Mailing lists (distribution lists) were added next, because users found that they frequently wanted to send mail not just to specific individuals but also to fixed groups of people. Professors Lee Sproull and Sara Kiesler[5] recall that:

> Large numbers of computer scientists around the country started to exchange ideas rapidly and casually on topics ranging from system design to programming bugs to movie reviews. Graduate students worked with professors and other students who could offer interesting problems and skills without regard to where these colleagues were located physically; some had a kind of free-floating apprenticeship. Scientists could choose their colleagues based on shared interest rather than proximity. A large electronic community formed, filled with friends who didn't know each other and collaborators who had never met in person.

It was amazing! Prior to e-mail, finding the right person who knew something about how to solve a problem took time. Requests for information were limited by assumptions about who you could or should ask. Requests were also limited by incomplete knowledge of each other's network of personal connections. Sometimes the bother of having to explain the whole context of a problem to someone else was itself discouragement enough not to reach out for help. E-mail revolutionized the distribution of information and the growth of knowledge within the research community. Once the *ANSWER* command (or Reply) was added to the e-mail programs, responding to an e-mail message became easy. There was no longer a need to retype the sender's address or to retype the message. If you needed to reference the original message or reference a reply in order to provide context for your new message, you could "quote" from what came before without retyping the text.

The speed of e-mail was one reason people came to use it as an essential communication medium. Within a matter of minutes or hours, people could get answers to their questions and go forward in their work without much of a delay. Distribution lists (*Listserve*) enabled the key learning to be widely shared. The data became available not only to the person who originated the request, but to all others on the e-mail distribution list interested in the topic.

Transcending time and space, e-mail and distribution list users found themselves part of a new virtual community. Hafner and Lyon[6]:

> The speed and ease of the medium opened a vista of casual and spontaneous conversation. . . . As the regulars became familiar to one another, fast friendships were cemented, sometimes years before people actually met. E-mail was uninhibiting, creating reference points entirely its own, a virtual society with manners, values and acceptable behaviors.

The results of the on-line interactions were important. The technology enabled participants to engage in breakthrough thinking. Equally important to the pioneers were the dialogs themselves. The technology enabled people to link up among their peers in a community of equals—many who, Hafner and Lyon note, "carried on as if they had known each other all their lives."

Claims, Evidence, and Counterpoint: Electronic Conferencing Systems

Collaborative work facilitated by computer-mediated communication proved to be tremendously useful to the scientific and research communities, and system developers looked for better ways to integrate their communications. In 1970, Murray Turoff designed and implemented the first computer conferencing system. It was structured as a Delphi discussion process, an iterative series of questionnaires and feedback. The purpose was to enable knowledgeable respondents to explore a complex topic. One advantage was that it created a permanent transcript of the discussion that could be archived as a kind of group memory. It could be called up time and again as a point of reference. The system evolved into a full-scale conferencing system, with personal messaging capabilities, discussion conferences, and a real-time messaging feature.

Sending a Message to the World: Usenet Newsgroups

On-line discussion forums, or Usenet newsgroups, were developed in 1981 as an alternative to services available through the ARPANET. They were similar to Turoff's conferencing systems and designed to host discussions around specific topics, organized according to a branching hierarchy (*alt, biz, comp, misc, rec, sci, soc,* and *talk*). Anyone with access to the Internet and free Usenet software could send out a specific, signed message to be seen by everyone else who "subscribed" to that group. The message would travel from a person's computer to a local Usenet "server"—a computer with a large memory that stores copies of all current Usenet messages. The server would then forward a copy of the message to a handful of other servers, each of which, in turn, sent the message to a few other systems. The system made it possible to post a message that could be seen by Usenet newsgroup users around the world, transcending time and space.

■ Phase Two, the Language

One major drawback was that most computer languages could not "talk" to each other, so finding and giving information was still difficult. Most organizations were still using computers for data processing. Those computers were not suited to free text verbal information and dynamically evolving information. A National Research Council committee observed that "Difficulties are: the researcher cannot get access to data; if he can, he cannot read them; if he can read them, he does not know how good they are; and if he finds them good, he cannot merge them with other data."[7]

Two trends led to the development of the Web: the development of the Internet protocols that made the global network possible, and the development of the computer-aided reading of electronic documents. One of the most important milestones was the creation of SGML, a highly sophisticated, complete system for describing digital document types.

SGML, a Rule-Governed Syntax

Charles Goldfarb invented SGML in 1979 as a system for formalizing the structure of documents. Much of the foundational work took place at IBM, where Goldfarb was trying to integrate legal documents. Until then, it was extremely difficult to interchange documents between different word processing packages. SGML provided a vendor-neutral, formal, international standard for information interchange. Roy Rada[8] explains:

> The syntax of SGML is based on tags that mark the beginning of logical components of the document. For example, the first tag to be entered into a document would signify that what follows is a general document. Security for the document could be set through the 'security' attribute and might, for instance, be useful for a confidential report. A heading at level 1 is specified with <h1>. Cross-references may be made in the text to a heading via the <hr> marker.

The appeal of SGML, Rada notes, is that a document prepared with SGML should be immediately useful to many other groups because they will be prepared to deal with it.

In 1986, SGML was adopted as a standard of the International Organization for Standardization (ISO 8879). Since then, it has been increasingly adopted as the international standard for data and document interchange in open system environments. HTML, the markup language of the Web, is a subset of SGML. It is basically a set of instructions for displaying documents and for linking documents together.

Hypertext: A Way to Get Information "Out of the System"

The other milestone was the creation of *hypertext*. The basic idea behind hypertext is that it provides a way to link information together in a way that makes sense to the individual using the system.

Again, the idea began with Vannevar Bush. At the close of World War II, *The Atlantic* published Bush's article "As We May Think," which offered a compelling vision for how computer technology could be used to enable the growth of knowledge.

In his essay, Bush[9] urged scientists to turn their energies from war to the task of making the vast store of human knowledge accessible and useful. Bush outlined his vision of a machine called the *memex*, which would be based on the principles of associative indexing. "Any item may be caused at will to select immediately and automatically another. This is the essential feature of the memex. The process of tying two items together is an important thing," he wrote. Bush envisioned ways in which the technology could help lawyers, physicians, and scientists access information and knowledge, resulting in better problem solving:

> Wholly new forms of encyclopedias will appear, ready made with a mesh of associative trails running through them, ready to be dropped into the memex and thereby amplified. The lawyer has at his touch the associated opinions and decisions of his whole experience, and of the experience of friends and authorities. The patent attorney has on call the millions of issued patents, with familiar trails to every point of his client's interest. The physician, puzzled by a patient's reactions, strikes the trail established in studying an earlier similar case, and runs rapidly through analogous case histories, with side references to the classics for the pertinent anatomy and histology. The chemist, struggling with the synthesis of an organic compound, has all the chemical literature before him in his laboratory, with trails following the analogies of compounds, and side trails to their physical and chemical behavior.

The "infostructure" Bush sketched out in 1945 included a proposal for what is now known as *hypertext*. All that was needed was a programming language and the right kind of networked computers. Ted Nelson, a visionary inventor, applied his knowledge to solve that problem.

Nelson coined the word *hypertext* and described it in a 1965 paper theorizing that, in the future, people would have access to a global network linking millions of desktop computers and containing all the world's knowledge. To access any of that knowledge, you could call up a precisely tailored document incorporating text, graphics, and video gleaned from computers scattered throughout the system. Nelson went forward and developed a hypertext coding prototype.

Many programmers were influenced by Nelson's work and by the concept of using hypertext as a way to get information "out of the system" onto people's computer screens. Van Dam and Nelson's Hypertext Editing System was developed in 1968 as a WYSIWYG (what you see is what you get) on a vector display. Van Dam's students, most of whom have become leaders in the computer industry and academe, continued to experiment with hypertext. By the late 1980s, a community of hypertext developers had emerged. They communicated with each other at conferences through a special issue of *The Communications of the ACM* and, most importantly, through a Usenet newsgroup called *alt.hypertext* that was open to anyone on the Internet.

Backstage Magic: Hot Spots

Several hypertext programs were developed for commercial and academic purposes. Most of the programs used "hot spots" in the documents, like icons or highlighted phrases, as sensitive areas. Touching a hot spot with a mouse brings up the relevant information. The network address of the new information is written into the document code but does not appear on screen. While reading through a document, people can skip to another hyperlinked piece of information with a click of the mouse. In 1987, Apple Computers introduced HyperCard, the first widely available personal hypermedia authoring system. The U.S. Department of Defense provided an added incentive to hypertext developers when they specified that all future manuals for parts for defense equipment must be provided in hypermedia form.

■ Pieces Coming Together

By the late 1980s, three pieces of the puzzle were coming together: a stable global network (the Internet), an international standard for document information exchange (SGML), and hypermedia authoring programs (to create hypertext). The moment was right for finding a supportive environment for innovation and a compelling reason to bring the technologies together. Enter Tim Berners-Lee, an Oxford-trained computer scientist who pursued a vision that would result in the World Wide Web and would change the world.

■ References

[1] Fernado Flores, "The Impact of Information on Business," *Address to the 50th Anniversary Conference of the Association for Computing Machinery,* San Jose, CA, March, 1997.

[2] Vinton Cerf, "Computer Networking: Global Infrastructure for the 21st Century" (http://Cra.org/research.impact)

[3] Katie Hafner and Mathew Lyon, *Where Wizards Stay Up Late: The Origins of the Internet* (NY: Simon & Schuster, 1996), pp. 146–147.

[4] Hafner and Lyon, pp. 144–145.

[5] Lee Spoull and Sara Kiesler, *Connections: New Ways of Working in the Networked Organization* (Cambridge: MIT Press, 1993), p. 11.

[6] Hafner and Lyon, p. 214.

[7] Quoted Lee Spoull and Sara Kiesler, *Connections; New Ways of Working in the Networked Organization* (Cambridge: MIT Press, 1993), p. 9.

[8] Roy Rada, *Interactive Media* (NY: Springer-Verlag, 1995), p. 78.

[9] Vannevar Bush, "As We May Think" (http://www.theAtlantic.com/atlantic/atlweb/flashbks/computer/tech.htm)

Test Site, Tools, and Cultural Consciousness

Imagine that you are working in a large organization, frustrated by missing information and imperfect communication, and that you invent a way to use existing technology to solve communication problems. Imagine further that your discovery is called the World Wide Web and that not only does it improve your organization, but people all over the world begin to use it in ways you never could have guessed. That is what happened to Tim Berners-Lee, who "invented" the Web. In this chapter, we'll see how Berners-Lee convinced his employer to let him go forward with his vision, how programmers across the globe grabbed his code from the Net and improved upon it, and how the Web began to affect American culture. We'll see why Berners-Lee's employer, CERN, created an ideal test site for these new technologies and how many of the Web's second order consequences extended far beyond Berners-Lee's control.

As with the previous chapter, this chapter leverages history to chart a solid course toward the future.

■ Phase Three, the Test Site and Tools

Tim Berners-Lee Needs to Get Himself Organized

In 1984, Tim Berners-Lee, an Oxford-trained computer systems designer, began a fellowship with the European Particle Physics Laboratory, known as CERN. CERN is the world's largest high-energy physics laboratory. It is funded by 19 European member states and is located near Geneva, with facilities on both sides of the Swiss-French border, and employs several thousand people. Berners-Lee was very knowledgeable about hardware and software system design, real-time communications graphics, and text processing. He went to CERN to work on distributed real-time systems for scientific data acquisition and system control. It was his second visit there. In 1980, he had spent a short time at CERN as a consultant and wrote a program for keeping track of software called *Enquire*. Berners-Lee, at that point, was motivated by a desire to keep track of pieces of information located on various databases and to be able to link them together in a pattern that would make sense to him. It was an effort, he said, to organize himself.

Berners-Lee shared Enquire with some of his colleagues. It was similar to Apple's Hypercard application except that it ran on a multiuser system. Previous hypertext systems worked across a disk or across a file system. Berners-Lee's hypertext program worked across the network to create a web of links between databases.

A Vision of Self-Managed Teams

Berners-Lee and his colleague, Robert Cailliau, began to talk about the need to use something like Enquire so that employees would have fewer frustrations when they tried to access documents or to learn about CERN projects. As Robert Cailliau recounts, CERN was a good place for such an experiment. The high-energy physics community is small but spread all over the world. The physics research laboratories of the world have many collaborations, and the exchange of data and documents is a "primordial activity." In addition, CERN and its fellow laboratories in the U.S. had adopted the Internet as the standard academic network.[1] Berners-Lee had a vision of improving how people communicated within this environment:

> In an exciting place like CERN, which was a great environment to be in . . . you have so many people coming in with great ideas, doing some work, and then leaving no trace of what it is they've done and why they did it. The whole organization really needed this. It needed some place to be able to cement, to put down its organizational knowledge.
>
> And that was the idea, of a team being able to work together, rather than a sequence of grabbing somebody at coffee hour and bringing somebody else into the conversation, or having a one-time conversation that would be forgotten, or a sequence of messages from one person to another.
>
> [The essential idea was] being able to work together on a common vision of what it is that we believe we are doing, and why we are doing it, with places to put all the funny little "this is why on Tuesday we decided not to do thats." I thought that would be really exciting, I thought that would be a really interesting way of running a team. Maybe we could work towards that goal: the dream of the "self-managed team."[2]

The Document that Led to the Creation of the Web: "Information Management: A Proposal"

In 1989, Berners-Lee wrote a proposal to persuade CERN management that a global hypertext system was in CERN's interests. It was called "Information Management: A Proposal." That proposal was the foundation for the original "WorldWideWeb" program.

Berners-Lee began the proposal by noting that good communication practices were valued at CERN and were an integral part of the culture. Although employees were organized into a hierarchical management structure, employees worked toward common goals and communicated very well. They shared information, equipment, and software across groups. "Information about what facilities exist and how to find out about them travels in the corridor gossip and occasional newsletters, and the details about what is required to be done in a similar way," Berners-Lee wrote. He observed that the working structure of the organization is a "multiply connected 'web' whose interconnections evolve with time." All things considered, Berners-Lee noted, the result was "remarkably successful, despite occasional misunderstanding and duplicated effort."

Defining the Specific Needs at CERN

The main problem was that most employees did not spend their whole careers at CERN. Like Berners-Lee, they circulated through, typically staying only two years or so. Consequently, information was always being lost. In the proposal, Berners-Lee[3] wrote:

> The introduction of new people demands a fair amount of their time and that of others before they have any idea of what goes on. The technical details of past projects are sometimes lost forever or only recovered after a detective investigates in an emergency. Often, [if] the information has been recorded, it just cannot be found.

As Berners-Lee was actually doing research, not simply observing or managing it, he knew precisely what sort of questions his colleagues had trouble answering. Those questions were: "Where is this module used? Who wrote this code? Where does he work? What documents exist about that concept? Which laboratories are included in that project? Which systems depend on this device? What documents refer to this one?"

An Eloquent Design for a "Future-Proof" Intranet

Berners-Lee received permission in 1990 to work on a hypertext system for CERN. In his proposal, he wrote that he envisioned a system that would enable people to:

- connect to various electronic conferencing systems;

- view an on-line employee telephone book with links to people, projects, and office addresses;

- construct a "Personal Skills Inventory," listing projects and areas of expertise;

- access documents linked by categories and projects, keywords, and authors;

- read newsgroups and create links from one newsgroup to another;

- share key learnings at the conclusion of projects;

- search the system for information; and

- generate mailing lists to keep people informed of changes.

In addition, Berners-Lee proposed that it might serve as a way to visualize where communication links were strong and where they were weak. "Perhaps a linked information system will allow us to see the real structure of the organization in which we work," Berners-Lee wrote.

Berners-Lee described in his original proposal, almost an entire decade ago, virtually everything associated with intranets today. Each element on the list above is now technically possible.

A Bold Synthesis of Emergent Technologies

One of the proposal's key strengths was its synthesis of how new, emergent technologies could be combined to offer solutions to common problems associated with organizational communication. For example, some people familiar with hypertext thought that it was too confusing, that programmers would get lost in the links and wouldn't have a clear path to follow. Berners-Lee proposed to use an SGML type of syntax. At the time, SGML was used primarily in a mode where a person would write an SGML file, put it in for batch processing on a mainframe, and expect a printed document hours later. Berners-Lee used the principles of SGML to separate hypertext code into its component parts, with an explanation of the form, function, and syntactical relationship of each part.

Berners-Lee looked to the future. He wrote that he wished to create a system that was "future-proof," meaning that it was portable, or supported many platforms, and was extendible to new data formats. The system would have universal access, meaning that documents could be accessed from anywhere; it wouldn't matter what computer system, platform, or operating system a person happened to be running. It would have an "unconstrained topology," meaning that the links could map to any existing database structure. Berners-Lee's ambition was to provide critical usefulness at an early stage.

Like "Pushing a Bobsled Up a Hill"

Anyone trying to implement an intranet today will probably be relieved to know that Berners-Lee had a tough time convincing CERN management, as well as his peers, to believe in his vision. In a speech Berners-Lee made to the British Computer Society in 1996, he recounted that there was a lot of pushing that had to be done. Berners-Lee compared the experience of creating the Web to pushing a bobsled up a hill and then watching as it gained speed and momentum.[2]

For the first two years, Berners-Lee recalled, "there was a lot of going around to explain to people why it was a really good idea." First, "the idea of doing SGML parsing and generation of something that could be read in real time was thought to be ridiculous." Then, there was a question of whether this work was truly on task. "There was also a strong feeling, and a very reasonable feeling, at CERN that 'we do high energy physics here.' If you want some special information technology, somebody was bound to have done that already; why don't you go and find it?"

So, faced with such challenges, Berners-Lee and Cailliau started to talking to people at conferences while trying to sell their own bosses on the merit of the work.

In 1990, with permission granted, Tim Berners-Lee wrote the first World Wide Web server and the first client, a WYSIWYG hypertext browser/editor that ran on the NeXTStep environment. The "WorldWideWeb" program was first made available within CERN in December and was made available on the Internet in the summer of 1991.

Critics of the WorldWideWeb program felt that HTML was too complex because people had to include angle brackets in the text that would tell the browser how to read the instructions for displaying the content. As Berners-Lee recounts, the feeling was that "you can't ask somebody to write all those angle brackets just because they want something available on an information system, this is much too complex." In addition, there wasn't manpower at CERN to create WWW versions for the Mac, PC, and UNIX systems. Berners-Lee's version could be used only on the NeXT platform.

A Universe of Network Accessible Information

Despite the criticism, the vision of a "universe of network-accessible information" resonated with other computer professionals. The whole idea was that there would be one common universe, one space. The Universal Resource Locator (URL), which starts with http, can be anything digital. The power of the hypertext link is that it can point to absolutely anything on the network. In the minds of programmers, it was an amazing tool. When a person creates a computer program, it is like creating a miniature universe in which the programmer is the master of the space. The computer does what you program it to do. You literally see what your mind and hands have created.

The World Wide Web provided a way to connect the universes and to expand the computing space. It offered a larger testing ground for the programmer's controlled experimentation.

The World Wide Web also offered an environment where programmers and system administrators could *show* their peers around the country and the world the incredible things they were creating with the code. It was a kind of "brotherhood" in the best sense of the term—like-minded people who felt a keen affinity for the problems and issues at hand, a mutual respect for each other, and a strong desire to build upon a body of programming knowledge, an evolving body of work.

The dynamics in the emerging, extended Web community were similar to the dynamics that characterized the Internet developer community a decade earlier. But now, the Internet made it possible for people to connect with peers anywhere on the globe. It did not matter if they worked in the U.S., in Europe, or anywhere else, so long as there were computers and access to the Internet.

A Web Developer's Community Forms in Cyberspace

Berners-Lee and Cailliau forged ahead and visited conferences where they told other programmers about the WorldWideWeb program. Those people went home and created versions for the Mac, PC, and UNIX system. System administrators in the U.S, Europe, and Asia who were reading the *alt.hypertext* newsgroup downloaded the software, played with it, and created their own web servers. Soon people around the world were building HTML documents and linking them to each other.

Berners-Lee's dream to provide critical usefulness at an early stage came true. It quickly became apparent beyond the CERN community that HTML documents were an ideal medium for publishing and annotating scientific papers, research materials, reference works, design specs, and white papers. Through 1991 and 1993, Berners-Lee continued working on the design of the Web, coordinating feedback from users across the Internet. Berners-Lee's initial specifications of URLs, http, and HTML were refined and discussed in larger circles as the web technology spread. One of the key learnings from the development of the Web that had been shown previously in the development of the Internet was that *innovation moves faster when people elsewhere are working on the problem with you. The trick was getting connected.*

The Big Morph: Berners-Lee's Web Editor/Browser → ViolaWWW Browser → (Mosaic Browser, the first "Killer App")

One problem, that of easily finding the documents on the Net, remained. Another innovator, Pei Wei, read about the Berners-Lee's WorldWideWeb program and wrote a piece of software called *ViolaWWW*. It was a World Wide Web client, code that allowed people to browse around the Web and look at web documents. Marc Andreessen and Eric Bina, students at the National Center for Supercomputing Applications at the University of Illinois at Urbana-Champaign, improved upon what the ViolaWWW code offered and created new code that would enable the browser to display graphic (GIF or JPEG) files. They called it *Mosaic*. It was the first web browser to interpret HTML and graphics files. It translated the HTML-formatted files, displaying them in a series of headings, lists, graphics, forms, and highlighted links.

Although people had been using the Internet for almost a decade, Mosaic was the first "killer app." It was easy to install, robust, and allowed in-line color images. Mosaic could not only track down HTML documents anywhere on the Net, but also could easily display them in a consistent way. Andreessen and his colleagues developed versions of Mosaic for Apple computers and Windows PCs, which opened the doors to the Internet for everyone, regardless of a computer's operation system. People didn't have to learn a set of commands to get themselves across the network, as was the case using telnet or FTP. Mosaic made using the Internet as easy as pointing a mouse and clicking on the hypertext.

■ Phase Four, Cultural Consciousness

In 1994, millionaire Jim Clark founded Mosaic Communications Corporation (MCC) with Marc Andreessen. Clark had once been an associate professor at Stanford, and he left in 1982 to found a company called Silicon Graphics, which became enormously profitable. In 1994, Clark quit as chairman of Silicon Graphics to join Andreessen. MCC later became Netscape Communications Corporation, and it hired some of the best young web programmers in the world. Three years earlier, the National Science Foundation had lifted restrictions against commercial use of the Internet. The lifting of the ban made it possible for a company like Netscape to exist.

By 1995, there was evidence that the Web was being used for a myriad of reasons—for commerce, for education and the arts, for distributing public information. There were many teachers, artists, librarians, students, statisticians, scientists, and government employees working on innovative ways to use the Web. A number of paperback technical reference books about creating HTML documents and internal web sites came on the market. The media, however, focused immediately on commercial applications.

New Communication Medium Begets New Marketing Model

The amount of media attention spotlighting the commercial potential of the Web somewhat distorted the fact that Web innovations were occurring in many areas of society. However, the media enthusiasm was understandable. The Web is not simply another channel for advertising, marketing, and direct distribution of products. It also offers a different, more direct way to reach consumers and to communicate with them. In 1995, <u>Donna Hoffman and Thomas Novack</u>,[4] professors at Vanderbilt University's Owen School of Management, reported that the Web was already beginning to profoundly change the economics of doing business. They wrote:

> Initial conjectures on efficiencies generated by online commercial efforts suggests that marketing on the Web results in 10 times as many units sold with 1/10 the advertising budget. It is about one-fourth less costly to perform direct marketing through the Net than through conventional channels. This fact becomes especially critical in the face of shortening technology and product life cycles and increasing technological complexity. Consider the example of SunSolve Online, which has saved Sun Microsystems over $4 million in FAQs alone since they reengineered information processes around the WWW.

The "Pull" Model

The Web created a different model for getting information into the hands of consumers. People using the Web select the documents they want for retrieval, a model of access called *information pull*. This contrasts with *information push*, where documents are sent to a preconfigured list of people, broadcast-style. The technology empowers users to pull information of value toward themselves while rejecting lower-value "noise."

For example, the SunSolve Online FAQ enabled Sun's customers to pull up the FAQ (frequently asked questions) on their computer screens, quickly scan through a list of questions and answers, and locate the pieces of information most useful at that particular moment. Customers could read the answer from the screen or cut and paste that section into a word processing document and print it out if they wished. It saved time and money, and reduced customers' frustrations with trying to search for the right person with the right answer. Because it was a computer file, it was also easy to update as new questions arose about the product. FAQs had long been part of the Usenet newsgroups on the Internet, and most of Sun's customers—computer professionals—were already familiar with that form of communication. What surprised so many people was that the new model of marketing communications – a computer-mediated "pull" model—could result in such substantial savings over other forms of marketing communication.

With the Internet as a catalyst, the marketing paradigm has begun a gradual evolution away from questions such as, How do we sell this, how do we push it onto the mass market and create mass demand? to, How do we find out what consumers want and need, and, at the same time, give them easy access to the right product?

The potential of the pull model was recognized by businesses migrating to the Web, as well as by on-line service providers such as eWorld, Prodigy, Compuserve, and America Online (AOL), which already had begun to bring advertisers, content providers, and millions of consumers to the Internet.

Virtual Spaces and the Desire to Connect

A key question emerged for the commercial online services and web sites: What is the best way to construct a virtual space from which people will want to pull information of interest to them? The answer to that question went through several stages. The first phase emphasized the wonders of the technology as a technology. The second phase emphasized content development —putting things of novelty or of real interest to consumers into the space. The third phase reveals a turn toward interaction and a focus on the people who use the technology. AOL CEO Steve Case notes:

> Content by itself is not king. Software in and of itself is not king. What really is king is the consumer and the way different technologies are brought together to provide services that have broad appeal. That's not just a technology question, it's a marketing question.[5]

As commercial on-line services evolved, it became apparent that some of the most value-added elements were the chat rooms and threaded discussion areas (or newsgroups), where people participate and contribute to on-line dialogs. Consumers wanted and needed more than information they could pull. They looked for opportunities to use the virtual spaces to communicate with each other—in just the same way that members of the research and scientific communities had been doing. Howard Rheingold eloquently explained the phenomenon in a 1988 essay, "Virtual Communities," and in his book, _The Virtual Community: Homesteading on the Electronic Frontier_, first published in 1991. Rheingold told stories about what was happening among people within the online communities and explained why thousands of people were joining in conversation on public Usenet groups on the Internet, on private on-line services such as the Whole Earth ELECTRONIC LINK (WELL), and on real-time chat areas called MUDs (Multiple User Domains).

Beyond Isolation: Finding Natural Synergies

More than simply virtual places to hold conversations, Rheingold observed that these technologies enabled the formation of communities. Adopting a schema proposed by Sociologist Marc Smith, Rheingold noted that people in virtual communities exchanged goods, just as people in the real world did. Sociologists recognize that *every cooperative group of people exists in the face of a competitive world because that group of people recognizes there is something valuable that they can gain by banding together.* Smith noticed that three kinds of collective goods bind people together in a virtual community: social network capital, knowledge capital, and communion. The millions of people who participate in on-line discussion areas find value in establishing relationships, in helping others or receiving help, and in getting answers to even the most esoteric questions. People who began to spend time in these virtual spaces found enormous synergy. Dave Carlson[6] remarks that "synergy is about balance. Each contributor to a synergistic relationship can gain from the other perspective, such that the benefit of the final solution is greater than its parts."

Howard Rheingold points out that the technology enabled people to experience such synergies first-hand. It also enabled them to actually become more than the selves they expressed in Real Life (IRL). Rheingold explains:

> I can attest that I and thousands of other cybernauts know [that] what we are looking for, and [are] finding in surprising ways, is not just information, but instant access to ongoing relationships with a large number of other people . . . . We reduce and encode our identities as words on a screen, decode and unpack the identities of others. The way we use these words, the stories (true and false) we tell about ourselves (or about the identity we want people to believe us to be) is what determines our identities in cyberspace. The aggre-

gation of personae, interacting with each other, determines the natures of the collective culture. Our personae, constructed from our stories of who we are, use the overt topics of discussion for a more fundamental purpose, as a means of interacting with each other. All this takes places on both private and public levels, in many-to-many open discussions and one-to-one private electronic mail, front stage role-playing and backstage behavior.[7]

A Critical Success Factor: The People and the Culture

Writers like Rheingold and Smith, who have tracked the evolution of public and commercial discussion areas, have noticed that *the* critical success factors have been the characteristics of the people who use the technology and the type of on-line culture they create. Writing about Usenet newsgroups, Stephen Steinberg[8] observed that

> The most reliable indicator of which newsgroups will foster intelligent discussion to be the presence of a core set of users— "experts"—who have been active in the newsgroup for a long time. These users embody the history and structure of the newsgroup.

> This is important because Usenet has a short institutional memory; a typical Usenet server receives over 80 megabytes of messages per day, and so can usually offer only the last few weeks of messages for each newsgroup. This lack of history means that the same questions are asked, the same arguments break out, and the same mistakes are made over and over.

> The group's experts serve as guides to ensure conversations stay on track, arguments are not repeated, and harsh personal attacks (known as "flames") are rapidly quelled. If the newsgroup is getting stuck on a question that was resolved months before, for example, the expert might post a message that explains what answer the group arrived at. If someone is posting insulting or offensive messages, the expert might send private e-mail reminding the guilty party of the rules of civility that prevail in the newsgroup.

Long-term users also help promote a sense of community. As you read more messages from a person, your mental picture of him or her becomes more fleshed out, you come to know the person behind the cryptic user ID. As personalities emerge, a newsgroup begins to feel like a corner cafe with regular customers, traditions, and myths.

If you have had first-hand experiences like these, you know exactly what Steinberg is describing. In fact, one of the greatest challenges is finding the right words to capture the experience. Like developing a strong friendship, it can be that amazing and that difficult to represent through words alone.

Information + People = Finding Solutions to Problems

Steinberg remarks that "in an earlier age, before people began to specialize in narrow fields, it was possible to have a friend who knew almost everything. Today discussion groups fills this role—it is a medium unrivaled for its ability to link the world's minds." And, some would add, to link hearts.

Some good examples of web sites that provide information and serve as a virtual space for communication about specific, problem-related issues are the _Parentsplace.com_ site for parents with young children, _The Intranet Journal_ for intranet developers, the _Tripod_ site for members of "Generation X," and _Salon 1999_ for people interested in ideas and culture. Rheingold's own web meeting place is _Electric Minds_, an attempt to create a large-scale electronic community devoted to science, technology, and their future effects on global society.

A decade ago, this kind of interaction was not possible for most people outside of the fields of science, technology, and academe. There was no way to broadcast a message over a wide terrain quickly and cheaply to a large group of people; no way to receive a quick response from the right person or people; no way to quickly locate a vital piece of information that is beyond your immediate physical reach. It is unfortunate that commercialization of the Net has enabled a number of people to display the some of very worst characteristics of this age, such as greed and excess. On the other hand, the commercialization and the mass marketing of the Internet has also enabled many people to gain first-hand experience with the new communication medium and has helped foster the beginnings of a distributed, diffuse Net culture.

Our culture and society are changing as a result of the new technology. Much of that change is being documented by the Public Broadcasting Service (PBS) series "Life On The Internet." The weekly series, hosted by journalist Scott Simon, examines the ways people use this new medium and its impact on all of us. The series web site includes transcripts from each of the shows— first-rate stories about how people are solving problems and connecting with each other—from doctors to family members to researchers.

Who is using the Internet and the Web today? There is much debate about that. One excellent source of demographic information comes from Jim Pitkow, a graduate student at Georgia Tech in Atlanta. In 1993, as a doctoral student in the Graphics, Visualization, and Usability program (GVU), Pitkow was writing his Ph.D. dissertation on the subject of human computer interaction, looking into the best ways for people to communicate with computers. However, he found that there were very little data on people who were using computers for communicating. What started as an interesting question has now become the world's largest collection of web data, the GVU's WWW User Surveys. It is updated every six months. While other pollsters scour the net and charge high fees for their findings, Pitkow and his graduate student colleagues put their information about the Web back on the Web, for free. Here is what Jim Pitkow explained to Scott Simon about why the group has not commercialized their work:

> The Web is a community and the surveys are a public service to the web community and we never want that fundamentally to change. Part of the notion here is that, if the cost of access to good information is expensive, then you're kind of crippling the adoption of this technology. And if you provide reasonable numbers for free, then you actually increase the adoption of this technology. Because you provide a valuable service, like we do, to the Web community for the Web community. After all, they're the people who filled out the surveys. Why shouldn't they have access to this? It's their data.[9]

Providing a value-added service in the spirit of "giving back to the user community" has won Pitkow and his colleagues much acclaim. Their findings reveal that there are some curious differences in trends between Internet use in North America and that in the rest of the world. Scott Simon summarizes:

> Americans, for example, are three times more likely to own their own computers than Europeans. There are more married people

than single people on line in the United States, in Europe it's just the opposite. They've discovered lots of other little differences on either side of the Atlantic, but in one area the international web population is moving in the same direction. Everywhere the demographics show that women are beginning to play a larger role than ever before.

Jim Pitkow remarks that one reason the on-line culture is changing is that women are now almost as likely to be on the Web as are men.

> Initially when we ran our first survey we had a 95% male population. And now we're finding we're around 70%. And the rate at which that is changing, itself is increasing. So we're rapidly getting into a more gender-balanced population. Additionally when we look at differences between the populations of the male versus female, the differences aren't that great. We find more difference between U.S. users and European users than we do between male and female users. So, even though there may be a little bit of imbalance, we're not talking about any major difference between the two populations, that we can see in our numbers. And this is very encouraging.

We can see evidence of this change in numerous sites that have been created to enable women to use the Web as a resource. Some of those sites are: _Women's Wire_, _Cybergrrl_, _WWWomen_, _A Woman's Space_, _Voices of Women Online_, _Herspace_, _Women@Work_, _Expect the Best From a Girl_, _Women Online Worldwide_, _Femina_ and _Mothers Who Think_. In fact, if you want to see open dialog, networking, problem-solving, and a lot of value-added content, these sites provide excellent examples.

Hammering Out the Rules: It's Easier on the Technology Side

One of the biggest problems on the Internet now is developing the rules—the rules of monetary exchange, the rules of discourse, the rules of conduct.

It is somewhat easier to manage the rules on the technology side. Internet protocols are governed by rules. HTML is a rule-based system of parsing a computer language. In fact, the rules are what enables the system to exist.

Like any rules, technology's rules change and evolve. Internet protocols and HTML are different today than they were in 1993; they have evolved—

and not without struggle. If you look at the debates about the evolution of the protocols and HTML, you'll find a lot of discussion about whether breaking the old rules is ruining a good thing. (See, for example, the debate about HTML in *Creating Killer Web Sites*).

The rules on the nontechnology side are more difficult to work out. With technology, you can push the rules only in increments; otherwise, the technology as a system falls apart. If you push too far, you'll know. Something won't work—the program won't run, the systems won't let the computers "talk" to each other.

It's different on the human side. The feedback loops in the human social system aren't as clean or as efficient as they are in a computer system. The effects of any particular action are delayed and are sometimes hard to see. We have to use language, like English, with its own set of rules, to talk about rules.

The struggle over rules governing the Internet has become a public issue involving industry, government, academe, and the media. There are many articulate and powerful participants in the debates. The diagenesis* that we see reflects the richness of our culture, as well as a wish to take elements of that culture and cement them, so as to create a stable foundation. The question is, which elements belong? This is an essential question because it will impact the "who" that "we" are on the Internet. (See, for example, the debates hosted by the Boston Review.)

Millions of people now know how to get on-line and use the technology but, as with any new medium, the issues of control are being worked out as the technology evolves. We're all making a gradual transformation—internet and intranet participants alike.

*The dictionary definition of *diagenes*is is "the process of chemical and physical change in deposited sediment during its conversion to rock." Cultural diagnesis is similar—the cementing of certain ideas and practices into our daily thoughts and activities so that, like rock, they provide a certain amount of cultural stability.

■ Meanwhile, Intranet Innovation Continues

Computer-mediated communication in the U.S. started in the 1970s and 1980s as conferencing and e-mail systems. The difficulty was in getting the systems to talk to each other. The web browsers and servers developed at CERN, the National Center for Supercomputing Applications, and Netscape were changing all of that.

So, while the culture at large adjusted to becoming increasingly networked, intranet innovation spread from CERN to other organizations and into corporate America.

The next chapter takes a look at what motivated the first intranet innovators to begin experimenting with web technologies within their organizations. We'll explore our first case study, the emergence of US WEST's "Global Village" and the US WEST Web Developer's Coalition. We'll see how certain individuals such as Peggy Tumey, Sherman Woo, and the founders of the Web Developer's Coalition shared a passion for improving the company through the application of web-based technologies. We'll also see how fast web technologies have evolved as a result of the enormous commercial money-making potential people perceived in web technologies.

■ References

[1] Robert Cailliau, "A Short History of the Web," text of a speech delivered at the launching of the European branch of the W3 Consortium Paris, November 2, 1995 (http://www.inria.fr/Acualities/Cailliau-fra.html).

[2] Tim Berners-Lee, "The World Wide Web—Past, Present and Future," transcript of a speech delivered at the British Computer Society, July 17, 1996 (http://www.bcs.org.uk/news/timbl.htm).

[3] Tim Berners-Lee, "Information Management: A Proposal," (http://www.w3.org/pub/WWW/History/1989/proposal.html)

[4] Donna L. Hoffman, Thomas P. Novack, and Patrali Chatterjee, "Commercial Scenarios for the Web: Opportunities and Challenges, paper submitted to the Journal of Computer Mediated Communication," August 7, 1995.

[5] David Kirpatrick, "Riding the Real Trends in Technology," *Fortune*, February 19, 1996.

[6] David Carlson, "A Natural Synergy," *Object Magazine*, August, 1996, p. 25 (http://www.sigs.com).

[7] Howard Rheingold, "A Slice of My Virtual Life," June 1992, sent via private e-mail to the author, October 7, 1992.

[8] Stephen Steinberg, "Travels on the Net," *Technology Review*, July 1, 1994, p. 20.

[9] Scott Simon interview with Jim Pitkow and Colleen Keyhoe for the PBS series "Life on the Internet," 1996, transcript at http://www.pbs.org/internet/demo/transcript/html.

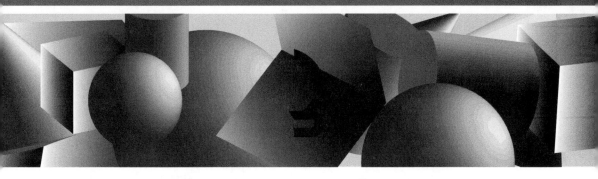

A Gradual Transformation
of Culture

As our story continues, we circle back to the focus of this book: intranets. As we saw in the last two chapters, during the mid-1990s, the American culture began gradually to change as more and more people began communicating through the Internet, forming electronic networks and virtual communities. On the Net, people were sharing resources and information, identifying new ways to make money or to save money through application of web technologies, hammering out the rules, and having a lot of fun.

This chapter takes a look under the corporate veil to discuss the first wave of intranet development. Led by information technology (IT) visionaries and "Generation X" rebels, the first corporate intranets, like the US WEST "Global Village," came into existence for many of the same reasons Berners-Lee had invented the Web. The technology itself was tremendously exciting, and people wanted to do something to improve organizational communication. The difficulties they found, however, illuminate why intranet development is the acid test of open systems computing.

■ Phase Five, Gradual Transformation

An Underground Intranet Movement Begins

In 1993, people began downloading copies of Mosaic from the Internet and passed them around from hand to hand and from department to department. People in companies all over the world began to see the potential of using web technologies to make it easier for employees to distribute and gain access to information. Intranets took off as a kind of underground movement.

The time was right. The infrastructure necessary for intranets to be widely implemented—PCs, LANs, WANs, and client/servers— was present in many organizations, providing a foundation for innovation. A major shift in the economy was underway, and the "learning organization" and "knowledge management" movements were rising.

A Convergence of Technology and Terminology: The Knowledge Economy

For almost half a century, management theorist Peter Drucker and others have been pointing to a radical change in the nature of work. In *Post-Capitalist Society*, Drucker argued that knowledge is replacing capital as society's basic re-source and that a market economy organizes economic activity around infor-mation. People who deal primarily with information are the expanding ranks of labor. Decade ago, Drucker noted, "knowledge workers" began to eclipse factory workers, just as those on the assembly line once replaced farm labor.

Drucker helped to draw attention to trends that economists actually started to identify in the 1950s. The industrial sector, which reached a peak during World War II, was declining steadily. By 1960, the information sector was al-ready larger (at more than 40 percent) than industry had ever been. (Today, it approaches over half the U.S. labor force.) Although scholars debate whether or not the "information economy" has truly replaced the industrial economy, Drucker's use of the terms "knowledge economy" and the "knowledge worker" had the effect of giving greater currency and weight to the phenomenon.

Other authors, such as George Gilder, pointed to the role of technology in the vast and sweeping economic changes. Since the 1970s, the growth of the information sector and the rise of the knowledge worker have been tied to the continuing proliferation of microprocessing technology. The most important social implication, James Beniger notes, was the progressive convergence of all information technologies—mass media, telecommunications, and computing—into a single infrastructure.[1] It was clear that the landscape in which people work and live was beginning to look more and more like an interlocked network of systems.

The Learning Organization

Peter Senge's 1990 classic, *The Fifth Discipline: The Art and Practice of the Learning Organization*, provided a vocabulary and road map to help organizations reinvent themselves in the context of the knowledge economy. Senge synthesized and eloquently articulated a set of ideas about stimulating organizational change and creating new forms of organizational life, ideas that had been evolving since the end of World War II. (Art Kleiner has captured that history in his poignant and inspiring book, *The Age of Heretics*). In the *Fifth Discipline*, Senge emphasized the importance of embracing systems thinking as a way to see underneath the dynamic complexity of organizational life. Senge also promoted the idea of "learning organizations" as places "where people continually expand their capacity to create results they truly desire, where new and expansive patterns of thinking are nurtured, where collective aspiration is set free, and where people are continually learning how to learn together." Senge and others provided a vocabulary and language that could be used to legitimately express ideas and visions about the need for organizational change at the turn of the millennium. In many corporations and organizations, people began talking about systems thinking, and the need for improved information and communication.

Knowledge Management

Tom Peters helped to push the idea of "knowledge management" further into the business community's spotlight. Peters was a former McKinsey consultant who received his MBA from Stanford Business School. He gained fame through his 1982 best-selling book, *In Search of Excellence,* which sold over 5 million copies. *In Search of Excellence* is based the academic practice of developing case studies. Case studies are an essential teaching tool in business schools all across the nation. The practice has been adapted as a corporate activity now known as benchmarking. It is the idea that by probing under the corporate veil, you can learn something of value from other companies and other industries that will enable you to succeed. It is, in essence, the sharing of best practices.

One of the most critical success factors is a person who can facilitate the transfer. This type of person loves to get connected with others, can ask the right questions and frame the responses in a way that creates enthusiasm and a desire for more information. Tom Peters, with his charismatic personality and gift for hyperbole, was the right person to bring the message to the marketplace.

The message of *In Search of Excellence* was: It is time to change your management paradigm. The old, traditional rules are not working. Those companies who exemplify excellence are doing things somewhat ahead of the rest. *In Search of Excellence* declared "disturbers of the peace" and "fanatical champions" to be the most vital people in the organization, and attacked the principles of "scientific" management.

Peters' book, *Liberation Management: Necessary Disorganization for the Nanosecond Nineties,* was published in 1992 as a kind of sequel to *In Search of Excellence.* It was far less theoretical than *In Search of Excellence,* and it amplified Peters' jazzy "sharing of best practices" mode. *Liberation Management* emphasized several key themes. They were:

- gathering information and disseminating information are signs of strength;
- knowledge hoarding is a sign of weakness;
- enabling communication and collaboration (particularly through technology) is a sound investment of resources; and
- teams and networks are the organizational structures of the future.

A large chunk of *Liberation Management* is about knowledge management. Peters examined over two dozen cutting edge knowledge management companies. He then created a typology of knowledge management activities that he used to rate 21 of those companies. His categories were: Learn From Clients, Learn From Outsiders, Learn From Each Other, and Systematic Knowledge Capture Device (technology).

Other excellent books by authors such as Mary E. Boone and Sally Helgesen presented similar themes. Assisted by Peters' tremendous energy in helping to push these concepts into the business marketplace of ideas, more media outlets began spreading the word. Publications such as *Fortune* began to publish long articles on the importance of knowledge management as a competitive strategy and began to profile leading edge practitioners whom Peters had profiled in his book, such as Buckman Laboratories International, Skandia, Dow Chemical, and McKinsey.

By 1994, the technology and the terminology was beginning to converge. For example, *Fortune*'s July 11, 1994 cover story was "Managing in a Wired World," and just three issues later the cover story was titled "Your Company's Most Valuable Asset: Intellectual Capital." Both covers stories were essentially about the same thing: using information technology to enable new forms of organizational structures and new forms of management.

Knowledge management is now a large and growing consulting and academic domain. There are several web sites dedicated to knowledge sharing and knowledge management, such as *The Knowledge Management Forum* and the *Community Intelligence Labs*. Over a thousand documents about knowledge management are on the Web alone. Yogesh Malhotra's *A Business Researcher's Interests* web site is one place you can literally see the exponential output in this field. In the area Malhotra has dedicated to Organizational Knowledge Management and Organizational Learning, there are over 500 links to papers, organizations, conferences, discussion areas, and articles about knowledge management and organizational learning.

Given the enormous amount of interest in this area, it seemed inevitable that corporations, companies, universities, and nonprofit organizations would embrace these concepts and re-think their operations. Interestingly, perception did not always match reality.

■ Case Study 1: U S WEST and the Electronic "Global Village"

U S WEST, the mid- and western states' regional Bell operating company, is a fascinating example of how intranet technologies rode into companies on a wave catalyzed by authors like Drucker, Senge, and Peters and began to take hold. Its lessons are highly instructive, and point to some of the central and

most difficult changes that intranet proponents face. Enter Peggy Tumey and
Sherman Woo.

Question: How Is Technology Changing the World, and How Is it Changing Our Industry?

In 1993, Peggy Tumey, a top financial officer at U S WEST in Denver,
wanted to find a way to help employees learn how new technologies would
affect the telecommunication services that the company offers. Tumey offered to provide support to a small team of people headed by a very insightful,
forward-thinking IT director named Sherman Woo. The team, including
consultants like Ryan Martens from BDM Technologies from across the
street, began by having discussions that led to the creation of a planning document. Their discussions about *technological and economic change* and *learning* were generative and imaginative.

The team planned a technology showcase where employees could have a
first-hand experience with new telecommunication technologies. Employees
would be able to drop by to learn about how new technologies work and how
they would be linked to the US WEST telephone network. The showcase
would have elements of sales training and consultative customer service—
employees could learn how consumers could use new technologies to improve their lives. It would be a place where people from all across the company with different backgrounds could come together to talk about the
company and new visions of the future. Peggy borrowed from media theorist
Marshal McLuhan's ideas about the centrality of information processing and
communication, and named the project the "Global Village".

A "Mirror World" Characterized by Systems Thinking and Shared Competitive Intelligence

Among the new technologies the team wished to showcase were the Web
and the Internet. The team, guided by Woo, set up an inexpensive Internet
demonstration in their first-floor offices. They created a kind of theater by
clustering several computers back to back in a circle and projecting computer
screen images from the Web onto large screens built from heavy cardboard.

The audience sat on an eclectic mix of comfortable, upholstered chairs and couches, many of which came from rummage sales. In a corporate setting like US WEST, the effect was unusual.

The team also developed their own web site. Besides being an example of a new technology, the team hoped that the Global Village web site could be like a "mirror world" for what was occurring in physical space. The site was designed with the hope that employees from all across the 14-state territory could join each other to work as virtual teams or to hold discussions in virtual rooms. The team saw that it was becoming essential to use technology to surrender knowledge to anyone with the skills to access and understand it. In their planning document, the team noted that it was becoming more crucial for employees to understand, respond to, manage, and create value from information. They argued that the new competitive telecommunications environment required systems-thinking skills and better competitive intelligence at *all levels.*

Providing Value and Becoming Evangelists

Funding for the physical technology showcase was not forthcoming. US WEST had other priorities, including reengineering the company a la Michael Hammer, changing its leadership, and expanding its reach into international markets and cable markets. However, the *electronic* Global Village, the company's first web-based intranet, was relatively inexpensive and was developed with the funds Tumey had earmarked for the group.

The on-line Global Village captured many managers' and employees' imaginations. Internet demonstrations at the Global Village offices resulted in several large-scale, web-based projects designed to streamline complex processes and to give employees better, easier access to data. One of Woo's largest projects gave mass marketing customer service representatives access to the company's massive, complex legacy systems through a web browser. Previously, the reps had to deal with a minimum of 12 different screens of information in order to assist customers calling to initiate or cancel service, order an additional phone line, or schedule a time for a service call. The web browser provided a single interface into all the various systems. A large project that demanded highly creative programming skills, Woo's legacy project met very real business needs.

At the same time, the Global Village staff continued as evangelists. They made it easy for employees to download web browsers off the US WEST network and made several web servers available for pilot projects that involved public relations and other business units. Employees began to create their own home pages and departmental web sites. Within a few years, there were over 50 other web sites besides the Global Village site on the network. One factor that contributed to the intranet's growth was the fact that US WEST already had a fairly extensive internal network of LANs and WANs.

The company—huge, bureaucratic, and extremely focused on top management's strategy—did not give much weight to the Global Village's original vision of technology-supported teamwork and collaborative learning. The main problem was not that the team was so far ahead of its time. Sherman Woo, a technology visionary, could perceive the potentials inherent in the Web before others, but much of the group's foundational thinking was a synthesis of books and articles that had been in print since the late 1980s and early 1990s. Peggy Tumey and her group were not fringe thinkers.

The overall problem was that the company was preoccupied with other things, and managers at all levels were rewarded for thinking about employees through the lenses of traditional command-control management. Many people in the company, across all 14 states, were reading Drucker, Gilder, Senge, Peters, and other authors and were talking with their colleagues about these ideas. Many had been Internet devotees since the 80s and knew a tremendous amount about the technical aspects of network-based and web-based computing. Yet, finding each other and making a dent in the corporate culture proved to be the largest challenge. It was not quite so easy or as jazzy as *Liberation Management* and the trade magazines would suggest.

And yet, the amazing thing was that the Global Village itself took hold. Largely because the Global Village was **funded on a project-by-project basis**, it was able to add staff, support users, and continue to teach US WEST employees and outside visitors about the value of the Web and web technologies. Today, it's probably one of the company's most undervalued assets. Visitors from around the world come to the Global Village offices to find out more about intranet design and implementation.

Capturing Key Learnings and Helping Each Other: The Web Developer's Coalition

In 1995, Ryan Martens from BDM Technologies, with several others, initiated a coordinating organization. Ryan, along with Kristina Jonell Yarrington, then a webmaster from Public Relations, Mike Vaughan, a webmaster from Capacity Provisioning/Service Assurance, and this author (a consultant working at that time within the Quality group), had been coming to each other for help on various technical and nontechnical issues. Given the number of web sites that had sprung up on the US WEST network, this group guessed that other people were facing similar problems. As a sideline project and not part of any of their official jobs, they founded the US WEST Web Developer's Coalition as a coordinating mechanism for sharing key learnings and technical expertise, and for addressing issues such as security, standards, budgets, and management support.

To announce their first meeting, they sent out a broadcast e-mail to people within their personal circles of contacts and to any employee who had ever had contact with the Global Village. It contained a description of the proposed coalition (very much in the spirit of an RFC), and an open invitation to anyone who wished to join. They designed and created colorful internal marketing materials, such as flyers and posters, which they distributed primarily to the Denver metropolitan offices. The centerpiece of their communication campaign was a web site where people could read about why the founders were motivated to create the Coalition and where they could fill out a membership form to get enrolled on the Coalition's e-mail lists.

The response was amazing. Over 400 US WEST employees replied via e-mail to signal an interest in joining the coalition. Over 100 people attended the first meeting, held at the Denver Convention Center, with Sherman Woo as the featured speaker.

The tremendous interest in the Web Developer's Coalition actually took executive directors in the IT group by surprise. Before the Coalition formed, most of the internal web development work within the company was invisible to IT senior management. However, the employees' interest in the Global Village and in the Coalition sent a clear signal of a strong demand for web-based computing all across the organization. One year after the first Web Developer's Coalition meeting, US WEST's CIO, Dave Laube, announced in an

October, 1996 press release that it was licensing 50,000 copies of a US WEST-customized version of Netscape Navigator for its employees.

"Always in human society there is what may be called a double reality," Kingsley Davis notes, "on one hand a normative system embodying what *ought* to be, and on the other hand a factual order embodying what *is*." In many ways, web development at US WEST illustrates that point. The work that began in 1993, just as Mosaic was being born, foretold the tremendous possibilities of intranet development for the company.

Peggy Tumey's career milestones have included several strategic initiatives, highly effective business process improvements, and recognition from her senior executive peers. Although her accomplishments are many, she notes that "the Global Village is my favorite accomplishment of my career."

At US WEST, the intranet initiative began with discussions by a small group of innovators supported by a smart senior-level champion about how the world was changing and how people in organizations needed to find better ways to communicate. US WEST was not an isolated instance. In corporations, professional organizations, and government agencies, teams of forward-thinking individuals with Internet access and a knowledge of computers were setting up their own intranets.

Fall, 1995: The Media "Discovers" Intranets

Other large "pre-wired" companies that created internal corporate intranets included EDS, Intel and Hewlett-Packard. The media, however, was focused on cybermalls, encryption, virtual reality, the "battle for the soul of the Internet," and Lotus Notes.

Then, in October 1995, Netscape Communications surprised the business press by announcing record third-quarter revenues of $20.8 million, more than half of which came from sales to corporations setting up internal webs. To bystanders, this was very big news. At that point, the media began to shift from a primary emphasis on the commercial uses of the Internet toward intranets.

The consistent message from the media has been how easy intranets are to implement. For example, *Fortune* magazine profiled Sherman Woo and the Global Village in a November 1995 issue called "The Internet Inside Your Company." In their rush to show how easy intranets are to implement, *Fortune* overestimated how many employees actually use the company's intranet on a daily basis and reported Global Village's vision for collaborative web-based computing as already occurring in everyday reality. The *Fortune* article offered typical intranet hype—not entirely a deception, but replete with exaggerated claims and extravagant examples.

In short, internal communication networks have been around since the beginning of network-based computing. Improving organizational communication was one primary reason why J.C.R. Licklider wanted to help develop the Internet and why Berners-Lee was motivated to create the World-WideWeb. The emergence of intranets only *seems* like a later development.

The Acid Test of Open Systems: The Future Looks Like a Question Mark

Yet, in many ways, intranets are the acid test of open systems computing and the visionary impulse behind web-based technologies. For over a century, organizations have been the playing field where materialism and idealism have battled. How will people choose to adopt intranet technologies? What human characteristics will be reflected in those technologies? What dreams and aspirations will be reflected in the intranets being brought into small companies, large corporations, and nonprofit organizations?

Up to now, technology in organizations has been implemented primarily from the top down. Technology objectives have reflected values of organizational control, the minimization of risk, and maximization of profits. With few exceptions, technologies have been introduced into organizations without the involvement of the majority of employees in conception, design, or evaluation.

Computer technologies have also been used to preserve artificial and outdated divisions of labor. Professor Shosana Zuboff has pointed out that until recently, information technologies have been leveraged principally by the managerial elite who perceive themselves as responsible for doing the thinking for the organization. The working caste, perceived as responsible for carrying out the orders, has not been given the same access to information or to the information technologies. In many organizations, technology—not people—have come first.

However, because of the Web, people are beginning to think about technologies in entirely different ways. People in companies all over the U.S. and the world are getting access to Web tools and are creating their own web sites and intranets, often initially without the knowledge or the explicit consent of senior management. Intranet champions do it because it is fun, because they have grown tired of waiting for the company to meet their communication needs, and because for many people, this type of work provides great opportunities for self-expression.

This is an *amazing* time in history. What happens from this point is up to individuals, groups, and organizations in the midst of making decisions about how they want to bring their intranets forward. Tom Peters' next book, which is about "breaking the rules," may give greater weight and currency to the idea of taking a project into your own hands and making it yours. Yet, small actions of creation and persistence made by people like yourself, in companies and organizations just like yours, will direct the technology toward the past or toward the future. Each step along the way, no matter how seemingly insignificant, will make a difference.

Meanwhile, the Technology Speeds Ahead

In terms of technology improvement, there have been many changes since Mosaic entered the market in 1993. Because the market is now perceived to be so enormous, the tools are becoming easier to find. Intranet developers no longer need to pull the pieces of the system together from scratch. Several intranet suites allow companies to quickly configure an internal corporate intranet by combining group conferencing, document management, electronic publishing, and workgroup-enhanced Internet access. RadNet's WebShare and IntraNetics intranet suite are excellent examples of open system intranet suites. They are easy to set up, and employees require no knowledge of HTML to contribute materials. Netscape communicates well with the development community, and the company has made a commitment to promote the application developers' products—regardless of whether the products come from big companies or small shops. (RadNet, IntraNetics, and Netscape demos are included with the CD-ROM packaged with this book.)

The Java Phenomenon

A very significant change is Java™. Java is a programming language created by James Gosling, one of the best programmers in the world, at Sun Microsystems. Version 1.0 was officially released by Sun in 1996. Java is a program designed to be included in an HTML document and to run inside a web browser. It can be used to create applets, tiny programs that can be embedded in a web page and downloaded over the Internet.

Before Java, web pages were not interactive. Once the HTML file was displayed on the screen by the browser, the page was static. Like a page from a book, the content did not change. PERL and C++ scripts for things like forms or animation resided on the web server (on the "server side"). So, for example, to submit information on a form and see results, you had to go back out on the network.

In contrast, Java enables a web page to deliver the applets along with the visual content. Because Java programs execute locally, they take advantage of a host computer's processing power without increasing the load on remote web servers.

The applets can do two things. First, they can bring the page alive. Applets can create scrolling banners, self-updating scoreboards, moving stock ticker marquees, and even shoot animated cartoons. If you have ever looked at a web page and a page from a four-color magazine and wondered why people kept saying that the Web is a superior communication medium, Java now makes the difference self-evident. From a multi-media standpoint (that is, the integration of visually compelling images and hypertext), Java is the Web's second generation "killer app."

With Java, the Power Gets Pushed to the End-User

Java has a second, equally important function. The applets are like just-in-time software that you can throw away after every use, and they don't take long to download. For example, prior to Java, if a person wanted to use a spreadsheet application, he/she either had to have the spreadsheet application loaded on their computer's hard drive, or they had to port over to another computer on the network where the application was loaded. Java enables a developer to write a small, useful spreadsheet applet that is executed by the web browser. A person can change the numbers and test assumptions, and create bar charts or pie charts, just as with a conventional spreadsheet. Java basically takes advantage of web technology's flexibility and universality, and it decentralizes networked applications.

Also, like HTML, Java is a platform-independent language. One applet can run on any platform with a browser supporting the Java Virtual Machine, which interprets and runs the Java byte-code. In addition, Java can be used to write more powerful stand-alone applications. Several large Java applications include a parts-ordering application at National Semiconductor, a purchase acquisition service at Dun & Bradstreet, a sports database dynamic linkage service at ESPN, and an on-line database access program at RR Donnelly. Java is similar to the programming language C++, but it's syntactically cleaner, less expansive in scope, and easier to learn. More importantly, Java may become the official programming language of the Web.

A Growing Interest in Extranets

Another development is the growing interest in extending the intranet beyond the organization's firewall to include business partners. "Extranets" are a kind of natural extension in the development of business-based networked communication. An extranet enables organizations to communicate electronically with external partners and customers. What makes this type of communication more feasible today than in the past are the open Internet standards such as HTML, Java, and JavaScript, which can be easily extended to partners and customers. As more and more business is becoming "virtual," the ability to use technology to support extraorganizational projects is becoming highly valued. PNF, Inc, for example, has already managed several extranet projects to provide intranet-to-intranet solutions to Wall Street firms. PFN's product, Continuum, replicates any information on a company's intranet to any other intranet, either inside or outside the firewall.

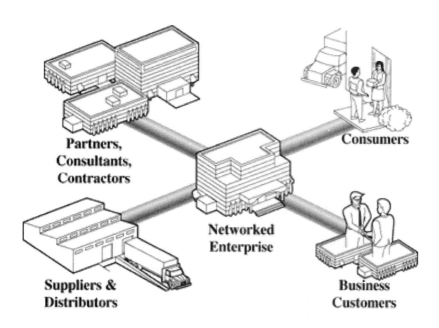

FIGURE 3.1

Extranets link organizations internally and externally to strategic partners, suppliers, distributors, and customers. (Copyright 1996, Netscape Communications Corporation. Used by permission. All rights reserved. This image may not be reprinted or copied without the express written permission of Netscape.)

A number of years ago, William H. Davidow and Michael S. Malone foretold the trend toward intraorganizational networks with their compelling and well-researched book, *The Virtual Corporation: Structuring and Revitalizing the Corporation for the 21st Century*. Virtual corporations are defined by the types of relationships that they have with suppliers, distributors, employees, and customers. Their use of information technologies distinguishes this type of business from what we have traditionally thought of as the modern corporation, for it increasingly relies on devices that "harness, integrate and effectively use new types of information."[2] Propelling this trend, Davidow and Malone note, is the desire to adapt in real time to the customer's changing needs, to become more customer driven and customer managed.

Intranet/extranet technologies can be used to support the profound changes that are in store for both the company and its distribution system and internal organization as the company evolves to become more customer focused and driven. In such a metamorphosis, there are no intermediate steps. The process of corporate revision, wrote Davidow and Malone, must be rapid and complete, involving all segments—from research and development to manufacturing, from marketing and sales to service and distribution, and from finance to information systems. Everyone needs to communicate.

Web-based applications that can be extended throughout the organization and across the firewall are, thus, becoming essential to organizational transformation.

Everyone's Talking

There are now numerous web sites dedicated to intranet development where people can find information about the latest intranet technologies and even post questions. Magazines such as _Computerworld, PCWeek,_ and _Webmaster_ include monthly columns about intranet technologies and their uses. Netscape's web site features an area dedicated to intranets that contains many demos, case studies, white papers, lists of seminars, press clippings, and a developer's discussion forum.

As measured by the amount of information becoming available, intranets are, as _Fortune_ put it, "The Next Big Thing." Beyond that, intranets are an important and significant development in the history of distributed computing and organizational development. It's top of mind at most professional conferences. What _is_ an intranet? How do intranets enable different and new forms of organizational communication? How are intranets different than groupware? The next chapter answers those questions.

■ Conclusion: Keeping the Purpose and the Pull Model in Mind

One thing to remember is that behind all of these activities there must be an underlying sense of purpose. When we look back at the history of the Internet, the Web, and the U S WEST Global Village, we can see that each project was driven by purpose. They were successful because they were purposeful. The Internet was created for the purpose of enabling the transfer of data across a distributed computer network. Behind that were other purposes such as Licklider's wish to enable people to use computers for rote work while freeing them up to become more informed participants in decision-making processes. Berners-Lee's purpose for creating the Web was to organize himself and to enable his colleagues to find answers to questions that were bogging down the work. Sherman Woo and his team created the US WEST Global Village with the purposes of helping employees see the link between new technologies and customers' needs, of distributing information more widely, and of enabling collaborative work.

Going forward, keep in mind that you'll need to scope the purpose of your intranet. The next chapters will help you do that. One rule of thumb is that the purpose of any new technology can be found in a question that is rooted in a problem we're trying to solve. For example, Berners-Lee's questions were, Where is this module used? Who wrote this code? Where does he work? What documents exist about that concept? Which laboratories are included in that project? Which systems depend on this device? What documents refer to this one? Those questions were rooted in the problem of separateness: the fact that CERN employees circulated in and out of the organization, reported to different bosses and work groups, and had a hard time tapping into the collective knowledge base. Berners-Lee's Web provided a solution to the problem. Its purpose was to enable people to connect to information and to each other.

The better you can see the problem, the better you'll be at developing the right technology solution and in predicting second-order consequences that flow from technology implementation. When we're not clear about the problem we're trying to solve, we tend to apply the technology in ways that not only exacerbate the main problem but also leads to a flood of hard-to-manage second-order consequences. A lot of companies want to implement intranets as a technology solution. Then they have a difficult time convincing management to buy into the system and lend ongoing support. They also have a hard time actively engaging employees to use the intranet. The situation seems to require them to "push" the technology at the employee base. However, if you probe through the corporate veil, you'll see that the more fundamental problem is often a communication problem—calling for a communication solution—which may or may not be focused around the technology as the driver. The model to keep in mind is the pull model of communication. What will motivate employees to pull the technology and the content riding on the technology to themselves and into their work? How will you know if they are actively engaged with the solution you've provided? The next chapters will provide a road map to streamline the process.

Take Aways from Section One

Five Phases of Ontogeny

The history of the Internet and the Web revealed five phases of ontogeny (*ontogeny* means "coming into being"). They were: Phase One: The Network; Phase Two: The Language; Phase Three: Test Site and Tools; Phase Four: Cultural Consciousness; Phase Five: Gradual Transformation. We can represent the five stages of ontogeny graphically as a flowchart like this:

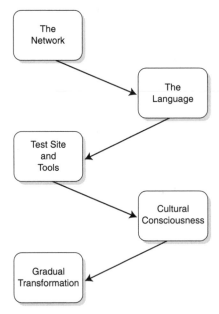

At each stage, we saw that there were important activities on the technology side as well as the nontechnology (or human) side. We can depict them as parallel activities radiating from each phase.

■ Parallel Activities on the Technology and Human Sides

PHASE	Activities on the Technology Side	Activities on the Non-technology Side
The Network	Creation of the network protocols to enable the transfer of data among machines	Vertical and horizontal distribution of resources (involving industry, academy, government). Networks of like-minded colleagues form to enable problem-solving. Effective use of RFQs and RFCs.
The Language	SGML + Hypertext = HTML	Berners-Lee's Proposal to CERN provides a rational argument why CERN should sponsor the work. Berners-Lee and Cailliau tell their story at conferences.
Test Site and Tools	Berners-Lee's web editor/browser → ViolaWWW → Mosaic web browser	Berners-Lee and Calliau: Web tools developed for NEXT computers. Beyond CERN: *alt.hypertext* participants and others develop tools for the MAC, PC, and UNIX.
Cultural Consciousness	Commercialization leads to technology race among Netscape, Microsoft, Apple, Sun, and others.	Commercialization leads to wide-spread first-hand experience of the Web as a communication medium and to further evolution of the Net culture.
Gradual Transformation	Further innovation in web-based technology, especially Java, which pushes power to the end users.	The concepts "Information Economy," the "Learning Organization," and "Knowledge Management" lead to new academic, consulting, and corporate activities focused around better distribution of information and knowledge.

■ Section One Questions

Sound, stable intranet development will follow that same progression through each of the five phases. Therefore, it is good to keep the following check list in mind.

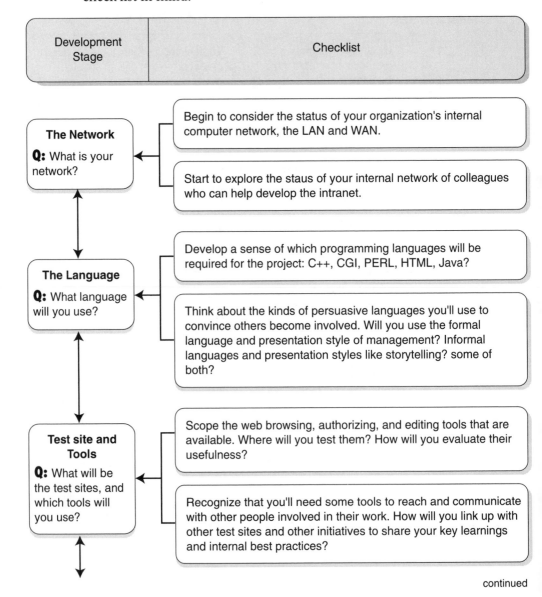

Development Stage	Checklist

The Network

Q: What is your network?

- Begin to consider the status of your organization's internal computer network, the LAN and WAN.
- Start to explore the staus of your internal network of colleagues who can help develop the intranet.

The Language

Q: What language will you use?

- Develop a sense of which programming languages will be required for the project: C++, CGI, PERL, HTML, Java?
- Think about the kinds of persuasive languages you'll use to convince others become involved. Will you use the formal language and presentation style of management? Informal languages and presentation styles like storytelling? some of both?

Test site and Tools

Q: What will be the test sites, and which tools will you use?

- Scope the web browsing, authorizing, and editing tools that are available. Where will you test them? How will you evaluate their usefulness?
- Recognize that you'll need some tools to reach and communicate with other people involved in their work. How will you link up with other test sites and other initiatives to share your key learnings and internal best practices?

continued

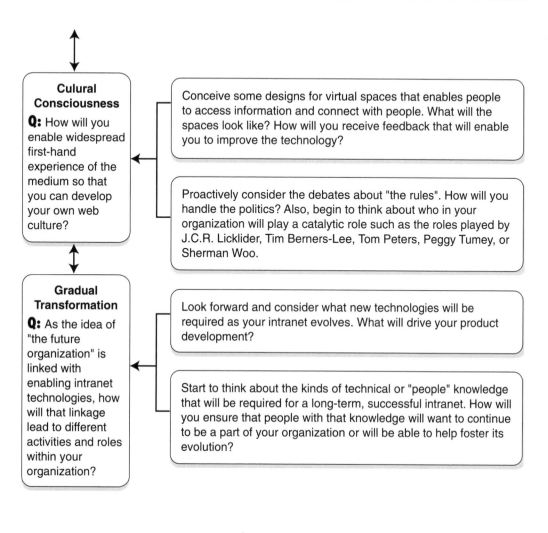

Culural Consciousness

Q: How will you enable widespread first-hand experience of the medium so that you can develop your own web culture?

Conceive some designs for virtual spaces that enables people to access information and connect with people. What will the spaces look like? How will you receive feedback that will enable you to improve the technology?

Proactively consider the debates about "the rules". How will you handle the politics? Also, begin to think about who in your organization will play a catalytic role such as the roles played by J.C.R. Licklider, Tim Berners-Lee, Tom Peters, Peggy Tumey, or Sherman Woo.

Gradual Transformation

Q: As the idea of "the future organization" is linked with enabling intranet technologies, how will that linkage lead to different activities and roles within your organization?

Look forward and consider what new technologies will be required as your intranet evolves. What will drive your product development?

Start to think about the kinds of technical or "people" knowledge that will be required for a long-term, successful intranet. How will you ensure that people with that knowledge will want to continue to be a part of your organization or will be able to help foster its evolution?

■ References

1. James Beniger, *The Control Revolution: Technological and Economic Origins of the Information Society* (Cambridge: Harvard University Press, 1986), p. 25.
2. William H. Davidow and Michael S. Malone, *The Virtual Corporation* (NY: Harper Business, 1992).

Inherent Potentials:
Four Intranet Models

There's a phrase in Buddhism, "Beginner's mind."
It's wonderful to have a beginner's mind.

Steve Jobs

Technology-enabled collaboration fueled the revolution in web technology development. Section One told the story of how all pieces of the puzzle came together to build the Internet and the World Wide Web. Drawing from that legacy of success, Section One concluded with a five-phase macro plan for intranet development.

Section Two, beginning with this chapter, focuses on how web technologies can be used to improve productivity and to eliminate waste. Within this section are answers to questions such as, What can web technologies actually do? How can the technologies be used to improve communication? How do web technologies compare to Lotus Notes? What are the essentials of good communication technology design? Are the political battles over Notes versus a web-centric intranet worth fighting?

To start the ball rolling, Chapter 4 clarifies some central intranet definitions and outlines four different models for web site development. They are: the Publication Model, the Asymmetrical Interaction Model, the Symmetrical Interaction Model and the Synchronous Virtual Environment Model. The Synchronous Virtual Environment Model is the most advanced of the four because it permits the most seamless on-line interactivity between people and information. Many organizations begin their intranets with the Publication Model, add interactivity, and evolve as the inherent potentials of the technology and employees' communication needs come to light.

If you are new to intranets, this chapter will help provide a framework for understanding the potential inherent in the technology. If you are already an expert, this chapter will give you some very helpful ideas about how to explain intranets to novice users. In fact, materials in this chapter can be extracted and used for presentations or demonstrations.

The models we keep in our heads strongly influence how we choose to go forward in an intranet project. Communication models, organizational models, and intranet models are often shadows, echoes, or iterations of each other. As we'll see, the best intranets have alignment between all three.

■ Defining the Term *Intranet*: A Distributed Hypermedia System

The term *intranet* can have different meanings. To some people, an intranet is basically the physical medium used to transport data. To other people, an intranet is a set of web pages with content. To others, it is a virtual place where a number of applications can be combined to provide improvements in organizational communication, work flow, and transaction processing.

All of those definitions are correct. However, intranets would not exist if it were not for the collection of web protocols and standards that define and unify the "languages" used to deposit and retrieve digital information from a web server.

The Web is defined by three standards: URLs, HTTP, and HTML. These standards provide a simple mechanism for locating, accessing, and displaying information.

Three different though complementary meanings of the term *intranet*:

1. the physical medium used to transport the data
2. a set of web standards and protocols used to create and transfer content
3. a sense of a "virtual place" where people exchange information and communicate

The Physical Medium: Client-Server Architecture

Let's start with the concept of an intranet as a physical medium. The architecture follows the Client-Server model.

A client is an application program (software) that goes out on the network, requests and retrieves files from servers, and displays the document in a standard format on the user's screens. Web browsers, like Netscape or Microsoft Exchange, are "clients." By the way, to be able to support an intranet browser, a PC needs a 486 processor and a speed of 66 MHz. (286-based PCs can- not run web browsers, and 386s run them, but slowly.)

Intranet servers are PCs or work stations that run web server software. A server's job is to house or store electronic files where they wait, ready, until someone electronically requests them.

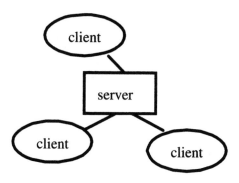

FIGURE 4.1

The web server "houses" the electronic HTML files. To access the files, a person uses a web browser to request data from the server. The data are sent to the person's computer and displayed in a standard format by the browser.

Data resides temporarily on the person's computer hard drive, and it can be saved to the hard drive if the user wants to keep a copy for future reference. Meanwhile, the original file stays on the web server, unless an authorized person changes it or removes it.

One advantage to client-server architecture is that several people can look at the same data at the same time. You can have dozens or even hundreds of simultaneous "hits" to an HTML file.

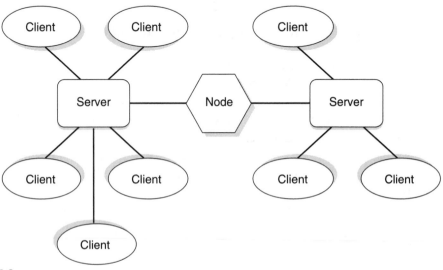

FIGURE 4.2

As Figure 4.2 shows, web protocols make it possible for people to access information from the same server and from several different servers almost at once.

A node is a point of connection in the network. Various groups within a company can each run their own web servers and make data accessible to any authorized person.

To construct an intranet, you need at least one computer to act as the server to house the files. The server requires an operating system and web server software. The server software typically consists of relational database and a set of configuration files to store pages and metadata (e.g., business rules, work flow constructs, and security access control mechanisms). Someone must prepare or configure the server to permit people to upload HTML files to the server where they can be stored. Files are not stored in just any random fashion; they are stored in hierarchical directories. Employees then require a client (web browsers) that enables them to request files and to have the data displayed on their computer screens.

Standard Web Protocols

How do the data get onto the server? How do they get to a person's desktop? The process for intranets relies on the same three standards that are used on the World Wide Web: URLs, HTTP, and HTML.

URLs, also called URIs (Universal Resource Locators), are a convention to specifiy the location of an Internet server. They are essentially the addresses of digital objects, such as documents, images, sound, and video. HTTP is a network protocol for transferring information and for enabling hypertext jumps. HTML is the language, or format, that is understood by web browsers.

When Tim Berners-Lee created HTML, it was limited in its presentation and layout capabilities. Just as any language, it has changed with use. HTML 3.2 and 4.0 now provide mechanisms to flow text around images, display tables, create client-side image maps and enable Java-based applets and applications.

Only a few years ago, people had to mark up their pages by hand, inserting the various HTML codes into the right places. Today, however, web editors have automated the HTML coding processes. People can create web pages without any training in HTML whatsoever. Web editors exhibit the WYSI-WYG approach to document production. A command in a WYSIWYG system is interpreted immediately upon being expressed. For instance, a command to center a line of text immediately centers the line on the screen. The actual center command is never explicitly visible in the text.

Given the high labor costs of entering HTML codes manually by typing them into a document, <u>web editors</u> have become extremely attractive, as they make the most of reusable code. There are many good ones on the market. The more expansive the creation of the information and the greater the volume of information, the greater the need to rely on digitized sources of common HTML coding structures.

TCP/IP

The computers that comprise the network are able to pass data through and to one another because they use another common protocol—that is, they speak the same language. That language is called *Transmission Control Protocol/Internet Protocol* (TCP/IP). All computers on the Internet and on intranets speak TCP/IP.

Hyperlinks

An intranet is much more than a network of networks with a variety of applications. Specifically, it is a distributed hypermedia system. Hypermedia allows multimedia information to be located on a network of interconnected servers. Users can travel from one piece of information to the next by clicking on hypertext links with a mouse.

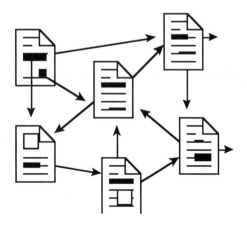

FIGURE 4.3

In a hyperlinked environment, selecting a link in one document moves you directly to another place in that document, or to an altogether different document anywhere on the intranet.

Hypertext allows us to assemble large collections of materials composed in various media and to link them in a variety of ways without destroying the integrity of the original.

Figure 4.3 illustrates how hyperlinks enable people to link documents together.

A hypertext link can be displayed as words, as an icon, or as an image (these are sometimes called *hot spots*). The links simplify the task of navigating and let the user direct the navigational path.

This is one reason why hypertext is a potential solution to problems that involve searching voluminous materials to find specific information. The links make the material accessible from multiple perspectives and through different search strategies. Users have greater control of how information is sequenced and can take an active role in pulling the right information to themselves.

The Web Page

The page or file that is displayed on a person's web browser can contain text, just like a page from a book. Because it is a digital document, it can also contain audio, video, photographs, illustrations, graphic enhancements, and Java applets (such as scrolling marques or animation). A web page can also become a virtual space to create a dynamic on-line discussion.

One of the things that makes the Web unique as a communication medium is that many different multisensory elements can be embedded right into a page.

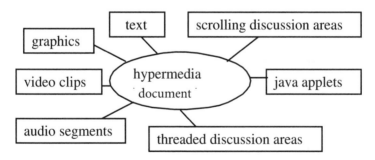

FIGURE 4.4
Web pages, as hypermedia documents, can include a variety of forms of communication.

A web page, once created, can remain static for the rest of its digital life. A web page can also change from moment to moment as new data get trans-

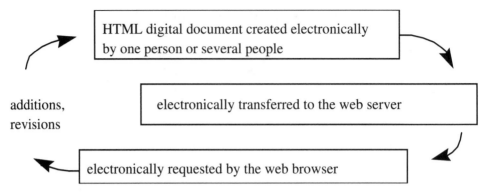

FIGURE 4.5
Digital documents can be constantly updated far faster than paper-based materials.

-erred from a digital file to the server to a person's web browser, and back to the server, and so on.

Web Sites

An intranet includes web sites. A web site contains web pages (documents written in HTML) that are hyperlinked. A web site's "home page" is very much like a book jacket or the cover of a magazine. It indicates what is found "underneath" that first page.

Yet, an intranet can be more than a set of web pages or web sites. It can include links to email applications, groupware databases (such as Lotus Notes databases), Oracle databases, and files stored in legacy systems. The beauty of an intranet is that the web browser provides a common interface to a variety of other applications.

Firewalls: Versions of Gateways

With an intranet, the network is protected by a firewall. Firewalls are gateway devices that act as gatekeepers between a company's internal network and the outside world. A gateway device is physically connected to multiple networks and/or understands multiple software standards between two networks. A gateway acts first like a language translator and enables users of otherwise incompatible networks to communicate.

A firewall selectively filters information passing between the networks. The firewall software examines the location from which data enter the system or the location to which data are going. Then the firewall software chooses, based on the instructions is given, whether to allow the transfer of the information. The firewall software also monitors the system and keeps logs so that a system administrator can know if anyone is trying to break in. Some firewall software offers encryption options that allow senders to scramble information in their files, making it illegible.

In the past, firewall software was primarily UNIX-based. System administrators had to type in commands and instructions. Today, more firewall software, such as <u>FireWall/Plus</u>, comes with user-friendly, graphical interfaces. It's easier to set up, especially for webmasters who are not UNIX experts.

The firewall software is being designed so that it can ensure that anyone from outside is blocked from sending files into the company's network or from retrieving corporate information via the Web. Some firewall software, like <u>SmartWall</u>, will even page the system administrator if it detects someone trying to log onto the system too many times with an incorrect password.

Now that we've covered the basic physical structure, let's look at our design options.

■ Four Models of Intranet Design

This section discusses four intranet models: the Publication Model, the Asymmetrical Interaction Model, the Symmetrical Interaction Model, and the Synchronous Virtual Environment Model. The levels of interactivity and the variety of features increase in each subsequent model. As we'll see, the Web is evolving from a publications platform to a high-value applications environment.

Here is an overview of the four models:

The Publication Model

Communication Type	Supporting Web Technologies	Types of Features
One-way static communication. "I publish, you read."	• Web standards and protocols (URL, HTTP, HTML) • Web server software • HTML editor software	• Product catalogs • Policy manuals • Internal job listings • Job aids • Training materials • Competitor profiles

The Asymmetrical Interaction Model

Communication Type	Supporting Web Technologies	Types of Features
Two-way, time-delayed didactic communication "I ask, you respond" or "You ask, I respond."	• All of the above plus • Tables • Forms • Scripts	• Self-serve HR benefits enrollment • Automated course registration • Supply requisition • Time reporting • Expense reporting • Internal surveys • Self-paced online tutorials • Diagnostic tools

The Symmetrical Interaction Model

Communication Type	Supporting Web Technologies	Types of Features
Multi-directional communication. Numerous feedback loops. "We all have a chance to talk and listen, ask and respond."	• All of the above plus • Threaded or scrolling discussion areas which enable people to post and respond.	On-line discussions for the purposes of: • Sharing knowledge, information and expertise • Building communities of interest or communities of practice • Product development by virtual teams

The Synchronous Virtual Environment Model

Communication Type	Supporting Web Technologies	Types of Features
Real-time, dynamic, multi-directional communication to support key business processes. "This is the way we work."	All of the above, plus hypermedia application-centric technologies such as work flow applications, relational databases, transaction systems, and document management systems, collaboration groupware.	Fully integrated communication applications and opportunities with hypertext links that make it easy to move from one application to the next. The virtual space supplements and complements physical space.

The next section looks at each of these models individually, pointing out the advantages and disadvantages of each.

The Publication Model: "I Publish, You Read."

In organizations, printed materials such as newsletters, policy manuals, and product specification sheets are typically distributed using a broadcast model of communication. People who are sources of information supply information to people who serve as editors or gatekeepers. The gatekeepers add, subtract or reform the materials and select the appropriate distribution media. The end user or the receiver basically awaits the distribution of information.

The receivers may signal either the sources or the gatekeepers of the need for further communication or information. Those signals can provide feedback to improve the nature of the communication and/or the content.

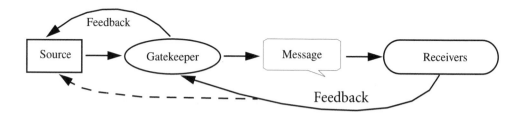

The sources and the gatekeepers are the producers of the information. The employees (the receivers) are basically consumers of information.

The nature and frequency of the feedback depends on different things, such as the size of the organization, the organization's culture, and the value placed on the act of communication itself.

An on-line Publication Model of an intranet follows that same basic design. Digital material is placed on servers by people who serve as coordinators or gatekeepers. End users await the distribution of information. Once the material is on the server, the end user can request, or "pull," it into his or her browser.

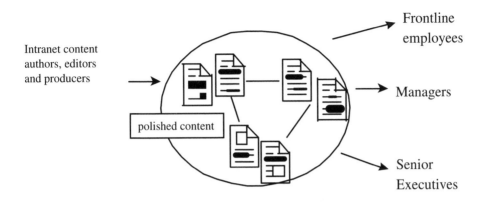

FIGURE 4.6
The Publication Model. Information production and distribution tends to follow traditional communication patterns and practices.

Intranets, therefore, can be somewhat like niche-marketed magazines. Information is "published" on web pages by people who act as writers or editors. People can "browse" to find what they need; they can search using search engines or indexes as tools. If a particular document or area on the web site is protected, a screen appears that requests the person to enter a password. Similar to reading through a magazine, users can scan the material and "pull" whatever interests them at the moment. The rest remains. Because the text is hyperlinked, the reader can jump from the magazine to pages from a dictionary, an encyclopedia, a bibliography, a directory, a video clip, etc.

The experience of using an intranet is, therefore, somewhat like going to a library or bookstore in search of material. With some goal in mind, you browse titles, scan contents, find references to other materials, ask for assistance. What you *see* in that space, what *you chose* to pick up in your hands, and your *level of interest* determines what you look at next.

Because the information can be linked to other information, it becomes far more useful. For example, an organization may publish a list of current projects that can be searched by key words. By typing in the term leadership, you would get a list of all projects involving that topic. By clicking one of the project titles, you would get a description of the project. By clicking on a contact person's name, you could enter the employee phone directory, which itself can have search capabilities. You can look up employees by name, department, or geographic location. When you find an employee, you get not only the data you would have found in a printed directory, but links to the employee's profile (or personal home page) and information about his or her department. The entry may include an e-mail link which enables you to send an email message directly to that individual. With adequate information on the servers and well-designed hyperlinks, the value of information that is "published" expands exponentially.

Chris Stone, a multimedia web developer and consultant, explains how this model was used to start the first intranet at a small software development company in Santa Barbara, California:

> Our "intranet" was actually the result of the Technical Support Department which started a centralized written database of bug fixes. Each week the Technical Support Department would get printed sheets with bug fixes. To get a bug fix into the sheet, you had to provide a bug report/fix in writing to the head of tech support. The head of tech support would compile the bug sheets—in order of the date the bug notice was received. The printed bug sheets would be distributed at the weekly tech support meeting. These sheets are static, non-searchable, and dated. Thus, you could go for days without knowing the answer to a bug, while the company actually had a fix the whole time. Multiple people would work on solving the same problem, not even knowing that others were already working on it or already solved it.
>
> Oftentimes with new releases, we would have catastrophic bugs that instantly created havoc. We would release a version, ship to 7,000 users and within five days all 7,000 users would have received the update disks and start calling in. It was sudden and intense. This is what software companies don't want the users to know, don't want happening, and need an instant fix for. That is why an intranet would greatly improve the handling of these situations. An intranet can provide a searchable database of bugs and fixes, update release information, etc., greatly improving productivity. Tech people can answer questions more confidently, customer support is improved and is consistent. So someone in tech used OCR to scan in the tech notes into a database and put it on the network—starting our intranet.

As Chris's example illustrates, consistency in communication among different members of the organization and customers is one of the compelling reasons to publish information on an intranet. Consistency and information integrity helps to make everyone feel more confident about the level of customer service provided.

One of the least appreciated functions of intranets is the capacity to support multiple information types. Consider the types of information that might be found on a competitive intelligence web site. There may be information abstracts such as competitors' profiles, histories, and financial information. There may be technical information, such as the company's own product specs, design documents, etc. In addition, we might expect to see analytical information, such as analyses of competitors' sales and marketing strategies, growth strategies, or R&D strategies. Figure 4.7 on the next page illustrates this.

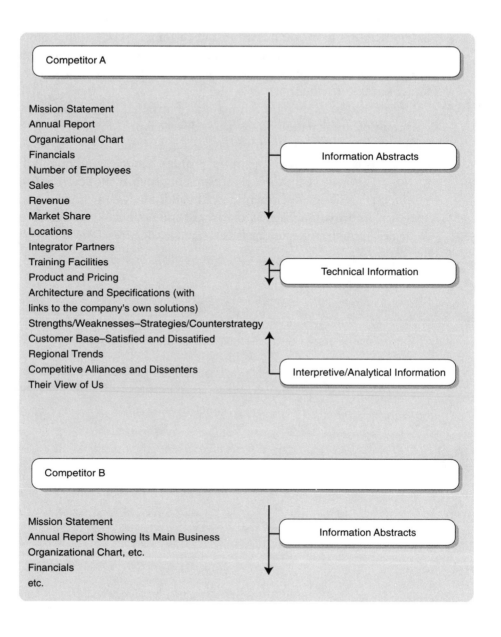

FIGURE 4.7
Example of Hypertext Index Page

Each underlined line would be "clickable." Employees can locate documents two different ways:

1. Scrolling through the index and locating what they are looking for.
2. Using the search engine.

All the content that employees might need, from information abstracts to technical information to interpretive/analytical information, can be accessed from one central location.

New web administrative tools are making web site administration significantly easier. Until now, the backend of content development and site administration was a laborious process. Content developers needed to know how to use HTML to create web pages, link content together, and keep the site fresh.

However, the web as a technology has matured very, very quickly. Templates, forms, and scripts residing in the background have eliminated the need to manually insert HTML tags into documents. The amount of information that can be included on a site and managed through time correlates to the quality of one's administrative tools, not to the amount of web site experience possessed by the site administrator. Companies can create state-of-the art web sites with evolution capability simply by making an up-front investment in web administrative tools or in an intranet suite like RadNet or IntraNetics, which allow people to publish online with no HTML exertise.

The hypercompetitive age is marked by the constant flow of information. When employees' computers are linked together through a client-server architecture, information dissemination can be fast, efficient, and purposeful. The network can enable greater coordination and knowledge sharing among counterparts and peers. Just at the moment when the need to share information is the greatest, web-based technologies offer a cost-effective, user-friendly solution.

Saving paper costs is one of the most compelling reasons to publish online. Kevin Han, a consultant at Just In Time Solutions, Inc., noted in 1996 that there is mounting evidence that the savings are substantial. Silicon Graphics saves $100,000 per day in printing and distribution costs through its intranet. More information is available at their web site. General Electric is saving $240,00 per year in printing costs for a single document by publishing it on the intranet.[1]

Intranets that are used primarily to publish information have a number of clear advantages, listed in the table below. Yet they also have some limitations.

Table 4.1   Publication Model Overview: Advantages and Limitations

Publication Model Advantages

- Saves printing costs.
- Information can be retrieved at any time of the day or night, from any place.
- Using a search engine, materials can be located easily, "just in time."
- People "pull" material that is of value to them while rejecting lower-value "noise" and leave the rest.
- People can follow self-directed navigation routes through the materials. The material can be delivered in sequence, it can be repeatable, or accessed in a random fashion.
- Material can be updated easily.
- Material can be archived for future reference.
- Graphics, color, photographic images, audio and video clips can be used to enhance the content and the presentation of the materials.
- Information can be linked together.

Publication Model Limitations

- Not truly interactive
- One-way communication. Users can't comment on things they are viewing.
- The value of the material to the end users can only be assumed.
- Feedback about the value of the material may be delayed and may be distorted.
- Most employees can download but cannot upload new materials.

What is Interactivity?

Interactivity is the essential feature of the next two models. Before going further, let's explore the concept of interactivity a bit.

Although the term *interactive* is frequently used when people talk about electronic media, true interactivity takes place only when participants "are acting or are capable of acting on each other."

The best example of interactivity is a face-to-face dialog between two people, where each person is listening *and* speaking. We also find interactivity in classroom settings and in meetings where participants are listening *and* responding. In situations where participants are encouraged to jump in and contribute, the nature of the communication can be highly interactive. Feedback can be immediate and direct. Participants can use the feedback to change or improve the communication in "real time," as it is happening. Interactivity is not simply a value-added feature of human communication. It is an essential characteristic of human communication.

However, right now, much of what we do with computer-mediated communication is not truly interactive. For example, SimCity, one of the most the popular CD-ROM titles on the market, allows users to raise taxes to see what would happen to the city's economics, but it does not allow people to introduce a new tax altogether. Compared to broadcast media such as television where people have very little influence over how the material is presented, SimCity is an interactive breakthrough. However, it is highly controlled interactivity. The designers actually created the program to prevent a user from making too many mistakes. The system was designed to anticipate error and correct the user's course.

When people are communicating in person, the nature of the interactivity is largely influenced by the context of the communication. Within the context of a party, a meeting of peers, a conversation between a husband and a wife, one would expect and hope for much interactivity. In the context of a lecture, or a conference with formal speeches, or a religious service, the situation discourages all but the lowest levels of interactivity between the speaker and listeners. The context of the communication informs the entire communication exchange. Nicholas Negroponte gives this now classic example:

"Okay, where did you hide it?"

"Hide what?"

"You know!"

"Well, where do you think?"

"Oh."

The scene comes from an MIT proposal on human–computer interaction submitted to ARPA 20 years ago by Chris Herot, Joe Markowitz, and Negroponte. It made two important points: Speech is interactive, and meaning —especially between people who know each other well—can be expressed in shorthand language that probably would be meaningless to others.

Why would we want to move toward computer-mediated communication if such interactivity is diminished? One reason is that non-computer-mediated communication is either time-specific or place-specific. It is fleeting.

Unless someone makes the effort to record the communication on video or audio tape, or creates a written record the way a court reporter would, the communication event is typically either entirely lost to memory or is preserved in a modified and incomplete form. People who were not physically present or cannot obtain a recorded version of the communication event can not really know what transpired. One of the greatest advantages of digital representation of information is that it can be transmitted through space and stored through time without loss.

Still, we should remember that the form of digital communication comes with some limitations. The discrete symbols no longer have a notion of locality or continuity. With in-person communication in the "natural world," continuity tends to simplify things for us. As Negroponte's example illustrates, our prior communication experiences with someone and our understanding of the context of the communication provide rules for making communication meaningful.

As we now move forward to explore the Asymmetrical Interaction Model and the Symmetrical Interaction Model, we'll begin to see how more and better interactivity can be built into web sites and intranets to make the on-line experience not only richer but more meaningful.

Asymmetrical Interaction: "I Ask, You Respond," "You Ask, I Respond."

In the on-line world, interactivity can be asymmetrical and asynchronous. The web technologies that enable this type of communication transaction are tables, forms, and scripts.

Tables, Forms and Scripts

Forms and scripts make it possible to collect information from employees and to transform inert data into useable information. On-line surveys and questionnaires, for example, are a highly efficient way to ask employees questions, collect answers, perform statistical analyses, and publish the results.

One of the most effective uses of forms and scripts is that of internal "benchmarking" surveys. Employees can fill out and submit questionnaires about their implementation practices, and in seconds receive an analysis of how their group compares to the other groups on the database, providing real-time data that can stimulate continuous improvement. Such on-line performance surveys can reduce the typical anxiety attached to performance measures and enable employees to see—literally— how they compare with the best. In 1997, Boeing launched an intranet site devoted to teamwork. The site provides learning that is "just in time, just for me," says Chuck Welter, an organizational development specialist at the company. As reported in *Fast Company*, the site provides a lot of self-diagnostic tools:

> The web site focuses on the most sensitive realities of life in teams. If a person is disrupting a meeting, for example, the site offers a menu of options. It also offers hands-on advice about learning from mistakes. It encourages leaders to call a meeting to discuss the following questions: What did we expect to happen? What actually happened? How did we respond?[2]

Here's another scenario. Many times customer service representatives will notice trends in the types of calls they are taking from customers. Often, those trends point to problems with order process fulfillment or problems with quality control. If you listen to customer service representatives, they'll say things like, "We sure seem to be getting a lot of calls about X." Or, "there must be a problem in the warehouse. I keep getting calls about Y." Ordinarily, the comments would either get passed to a supervisor or recorded on paper-based logs. With an intranet, the customer service reps would be able to pull up a form that enables them to submit information in real time about the problems. By doing this, the trends they are observing personally or together as a group can become hard data used to improve the process or improve the quality of the product. People don't need to know any HTML to submit information. They simply type it into a box on the web page, click SUBMIT, and are finished.

Companies such as Fluor Daniel, Oracle, and Texas Instruments have employed forms and scripts to completely automate their human resources (HR) and training registration processes. Employees can log onto the intranet, browse through menus and descriptions, and register for the types of benefits or types of courses they wish to select. The system enables employees' selections to be automatically processed. For example, the Wisdom-Link™ System, created by International Learning Systems, not only enables employees to create self-directed "Learning Profiles" and to register for courses, seminars, or workshops, it also provides the corporate training de-

partment with automated class lists and enterprise-wide employee competence profiles.

According to <u>Watson Wyatt Worldwide</u>, HR departments are moving
quickly to take advantage of intranets. In their 1997 survey of 323 companies, 57 percent of the companies said they plan to use intranets for HR purposes within the year. Of those companies that have already placed some HR
applications on the web, 60 percent said they planned to add additional applications within the next six months.

The types of information currently on intranets that Watson Wyatt
Worldwide surveyed were:

> Job posting/application—70%
> Corporate communication—57%
> Benefits information/enrollment—32%
> Training—24%
> Other—19%
> Thrift/savings/401(k)/profit sharing—18%
> Performance appraisal/management—6%

"Most HR departments initially ventured onto their company intranets
with simple on-line documentation like employee handbooks or job post-
ings," says Steve McCormick, Ph.D., virtual HR practice leader in Watson
Wyatt's Washington, D.C., office. "Now many are adding more complex HR
transactions, such as annual benefits enrollments and ongoing status changes."

Innovative benefit managers at highly networked companies such as
America Online, Apple, MCI, Oracle, and Texas Instruments have already
done so, with rave reviews from employees. Indeed, 84 percent of companies
with no existing web applications surveyed by Watson Wyatt Worldwide said
they would probably move their benefits enrollment online in the future.

In addition to creating materials that employees can pull, information on
the system can also be "pushed" to employees. For instance, if something
changes at the organization—a new policy, a new procedure, a new rate increase, etc.—the system can send an e-mail "alert" message to the employees
with an embedded hypertext link that points the employee to supporting materials. Such messages can be targeted to specific individuals or employees,
using various need-to-know criteria.

Here is a wonderful example of an integrated "push" and "pull" delivery scenario developed by Elliott Masie,[4] the dynamic president of The Masie Center, a technology and learning think tank in New York.

> Meet Karen the Learner. She needs to learn how to present a new mutual fund package to a prospective customer. Karen works 2,350 miles from the home office. She needs technology to help her learn this important task.

> Old Model: An instructional designer would author a step-by-step lesson for Karen to take. The lesson would have good motivational elements. Karen would be presented with several modules of information. She would have a chance to test her understanding of the content, and there would be a clear beginning, middle and end. The organizational investment in this training material would be front-loaded, with the 100+ hours of authoring and coding done prior to release.

> New Model: Karen gets an e-mail about the new program. She clicks on a link in the e-mail called *Briefing Link*. This launches Karen's web browser, connecting her to an intranet. Upon connection, the intranet server displays a series of pages of content for Karen based on her position, the specific e-mail that she just received, and the latest sales reports from the field. The content would change if she did the same action 2 weeks into this sales campaign. The changes would be dynamically adjusted, not hard-coded with an authoring system.

> In other words, Karen's training session would be On-the-Fly Content, assembled according to a series of formulas, using content that is on file in other parts of the enterprise's computer systems. The "authoring" process would be less focused on creating a clear instructional pathway for Karen and more on building formulas that would gather the information she might desire for learning.

Masie makes the point that this kind of scenario is made possible because of a couple of core web technologies: web-based authoring systems for content creation, dynamic scripts that generate customized learning profiles, and feedback loops that permit employees to provide real-time feedback to con-

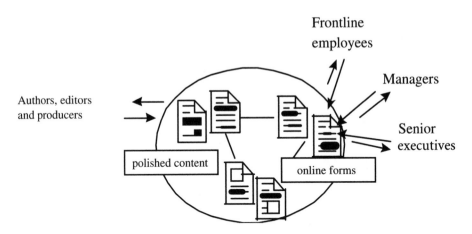

FIGURE 4.8

The Asymmetrical Interaction Model. Employees can not only read materials, they can fill out forms and submit information. The double set of arrows indicate that creating information and consuming information are discrete activities: There is a lack of temporal concurrence. Someone produces the bulk of the materials at one point in time; users interact with the materials at another point in time.

tent creators. The feedback can be used by the participants themselves to help build knowledge bases as they are needed.

This intranet model has become extremely popular. There are now dozens of examples of how companies are moving beyond the publication model and are adding greater interactivity on their web sites and intranets. Netscape has organized some very good demos on the part of their web site dedicated to intranet development. Among the demos, you'll find these applications:

- **Expert finder**. KnowledgeNet searches for people in the organization according to area of expertise. Internet Media Services first developed this application for Hewlett-Packard.

- **Management and tracking of internal requests**. The Lawson Insight Internal Procurement Center provides employees with a secure, web-based, self-service vehicle for processing internal requests for maintenance, repair, and operating supplies (MROs).

- **Client-focused productivity applications**. Oblix uses Netscape SuiteSpot servers (Directory, Calendar, and Mail) to provide applications such as organizational charts, group creation and management, document sharing, and facilities scheduling.

- **Legacy data access**. SimWare and Teubner & Associates have created a streamlined method to integrate legacy systems into their intranets.

- **Decision support**. Arbor Software's Essbase Web Gateway enables people to submit information onto tables and forms to generate decision support materials.

- **Human resources applications**. Austin-Hayne provides applications to automate such HR functions as a job listing center, company directory, and employee data.

- **Employee time tracking**. Internet Media Service's AppFoundry application, Tock, provides web-based time sheets.

- **Purchasing analysis tool**. Booz-Allen & Hamilton's Strategic Sourcing/Decision Support System provides a mechanism for identifying, analyzing, and diagnosing opportunities to improve corporate purchasing performance.

- **Leveraging of client-server applications**. OneWave demonstrates how to migrate PeopleSoft, Baan, and SAP solutions to intranets.

Many asymmetrical, asynchronous applications are being created for intranets. The explosion of these types of applications is a sure indicator that intranets are becoming more central to the operations side of businesses and organizations.

Sun Microsystems is an outstanding example of how a single company can leverage an intranet investment. In Chapter 1, we talked about how Sun was one of the first companies to perceive and exploit the economic potential of web-based FAQs to improve customer service. Today, we can also look to Sun for outstanding examples of operations-centered intranet development.

A detailed description of what Sun has achieved with its intranet is available on its web site. There, you'll find a narrative tour of Sun's intranet (dubbed SunWeb). The tour includes descriptions of the SunSoft on-line literature fulfillment process; SunDocs individual product manuals; SunSoft Field Marketing to help keep customers current; SunExpress, a comprehensive product catalog on the Web for easy, worldwide access; Catalyst Catalog On-Line about third-party software; Sun Information Resources, which uses

Oracle Financials to distribute reports and track assets; Sun competitive analysis data available to all Sun employees; SunSoft price books accessed by sales representatives worldwide; downloadable Java software, saving on CD pressing, packaging and fulfillment; Catalyst Flash developer newsletter, the CheckMate automated check processing tool that saves in excess of $100,000 per year; SunTea Expense Reporting, which saves $2.5 million a year; and Saltool, an automated system for processing employees' raises. The variety of applications is impressive. Sun estimates a savings on documentation distribution through the intranet at $25 million dollars a year.

Making the decision to automate processes usually requires the right configuration between the database and the web server platform. Your organization may already have data stored on databases that are web-enabled, such as Oracle databases, Microsoft SQL databases, or Microsoft Access databases. A "web-enabled" database is one that offers a connection between the data and the page that is displayed in the browser. Depending on your objectives, your organization may need to think about starting a new database for the sole purpose of aggregating data and using them on-line. You may need to upgrade the version of your database or convert data in a database that is not web-enabled to one that is. There are times when "middleware" is necessary. Middleware, while dependent on the database you use, is also dependent on the server you have running your web site.

These are just a few examples. Lynda Rathbone, popular on-line instructor at Zdnet University (ZDU) reminds us of several important technical questions intranet developers need to bear in mind. If the information is in a database already, should that database be put online? Does the data need to be copied into a more robust database? If so, can they be combined with other data in the same database?

We live in an information economy. One problem is that information is usually impossible to get, at least in the right place and at the right time. The Publications Model and the Asymmetrical Interaction Model are two steps forward in enabling people to manage information more efficiently.

Table 4.2   Asymmetrical Interaction Model Overview: Advantages and Limitations

Asymmetrical Interaction Model Advantages

All of the many advantages listed in the Publication Model (e.g., saves printing costs, information can be retrieved at any time of the day or night and from any place) *plus*:

- Disintermediation—the removal of barriers between employees and internal groups offering a service to employees.
- Streamlines paper-based processes.
- Can eliminate process steps and redundancies.
- Employees using the systems don't need to have any HTML skills to contribute data or information.
- The data generated from people's individual responses can be aggregated and analyzed.

Asymmetrical Interaction Model Limitations

- Use of the system is characterized by staccato patterns of somewhat disconnected "hits."
- The value of the materials to the end users is typically measured quantitatively by cost savings or by numbers of "hits" or transactions.
- Feedback about the value of the material is delayed and may be distorted.
- Most employees can download but cannot upload new or revised pages.
- Communication is highly didactic: intended primarily to instruct, or to solicit data, but not to learn or to foster new knowledge.
- Interaction is computer-centered. People interact primarily with the system, not with other people.
- Materials must be designed to ensure employees' completion of each task and to ensure appropriate time-to-task completion.
- There are a number of challenges in gaining employees' acceptance and trust of an on-line system when they have come to rely on paper and people as their primary, preferred communication media.

Symmetrical Interaction Model: "We All Have a Chance to Talk and Listen."

The Symmetrical Interaction Model emphasizes dynamic interactivity. This type of intranet includes open communication areas where people can "write" as well as "read." Therefore, some of the content can be dynamic and can change with only momentary delay. Such dynamic communication is made possible through several web technologies: on-line bulletin boards or "discussion areas," and real-time conferencing.

On-line Bulletin Boards, or "Discussion Areas"

Open communication environments give people the opportunity to communicate on a many-to-many or few-to-many basis. Discussions are organized by topic and topic subhead (sometimes called *threads*). People who post and respond to messages are identified by name. In a sense, the topic of the discussion group is the "address" of the "place" where people meet to communicate. Though you can't pick up the phone and ask to be connected with several people in world who are highly knowledgeable about a topic, you can, however, join a discussion group and take part in an on-line dialog where you will find resident expertise.

The chances of finding the right person with the right answer are magnified many times over the old methods of finding people or information. An on-line discussion may feature only a few topics when it first begins, then grow to include several dozen. A search engine built into the system can help people find information quickly and easily.

Intranets that include discussion groups can be somewhat like corridor conversations about various topics. People can join the conversations as participants or just "listen in." Just as some corridor conversations become closed-door meetings, some discussion areas may be designed to require a password.

There are two types of on-line discussion formats. One is the threaded discussion format:

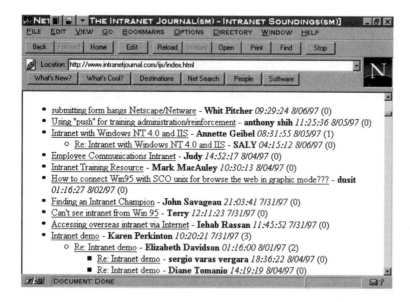

FIGURE 4.9
Source: Intranet Journal, http://www.intranetjournal.com

To view the text of a person's post or response, a participant clicks the header or subject line. A new window opens, showing the text of the person's post. Usenet newsgroups are formatted this way. One advantage to this format is that participants can get a quick overview of the discussion. If you don't want to view the text of each message, you don't have to do so.

The other type is the scrolling discussion:

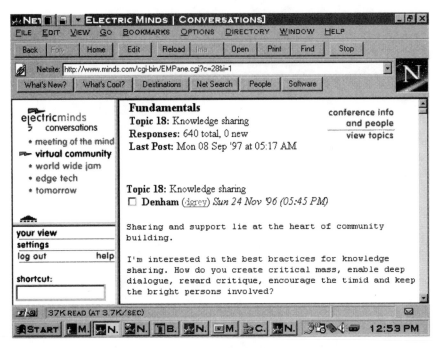

FIGURE 4.10
Electric Minds, http://www.minds.com

This type of on-line discussion looks somewhat like a transcript of a real conversation. One advantage of this format is that users don't have to click open the posts that interest them. The entire text of the discussion is presented at once.

Real-Time Conferencing

Real-time discussion areas are also possible. People communicate in real time by typing messages that appear immediately on a window on all of the other participants' screens. Comments can be anonymous, unless a participant wishes to attach his or her name to an idea. The participants' contributions can be saved in digital form and can be forwarded, archived, and retrieved. The session can literally be restarted and re-entered at any future date.

The ability to converse on-line is especially useful when people wish to brainstorm, engage in scenario planning exercises, or participate in focus groups.

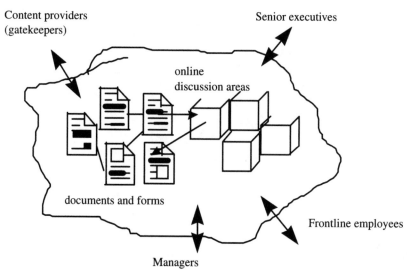

FIGURE 4.11
The Symmetrical Interaction Model

Communication flows in many directions. The intranet becomes a "virtual space" where members of the organization can access information *and* can communicate with each other. Every participant is offered the opportunity to "read" as well as to "write."

The intranet can be organized so that all of the discussion areas are located in one section, or the discussion areas can be organized around specific group interests or practices, with supporting content hyperlinked to the appropriate discussion.

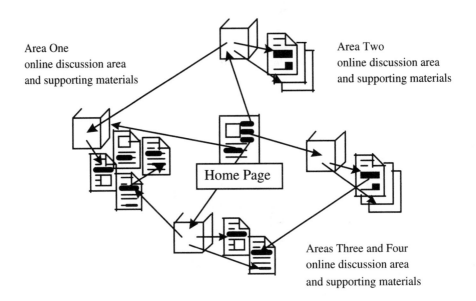

Area One
online discussion area
and supporting materials

Area Two
online discussion area
and supporting materials

Home Page

Areas Three and Four
online discussion area
and supporting materials

FIGURE 4.12
In the Symmetrical Interactive Model, you can create links among discussion areas and documents.

An example of how this sort of model would come to life on an intranet can be found on the Netscape web site where you will find a demo of National Semiconductor's intranet. The demo highlights how National takes advantage of discussion groups to create "Communities of Practice." National creates semiconductor products used for moving and shaping information. The company is headquartered in Santa Clara, California and has over 22,000 employees worldwide. To capitalize on the expertise of its employees in developing new products in more productive ways, National established Communities of Practice—groups of engineers who share knowledge, tools, design methodologies, successes, and key learnings—to develop their design engineering competence.

One of the things that the Netscape/National demo illustrates very nicely is how people can use a discussion area to communicate with their counterparts on a many-to-many basis and can then communicate on a one-to-one basis via e-mail with a simple click of a hyperlink. The ability to switch from group discussion to one-to-one communication makes this type of intranet extremely attractive to people who are working together to solve problems.

These kinds of intranets can be used to help employees learn and to increase their speed and proficiency. Research on teaching and learning shows that people don't learn new skills or ideas just by being exposed to them. Learners must be prepared to learn; they must have the mental preparation and requisite skills to understand and master new ideas. Listening to networked discussions may help produce this "absorptive capacity" in employees, both old-timers and new employees.

Let's take a look at how discussion areas compare with e-mail, document libraries, and expert directories with regard to organizational knowledge sharing.

As interactivity increases, so does the potential of web-based technology to enable organizations to eliminate redundancy, share good ideas, create virtual teams, and improve problem-solving.

In terms of implementation, most intranet development is now just on the cusp between the Asymmetrical Model and Symmetrical Model. For many employees, participation in online discussions is a brand-new form of communication with new rules to learn and new communication norms to work out.

Table 4.3   Web-based Protocols

Objectives	Internet Access	Virtual Library	In-House Expert Directory	E-Mail	Discussion Groups
Fairly interactive ⟶ Highly interactive					
Rapidly identify problems and create action plans				✔	✔
Increase diversity of contributors to problem identification and solution			✔	✔	✔
Quickly identify people with experience or knowledge on topics, issues, problems, or solutions			✔	✔	✔
Organize teams of people who are geographically separated			✔	✔	✔
Expand set of analytical tools to problem-solve	✔				✔
Enable direct, unfiltered communication unimpeded by gatekeepers	✔			✔	✔
Capture, store, and share new knowledge		✔			✔
Enable cross-organizational communication			✔	✔	✔
Create shared vision, common ground				✔	✔
Access and retrieve static information	✔	✔			✔

Table 4.4 Symmetrical Model Overview: Advantages and Limitations

Symmetrical Model Advantages
- Discussion groups accelerate information flow. Time delays associated with mail, fax, telephone tag, or face-to-face meetings are shortened considerably.
- People don't have to be available simultaneously for communication to occur. The message can be posted at the convenience of the author and read at the convenience of the other participants.
- Informal communication can become regularized; previously ad hoc communication can become more fine-tuned.
- Because discussions are captured in digital form, they can be accurately referenced at some later point in time or "mined" for key insights or shared knowledge.
- Employees can provide real-time feedback about materials published on the intranet or about other matters.
- Employees can "raise their hands electronically" and ask for help from their peers.
- Employees can document key learnings, failures, and successes as they occur, and make that information available to many others.
- By placing hypertext links to other documents into their posts, employees can enrich discussions and provide evidence for claims.

Symmetrical Model Limitations
- For most organizations and companies, the concept of many-to-many communication is foreign.
- Decisions must be made about such issues as authenticating users, keeping discussion areas open or closed, and how best to moderate discussions.
- There is a certain amount of chaos that comes with dynamic interactivity. Decisions must be made about creating some order out of that chaos.
- Users need to be supported by people who work behind the scenes to moderate discussions, keep links to content fresh and accurate, etc.

Synchronous Virtual Environment Model: "This is the Way We Work."

The Synchronous Virtual Environment Model is a "fourth-generation" intranet where the virtual space is customized for each potential participant and where different forms of technology-enabled communication are occurring or existing at the same time.

To clarify a couple of terms, *asynchronous communication* is delayed in time and disconnected in space. Letters, voice mail, e-mail messages, and online discussions are examples of asynchronous communication. *Synchronous communication* takes place in real time. Telephone calls or in-person communication are everyday examples of synchronous communication.

One challenge in describing this type of model is that there aren't any easily accessible intranet examples that we can examine. Prototypes are in development at Xerox Palo Alto Research Center (Xerox PARC), IBM, and Microsoft, but they aren't available on any public platform right now.

The closest illustration is Apple Computer's "Knowledge Navigator" video, which was produced in 1987. The Knowledge Navigator is a five-minute video that depicts a future computer with capabilities such as voice recognition, integrated telecommunications, video conferencing, and a humanlike agent that carries out tasks for the user. The video shows a somewhat harried male college professor using the Knowledge Navigator to prepare a multimedia lecture at the last minute, retrieving research papers, running a simulation, and contacting a colleague who agrees to show up at the class (over a live video feed) to answer students' questions. Our hero is able to keep several windows open on the computer at once, switching back and forth in a seamless, natural way as he attempts to get things aligned for class. There is no need to exit from one application or system to use another. Everything he accesses through his computer is coinciding, congruent, and in conformity to his needs.

The Synchronous Virtual Environment Model embraces a concept called *calm technology*, discussed in "*Designing Calm Technology*" by Mark Weiser and John Seely Brown, two eminent technologists at Xerox PARC. Calm Technology engages both the center and the periphery of our attention, and, in fact, moves back and forth between the two. A calm technology will move easily from the periphery of our attention, to the center, and back.

According to Mark Weiser and John Seely Brown, this type of computer-based interaction is fundamentally calming, for two reasons. First, by placing things in the periphery we are able to attune to many more things than we could if everything had to be at the center. Things in the periphery are attuned to by the large portion of our brains devoted to peripheral (sensory) processing. Thus, the periphery is informing without overburdening. Second, by recentering something formerly in the periphery, we take control of it.

John Seely Brown's advocacy of this type of computing is based on research at Xerox PARC on the ways in which people work every day. Important communication, Seely Brown reminds us, happens near the water cooler where people gather to talk informally. Likewise, when people attend conferences, they greatly value the opportunity to network before and after the formal presentations. If we attend to the importance of this sort of communication, Seely Brown argues, we must shift the focus of human computer interaction to designing the social and information periphery, as opposed to just its center.

This is the cutting edge of intranet development. Such intranets will require expanded, shared-Ethernet LAN pipes with higher bandwidth alternatives using different configurations of switches or routers. In addition, just as one cannot place a phone call to another person who doesn't own a phone, one cannot hold a video conference or collaborate with another person on editing a document unless they both possess the same software and network connectivity. Thus, the true value of this type of technology won't become expressed until a critical mass of people are equipped to communicate in this fashion. Bundling all the various components will be essential. One development on the technology side that will enable this model to become reality is Java, discussed in Chapter 1, which enables applications to reside on the network.

Another catalyst will be eXtensible Markup Language (XML). XML was developed in 1996 by on-line publishing experts from industry and academe under the auspices of a World Wide Web Consortium (W3C). The working group, chaired by Jon Bosak of Sun Microsystems, included members from SoftQuad, Adobe, IBM, HP, Microsoft, Lockheed Martin, NCSA, Novell, Sun, Boston University, Oxford University, and the Universities of Illinois and Waterloo.

XML is an extremely simple dialect of SGML. The goal is to enable generic SGML to be served, received, and processed on the Web in the way that is

now possible with HTML. It has been designed for ease of implementation
and for interoperability with both SGML and HTML It provides a standard
way of adding custom markup to information-rich documents so that complex documents can be rendered and published in any way. Today, HTML
provides a way of representing and publishing structured information.
Whereas HTML is easy to use, its simplicity places serious constraints on the
degree to which publishers and users can utilize business-critical documents
and databases. One of the reasons XML was developed was to solve the problem of integrating structured information, such as that in SQL databases,
into the fabric of web pages. XML provides the means to publish and receive
any information, regardless of format or origin, in any way that the authors
wish.

   A couple of economic and social trends will speed development of the Synchronous Virtual Environment model. <u>Wired magazine's experts</u> predicted
in 1996 that the number of telecommuters would triple in the next 15 years
to 20 percent of the U.S. work force, driven by stricter air-quality regulations,
improved communications networks, and rising demand for adaptability in
the business world. Companies will want to get people into the field so they
can be more responsive to customer requirements, and such a technology
model will enable that desire. This is not web-centric work but rather web-
augmented work.

■ Review

Purposes of Intranets

Intranets are being designed and developed for a variety of interrelated
purposes:

- to make available information that was previously unavailable or
  distributed in hard copy form
- to facilitate work for cross-platform users
- to provide personalized or self-selecting views of information

- to facilitate work for mobile users
- to tie together disparate systems and information
- to enable new ways to do business

An "Intranet" is ...

A distributed hypermedia system
within an organization
that enables people to:
    access information
    communicate with each other
    share what they know
    learn from others

Therefore, it changes:
    peoples' roles
    peoples' activities
    peoples' jobs

And ultimately:
    can transform an organization

How Do Differences in Design Emphasis Change the Experience of Using an Intranet?

Model	Emphasis	Experience feels somewhat similar to:
Publication Model	content	Being in a library, browsing and reading through publications.
Asymmetrical Interaction Model	transaction	Filling out and submitting forms, report surveys, questionnaires. Using a CD-R
Symmetrical Interaction Model	dialog	Attending a group meeting, workshop, seminar, or national sales meeting.
Synchronous Virtual Environment Model	coordination	Being a participant in various forms of communication activities with the inte of achieving certain outcomes.

■ New Models for Organizational Communication

If you apply these four web technology models to the way we traditionally view organizational communication, you come up with different ways of thinking about communication. Information is no longer defined by what *it alone* can do. Rather, information is viewed as part of a larger pattern of communication. The next chapter discusses how to use the new technologies to create a learning organization that has the energy and capacity to rise to the challenges we're facing in the 21st century. We'll look at why it is important to understand people's learning styles and to recognize that not all people process information the same way.

■ References

1. Kevin Han, posted reply to Janis re: Saving paper costs from intranets and Internets, IABC discussion group, http://ww.iabc.com, May 30, 1996.

2. "How Boeing's Leader's Fly," *Fast Company*, June–July, 1997, p. 126.

3. "HR Departments Embrace Web-Based Technology," International Association of Business Communications. Communication World Online, March 14, 1997. http://www.iabc.com/cw/news/i_f_m97/March1497.htm.

4. Elliot Masie, The Masie Center, "The Next Learning Trend: On-the-Fly," Contact 800-98-MASIE or http://www.masie.com.

Web-Based Organizational Learning

Having a treasure trove of web technologies is great. Web technologies can enable people to publish on-line documents, to streamline information transactions, and to hold on-line discussions in which everyone can speak and listen. The last chapter also provided some examples of how web technologies can be applied to real business issues and problems, such as the management of HR information and registration.

This chapter goes beyond the last one to explore the question, How can we leverage all of the web tools available to us in order to improve an organization and build capacity? This chapter argues that there is a set of drivers within the hypercompetitive environment that is forcing us to rethink all of our organizational practices—from how we communicate information to employees to how we enhance problem-solving skills.

Successful organizations, it is said, integrate learning into the way people work, continuously increasing skills and knowledge. And yet, for the past century, "thinking" has been an activity defining the managerial class, whereas "carrying out orders" defined the rest of the employees. If that division is to dissolve, we must ask ourselves questions like, What is thinking? What is knowledge? How do people learn? This chapter explores such ques-

101

tions and proposes that web-based technologies are one of the few sure things that can foster new ways of problem-solving necessary for work in the 21st century.

■ The Hypercompetitive Landscape and the Need to Change

Within the competitive landscape, technologic forces are coming together to shift the economic ground. As Professor Richard D'Aveni writes in his award-winning book, *Hypercompetition*:[1]

> Competitive advantages, once considered unassailable, have been ripped and torn in the fierce winds of competition. Technological wonders appear overnight. Aggressive global competitors arrive on the scene. Organizations are restructured. Markets appear and fade. The weathered rule books and generic strategies once used to plot our strategies no longer work as well in this environment.

Peter Schwartz and Peter Leyden note that, beginning with the recession of 1990 and 1991, American businesses began going through a "wrenching process" of reengineering, downsizing, outsourcing, and creating the virtual corporation. However, despite all of these techniques, they note, productivity has become one of the "great quandaries stumping economists throughout the 1990s." Schwartz and Leyden[2] write, "Despite billions invested in new technologies, traditional government economic statistics reflect little impact on productivity or growth."[11]

Floating around the business press and consulting circuits is the claim that if businesses invest in new technologies, they can boost the productivity of their workers. The phrase is almost trite. However, the sorts of web-based technologies just discussed in the previous chapter *can* have a profound, long-lasting impact on organizations and can improve companies' chances to compete.

The drivers of this model are increased customer satisfaction, decreased costs, rapid competence development, and the need to shift the responsibility for learning to the learner—making learning continuous. The outcomes are improved organizational responsiveness to changing economic conditions and changing needs of customers, enhanced organizational capacity (perhaps even abundant capacity), and improved problem-solving skills. The mediator between the drivers and the outcomes is web-based communication technology.

Scanning the Horizon of Possibilities

Drivers	Outcomes
Increased customer satisfaction and improved customer relations. Increased customer retention.	Improved organizational responsiveness to changing market conditions and customer expectations.
Decreased operating costs.	Decreased unnecessary redundancy and duplication; elimination of waste.
Rapid competence development.	Enhanced organizational capacity.
Shifting the responsibility for learning to the employee; making learning continuous.	Improved problem-solving skills transferable from one activity to the next.

Guardians of the Knowledge Base

How can we achieve such outcomes when, traditionally, "thinking" has been the role and responsibility of upper management? As Shoshana Zuboff explains, the functional hierarchy—the organizational form of the 20th century—was invented to meet the business challenges of increasing throughput and lowering unit costs. It proved to be so successful, we are having a difficult time dismantling it, even in the face of the tornado. Professor Zuboff teaches:[3]

> Business processes were divided into separate functions—manufacturing, engineering, sales and so on. Other innovative features included mass-production techniques, the minute fragmentation of tasks, the professionalization of management, the growth of managerial hierarchy to standardize and control operations, and the simplification and delegation of administrative functions to newly contrived clerical workforce. Collectively, these components

were incredibly successful; they came to define the modern workplace.

Prior to industrialization, "workers" did work that was very complex. But the coming of the machine age brought with it a different form of work for a different kind of economy.

> *It has been reported that when Charlie Chaplin's "Modern Times," with its depiction of a man meshed with a machine and reduced to machinelike jerkiness of movements, was shown to audiences in industrial Pittsburgh, they did not find it funny.*
>
> **George F. Will[4]**

Work such as assembling pieces of an automobile airplane, disassembling thousands of cows in meat-packing plants, or processing forms did not require exclusive engagement with the whole product. Enter Frederick Taylor (1856–1915) who conceived of scientific management. As "scientific management" grew in popularity through the 20th century, the industrial hierarchy, Professor Zuboff notes, rested on the premise that "complexity could constantly be removed from lower level jobs and passed up to the management ranks." Front-line workers became progressively involved in the overall business of the firm as their jobs were narrowed and stripped of opportunities to exercise judgment.

During the 20th century, such a model of organization was seen as rather good and benign. For example, Peter Drucker calls our attention to results such as these:[4]

> By applying Taylor's Scientific Management, U.S. industry trained totally unskilled workers, many of them former sharecroppers, raised in a pre-industrial environment, and converted them in 60 to 90 days into first-rate welders and ship-builders.

People in management came to own organizational knowledge, communicating downward what lower levels needed to know. Professor Zuboff:

> The manger's role evolved as guardian of the organization's centralized knowledge base. His legitimate authority derived from

being credited as someone fit to receive, interpret and communicate orders based on the command of information.

Traditional Organizational Communication

Traditional organizational communication is, therefore, typically linear. Employees respond to the source of the communication, to a gatekeeper, or to other employees. Instances of communication tend to be discrete; that is, they are not easily linked across the organization to other instances of communication. Often, communication takes place as if in silos. Messages travel up and down the organizational hierarchy, with gatekeepers mediating what can and cannot be passed along. Cross-organizational communication, if it occurs, is rarely cross-hierarchical.

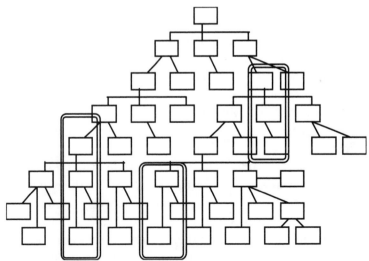

FIGURE 5.1
Traditional organizational communication. A multilevel pyramid of authority clearly defines how each level communicates with and supervises the other. Communication travels in linear directions, which some people call stovepipies.

Today, the transformation of the organization to adapt to the new rules in the new economy involves a fundamental change in the ways in which people use information and communicate. As Moira Gunn[5] wrote in *Wired:*

The corporation as we know is dying. There weren't a lot of great corporations before the industrial age, because they couldn't communicate plans up and down. Napoleon's army showed how to organize a big group of people to do anything. They key was command and control. You couldn't tell the whole plan to everyone, so you'd communicate only the part that was needed to get the job done. The first modern corporations modeled themselves on this. But now, that doesn't work; all the data is networked and available to everybody. Decisions can be made at a far lower point in the organization. But people in their hearts still want to act like Napoleon.

The Effect of Technology on Organizational Communication

Several excellent books have been written about how information technology changes how people actually communicate in organizations. Among them are two classics: Shoshana Zuboff's groundbreaking book, *In the Age of the Smart Machine* (Basic Books, 1988) and a book by Lee Sproull and Sara Kiesler, *Connections: New Ways of Working in the Networked Organization* (The MIT Press, 1993). Zuboff, Sproull, and Kiesler base their arguments on solid, empirical evidence gathered from research projects they conducted in the field.

In *The Age of the Smart Machine*, Zuboff describes how a computers have changed organizations both for the better and for the worse. She argues against using computers to simply automate work-related tasks because automation tends to strip away the meaning of work for most people who have had technology imposed upon them. Zuboff argues that we ought to use information technologies to "informate"—to surrender knowledge to anyone with the skills to access and understand it.

In part of the book, Zuboff describes how a conferencing system brought employees together from different functional areas and diverse social backgrounds. The remote and textural qualities of the computer eliminated people's advantages or disadvantages over one another. Employees who regarded themselves as physically unattractive reported feeling more lively and confident when they expressed themselves in an on-line discussion. Others with soft voices or who were small of stature felt they no longer had to struggle to be taken seriously in a meeting. The online discussions became "sociological events" because they brought together in conversation people who otherwise would have been separated by position or prejudice. One employee[6] communicated to Zuboff about the online discussion

> ... lets me talk to other people as peers. No one knows if I am an hourly worker or a vice president. All messages have an equal chance because they all look alike. The only thing that sets them apart is their content. If you are a hunchback, a paraplegic, a woman, a black, fat, old, have two hundred warts on your face, or never take a bath, you still have the same chance. It strips away the halo effects from age, sex, or appearance.

These are the sort of communication opportunities Zuboff would like to see companies making available to more employees. "Exploiting the informated environment ," Zuboff writes, "means opening the information base of the organization to members at every level, assuring that each has the knowledge, skills and authority to engage with the information productively. The revamped social contract would redefine who people are at work, what they know and what they can do."[7]

When such opportunities are made available, information technologies can be leveraged to add a new dimension of reflexivity. The technology makes its contribution to the product, but it also reflects back on its activities and on the system of activities to which it is related. "Information technology not only produces action," Zuboff writes, "but also produces a voice that symbolically renders events, objects and processes so that they become visible, knowable, and shareable in a new way."[8] Where automation effectively hides many operations of the overall enterprise from individual workers, information technology tends to illuminate them. It can quickly give any employee a comprehensive view of the entire business or nearly infinite detail on any of its aspects.

With an intranet, the company's own organizational learning cycle can become shorter and quicker. In the past, companies often experienced a lag between the problem identification and solution. Employees traditionally have had to rely on intermediaries to signal breakdowns in processes, procedures, or communication. As a consequence, vital information about the need for change, or the urgency attached to the need, was often lost or diluted through the organizational gatekeeping process. Computer-based performance support systems can enable direct, immediate communication between frontline employees, support service employees, and management.

Web technologies are dramatically altering this traditional view of communication. Rather than silos, communication facilitated by intranets resembles networks:

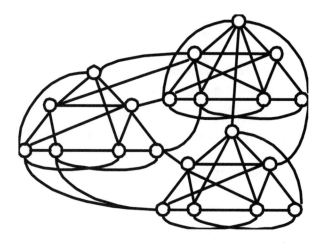

FIGURE 5.2
The Networked Organization. Documents are linked electronically. People are linked through the sites.

Chris Stone explains how intranets can become the catalyst for better organizational communication:

> A company with poor internal communications is like a circle with paths crisscrossing throughout—random, disorganized, and inefficient, and sometimes never connecting the points that really need to be connected. For example, the development department letting [the] shipping department know when a release is expected [to be] ready for shipping. An intranet becomes the center of the circle and the circle becomes a gradient fill—everyone has access to a centralized interactive database of information (the gradient fill representing various levels of access to protected information).

How difficult is it to achieve this kind of open communication? Sproull and Keisler demonstrate in *Connections* how computer-based communication can alleviate barriers and distortions in organizational communication and can create opportunities for new communication among people. They also show how it can create new problems that require discussion. One of the complications is securing management buy-in. Remarking on the types of management responses to information technologies they have witnessed, Sproull and Keiser write:[9]

> New computer-based communication technology has prompted some managers to invoke the following organizational objectives: a clear chain of command reinforced by routing all network messages through the hierarchy; rationalization and control of information exchange by blocking certain channels of communication; reduced inefficiency and waste by forbidding extracurricular messages or work messages outside a person's responsibilities; and improved security by surveilling message files.

> The same technology has prompted other managers to initiate or intensify a different set of objectives: a flexible, internally motivated, continuously learning workforce; a strong internal culture to support information sharing and participation in problem solving; delegation or shared responsibility in recognition that dispersed activity requires local information; and creation of dynamic procedures, structures, and groupings to amplify expertise and technologies."

Companies and managers who take the second approach are often those who take the long view and who think of increasing employee participation by electronic communication as a capacity-building strategy with implications for long-term performance. Three components of such a strategy are: creating connections among employees, building new skills, and increasing employees' links among employees.

Throughout the rest of this book, we'll be exploring whether an open communication environment makes sense for your organization, and we'll look at specific strategies you can use to achieve a Symmetrical Interaction Model, if it's right for you. The next section of this chapter continues our discussion of technology models and what they imply for organizational learning patterns and practices.

■ New Models For Learning

One of the central advantages of evolving your intranet beyond the first two models is that it can be used to improve the ways in which employees learn, train, and improve their performance. With a web, learners have greater control over what they learn and when they learn it. There is greater retention of the material. On a well-designed system, information comes alive as employees pull the materials to themselves.

As Vannevar Bush wrote:

> The human mind operates by association. With one item in its grasp, it snaps instantly to the next that is suggested by the association of thoughts, in accordance with some intricate web of trails carried by the cells of the brain. It has other characteristics, of course; trails that are not frequently followed are prone to fade, items are not fully permanent, memory is transitory. Yet the speed of action, the intricacy of trails, the detail of mental pictures, is awe-inspiring beyond all else in nature.

Research on the ways in which people learn reveals that, while learning, people often switch quickly from one question or request to another. Intranet-based performance support enables people to switch quickly from one piece of information to another, until their inquiry is satisfied.

While one might assume that the level of inquiry can be only superficial, research by Gloria J. Gery and others reveals that the level of inquiry is often very deep. As employees' control over the variables, processes, procedures, and information increases, employees often seek *more understanding* of the concepts, rules, principles, and relationships.

Sometimes it is hard to see such in-depth learning occur, as the required sequence, depth and repetition of information will vary for each individual. Moreover, individuals may not be internally consistent about the way they go about the process of inquiry and application. Yet, when the computer-based performance support system is well designed, when the systems' capabilities meet the employee's needs, the beneficial effects are manifested in a variety of important ways. Evidence of the system's value is demonstrated through increased skill, knowledge, motivation, and confidence. Each of these elements, by the way, can and should be measured, so that the system's effectiveness can be continually monitored and improved. We'll talk more about measurement later in this book.

The overall advantage to an intranet-based performance support is that learning can be systematically integrated with the work. Faced with a problematic situation—a question—an employee can find the resources needed in order to improve performance.

Experience-Based Learning

Earlier in this century, John Dewey's work at the Laboratory School at the University of Chicago offered a theory of learning that today is being revisited by leading thinkers in the fields of education and learning. Dewey, a philosopher and student of public policy, believed that the scientific model of learning by memorization or by abstraction was not the right way to teach students how to think. In 1916, Dewey wrote *Experience and Education*, arguing that all learning required the transactional interaction between the individual and the environment.

For Dewey, experience is paramount—i.e., the interaction of the individual with the environment as a testing ground for ideas. Dewey's model of inquiry posits that inquiry is triggered by a "problematic situation." A problematic situation is anything that blocks the flow of spontaneous activity and gives rise to thought and further action aimed at reestablishing that flow. That problematic situation could be some kind of conflict, a different interpretation of a situation, or an alternative interpretation of the facts. The problematic situation is the stimulus to a process of inquiry.

The model can be depicted this way:

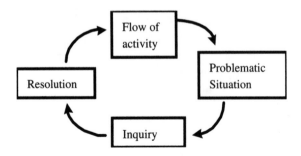

FIGURE 5.3
Experience-based Learning. This model sees people not as passive recipients of information, but rather as active learners whose processes of inquiry actually help to construct the foundation for the next stages of learning. The length of the cycles can be long or short, depending on the situation and context.

If we use this model to design intranet-based performance support, employees would have the option of: (a) turning to other people within their immediate, physical work space for help, (b) turning to the system for help; or (c) using a combination of in-person human and computer-based support.

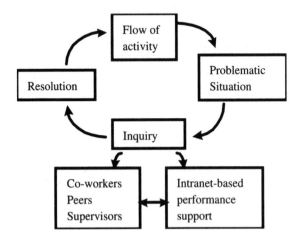

FIGURE 5.4
Web-Augmented Learning

By leveraging an organization's investment in intranet technologies, we have an opportunity to change from traditional, formal, structured, and classroom-based training to continuous learning and knowledge sharing.

The Role of Tacit Knowledge

For a long time, a rationalist philosophy of education has dominated most of our ideas about how people think and learn. Conventional wisdom has held that teachers are experts who transfer their knowledge to the student, who is considered to be empty vessels. Our concerns for effectiveness, behavioral change, skill acquisition, and speed pushed the learning model further and further away from Dewey's idea of experienced-based learning and inquiry toward a mass-consumption model of training delivery. What learners actually brought to the table was considered less important than training outcomes than the kinds of things that could be measured and quantified.

Today, that philosophy is under attack. A whole community of educational researchers have rallied around the idea that thinking and acting are intimately related and that learning is "situated," meaning that learning is not abstract or self-contained but is constructed in particular social and historical contexts. Knowledge, in other words, grows out of a particular activity, context, and culture, and is being continuously reconstructed in use. Learning is fundamentally a social activity. We learn from various members in communities in which we are socialized. This kind of social learning goes beyond acquisition of knowledge that is explicit. It includes the acquisition of "tacit knowledge," a term coined in the 1960s by philosopher of science, Michael Polanyi.

Polanyi, like Dewey, believes that people create knowledge through experience. Polanyi termed this "indwelling"—knowing something through self-involvement. Polanyi's ideas stood in sharp contrast to the scientific model of learning, where knowledge derives from the separation of the subject from the object of perception. Much of our knowledge, Polanyi argued, is the fruit of our own purposeful endeavors in dealing with the world.

For Polanyi, the "tacit" level of knowing was a kind of out-of-awareness level of activity and close to impossible to put into words. But in the 30 years that have passed, others have argued that "tacit" knowledge is coded into people's activities. We acquire it through observation, through language, and through peripheral participation in the communities to which we belong. Passing on knowledge is like passing on language.

Among two of the most prominent researchers in this area are Ikujiro Nonaka and Hirotaka Takeuchi. They were both professors at Hirotsubashi University in Japan, where they began to study how companies create new knowledge and use it to produce successful products. Their book, *The Knowledge-Creating Company* includes fascinating case studies from companies such as Matsushita, Honda, Canon, Nissan, and 3M, showing how tactic knowledge can be converted into explicit knowledge.

Becoming An Apprentice: Matsushita's Home Bakery

One of the best case studies in *The Knowledge-Creating Company* describes how designers at Matsushita wanted to design a technology called *Home Bakery*, an automatic machine to bake bread. When the designers couldn't perfect the dough-kneading mechanism, a female software programmer, Ikuko Tanaka, apprenticed herself with the master baker at Osaka International Hotel. She gained an understanding of kneading, then conveyed this information to the engineers by creating a mental image of "twisting stretch." The skill of kneading was then materialized into specific mechanics, such as the movement of the propeller, which kneaded the dough, and design of the special ribs. The first prototype resulted in bread with overcooked crusts and raw insides.

Calling upon her experiences with the master baker and how she learned from trial and error to produce bread as good as his, Tanaka guided the engineers' redesign. She would say, simply, "move the propeller faster" or "make the propeller move stronger." Several months later, when the prototype still wasn't right and the team was getting nervous, somebody else recalled that it was possible to mix the ingredients and add yeast at a later stage. This improved the quality of the bread and lowered the manufacturing cost of the product. Nobody "discovered" this; they just remembered that method of baking.

By finding ways to share their tacit knowledge through communication, the Matshusita team developed a product that was so successful, *Fortune* magazine put it on the cover of its October 26, 1987 issue.

With books like *The Knowledge-Creating Company* and examples such as these, the field has moved beyond the theoretical level to the practical level.

The best way to learn is through interaction and exchange with one's peers. There is no one direct path to acquire knowledge; it is a circular and repetitive process. Ikuko Tanaka may have been "trained" in the discipline of software programming, but she was not trained on becoming an apprentice. That was *her* solution to the design problem. Rather, Matsushita defined their employees' roles as problem-solvers and created the environment for collaborative, reality-based learning.

No one on the team was insulated from the reality of the situation—i.e., competitors about to introduce a similar product, the need to balance manufacturing costs against profit margins, etc. All of those business issues were communicated to the team and became part of the context in which the team worked. In fact, those facts of corporate life gave the team something to push against to gain more energy and momentum. Had they not learned of the risks involved for the company in attempting this product, the team might have become "self-referential," with success defined too narrowly.

At the very heart of the Matsushita Home Bakery success story is good, creative, person-centered communication. As the old, rational model of education is dying out, we are beginning to focus on a new set of questions: How do we become sensitive to other people's points of view and learn to explain and/or modify our ideas so that they can be communicated to others who are not just like ourselves? Studies by cognitive scientists provide growing evidence that each human being perfects a specific set of cognitive operations (and not others) as a result of personal adaptations to his/her life experiences. How, then, do we communicate and share knowledge? One first step is to try to better understand the person or people with whom we wish to communicate.

■ Learning: The Constant, All-Encompassing Central Life Task

Back in the 1970s, researchers Herman Witkin and Charles Moore wrote a book called *Field-Dependent and Field-Independent Cognitive Styles and Their Educational Implications.* It challenged the idea that we all, by nature, are "rational" learners. According to Witkin and Moore, persons who utilize a field-dependent or field-sensitive orientation process information from their entire surroundings. In the classroom, they are as concerned about the human relational interaction and communication styles of the instructor as they are about the delivery of the content; they do not see the two as separate.

Field-Dependent vs. Field-Independent Students Expectations of Teachers

Field-Dependent Orientation	Field-Independent Orientation
• To identify with values and needs of students.	• To identify with goals and objectives of
• To minimize professional distance.	• To maximize professional distance.
• To provide guidance, modeling, and constructive feedback.	• To encourage independence and flexibil
• To provide verbal and nonverbal cues to support words.	• To provide commands and messages dir and articulately.
• To seek opinions when making decisions and to incorporate subjective criteria.	• To make decisions based on analysis of problems and objectives.
• To give support, show interest, and be emotional.	• To focus on task and objectives.

Modified from James A. Anderson and Maurianne Adams, "Acknowledging the Learning Styles of Diverse Student Populations: Implications for Instructional Design," *New Directions For Teaching and Learning* (San Francisco: Jossey-Bass, 1992), p. 24.

Since the 1970s, many, many scholars and researchers have used this framework to explore gender and ethnic issues in the classroom. Females tend to exhibit a relational style of learning (field-dependent) while men tend to exhibit an analytic style (field-independent).

Specifically in regard to web-augmented learning, Witkin and Moore compel us to acknowledge that the information people take in as part of their "experience" is highly varied. There is no one right way. Our forms of thinking exist in a continuum:

Analytic ----------- Relational
Deductive --------- Inductive
Verbal ----------- Visual

There is a requisite, essential variety in the ways in which human being think. For a long time, we have stressed one domain of thinking—the analytical style—over anything else because it fit the machine-based way of experiencing the world. The ability to be task-oriented, to not be greatly concerned about the opinions of others, to disembed information from the total picture, and to persist at unstimulating tasks was highly rewarded. Work in the 20th century required it.

Learning Styles and Preferences

In the 1980s, David Kolb, now a professor at Case Western Reserve, developed his Experiential Learning Theory. Like Dewey's model, it was based on an expanded view of human intellectual capacity that involves testing ideas in actual experience.

According to Kolb, the analytical style was simply one of four different learning styles. For Kolb, human learning and personal development are parallel processes that involve the continuous integration of a number of factors that give meaning to life's circumstances. Kolb specifically names these systems (or modes) as follows: concrete experiential (CE) , reflective observation (RO), abstract conceptual (AC), and active experimentation (AE).

Learning Strengths and Preferences

Concrete experiential (CE)	People-oriented, finds theoretical approac es not helpful, prefers to learn from new experiences, games, role, play. Peer feedback, discussion, and coaching are impor tant.
Reflective observation (RO)	Enjoys taking an observer role to see different perspectives on an issue. Makes careful observations before making judgments. Looks inward for the meaning of things. Logs, journals, discussion, brainstorming, and thought questions that provide an opportunity to reflect are very beneficial.
Abstract conceptual (AC)	Highly conceptual and analytical. Prefers symbols to people. Learns by logical analysis of ideas. Desires clear, well-structured presentation of ideas, and learns best in authority-directed, impersonal situations. Enjoys lectures, projects, analogies, and model-building; dislikes role-playing or simulations.
Active experimentation (AE)	Has a great ability to get things done. Enjoys opportunities to practice and receive feedback. Will take risks, but likes individualized, self-paced learning opportunities.

Kolb affirmed all major aspects of active learning, accounting for a variety of individual and culturally-based differences. Individuals, Kolb believed, exhibited a combination of learning styles, and he proposed that learning situations be created that would enable people to enrich their cognitive abilities by experiencing a flexible learning environment. As shown in Figure 5.5, at either end of the intersecting axes are bipolar dimensions representing on one hand how we take in or perceive information (the vertical axis on a continuum from concrete to abstract) and on the other hand how we process or transform what we take in (the horizontal axis, on a continuum from reflective observation to active testing or experimentation.

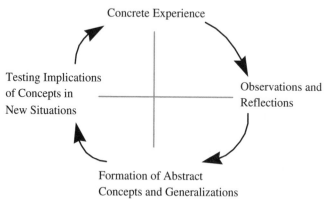

Concrete Experience

Testing Implications of Concepts in New Situations

Observations and Reflections

Formation of Abstract Concepts and Generalizations

FIGURE 5.5
The Experiential Learning Model

Over the past decade, many different people have adapted Kolb's Experiential Learning Theory and models. As with any diffusion of theory, inevitably, differences in interpretation arise. There were two stands of thought interwoven in Kolb's work: (a) the use of scientific methods to identify and label individual learning styles, and (b) the idea that learning is a continuos process grounded in one's interpretation of the world; a constant, all-encompassing central life task

The Segmentation Approach

In his work in the 1980s, Kolb demonstrated how individuals can be classified into one of four learning styles, based on a mathematical computation that derives from the individual's score on a self-report survey. Learning styles are then described in terms of individual behaviors. Kolb's original survey measures preferences for perception and processing. Subsequent surveys created by other individuals and groups focus on particular situations. (Several are available on the Web. Search Alta Vista (*http://altavista.digital.com* with the keyword" Learning Style Inventory.")

Learners can then be described as being like members of market segments. If you understand your target's learning styles and preferences, what sort of situations they enjoy, what sorts of learning media they feel comfortable using, you can design a program geared to their preferences.

International Learning System (ILS) has been doing research in this area since 1994 and has created its own proprietary survey to identify the types of learning styles and learning situations that are unique to particular groups of employees. Its data and analysis helps ILS create learning opportunities that increase employees' speed to proficiency. Some of the ILS segments are "Learn From Others on the Job," "Self-Directed/Self-Paced," "Classroom," and "Group/Team."

Knowledge about employees' preferences and least-preferred methods enables organizations to avoid wasting resources. For example, ILS completed a study for a large corporation interested in accelerating learning and employee development. The study revealed that employees' preferences for learning nontechnical skills were one-to-one training with someone who is qualified; learning from other people working on similar issues, tasks, or projects; asking a co-worker or someone who knows; and reviewing best practices, examples or others' key learnings. For the group surveyed, the least-preferred methods included role plays, listening to an audio tape, and figuring something out by trial and error.

In 1997, ILS began broadening its learning segmentation research to assess employees' knowledge of and interest in new technologies. Through its survey research, ILS identified a learning segment of people who prefer Internet/Intranet learning situations. ILS has been finding an ever-growing number of employees who indicate on their learning segmentation surveys and in interviews that they would like more computer-based and intranet-based learning.

The Continuos Approach

Intranet-based learning makes sense from another learning styles perspective. Bernice McCarthy, founder of Excel Inc. and author of several books, including *About Learning* (Excel Inc., 1996), developed The 4MAT® System for Teaching, Learning, and Leadership. Kolb's Experntial Learning Theory, specifically his cycle of interaction between Concrete Experential (CE), Reflective Observation (RO), Abstract Conceptualization (AC), and

Active Experimentation (AE) modes of personal adaptation, is the theoretical basis for 4MAT. McCarthy, drawing heavily upon brain studies and the work of John Dewey, David Kolb, and Carl Jung, created a pedagogical model which assumes (1)that individuals learn in different yet identifiable ways, and that (2) engagement with a variety of diverse learning sets results in higher levels of motivation and performance. While McCarthy has slighly changed the articulation of Kolb's theory to incorporate other theories and to reflect more recent research, each change was an extension of rather a departure from Kolb's original concepts. Rather than taking a mathematical approach, McCarthy emphasizes the independent yet related nature of all four of Kolb's aspects of style. McCarthy identifies four types of learners:

- **Type One Learners** are primarily interested in personal meaning. They are imaginative learners—feeling and watching, seeking personal associations, meaning and involvement. Their key question is, Why? People communicating with Type One need to *create a reason*.

- **Type Two Learners** are primarily interested in the facts as they lead to conceptual understanding. They are analytic learners—listening to and thinking about information; seeking facts, thinking through ideas; learning what the experts think, formulating ideas. Their key question is, What? People communicating with Type Two need to *provide facts that deepen understanding*.

- **Type Three Learners** are primarily interested in how things work. They are common sense learners—thinking and doing learners. They like experimenting, building, creating usability, tinkering, applying ideas. Their key question is, How? People communicating with Type Three learners need to *create situations to let them try it*.

- **Type Four Learners** are primarily interested in self-discovery. They are dynamic learners—doing and feeling learners. They seek hidden possibilities and enjoy exploring, learning by trial and error, self-discovery, creating original adaptations. Their key question is, If? People communicating with Type Three learners need to *allow them teach it to themselves and others*.

Most schools and organizations, McCarthy notes, focus on teaching people concepts with little regard to other fundamental questions:

- Why is it important?

- How can I use this in my life?

■   What are the possibilities?

McCarthy's system stresses that people are constantly asking questions that fuel their desire to learn and to know and to grow. Good learning situations address not just one of the questions but all four, and they provide groups of learners an opportunity to create meaning, to add to their repertoire of explicit knowledge, to find ways to apply what they have learned and know, and to find additional   opportunities for application.

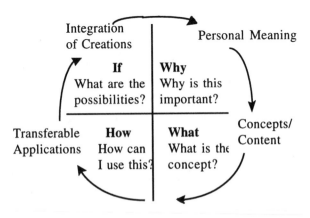

FIGURE 5.6
Bernice McCarthy's The 4MAT System

Source: From "The 4MAT System: Teaching to Learning Styles with Right/Left Mode Techniques" by Excel, Inc. Used by special permission. Not to be reproduced without express written permission of Excel, Inc.   23385 Old Barrington Road, Barrington, Illinois 60010; (847)382-7272; http://www.excelcorp.com.

To review, from Bernice McCarthy's work, five key points relate to developing intranets:

1. Human beings perceive experience and information in different ways.

2. Human beings process experience and information in different ways.

3. Our own perceiving and processing techniques form our unique learning styles.

4. We need to learn in all four ways to be comfortable and successful part of the time while being stretched to develop our other learning abilities.

5. Each individual will "shine" at different places in the learning cycle, so we will learn from each other.

■ Intranet-Based Learning: A Kaleidoscope of Features

An intranet can include an incredible variety of materials that are appropriate for different learning styles. Using the models discussed in the previous chapter, an intranet can help people to communicate, construct meaning, learn new things, and to discover opportunities to apply what they know. Multimedia by definition involves knowledge represented in different forms: graphics, film clips, video, spoken and written text. Even without expanded bandwidth, a corporate intranet can include powerful visual messages.

Some examples are listed in the flowchart that follows. The left-hand column summarizes various needs that emerge when employees are faced with a new or complex task. They are phrased in the form of a question. The right-hand column lists the kinds of things an employee would be able to find on the system.

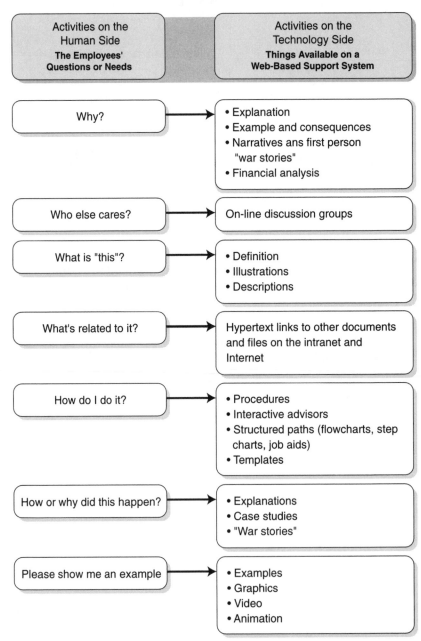

Activities on the Human Side **The Employees' Questions or Needs**	Activities on the Technology Side **Things Available on a Web-Based Support System**
Why?	• Explanation • Example and consequences • Narratives ans first person "war stories" • Financial analysis
Who else cares?	On-line discussion groups
What is "this"?	• Definition • Illustrations • Descriptions
What's related to it?	Hypertext links to other documents and files on the intranet and Internet
How do I do it?	• Procedures • Interactive advisors • Structured paths (flowcharts, step charts, job aids) • Templates
How or why did this happen?	• Explanations • Case studies • "War stories"
Please show me an example	• Examples • Graphics • Video • Animation

continued

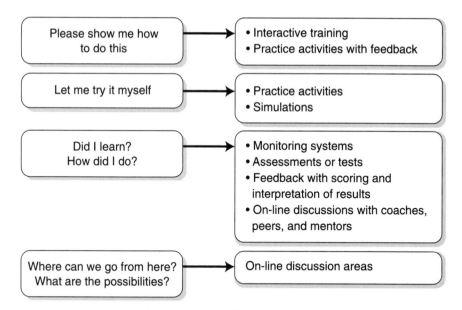

The purpose of the technology, therefore, is to help people get to the heart of whatever problem they are trying to solve. Use is driven by pressures and demands experienced by people themselves. People pull the technology and content to themselves because it solves an immediate real-time problem.

■ Enhancing Communication and Problem-Solving in the 21st Century

The return to Dewy and experience-based learning is an interesting development in our culture. At the Doors of Perception 2 conference in Amsterdam in 1994, John Perry Barlow[12] reflected on experience as the foundation for knowledge:

> *We have to peer through the fog of information until we can again see the reality. Right now we are unclear about the difference between information and experience, and I'm here to tell ya—there's a big one. This is not known to many people who have grown up in the informatized world. The average American lives in a condition where the majority of his or her cognitive activity is stimulated by information and not experience. But experience happens to you. Information is about what happened to somebody else. Information therefore sits between us and the Thing Itself. It separates and, as Nietzsche told us, "that which separates is sin." Information puts you at a distance, it makes you passive and helpless. Experience is something that you can probe interactively and question in real time.*

This is good council. Information that resides on an intranet and creates distance between people does no more than reinforce organizational hierarchies. Intranets can never substitute for person-to-person communication, but they can become a powerful platform or environment for learning. With intranets, learning can take place out in the open in a virtual space accessed by many, and it can include more people and a greater diversity of people. At times, the interaction may not feel like learning at all, but rather like an extension of one's curiosity and competence.

Work in the 20th century demanded a rational, analytic style of thinking. Webs of meaning and webs of relationships weren't quite so important. Work in the 21st century will be focused less around durables and more around intangibles. Daniel Burrus, author of *Technotrends*,[13] offers this list of abilities and competencies required for the 21st century. People will need the ability:

To demonstrate adaptability in a rapidly changing environment.
To communicate orally.
To apply negotiating skills while demonstrating personal responsibility
To work in collaboration with others (teamwork)
To identify the benefits of being observant
To identify the benefits of being of service to others
To focus and apply creativity in problem solving
To demonstrate technological literacy in problem solving
To apply computer technology to enhance task performance
To find and communicate paper-based and digital information
To apply memorization techniques
To learn new skills and assimilate new ideas quickly
To take initiate and be self-directed
To apply abstract thinking techniques
To identify problems and develop solutions.

Into this demanding situation, we must bring our requisite, essential variety in the ways that human beings think. We must also provide the right tools to accomplish that.

This chapter has argued that our ways of thinking are analytical and relational, field-dependent and field-independent, concrete and abstract. Our thinking is rarely linear and bears no resemblance to traditional models of organizational hierarchy. Rather, our thinking is fluid and connected; with one idea in its grasp, our minds leap to make another link. Given this way of thinking, what kinds of communication technologies are best suited for the organization of the 21st century? How should they be designed? In the next chapter, we'll compare Lotus Notes and web-based intranets, focusing on technical and nontechnical issues.

■ References

[1] Richard D'Aveni, *Hypercompetition: Managing the Dynamics of Strategic Maneuvering* (The Free Press, 1994), p. 1.

[2] Peter Schwartz and Peter Leyden, "The Long Bloom; A History of the Future, 1980–2020," *Wired*, July, 1997, p. 120.

[3] Shoshana Zuboff, "The Emperor's New Workplace; Information Technology Evolves More Quickly Than Behavior," *Scientific American*, September, 1995, p. 202.

[4] George F. Will, "A Faster Mousetrap," a review of *The One Best Way*; Frederick Winslow Taylor and the Enigma of Efficiency, *NY Times Book Review*, June 15, 1997, p. 10.

[5] Moira Gunn, "Gunn Club," *Wired*, July, 1997, p. 136.

[6] Shoshana Zuboff, *In the Age of the Smart Machine* (NY: Basic Books, 1988).

[7] Shoshana Zuboff, "The Emperor's New Workplace; Information Technology Evolves More Quickly Than Behavior," *Scientific American*, September, 1995, p. 203.

[8] Shoshana Zuboff, *In the Age of the Smart Machine* (NY: Basic Books, 1988), p. 9.

[9] Lee Sproull and Sara Kiesler, *Connections: New Ways of Working in the Networked Organization* (The MIT Press, 1993), p. 175.

[10] Vannevar Bush, "As We May Think," http://www.TheAtlantic.com/atlantic/atlweb/flashbks/computer/tech.htm.

[11] James A. Anderson and Maurianne Adams, "Acknowledging the Learning Styles of Diverse Student Populations: Implications for Instructional Design," *New Directions for Teaching and Learning* (San Francisco: Jossey-Bass, 1992), p. 22.

[12] John Perry Barlow, "@Home on the Ranch," speech given at Doors of Perception2@HOME Conference, November 4–6, 1994, Amsterdam, sponsored by the Netherlands Design Institute and the Institute and Mediamatic (http://www.mediamatic.nl/Doors/Doors.html).

[13] Daniel Burrus, *Technotrends* (NY: HarperBusiness, 1993), p. 241.

Lotus Notes vs. the Web:
a Comparison

Lotus Notes has become a very popular groupware product. Lotus Notes is a groupware infrastructure that includes a "fat client," the Notes desktop software installed on employees computers, and a Notes server which houses the files and directories, and contains the transfer protocols. Notes runs on a company LAN and requires TCP/IP.

Because Lotus Notes enjoys a considerable market share, intranet champions often should be able to explain the advantages of intranets as compared to Lotus Notes, either because the organization already uses Notes or because Notes is being considered as one of the technology options. This chapter outlines the relative advantages and disadvantages of each. One of the central arguments in this chapter is that although Notes and intranets seem to share similar features, such as discussion areas, their designs are very different; thus, there are important implications for organizational communication. Understanding these difference can help you avoid a very costly, long-term mistake.

If you aren't facing the Lotus Notes versus intranets debates, this chapter can further your understanding of intranets. By comparing intranets to another similar yet different technology, we can develop a clearer, sharper picture of an intranet's value.

■ More and More Alike: A Convergence of Features

One challenge in comparing intranets and groupware like Notes is that the two are growing more alike. Both can feature applications such as e-mail, discussion groups, document management, and work flow applications. Both can include security features such as password protection. In fact, in terms of *features*, groupware and intranets are coming close to resembling each other. Intranet developers are creating more and more web-based applications that have the same qualities and ease of setup as do groupware applications. It is not difficult to include features to intranets that have made groupware so attractive—search capabilities, threaded discussion areas, and forms.

Groupware companies are also adding web browser/editor features to their packages. Lotus' Domino enables organizations to publish information residing on the Notes server to a web-based intranet or to be the Internet. Groupware and web-based intranets are not incompatible. In fact, it is not uncommon for some organizations to use both.

Notes Selling Points

One of Notes' advantages is its single, consistent user interface that is provided right out of the box. The Lotus Notes "workspace" consists of six on-screen tabbed desktop "folders" where users can arrange icons representing Notes databases. Your tax group and your HR group, for example, each may be using several custom-designed Notes databases of their own, in addition to shared corporate databases that everyone sees. But, the onscreen desktop, and the look and feel of Notes will be very similar whether you work for tax, legal, HR, etc. There is no need to debate how the desktop design will look— whether there should be graphics and text, or graphics alone. Everyone's desktop will look basically the same.

A second advantage to Notes is that it provides an application development environment that enables developers to create customized databases without a lot of coding trouble. The high-level scripting language speeds the setup of custom databases. Consequently, an organization's Notes developer can quickly customize prebuilt applications (such as document libraries, form-based approval systems, project tracking applications, and status reporting systems) to suit the needs of the group.

Notes: A Prepackaged Product

We can see that Notes is very much an external "product." That is, the *majority* of the development work occurs apart from the end user's environment. As a one consequence, organizations and employees must adapt to the technology's requirements.

First, the product itself drives the type of roles required to use it. Notes requires four "standard" roles—an administrator to set up and maintain the server, a database manager who controls access, a certifier to create IDs for Notes users, and an application developer to customize databases. Although one person may be responsible for a combination of roles, each task is essential for Notes to perform as it was designed. Notes users typically just take advantage of the technology that's been given to them. Often, a "Notes consultant" will criss-cross among the groups, bringing information needed to improve the product or to catalyze ROI.

Second, because Notes is so robust, user training is essential. There are many steps a user must learn to operate Notes. These include how to get a database on the workspace; how to use different views within each database; how to create hyperlinks and attachments; how to import information onto documents; how to create a topic, a subject, a message and a reply on a discussion database; how to use a password and user ID; how to use dial-up features to access the Notes servers; how to replicate databases; and so on. Notes manuals are thick with instructions. The steps are not impossible to figure out on one's own, but self-training becomes burdensome because most people have so many other demands on their time. Without user training, Notes' inherent potential as an effective workplace tool is wasted. Unfortunately, this is the case at many large companies now using Notes.

Intranets: An Internal Product

With intranets, ownership of the "product" is much more distributed. Development tends to take place much closer to the ground, and the workplace *is* the laboratory for development. Intranet technologies, particularly Java, are basically tools that let people build their own products. With intranets, at least some of the development burden shifts from the software company that sells the product (i.e., Lotus, Novell, or Microsoft) to the organization itself.

■ Technical Advantages of Intranets

If more programming and design effort is required for intranets, what are the advantages that offset the costs? According to David Berlind,[1] from a technical perspective, there are several advantages.

1. Web browsers provide a common interface to a variety of applications. For example, simultaneous access to internal web pages and web sites, Lotus Notes databases, Oracle databases, and files stored in legacy systems. They have the potential for generating savings over more proprietary interfaces.

2. Web browsers provide users with universal access. They run on different operating systems and present a common interface to all applications. Building a groupware application, on the other hand, requires that a programmer develop one version of an application for each desktop operating system. A company then is forced to support a variety of desktop operating systems and deal with multiple versions of a system. This adds to the development time and administration challenges.

3. Intranet applications can also be more flexible. With traditional applications, a programmer has to determine how information will flow before designing it. Users then must follow each step in the design. An intranet's hyperlinked environment, on the other hand, gives users more freedom in choosing how to access information. Users can piece the data together in almost any way imaginable.

In short, intranets have a number of technical advantages.

- Intranets allow system managers to leave all the data on the system where they exist. They do not have to convert data to another system.

- The web browser minimizes the number of interface mechanisms that people have to know how to use.

- The amount of training required for intranet participation corresponds to the nature and purpose of participation. People who use the intranet only to look at documents and to post to newsgroups need very little assistance because the point-and-click hyperlinks are so easy to use and because they enable multiple navigation paths.

Several good products, such as <u>RadNet's WebShare</u>, <u>IntraNetics</u> and <u>WisdomLink</u> (which are included on the CD-ROM) take much of the development headaches out of intranet development. Because they are browser-based and designed from open architecture principles, the applications are compatible with any existing information technology infrastructure. Information technology managers do not have to worry about RadNet's WebShare, IntraNetics, and/or WisdomLink being incompatible with Microsoft BackOffice, of Netscape Suite Spot or Oracle databases. An organization can leverage what it already has—fit the RadNet's WebShare, IntraNetics, or WisdomLink package into the existing infrastructure, and continue to add other intranet applications as needed. They have the convenience of a product like Notes but enable the organization to take control of the desktop.

■ Explaining the Nontechnical Differences Between Intranets and Notes

Clearly, there are some compelling technical advantages to intranets. There are other important nontechnical advantages as well. The best way to compare the differences between Notes and an intranet is to get a feel for each system on your own computer and to observe over time how your patterns of working and thinking are enabled by either technology. Because that method isn't practical for most people, one option is to describe what it would feel like to use either Notes or an intranet.

Notes feels like a huge building—like a beautiful mansion or hotel. Each of the rooms (the databases) within it are somewhat guarded, or private. Users are required to have permission to enter any database. Once they are "inside" any particular database, they can do a wide variety of things such as make documents available to other users, fill out and submit forms, hold on-line threaded discussions, or import information from outside the organization.

Notes makes it easy for people to move information *laterally*—from one source to another source, from one database to another database, from a Notes database out to a web site. But, particularly in large organizations, only Notes Administrators with permission access to all of the databases can "see" the full picture and how the information might fit together. One advantage of Notes is its built-in security features. However, by the nature of its design, the technology does not facilitate wide cross-fertilization of information across groups. It simply was not designed that way.

Because Notes makes use of hyperlinks, it is possible to point a user to another piece of related information stored in the same database or in a different database, on the same server or on a different server. Yet Notes promotes a certain forms of thinking that are still fairly linear and hierarchical.

The ability to construct meaningful, rule-governed categories of information is one of the critical success factors for Notes implementation. Those categories must be good enough so that every member of the end-user population can use them as guideposts to locate the right pieces of information.

When data of any sort are placed in databases for storage, they are filed in a directory system, and information is found by tracing it down from category to category. Although you can place duplicates in various Notes databases, you have to have rules about which path will locate it, and the rules are somewhat cumbersome. Moreover, if the databases are password-protected, a person who has found one item in one database on one server must emerge from the system and re-enter on a new path.

As anyone who has ever used a bad card catalog system in a library knows, if the categories are off or if the cards are poorly cross-referenced, it's very difficult to locate the right or the best piece of information quickly. If the path is misleading or nonexistent, there's the chance that the piece of information you need will be out of your sight, and thus out of reach.

Some Notes databases can be created to allow full text searches of all materials on the database, so that the user's ability to conduct a search can offset the lack of quality of the categories. But, even when that feature is enabled, you can search only the databases to which you have been granted access. It's analogous to being able to search only a certain section of the library. intranets can be just as closed as groupware platforms. In fact, you can keep parts of an intranet out of reach to everyone except to those people who know the URLs and/or have a password. Also, intranets can be constructed to be far more open than groupware platforms. An intranet's central advantage over groupware is that it can enable people to create their own paths or trails through the information. Although an intranet may start out as basically a groupware-like application, it is based on open system architecture and can be configured and reconfigured as it evolves.

Two Different Models of Organizational Communication

The models of communication that Notes and intranets support, therefore, are different. The Notes manager is like a innkeeper who concentrates primarily on the questions, Who can have access? and Should we build more rooms? An intranet champion, in contrast, can be more like an architect or a master gardener who focuses on creating a space for communication based on the employee's needs.

The central questions are, Who is the audience for this information and how will the information help them? and then, How should we build this communication environment?

Web development skills, particularly programming skills, are essential to intranet design. The fundamental difference between an intranet and groupware is that the *vision* of what *you* want to do with the technology drives the supporting roles, not the other way around.

That is one reason that a clear concept of what you want to accomplish with the technology is so crucial. If it is the case that streamlining processes is the goal, or that having tightly secured electronic environments for team-based projects is the goal, then groupware like Notes is a very good investment.

However, if a goal is to enable breakthroughs in thinking—the "ah ha's" that result from serendipitous linking of ideas or pieces of information or people through a diffuse, extended network, the technology design must be open enough to enable that. With an open hypermedia system (an intranet), the "ah ha's" are a genuine possibility.

The Bottom Line: What Are Your Objectives?

The bottom line is that neither Notes nor an intranet is a "perfect" or "complete" technology. Different technologies will promote and support different behaviors and different ways of thinking. Although vendors are claiming that groupware and intranets are really two different versions of the same thing, the truth is that they are not the same.

Using the hotel and gardening metaphors may help you decide how to put the pieces together. The Notes technology will enable you to:

- Offer people very nice virtual rooms where small groups can bring hypermedia resources that will help them work together.
- Take a process that in the real world is time-consuming and create and orderly, efficient check-in, check-out system.
- Secure information with a sophisticated security system that is provided for every single database and a password provided for every licensed user.

You can also accomplish the same three goals with an intranet using web-based technology. The challenge is in the construction of the intranet technologies, because you have so many more design options. However, with an intranet, you can also:

- Provide a space where all of that great knowledge being created by individual groups in their private spaces can get linked together.
- Cultivate the cross-fertilization of ideas and information to avoid duplication of efforts and to generate new questions, leading to better solutions and breakthrough thinking.
- Permit employees to become very involved with the design of the technology so that it feels right and meets their needs.

- Provide a lot of people in the organization with a "thin client" (a web browser) instead of a "fat client" (Notes desktop), saving the expense of computer upgrades, memory shortages, and complicated software installation.

We need to design our systems in such a way that there can be virtual places that function like the "commons." In real life (IRL), commons are tracts of land, usually in a centrally located spot, belonging to or used by a community as a whole. The term *commons* can also mean a building or hall for dining, typically at a university or college. A lot of learning and a lot of information-sharing takes place in the commons, in those places where people can see each other and connect.

■ Intranet: Like a Farmer's Market

Dave Carlson, IT expert and president of Ontogenics Corp, offers the metaphor of a farmers' market as a way talk about intranets. This metaphor is another good way to understand the comparative benefits of an intranet.

Have you ever been to a farmers' market? The main purpose is to enable financial transactions between produce suppliers (the "farmers") and customers. Suppliers offer their produce and products, and customers give them money in exchange. In that sense, a farmers' market is somewhat like a supermarket. It's a place to make an economic transaction. However, there is always so much more that happens at a farmers' market.

Farmers' markets are often perceived as community events where people can see each other, meet, circulate, and talk. Although people engage in economic transactions, their social interactions and social transactions can be even more important than actually purchasing food or flowers or honey. There is also an element of surprise and unpredictability. At Farmers' markets, the produce is fresh, locally grown, and seasonal. The supply is never static.

The merchants sit in close proximity to each other, learn from each other about things like presentation and pricing, and continually adapt. Merchants and customers alike circulate in and out of the space; their comings and goings driven by their immediate need to sell and/or to buy.

Intranets that feature an open systems design can be very much like farmers' markets. The information exchanges may have multiple dimensions— some very pragmatic and goal-oriented dimensions, some far less structured but no less important. The information and knowledge can be very "fresh." In this sort of design, what gets put on the system is typically highly reflective of people's immediate and most pressing information needs. It is not based on what the grocer has interpreted from a sheet of data or what a central authority says that the store needs to push.

As Dave Carlson points, out, "some people like grocery stores. At the supermarket, a structured and controlled environment, the produce and products and prices are generally predictable. Many people like the predictability and the ease of selecting products and then making a streamlined purchase." On the other hand, some people really like farmers' markets, particularly because they allow people an opportunity to become a participant in the flow of community life. They also provide a way for people to observe changes in each other and in the community.

The good thing is that one type of market is not exclusive of the other. It is possible for each type of market environment to sit side by side, providing value to a wide base of customers who like having a choice. Lotus Notes is more like a well-lit, very orderly supermarket. An intranet is more like a farmers market, and it can be either very orderly or very disorderly. (The design is up to you and to the people who'll use the space.)

These metaphors raise some interesting questions that any intranet developer should ask: What is the nature of the "information transaction" that will be talking place on the system? How much structure and how much "chaos" or spontaneity are you looking for? What is the sort of electronic environment and culture you wish to create? Why do you think any of your "customers" would make an effort to get to or use the space? What are *they* looking for?

■ Political Battles About Notes and Intranets

As many people who have already implemented either Notes or an intranet know, discussions about Notes versus intranets, and vice versa, tend to get heated and can become emotionally charged. The political conflicts can be discouraging.

There seem to be two reasons why people go to battle over these technologies. First, learning how to implement and manage one information technology is challenging. Learning about multiple technologies is even more challenging. Some people would rather not see the merits of the other side's technology because it creates additional pressure to learn and perhaps to adapt to something new.

Second, both Notes and intranets require an investment in resources. The capacity for individuals to learn and the amount of resources available to improve an organization are typically greater than most people realize, but they are not infinite. Rare is the organization that can dedicate a lot of manpower to managing a fully functional enterprise-wide Notes system and a fully functional, enterprise-wide intranet. Choices should be made. The debates, therefore, do need to take place.

There are ways to make the debates less acrimonious. Chapters 15 and 16 discuss how technical and nontechnical people can come together to co-create an intranet. Going forward, the right question to ask is not, Is this the best technology? but, Will our organization be improved with a technology? In some people's eyes, Notes is the "best technology." But best for what? And best for whom? What is your mental model of the technology and its capabilities?

■ Trying to Create a Virtual Workspace: A Pattern Language

Chapter 4 discussed how intranets can be used for more than tools to automate work processes. They can become virtual places for people to meet and communicate on-line. One person helping to foster vigorous discussion about designing places—virtual and real—where people feel comfortable and healthy is <u>Christopher Alexander</u>, the president of the Center for Environmental Structure and Professor of Architecture at the University of California-Berkeley. At a conference in Amsterdam that focused on interactivity and design, <u>Alexander told his audience</u>:[2]

> In my view, the biggest problem in architecture in the second half of the 20th century is the connection between people and the physical world—the building of streets and so forth. Essentially,

what we miss right now is the connection that one could call `belonging' or possession in the true emotional sense.

For the past 30 years, Alexander has approached the design of buildings by first attempting to understand the ways in which people live and experience their world. He argues that most architects have not designed for people; they have designed for themselves—for their colleagues in the field of architecture. The consequences have been several. In *Notes on the Synthesis of Form*, Alexander writes that we have a legacy of poor design that is shown in several problems:

- Inability to balance individual, group, societal, and ecological needs.
- Lack of purpose, order, and human scale.
- Aesthetic and functional failure in adapting to local physical and social environments.
- Development of materials and standardized components that are ill-suited for use in any specific application.
- Creation of artifacts that people do not like.

Alexander is not just a theoretician. He is a practicing architect, a professor and the author of many books including *Notes on the Synthesis of Form*, *The Production of Houses*, *Linz Café*, *The Timeless Way of Building*, *The Oregon Experiement*, and *A Pattern Language*. In his books and speeches, Alexander argues that people should design for themselves their own houses, streets, and communities. The most wonderful places in the world were made not by architects but by people. In Amsterdam, Alexander said:[2]

My question is: what does it really take to build up a world in which our houses sustain and enlarge childish, innocent life in us? One of the most obvious things that comes to mind when one compares mass housing, tract developers' suburban homes, public housing and expensive architect design houses, for example, is the question: what if people did this for themselves? If they really got involved in making, shaping the environment? Things would be a lot better. Of course, this is what happened for centuries at virtually all times in most cultures.

Yet, doing so today is "radical," Alexander explains, as it requires innovations in construction, administrative, financial, and other processes that allow for both fluid construction contracts and efficient management of time and money. Historically, the modern ``rational'' design was a contributing factor toward the professionalization of design. Rational design is separates designs from products, uses analytic models, and focuses on methods that only those with sufficient formal training may apply. Whereas rational design was in many ways a major advance over traditional methods, Alexander argues that the notions of analysis and synthesis have been badly construed in architecture and artifact design. They may be efficient, but they are counterproductive in the long run because they don't last. People end up tearing down what they recently built only to begin again, to simply continue to try to adapt themselves to poor design.

In his remarkable book, *A Pattern Language*, Alexander tries to give us a language to help people articulate and communicate the kinds of design patterns that they need to live healthy lives and to maintain social networks. The book contains many references to studies from sociology, anthropology and organizational development—some going as far back as the 1800s. *A Pattern Language* is as much a philosophy of "the good life" as a book about designing towns, buildings, gardens, cafes, children's bedrooms, bathrooms, and homes.

Although his books are written primarily in the interest of architects, Alexander's books have been taken as having a fundamental importance to computer programmers, software designers, and web application designers. It turns out that the same organizing principles apply to computer programs as to buildings. Variants of Alexander's decomposition algorithm have been applied to object-oriented (OO) software. A good overview can be found in Richard Gabriel's book, *Patterns of Software* (New York: Oxford University Press, 1966; with a foreword by Christopher Alexander). Gabriel illuminates some of Alexander's key insights—"the quality without a name," pattern languages, habitability, piecemeal growth—and reveals how these influential architectural ideas apply equally well to the construction of a computer program.

■ Your Intranet Design Principles

How do people in your organization think about communication within the organization? How do they think about the structure and function of the organization? Does "farmer's market" sound too strange or foreign? What terms and metaphors would resonate in your organization? Starting from this point in the book, the focus will turn to issues around communication with employees about what would motivate them to use an intranet on a continuous basis.

In Section Two, we looked at web technologies and what they can offer. We compared Notes to an intranet, arguing that the design of a technology strongly influences the types of communication that will occur with its use. Some questions emerged: Who is the audience for communication and how will the information enable them to solve problems? How should we build a communication environment that meets employees' needs? The discussions in the next four chapters in Section Three will provide tools and methods for designing and building an intranet that doesn't feel forced or artificial.

■ References

1. Berlind, David, "Intranets Could Solve Many IT Issues," *PC Week* 13, no. 3 (January 22, 1996): 68.
2. Christopher Alexander, "Domestic Architecture," speech at Doors of Perception 2@HOME Conference, November 4–6, 1994, Amsterdam, sponsored by the Netherlands Design Insitute and the Institute and Mediamatic. http://www.mediamatic.nl/Doors/Doors.html.

■ Section Two Questions

In Section One, we saw that at each stage in the history of the Internet and World Wide Web, there were important activities on the technology side as well as the non-technology (or human) side. We depicted them as parallel activities radiating from each phase. Sound, stable intranet development follows that same progression through each of the five phases. Drawing from key learnings discussed in this chapter, keep the following checklist in mind.

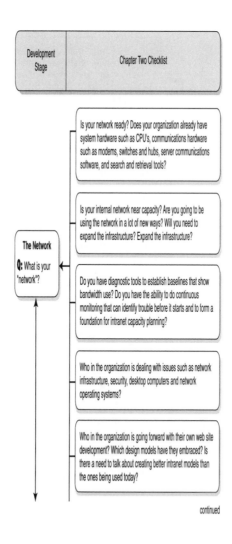

Development Stage	Chapter Two Checklist

Is your network ready? Does your organization already have system hardware such as CPU's, communications hardware such as modems, switches and hubs, server communications software, and search and retrieval tools?

Is your internal network near capacity? Are you going to be using the network in a lot of new ways? Will you need to expand the infrastructure? Expand the infrastructure?

The Network

Q: What is your "network"?

Do you have diagnostic tools to establish baselines that show bandwidth use? Do you have the ability to do continuous monitoring that can identify trouble before it starts and to form a foundation for intranet capacity planning?

Who in the organization is dealing with issues such as network infrastructure, security, desktop computers and network operating systems?

Who in the organization is going forward with their own web site development? Which design models have they embraced? Is there a need to talk about creating better intranet models than the ones being used today?

continued

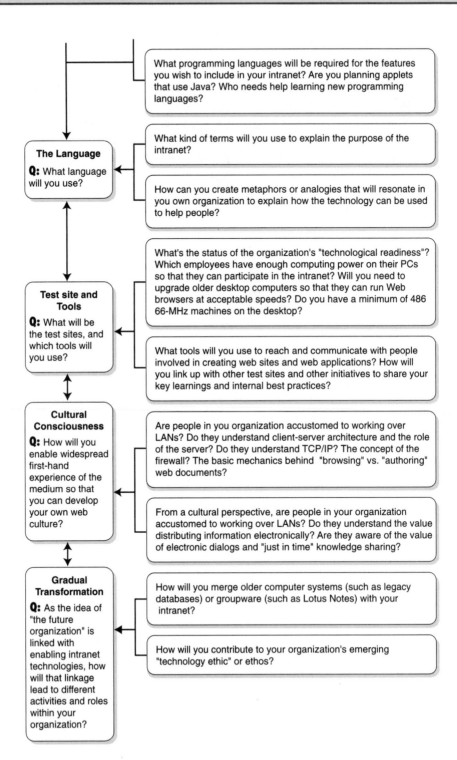

What programming languages will be required for the features you wish to include in your intranet? Are you planning applets that use Java? Who needs help learning new programming languages?

The Language

Q: What language will you use?

What kind of terms will you use to explain the purpose of the intranet?

How can you create metaphors or analogies that will resonate in you own organization to explain how the technology can be used to help people?

Test site and Tools

Q: What will be the test sites, and which tools will you use?

What's the status of the organization's "technological readiness"? Which employees have enough computing power on their PCs so that they can participate in the intranet? Will you need to upgrade older desktop computers so that they can run Web browsers at acceptable speeds? Do you have a minimum of 486 66-MHz machines on the desktop?

What tools will you use to reach and communicate with people involved in creating web sites and web applications? How will you link up with other test sites and other initiatives to share your key learnings and internal best practices?

Cultural Consciousness

Q: How will you enable widespread first-hand experience of the medium so that you can develop your own web culture?

Are people in you organization accustomed to working over LANs? Do they understand client-server architecture and the role of the server? Do they understand TCP/IP? The concept of the firewall? The basic mechanics behind "browsing" vs. "authoring" web documents?

From a cultural perspective, are people in your organization accustomed to working over LANs? Do they understand the value distributing information electronically? Are they aware of the value of electronic dialogs and "just in time" knowledge sharing?

Gradual Transformation

Q: As the idea of "the future organization" is linked with enabling intranet technologies, how will that linkage lead to different activities and roles within your organization?

How will you merge older computer systems (such as legacy databases) or groupware (such as Lotus Notes) with your intranet?

How will you contribute to your organization's emerging "technology ethic" or ethos?

Contexts for Intranet Communication

We owe almost all our knowledge not to those who have agreed, but to those who have differed.

Reverend C.C. Colton

In the last chapter, we talked about intranets as being somewhat like farmers, markets in that they provide a space for co-mingling of ideas and people. People enter such a marketplace for a variety of different reasons; they return if the space has met or exceeded their expectations. Section Three, which starts with this chapter, focuses on ways to develop an intranet that employees as internal customers will select and use consistently as a "preferred product." Most of the case studies in this book are here in Section Three. The case study key learnings illuminate the benefits of engaging with employees throughout the design and development phases.

Here in Chapter 7, we look at how the computer industry has begun to place significant emphasis on user-centered design. More and more, customers are being perceived as "engines of innovation." We'll look at how and why this is happening, then discuss how intranet development can improve

145

if these ideas are transferred from the marketplace to internal web development.

■ A Dynamic, Fluid Marketing Model

For many years, technology specialist groups inside organizations have maintained responsibility for purchasing or creating new technologies and delivering them to the employee base. Employees rarely had a say in what technologies they would like to use on the job, or how they would like to use them. For a decade now, evidence has been mounting that this method does not work well.

To avoid implementing internal web sites no one will use, it's important to involve employees in the technology design, development ,and implementation. More than a philosophy, it's good business sense. Paul Kazmierski, an industrial psychologist and professor at the Rochester Institute of Technology in Rochester, New York, argues that if you don't take people needs into account when designing technology, "employees can't or won't do their jobs, turnover will increase, and productivity will decrease, all of which will lead to lost revenue."

There is a better, smarter way. Since the late 1980s, high-tech companies have been following a dynamic marketing model that stresses ongoing interaction and dialog with customers and other participants in the marketplace. The objective? Improve products, speed product-to-market cycle time, and develop loyal customers.

This model of market relations has proved to be so reliable, several high-tech companies have developed special labs to watch people at work using product prototypes. Some companies, like Xerox, employ anthropologists and ethnographers to watch people in their "natural" workplace settings. Other companies go even further. As Elizabeth Weil reported in a wonderful *Fast Company* article, "The Future is Younger Than You Think," adult leaders of the 20th century are beginning to pay a lot of attention to young students still in high school, who have grown up with technology and who, the executives believe, will help their companies create technologies for the 21st-century workplace. Compaq, Autodesk, and Xerox are inviting kids into their companies as ad hoc consultants to help the companies predict and create new products that appeal to future generations of employees.

We have not seen the same kind of attention focused on internal "customers" (i.e., employees), for a couple of reasons. If a high-tech product fails in the marketplace, the consequences can be great. Investors, R & D groups, engineers, the manufacturers, senior management and front-line employees all take a hit. That type of failure is public and measurable. The failure of internal communication technologies, in contrast, are almost always private failures. Though the consequences are real, they often go unnoticed and undocumented.

Whether the failure is noticed or not, it is not necessary. Intranet developers can break open the seams of "business as usual" to rethink the process of intranet development. You don't need to hire a group of media-savvy high-schoolers to lead you toward the future, though you may have fun and learn a great deal. Nor do you necessarily require a person with a Ph.D. to study the workplace as though it were a village in a foreign land—though people trained in interpretation and analysis can often be very instrumental in catalyzing change.

The central argument of this chapter is that your organization's existing employees have a lot of valuable ideas about improving communication and information flow, and if you begin to listen *with intent*, you will secure your intranet's "value proposition." Here, we'll examine four different case studies, lay out the Intranet "Value Triad," and make the case for engaging with employees as internal customers during all phases of internal web site development.

Let's start by looking at how and why the U.S. Army, formerly one of the most bureaucratic institutions in nation, decided to stop pushing new technologies and systems at their troops and began to use a model of collaborative design and implementation instead.

■ Case Study 2: Creating the Army of the Future, "Force XXI"

For the past several years at <u>Ft. Hood</u> in Texas, the U.S. Army has been testing an integrated, concurrent process of technology development. The process includes technology "Acquirers, Requirers, Users, and Builders," experts from each group all working together. Involving soldiers is an essential element in the program. As <u>William Perry</u>, U.S. Secretary of Defense, commented in a speech at ACM '97, the Army discovered, much to people's surprise, that soldiers can not only use and maintain technology, they can find new, ingenuous ways to employ it. "This was contrary to expectations and assumptions," Perry admits. "But, our development cycle is significantly shortened."

This is important news. Ft. Hood is the Army's premier installation to train and deploy heavy forces. In an age when military superiority is intimately linked to technologic superiority, it is not at all surprising to find that the Army is focused on technology. Bruce Sterling's eye-popping *Wired* article, "<u>War is Virtual Hell</u>" illuminates the dark side of the force—the intentions and technologies of the "cybercolonels" who spend millions to create virtual fighting simulations. However, as you would expect with an organization as large as the Army, there is much more happening within it's jurisdiction than a single emphasis on cyberwar games. With Force XXI, the Army is focusing on technology *and* on the people who use that technology.

Since 1992, the Army has been in the process of creating <u>Force XXI</u>, (Force 21) the "transformed Army of the 21st Century." The initiative began with a series of simulations and exercises called *Louisiana maneuvers* (LAM). The central and essential feature of this Army will be its ability to exploit information. The Army believes that information and digital technologies are creating such a synergistic effect among all of the Army's operating systems, organizations, and components that the Army's capability will be enhanced by an order of magnitude. The Force XXI "system of systems," will provide a constant flow of information to and from all combat units.

Information technology is not the only focus. Soldiers are seen as even **more** important than the sophisticated technology the Army is creating for the 21st century. In "<u>The Army in the Information Age</u>," General Gordon R. Sullivan and Lieutenant Colonel Anthony M. Coroalles assert that

> The Army has one tremendous resource as it faces the 21st century: soldiers that can think. They constitute more than a half million smart weapons in the Army inventory. Each one can make decisions under adverse conditions, track on multiple targets, fire and forget, and each one possesses a virtually unlimited reloading capability. Because each one also can make moral choices, they are individually more precious than any number of Comanche

helicopters, multiple launch rocket systems, or counter-battery radars.

As suggested by the Roman numerals in its name, in many ways Force XXI is a return to history, to a time when great militaries were known by the character, quality, and courage of the members of its armies, to a time before the Army became technologized and statistics were used as the primary method to know and manage the front lines. For over 30 years, the military technocracy tended to view people at the front lines as bits and pieces in the machinery of war. Today, in the post-Cold-War world, the Army's mission is different, as are its doctrine and its view of people and information. The underlying idea is to create an infrastructure with coherent data and coherent standards so that *the people* can have more power.

Adjusting to Change Through Proactive Means

The Force XXI statement of purpose notes that, "we live in a volatile, uncertain, chaotic, and ambiguous world that demands a force capable of performing missions across a full spectrum of conflict and operations *other than war*." The role of the Army and its troops has changed, and is changing. The Army is taking a central role in managing domestic crisis situations, such as helping restore communities in the aftermath of floods and hurricanes.

In addition, the Army recognizes that the geopolitical future is uncertain, and the only certainty is change. For example, Secretary Perry points out that although the Soviet Union has collapsed, the old, morbid systems in Russia present a huge challenge. Quoting the philosopher and cultural critic Antonio Gramsci, Perry reminds us that "The old has died, but the new has not yet been born." So, instead of containment, a "holding strategy," the military seeks "engagement" with small, new nations to demonstrate how the military can support economic growth.

This is a very different role, and it is predicated on the idea that we will never return to the kind of geopolitical stability and predictability that marked earlier periods in our history. As General Gordon R. Sullivan states, "I will tell you, we are using every means available to project ourselves into the future . . . we are reading everything we can about the world of the 21st century. And then we are trying to create the worlds of the 21st century and force ourselves into the 21st century."

Dr. Margaret Wheatley, president of the Berkana Institute and author of the pathbreaking book, *Leadership and the New Science : Learning About Organization from an Orderly Universe*, has been involved in discussions about Force XXI and its requirements for success. Force XXI, Dr. Wheatley notes, reveals how a large organization can become well-ordered via open and flowing information and communication—as opposed to hierarchy, rank, authority or inflexible rules. According to Dr. Wheatley,[1]

> With both the Louisiana Maneuvers and Battle Labs, the Army has created the means for the organization to see and experience for itself how it could learn from itself and change. Important initial conditions for experimentation and learning, and the means for broad involvement have been created. The inspiration for continued change comes not from the leadership, but from the successes that are occurring in many places around the organization. In this way, the organization provides its own inspiration, and also establishes its own pace of change. People learn what is possible by listening to the experiences of their peers, rather than the inspiring words of their leaders. As they are able to reference more and more of these stories, the organization changes its beliefs about itself. It comes to know itself as capable of change, even in an organization as tradition and policy-bound as the U.S. Army.

Case Study 2: Key Learnings

Why did the Army decide to begin to focus on two things simultaneously: information technologies **and** the people who use them? It stemmed from the recognition that the world is changing, quickly and dramatically.

The Army was smart. It faced the signs of change, including the decision Congress made in 1995 to close over a dozen bases and hospitals. Military leaders decided that the Army would not melt away; instead, they identified where the Army could make unique contributions; and they then defined an important role for the Army in the future.

Next, the Army created a plan: develop communication systems that would not only (a) handle the complexity of routine tasks like surveillance and data transmission, but (b) would also be flexible to accommodate information spawned from uncertain, even chaotic situations. It was decided to

use information technologies to become "future-proof." Instead of chan-
neled flows of information, Force XXI's "system of systems" transmits information in all directions simultaneously and provides numerous mechanisms
for feedback and two-way communication.

Wrapped around this is the explicit acknowledgment that the military is
participating in the creation of geopolitical realities—not merely responding
to external forces. The Army is creating the environment through its strong
intentions, such as "preventive defense." Like proactive medicine, it involves
proactive tactics that create the conditions for peace.

The Army clearly outlined the requirements for success in its new role.
First, it required state-of-the art information technologies that its troops
could adopt and adapt through a process of continuous improvement—as
opposed to discontinuous innovation. Second, it decided that it required
trained, quality personnel who could do more than carry out orders. The
Army of the future needed people who could think, reflect ,and respond appropriately to fluctuating conditions.

The main point is that the Army did not simply arrive at the conclusion
that involving soldiers in its new, integrated, concurrent process of technology development was a good idea. If they arrived at the conclusion by recog-
nizing that it no longer had *the luxury* of developing new technologies apart
from the people expected to use them to perform their jobs. For the sake of
speed and survival, the Army was forced to abandon its old model and begin
to involve soldiers as partners in an integrated, concurrent process of technology development.

Though the Army may appear foresighted as compared to many other
large organizations, it is following in the wake of the computer industry,
which began abandoning the old model over a two decades ago. The change
was stimulated by marketing visionary Regis McKenna, who helped launch
some of the most important technological innovations of the last two decades, including the first microprocessor, Intel Corporation, the first personal computer, the Apple computer, the first recombinant DNA genetically
engineered product for Genentech, Inc., and the first retail computer store,
The Byte Shop. This method is called *market relations.*

■ A "Market Relations" Approach

In 1970, Regis McKenna, founder of the <u>Regis McKenna Group</u>, began working with high-tech companies like Intel and Apple to try to change how they marketed high-tech products. Traditional marketing approaches such as advertising and brand-awareness failed when applied to products like computers. This was partly because of the "FUD factor"—that is, the fear, uncertainty, and doubt that can plague people trying to make a decision about such an unfamiliar set of products and services. McKenna conceived of a different approach to high-tech marketing and advertising based on a model of dynamic two-way communication rather than traditional advertising's model of one-way communication.

The fundamental idea of market relations is to build and manage relationships with all the members that make up the high-tech marketplace, not just the visible ones, like customers. The method requires setting up formal and informal communications with a variety of different groups—customers, reporters, analysts, hardware and software partners, distributors, dealers, systems integrators, user groups, vertically oriented industry organizations, universities, standards bodies, and international partners. The method requires improving not only external communications but also internal exchange of information among the sales force, product managers, strategic planners, and the staffs of customer service and support, engineering, manufacturing, and finance.

The central tenet in this approach is that direct, honest information about your product is very, very valuable. The feedback permits you to identify areas for improvement before your competition has an opportunity to leapfrog ahead. As McKenna points out, companies rarely get it right the first time. For example, the first Macintosh and the first release of Windows simply were not right—both needed major overhauls before they captured enough attention to make the products runaway successes. This was possible, McKenna states, only because Apple and Microsoft kept in close touch with their customers and the other participants that make up the PC marketplace.

McKenna's continual and constant emphasis on the importance of communication with customers shifted the marketing paradigm from a "push" process to a dialogic "pull" process. It was just one of the things that has helped to fuel the adoption of participatory design techniques.

■ A Concurrent Wave: User-Centered Design

At the same time that McKenna was making his case for more and better communication between high-tech firms and customers, people from cognitive science and computer programming started to talk and write about specific techniques for improving software and hardware design. Inspired, in part, by Donald A. Norman's book, *The Design of Everyday Things*, software designers and computer experts began to develop several techniques to improve things they hoped consumers would buy and integrate into their workplaces and homes. Techniques introduced in the 1980s included user-centered design (1986), user-centered requirements analysis (1988), contextual inquiry (1988) and joint application design (1989) .

The methodologies use an incremental, iterative process in which any given step can feed back and modify decisions made in the preceding one. As others[2] have pointed out, this iterative or "spiral" idea, suggested by Boehm in several technical publications the 1980s, is the main trust of the current wave of rapid application development methods such as object-oriented modeling and object-oriented design.

Such methods have grown in popularity because they have helped high-tech companies respond in a proactive fashion to hypercompetitive conditions within the computer marketspace. Karen Holtzblatt and Hugh Beyer, creators of Contextual Inquiry and founders of InContext Enterprises, explain that "to be innovative means to address important needs in new ways. Since existing products cannot act as a model, guidance must come from users themselves."

Digital Equipment, for example, uses Holtzblatt and Beyer's interactive Contextual Inquiry. Instead of simply product testing what specialists have created, the experts build on users' strengths by doing all their work with them in their own context, on their own problems. The method is highly interactive. Holtzblatt and Beyer report that

> If we wish to validate a model of how they work, we do not show and walk through the model with them. Instead, during an interview about their own work practice, we respond to their description of their work by drawing a picture. This picture is one of our models which responds immediately to what they just said about their own experience. It is a conversation aid, not something to be learned.

The method is essentially dialogic. Holtzblatt and Beyer promote constant circulation of data collection, interpretation, and analysis, with several data integrity checkpoints along the way. The theory is, if you learn from users and get close to them, you'll improve product design and increase customer satisfaction.

These kinds of methods provide good alternatives to traditional application design development methods, which have been characterized by high costs, missed programming schedules, cost overruns, inflexibility of programs, and programming backlogs. However, the methods are of little value unless they are accompanied by a communication ethos that is grounded in communicating and respect. The methods require that people are able to make free and informal choices with a minimal amount of defensive interpersonal relations or organizational routines. They involve a commitment to, and a close monitoring of, choices.

Customers as "Engines of Innovation"

Malcolm Gladwell,[3] writing for *The New Yorker*, provides a fascinating account of how NetObjects developed Fusion, an outstanding HTML editor, by incorporating suggestions from its customers. Samir Arora, co-founder of NetObjects, disclosed that he was motivated to create Fusion because he knew from his own experience and that of his friends that the tools web designers were using to create dynamic web sites were too primitive. HTML coding ate up too much valuable time. In 1994, Arora decided to create software to automate HTML. To do so, Arora followed the same development model Tim Berners-Lee used to create the Web and the one that Regis McKenna writes about in his books—that is, Arora solicited feedback and then integrated the best ideas into the product design.

Gladwell describes how this happened at NetObjects. The programmers at NetObjects began with a prototype—a beta version—they gave to about a hundred carefully chosen web designers for comments. They adjusted the software based on the feedback they received from their group of 100. About five months later, NetObjects began shipping this first version, Fusion 1.0, to distributors. Over the next few weeks, customers' e-mail messages arrived offering more suggestions and complaints. The company also sent out "evangelists" to Internet companies and conferences, looking for feedback. That feedback was analyzed and incorporated into version 2.0.

A few months later, the company finished the beta version of Fusion 2.0 and it, too, was sent to a select group of 400 customers. The 400 beta testers sent between 100 and 200 e-mail messages per day to the company, some of which were highly detailed. The best were forwarded to the relevant designers and engineers. Their suggestions and criticisms were then incorporated into the final version of Fusion 2.0.

Just as William Perry and other military leaders were surprised by the quality of ideas soldiers have offered about improving technology design, the designers at NetObjects were pleasantly surprised by their customers' ideas as well. Samir Arora remarks that many of the suggestions would never have occurred to staffers on their own, if for no other reason than that many web designers are using Fusion in ways that were impossible to predict. For example, just after the release of 1.0, the company learned that people were using Fusion to do web-casts —creating a live web site and constantly updating the site on the Internet. There was a problem, though. Every time the site was updated with a new picture—text or audio—Fusion would laboriously re-send all the data on the web site. When the web-casters pointed this out, NetObjects revised the code. In version 2.0, when a site is updated Fusion sends out only the new data. Gladwell reports that of the 100 new features Fusion 2.0, 80 are a direct result of this kind of user suggestion.

As computers and computer applications become more and more essential to the way we live our lives in the dawn of the 21st century, more and more people are concentrating on these kinds of issues. In fact, user-centered participatory design is more than a trend gathering momentum, it's a booming field. *Bringing Design to Software* by editors Terry Winograd, John Bennett, and Laura De Young, reveals how fast and how far the field has matured. The book features the insights of experienced software designers and developers, including Mitchell Kapor, David Liddle, John Rheinfrank, Peter Denning, and John Seely Brown. Other luminaries such as David Kelley, Donald Schon, and Donald Norman discuss the ideology and philosophy of user-based design. Case studies about the creation of Mosaic, Quicken, Macintosh Human Interface Guidelines, and Microsoft Bob reveal the intricacies behind this burgeoning field.

The learning is taking place so quickly, conferences have become an essential medium to share knowledge and information. Computer Professionals for Social Responsibility sponsors an annual Conference on Participatory Design. ACM, the oldest, largest professional society for people interested in computers, includes a vibrant and growing special interest group (SIG) for

Computer–Human Interaction (CHI). In 1997, <u>SIGCHI</u> had several hundred members, including user interface designers and users, software developers, managers of human–computer interface projects, human factors practitioners, interface evaluators and testers, industrial designers, teachers, researchers in human–computer interaction and professionals in other areas seeking to gain an understanding of how CHI relates to their specialties. SIGCHI is one of ACM's fastest growing subgroups and the SIGCHI annual conferences attract people from all across the world interested in sharing key learnings with their colleagues. Credentialed experts such as Holtzblatt and Beyer even offer day-longer seminars on their methods and techniques.

Malcolm Gladwell remarks that "as technologies become more complicated and users more sophisticated, customers are no longer the passive recipients of innovation. In many ways, they are the engines of innovation." This is a different way of looking at the process of innovation—innovation driven by market needs, not by spark of individual creative genius alone.

There is an implicit social contract at work here. For example, NetObject's customers improved upon but did not invent Fusion. They wanted better tools and demanded a better product, so they provided valuable guidance and feedback in the development process, with nothing but the hope for a better tool in return. NetObject set up the conditions to develop the product and bring the innovation to market. Clearly, one party could not exist without the other. Both parties experience benefit from the relationship. As we will see in the next section, this type of interdependence between people who use technology and people who create technology is beginning to characterize cutting-edge intranet development, as well.

■ Engaging With Employees as Intranet Customers

Though intranet development is focused on internal communications, not on bringing a product to the marketspace, the same principles can be used to better understand the needs of internal customers.

Carol Hildebrand, a senior editor at *WebMaster* magazine, argues persuasively in her article "<u>Face Facts</u>," that successful intranet developers focus on employee needs and respond to their requests. Successful developers, Hildebrand notes, give users the information they want, bundle it in ways that make sense to most users, and get employees to that information as quickly as possible.

Focus groups and surveys are playing an essential role in the intranet development process. Hildebrand interviewed Cynthia Casselman, manager of strategic communications and an intranet development partner at Xerox, responsible for Xerox's Webboard. When Casselman started intranet development, she ran 12 focus groups and surveyed 1,500 Xerox employees to learn how they thought about, prioritized, and categorized information. Based on the results of those studies, she built a home page with 11 icons. A year later, the group's studies showed that the employees wished to see some changes made on the site. Casselman and her team eliminated several icons, changed others and leveraged specific meanings that would resonate within the Xerox culture.

The employees' responses to the site also motivated the Xerox team to identify and plug some big gaps in the information structure. For example, they created an icon called Benefits and Resources for an area that contains HR information such as administrative forms, benefits material, and support resources. They also reorganized information into two other categories: "Customers and Marketplace," which combines external links to industry news, competitive intelligence, and competitors' Web pages with Xerox's internal market information; and "Values and Direction," which focuses on the strategic direction and values of the company. You can see screen shots of the changes on a link off of Hildebrand's article.

Good design goes beyond information architecture and useablity studies, however. Developing content holds a second, overlapping set of challenges. Good communicators research the needs of their audience instead of falling back on assumptions about what employees need to know or understand. Mik Chwalek, partner in charge of knowledge strategies at Coopers & Lybrand LLP, spoke with Carol Hildebrand for the "Face Facts" article and disclosed that before beginning her redesign of C&L's intranet, Chwalek was determined to find out what her users wanted. Her team completed an extensive survey of more than 500 users, from clerks to partners, asking questions about what kind of information content they needed and how often they needed it. Then the team surveyed librarians and information professionals at Coopers & Lybrand, asking which information was popular. When her team put the two surveys together, the results validated what the team had suspected. People at Coopers & Lybrand, says Chwalek, need information about companies and industries: news, credit reports, Securities and Exchange Commission documents, financial statements and stock research.

Surveying employees to determine their information needs is not that difficult, and it's a good place to start. Uppermost, however, is the identification of core objectives.

■ Begin With the End in Mind

World-renown authors like Anthony Robbins and Steven Covey continually remind us that successful people always start with the end in mind. Intranet and web site developers can benefit from that advice.

Currently, there are numerous Intranet goals circulating through the Intranet community and media. Intranets and internal web sites are being funded with the intention of:

- Reducing and cutting costs (e.g., cutting printing and paper distribution costs)

- Decreasing the amount of administrative, secretarial, or service-based human support requested by employees (e.g., decreasing the number of times employees call a HR staff to request help or information)

- Increasing sales (e.g., by speeding up the process by which salespeople can qualify potential customers, or by developing better competitive intelligence about others' products, prices, and strategies)

- Increasing speed to proficiency (e.g., by making training materials available at any time of the day or night, by allowing people to become self-directed learners)

- Decreasing the amount of time required to accomplish a task (e.g., by eliminating redundant steps in a work process)

- Improving quality (e.g. by enabling employees to call management's attention to quality-related issues) and

- Improving information access (e.g., by enabling employees to search for, request, and retrieve digital information electronically)

Each one is an attractive goal or end state. Almost everyone today wants to do more business, increase profits, cut costs, eliminate waste, increase speed, enhance quality, and improve skill and competence levels. One common assumption is that if the company creates a robust computer network and puts a well-funded intranet in place, it can achieve such goals. "If we build it, they will come, and we will be able to accomplish X goal" (cut costs, etc). Yet, this is one of the worst assumptions an intranet developer or sponsor can make.

The Goal: Consistent Use Overtime

The right metric for intranet success is consistent use over time. When employees choose to use the Intranet on a consistent basis to satisfy their information and communication needs, the technology provides value to the organization. Only then can goals such as improving sales, improving quality, or increasing speed be realized. When employees decide not to use the Intranet, or to use it only because they are forced to do so, the value proposition can not hold.

For example, some companies have justified intranet budgets by looking at the amount of money that will be saved when materials such as company newsletters, training manuals, internal phone directories, and benefit information is published on-line instead of in paper. The goal is to cut costs and eliminate waste. Yet the intranet sponsors find that employees still rely on paper copies, even when the copies are outdated or incomplete. Employees will ask a co-worker for an old copy of an employee directory and take the chance of not finding the right information rather than going directly on-line as their first option.

Employees do not circumvent the Intranet out of insubordination or an unwillingness to embrace change, but rather because in their experience, going online to use the Intranet to locate and view the information is too cumbersome and time-consuming, as *compared with the methods they already know and have come to trust*. In these sorts of situations, people will work around the technology, as though it is a barrier to the accomplishment of their goals, rather than perceive the technology as a tool to achieve their goals.

■ Working Around the Technology

Studies by anthropologists and sociologists who have examined work practices tell us that people are very good at creating "workarounds." Employees find ways to accomplish their task objectives, even if that means going around processes and procedures designed to make employees more productive or efficient.

Back in the 1940s, sociologist William Foote Whyte[4] did a field study of Phillips Petroleum Company plants in Oklahoma City. Whyte revealed how the foremen insisted on giving workers detailed instructions and "refused to acknowledge that [they] might know more about some aspects of operations than did a chemical engineer." Yet, Whyte observes, the workers tended to think and act rather like scientists. They took actions, observed apparent consequences, and "adjusted to varying conditions based on observations of the results achieved." They had also learned from experience that following the foreman's instructions would not produce the desired results. So, they "boiler-housed" their records. The workers wrote down the steps the foremen prescribed but went on to operate the plant as they saw fit, thereby confounding the chemical engineers' attempts to use production data to learn to improve the plant's productivity. Workarounds, Whyte pointed out, actually have their basis in rule-governed experience. Management keeps trying to do the thinking for its workers; workers keep "resisting" and think for themselves.

Another story Whyte told was how U.S. agriculture experts tried unsuccessfully to increase the productivity of small corn farms in the Puebla region of Mexico. The experts believed that the farmers could improve production if they applied a model of farming developed in the American corn belt. However, only a quarter of the corn farmers in the region participated. Whyte reveals that this was not because of "traditionalism" or "resistance to change," but because the farmers were "making twice as much money by following their own methods." Contrary to the tractor-based American model, they planted beans between the rows of corn, "making more efficient use of fertilizer, which now served two crops instead of one." Their method did not fit the technology the Americans so ardently promoted, so it didn't fit the American's mental model of farming. However, it provided a real, measurable economic advantage to the farmers.

In his work for the past 50 years, Professor Whyte has been encouraging us to learn two important lessons about the ways in which people work. First, local knowledge should be valued, even when it contradicts professional expertise. Second, scientific models and methods should be reinvented to suit the local context.

Researchers like Whyte in academe validate and articulate what many of us already know from our everyday work experience: We use what works for us, and if something is not working, we'll find another way. People are problem-solvers by nature and most of our problem-solving relies on schema or patterns of problem-solving we carry around in our heads. We do what seems sensible within our context, our environment, our culture. Yet a great deal of organizational life, as Dilbert cartoons brilliantly illustrate, seems to revolve around frustrating employees' attempts to work sensibly.

When intranets were in their infancy, many people created web pages and web sites out of a sense of frustration with other communication channels and methods that were not working very well within their companies. The web was their workaround. Those early web sites, designed by the same people who felt a need for change, tended to satisfy the creators' needs. Today, however, internal web sites and intranets are no longer an underground phenomenon in most organizations. They have budgets and sponsors. They are tied to strategic goals and objectives. They are frequently "owned" by specialist groups within the organizations. In the process of becoming "legitimate," web site and Intranet design have been removed from the workplace and have been handed over to technical specialists who are generally unfamiliar with how people actually do their work every day. This detachment has been a fundamental mistake.

■ Intranets Do Not Exist in Isolation

In the consumer world, products compete for shelf space and for market share. In the work world, intranets compete for mind space. No intranet stands alone by itself, the only object or technology within an office or cubicle. From the employee's perspective, an Intranet is yet another communication platform that is added to the universe of workplace communication media. That communication universe is already well populated. Let's explore this universe for a moment.

First, the workspace includes oral communication. Communication events and opportunities that rely primarily on verbal speech include:

- phone calls
- one-to-one meetings
- small group meetings
- small group presentations
- large group presentations

We also use written communication. Text-based communication includes communication opportunities such as:

- letters
- memos
- newsletters
- manuals
- hand-written notes

The communication universe also contains media-centric communication events and opportunities, using technologies such as:

- video
- videoconferencing
- audio tapes
- voice mail
- conference calls
- e-mail
- CD-ROM
- fax

As Figure 7.1 illustrates, internal web sites are one among many different communication options and opportunities.

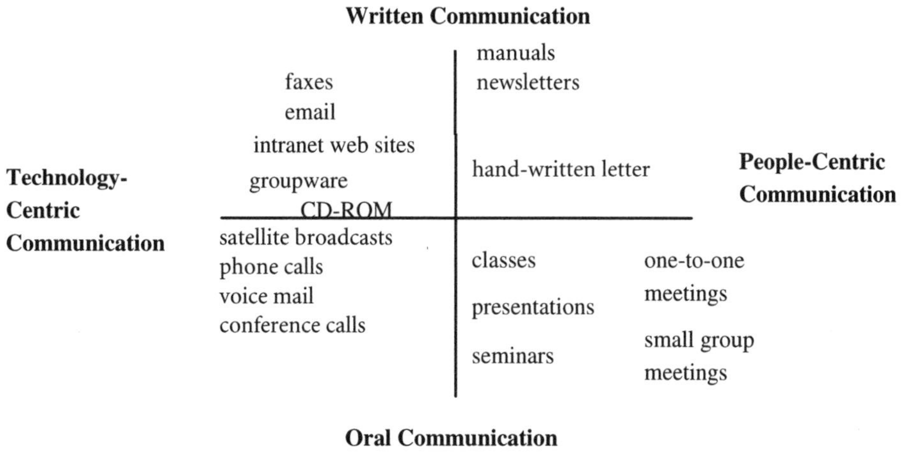

Written Communication

	manuals
faxes	newsletters
email	
intranet web sites	
groupware	hand-written letter
CD-ROM	

Technology-Centric Communication   **People-Centric Communication**

satellite broadcasts
phone calls   classes   one-to-one meetings
voice mail   presentations
conference calls   small group meetings
seminars

Oral Communication

FIGURE 7.1
Within the workplace, there is a variety of different communication media and communication opportunities.

■ Know the Benefits

Each of these communication tools has its own form of media richness and own set of advantages. Print, for example, has the highest degree of portability, whereas e-mail has the highest degree of message delivery speed. CD-ROM has the highest degree of multimedia intertextuality, whereas face-to-face communication provides the greatest opportunity to use feedback to alter the communication. To better understand the unique features that make intranets an attractive communication platform, let's compare the strengths and weaknesses of three different communication media: classes, CD-ROM, and intranets.

Classes and seminars are delivered to groups of people. The information is delivered in a linear sequence. Once you say something, you can't repeat the moment exactly the same, nor can you delete it. The communication is time- and place-specific, which means that unless satellite broadcasts or video tape are used, the participants must be physically present. It is an interactive event: The participants may contribute their thoughts and ideas. They may even influence the presenter to completely change the content of the presentation to accommodate the particular needs of the audience. In some situations, it's even possible to reverse the roles of speaker and audience.

CD-ROM is delivered to individuals at their specially equipped computers. The information can be delivered in sequence, but it can also be made repeatable or random. CD-ROMs are portable from one specially equipped computer to another, from one place to another, extending time and place. The content can combine many forms of communication such as text, still graphics and photography, animation, video, and audio. Authors can push the envelope of intertextuality. However, CD-ROMs are not interactive. People may be free to chose a variety of paths through the content, but they cannot add content to the CD-ROM or change it in any way.

Intranets deliver materials to individuals at their computers. Like material on a CD-ROM, information can be delivered in sequence, and it can be repeated or random. Because the material is digital, it can be stored, archived, and retrieved. Unlike a CD-ROM, it requires no special hardware, only special browser software, so it extends time and space even further. The material is not entirely portable, however, as access to the network is required. Content can be highly interactive and dynamic. Participants on an internal web can add material, create new material, and even edit existing material. On a discussion groups, participants can engage in a series of linked messages and responses. So, whereas the intranet content is delivered to individuals, discussion areas on intranets can foster dialog and conversation, similar to a gathering of people. Yet much of the sensory richness that comes with interpersonal communication—sight, smell, touch, and hearing—is not possible with computer-mediated communication unless it includes video feeds, which permit us to see and hear each other.

Though these differences may seem obvious, most of the time we fail to compare advantages and limitations of different media. We need to ask the question, Where does this medium, the intranet, fulfill a particular kind of information or communication need? The case study in the next chapter reveals how a team at U S WEST successfully asked and answered that question.

■ References

[1] This quote appeared on the ForceXXI web site at http://204.7.227.75.443/force21, May 1, 1997.

[2] Nada Korac-Boisvert and Alexander Kouzmin, "IT Development: Methodology Overload or Crisis?" Vol. 17, *Science Communications*, September, 1995.

[3] Malcolm Gladwell, "Just Ask for It: The Real Key to Technological Innovation," *The New Yorker*, April 7, 1997, pp. 45-49.

[4] William Foote Whyte, *Social Theory for Action: How Individuals and Organizations Learn to Change* (Newbury Park, CA: Sage, 1991).

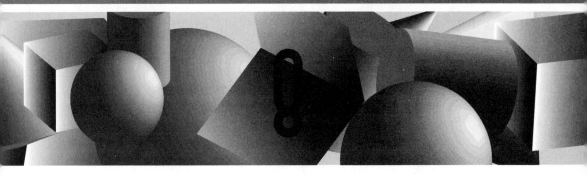

A "Preferred Product"

The context of communication is essential. We saw in the last chapter that intranets complete for mind space within a universe of communication options and opportunities. For an intranet to succeed, the benefits of the system relative to other choices must outweigh any costs or deterrents. This chapter contains a case study that illuminates how a communications team successfully identified the ways in which an intranet could be combined with a variety of other communication media to improve productivity in a large corporation. After the case study is explored, the situation is extended further into the future to propose a model for electronic commerce and a "knowledge value network." The model turns the traditional value chain on its head and proposes a model better suited for the economics of the 21st century—one that plays up the potentials inherent in web technologies.

■ Case Study 3: Redesigning Communication at U S WEST's MegaCenters

Occasionally, a major change in business operations provides the occasion to examine communication practices and look for opportunities to develop intranet applications. That was the case with the Mass Markets Groups at U S WEST. In 1994, U S WEST reengineered its call centers from 500 call centers in 14 states to 30 MegaCenters in 6 states. It proved to be an ideal opportunity to examine the potential usefulness of an intranet.

Call centers are staffed by customer service representatives sit at computer monitors wearing special headsets and take calls from customers who wish to open and close accounts, change telephone services, report service problems and schedule repair. The decision to change from 500 local centers to 30 regional centers had significant ramifications for the employees. Many call center employees lost their jobs and many other employees who chose to stay with the company had to move their families and relocate to other states.

The change also affected communication in very significant ways. Prior to the change, informal communication networks provided one of the most important sources of information and knowledge. Service representatives, capacity and provisioning engineers, and field technicians passed along information and gossip about their area's telephone networks. For example, employees within the local centers would hear about where there was trouble with the network, such as a section of buried cable, and would hear about how the buried cable specialists were trying to fix the problem. When the MegaCenters were created, service representatives no longer responded to calls coming exclusively from one geographic area. They took calls from a much wider territory. With the relocations, informal networks dissolved. Service reps were no longer physically co-located with engineers or field technicians; they sat in cubicles in one of the 30 MegaCenters populated almost exclusively with other customer service representatives.

Linda Pancratz, a foresighted vice president of Mass Markets Service Delivery, looked at the reengineering initiative as an opportunity to explore how to create more effective communication systems. She recognized, first of all, a need to create an information system that would enable the service reps to be knowledgeable about the *entire* network, not just one local area. She also wisely perceived the importance of communication in creating a strong

MegaCenter culture, one that would support employees' performance objectives.

Kristina Jonell Yarrington was a key player on the Communications Design Team. Kristina and the team were responsible for developing a communications process that would be: easy to use, fast, measurable, easy to replicate, and would enable employee choice, incorporate a mix of communications tools, and allow two-way communication. The team was purposefully cross-functional; it included representatives from Public Relations, the Systems (IT) group, Methods and Procedures, the union, and the Business Resources group, as well as several Mass Markets service representatives and managers.

One of the team's first questions was, What kind of information is coming into the Centers? Rejecting the idea of a formal study as too limited, the group designed the "In-Basket Study" and shadowed a group of service representatives for a week. Kristina recalls that:

> We looked at everything the reps used—e-mail, voice mail, memos, newsletters, and even though only a few centers had email or voice mail, we found that we were already bombarding the service reps with information. For example, whenever Mass Markets made a systems change on the network, the reps would receive e-mail, followed by voice mail, followed by a thick paper document. The service reps told us "We're getting information, but it doesn't help us." It was a paradox. Too much information, but not enough. In addition to that, we also found "delayed" communication needs. How do you store all this information and then retrieve it when you really need it?

To complement and supplement the "In-Basket Study," the team also conducted several focus groups with service representatives. The reps were very clear about what they did and did not need. They made statements like:

> "Give me information to help me do my job."

> "Give me the time to read the information and gain knowledge."

> "Give me the capability to access what I want when I want it. Don't think for me."

"Don't read it for me and decide what part I need to know. You don't know how the job really works and what I need to do the job."

"I want to use my computer as a library resource to access the information I need."

"Don't just focus on corporate information – give me local information too."

In short, the representatives were requesting information to meet their needs. They wanted fewer information mediators and interpreters, and wanted more "local" information about things happening within their own groups and MegaCenters.

When the research phase came to an end, the team began to craft a blueprint to link the right people with the right information at the right time with the right technology to deliver appropriate communication solutions. They defined a "communications tool set," which included the video display system, print, face-to-face communication, e-mail, satellite broadcasts, fax broadcasts, audio cassettes, and a part of the US WEST intranet, then called *The Link*. Within the context of the MegaCenter communications, the group perceived that each medium possessed a different benefit. For example, the video information network (VIN) – television monitors that hung from ceiling joists—was good for proving short, simple messages and for broadcasting news about urgent information, while the web-based electronic library was good for stable, long-term information required for detail-oriented problem solving.

The Communication Matrix

The team then created a matrix of communication channels, target audiences, and immediacy needs, indicating which medium made the most sense in any particular situation. The matrix is reproduced in Figure 8.1 below. For instance, the team believed that if a piece of information was extremely urgent and critical, face-to-face communication was the most appropriate medium. The service representatives were bombarded with information from a number of different broadcast media, and they had disclosed that the way they would know if something was *truly* important was if someone delivered the news in person and took the time to check the receivers' understanding and comprehension of the news.

There were other instances where the intranet, The Link, was most appropriate. For example, the team perceived that the intranet would be helpful when all service representatives needed to see an important piece of information, when they needed to self-educate themselves about something new, or when they wanted to review detailed materials located in the electronic library to solve a customer's problem.

Immediacy Scale	Target Audience		
	One Person	Subgroup	Entire Group
Right Now	Face-to-face VIN	Face-to-face VIN	Face-to-face VIN
Soon	E-mail Face-to-face Voice mail Audio cassette Fax	E-mail Face-to-face Voice mail Audio cassette Fax	Printed manuals E-mail Face-to-face Voice mail Audio cassette Fax Physical bulletin board Intranet
Later	E-mail Face-to-face Voice mail Audio cassette Fax	E-mail Face-to-face Voice mail Audio cassette Fax	Printed manuals E-mail Face-to-face Voice mail Audio cassette Fax Physical bulletin board Intranet

FIGURE 8.1
Communication Matrix for U S WEST Mass Markets MegaCenters

Communication in the "Right Now" category included things that would affect customers in the space of a day to a week. For example, cut cable, new products, billing errors, system problems, a disaster, or a significant company event. Things that fell into the "Soon" category included information that generally affected customers or employees in 2–4 weeks. Communication that was defined as nonurgent, "Later," concerned things that did not directly impact customer service on a day-to-day basis, for example, personal improvement opportunities or team building workshops.

The team strongly believed that an intranet could be used to improve communications with the MegaCenters. To help the team convince senior management to fund the development of a web site to support MegaCenter communications, Sherman Woo, the IT visionary behind U S WEST's Global Village, helped Kristina and the team create a customized web site demo. The demo illustrated the web's key benefits to MegaCenter employees ,such as the fact that information could reside anywhere, that the web provides cross-platform capability, that updates could be made within minutes of a change in the system's status, and that the web can convey both simple and complex information through the use of text, sound, graphics, and video.

In addition to the demo, the team also created a "Day in the Life" multimedia scenario to demonstrate how the communication system would actually work. The scenario was acted out by employees who had been involved with the team from the very early stages of the project.

This is a modified version of the script (names have been changed, proprietary company information has been removed):

"A Day In the Life" Script

It's 8:00 on August 29th and I walk into the office to start the day. As I'm walking to my desk, I look up at the TV monitors to alert me of critical information and news. Here's what I see.

(Video Monitor scrolls important news items)

The two items that catch my attention are the fiber cut in Aurora and the news about the new service, Personal Locator, we are going to begin deploying in Boulder. Both of these things will impact the way I work with my customers today.

As I sit down at my desk, the first thing I do is check my voice mail. Here's what I hear on a message from my Customer Service Manager, Patricia Andersen. The new sales bonus structure is being announced tomorrow and Patricia wants to make sure our group remembers to attend the lunch time presentation.

(Dial Voice Mail, play message)

After listening to my voice mail messages, I then want to tap into my other personal messages on e-mail. When I get into the system, I see this message from Clarence Denton, one of the Denver Learning Consultants.

(Open E-Mail, view message)

Since Clarence wants to know if I'd be interesting in lending my perspective to the "Dealing With Angry Customers" segment of the Advanced Sales course he's working on. I send a quick reply, "Count me in." It's now 8:05 and I have ten minutes to lean more about the fiber cut and the new Personal Locator service before going on-line with calls at 8:15. I know that all the information I need will be on our intranet, The Link, so I click on the Link icon on my computer desktop screen.

(Show screen shot of home page)

The first thing I see is the What's Up page for my local area. This page flags today's important items for my Megacenter. I decide to get details on the fiber cut, so I click the blue words "fiber cut."

(Show "fiber cut" page)

This automatically takes me to a different section of the web site where I read a paragraph about where the cut is and the expected down time. I now feel armed with the information I need to help customers in that area of Aurora where the repair will take place. I click the arrow to return to go back to the previous web page.

(Show "What's Up—Big Picture" page)

Having scanned the headlines for my MegaCenter's news, I now go to the "What's Up - Big Picture" page to check out regional and corporate-level critical items. Here I see the item about the introduction of the Personal Locator service. I click on the icon for the new service and find myself reading an internal press release about the new service introduction.

(Show internal press release about the Personal Locator service.)

The article includes a hyperlink to a previous article published last month about the advanced technology computer networks that cre-

ate the foundation for this new service. I click on the hyperlink and suddenly I'm reading the announcement published weeks ago that didn't interest me very much then, but is important to me now. I then click on the arrow to go back to the previous page.

(Show Personal Locator service data page.)

I need more detail about the service so that I can start selling it to our customers, so I click on the hypertext that says "Click here for more information."

Here I read more specifics of the service. I see a list of features, and then a list of benefits to the customer. This is an interesting product. Curious to see what the customer might have seen on local TV commercials, I click on the icon.

(Show video clip playing through the web browser.)

I notice that the webmaster has created a place for us to provide feedback from customers about this new service. If my customers voice their opinions to me, I have a way to route their comments immediately and directly to the Marketing Group.

I now want to see how the new service will be deployed beyond Boulder to the rest of Colorado, in case anyone from outside Boulder who might have seen the commercial calls with that question. I click on "Deployment Schedule" and then "Colorado" and view the schedule. With this information, I feel confident that I now have the knowledge to tell customers about this new product.

It's now 8:15, time to start talking to customers.

The "Recipe Book"

Considering all of the various options within the communication system illustrated by a "Day in the Life," the team wrestled with the question of how to teach potential content authors and message sources how to leverage all their various options. The team considered creating flowcharts, but, as Kristina pointed out, "so many other groups were *already* using flowcharts." Therefore, the team created a "Recipe Book," which provided a very basic five-step guide to maximizing options within the communication system. Here is an example:

STEP 1	Determine message	Fiber cut in Aurora
STEP 2	Identify target audience	All Denver MegaCenter employees
STEP 3	Identify immediacy	"Right now"
STEP 4	Select tool	Alert on video information network (VIN) with details on the Web
STEP 5	Create and distribute message	

The method is elegant in its simplicity. The team saw that producing high-level and high-cost communication was not always necessary. When the issue was speed of receiving information, the team concentrated on rapid delivery of useful content, rather than glitz. This type of approach saves time and money, and supports "speed to proficiency."

Case Study 3: Key Learnings

This was an interesting approach to intranet development, particularly because the initial intention was not to develop the intranet, but rather to improve communication overall. The project was exemplary because it focused on employees' information and communication needs first, tools and techniques second. The project involved employees and key stakeholders (such as union leaders) right from the beginning, so that the team was able to avoid making erroneous assumptions about the value of the communication system as seen from the employees and other stakeholders' point of view. The first deliverable was partnership. The overall goal was to communicate, not manipulate, and the mechanism was dialog, not monologue.

One of the greatest advantages of the team's "tool box" approach was that it forced the group to acknowledge all of the other communication options and methods besides the intranet already being used by the service representatives. Kristina remarks that the team thought very hard about the question,

How do we alert service reps to go to the web when that's the place to find a certain kind of information? They realized that it would be important to use complementary and supplementary media, even building redundancy at times, so that the representatives would make a smooth, anxiety-free migration to the web as a preferred communication medium.

■ Uses and Gratifications

As the U S WEST case study illustrates, the intranet, as a communication medium will compete within a universe of communication options and opportunities. The good news for intranet advocates is that even within this well-populated universe, there is much room for improvement. Communication in most organizations is far from perfect.

The case study also illustrates the principles of the "Uses and Gratifications" theory, which says that people will, in a virtually seamless fashion, switch between one communication medium and another as they go about the day, accomplishing tasks large and small. Uses and gratifications studies tell us that there is a method to the way each of us uses communication media, and a purpose behind it. The audience is active and its media use is goal-oriented. Therefore, no communication media—whether telephone, print, radio, television, or the computer—exists in the workplace in isolation. Each exists side by side with other communication media and other communication options. We are not passive consumers of media: we use media that suits our purpose at a particular point in our day.

In addition, as this case study and the examples from the U. S. Army and NetObject's Fusion software illustrate, people use technology for purposes designers never anticipate. Studies of how people use communication technologies and integrate them into the fabric of their lives reveal that people use communication technologies for many reasons:

1. For surveillance (e.g. to obtain information about the internal and external environment)
2. To supplement or substitute for interpersonal interactions (e.g., sending e-mail instead of a face-to-face meeting)
3. To gather content for interpersonal interactions (e.g., to get interesting things to talk about)

4. To form and/or reinforce self-perceptions (e.g., to be seen as "an expert" or a "team player")
5. To learn appropriate behaviors (e.g., the norms and rules specific to a particular organizational culture)
6. For intellectual stimulation and challenge
7. As a less costly substitute for other media (e.g., posting a link to an article on-line instead of mailing photocopies to each member of the group)
8. For networking and mutual support
9. For self-improvement and self-directed learning
10. For entertainment
11. For "company" and safety (e.g., to be able to join others in a virtual community of practice)

Technology and content that is well-designed can be put to all of these different uses. In regard to the U S WEST case study, we could envision a service representative using The Link to satisfy every one of these different needs. In the right context, with the right set of features, an intranet can have a significant affect on productivity **and** organizational culture.

■ A Web of Commitments

This case study also illustrates that people rarely work in isolation, and most of our interaction with each other at work is far from mechanical or impersonal. In our daily work practices, though we don't always see it, there is room for change and negotiation among activities and processes. Small as they often are, these acts of negotiation permit us to navigate through tasks, flexing to accommodate changes that are internally and externally generated. We are always bringing other people and other objects or artifacts from the periphery to the center, as required.

Whereas we have latitude in our patterns of activities, our social roles constrain our communication needs, opportunities, and choices in very significant ways.

Since the 1970s, <u>Fernando Flores</u> and <u>Terry Winograd</u>, two leaders in the field of information technologies, have emphasized the importance of paying attention to human behavior when designing any form of computer-based performance support. They contend that efforts such as traditional process mapping fail to describe how work actually gets done in the Information Age. In real life, people continuously negotiate with one another, juggling priorities while trying to make good on past promises. Work, therefore, cannot be described as a linear information flow, but rather as a web of commitments among human beings. *The basic building block of all commitment webs— indeed, all work—is the person-to-person transaction.*

In the scenario above, for example, the customer service representative engages in a number of person-to-person transactions with other people, including her supervisor, a learning consultant, and customers on the phone. The technology played an instrumental role in facilitating those transactions.

One of the intentions of the project was to improve the MegaCenter culture. Culture is a term that is difficult to define. As Raymond Williams has noted, culture is one of the most complex words in the English language. Unfortunately, the phrase *organizational culture* is tossed around so much by organizational consultants, it's become almost meaningless.

Essentially, culture is a "structure of feeling." Organizational cultures are made through complex and interrelated processes of limits and pressures. These processes work so well, they seem natural and unexceptional. To understand organizational culture is to understand the interplay between people's behaviors, values, and attitudes, *and* the material conditions—or economics—that support the production of work. Employees' activities are situated in particular idealistic and materialistic contexts.

■ The Role of "Knowledge Workers" in Organizational Change

During the project, the communication team came to appreciate how much the representatives knew about customers' perceptions of U S WEST advertising and marketing campaigns. In their roles as customer service representatives, talking with customers all day long on the phone, the reps frequently received comments from customers that were related to U S WEST's marketing and advertising.

For instance, in almost any setting—not just U S WEST—customers may perceive television commercials as glitzy but lacking sufficient product information. Often, when products are co-branded, customers have difficulty knowing who "owns" the product. Customers may respond favorably to marketing and advertising materials in the context of focus groups held in office buildings downtown. Yet, in the context of their own homes, with all the distractions of "real life," the customers often have trouble cutting through the clutter.

The customer service representatives at U S WEST were highly sensitized to these problems because what US WEST did in terms of marketing and advertising directly affected their abilities to, first, respond to customers' requests for service and, second, to try to persuade customers to consider purchasing additional U S WEST services.

Prior to the intranet, there really was no way for the customer service representatives to communicate any problems with marketing or advertising to the marketing groups. The intranet, however, provided a way for them to send that information directly to the marketing group.

This involved a change in roles from "downstream" in the process to "upstream." Traditionally, communication between customer service representatives, customers, and marketing groups is linear. Figure 8.2 illustrates the communication pattern.

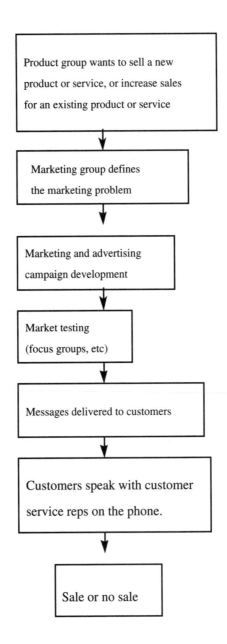

FIGURE 8.2
Linear Communication Between Customers, Customer Service Reps and Marketing

Perhaps the greatest inherent liability in this sort of linear model is that "data" passes too easily as valid representations of reality. Much data is collected and analyzed, but there are few opportunities to get underneath the data to more fully understand customer's perceptions of the company, its products, or its services.

The intranet provides a way to get more information about how customers are responding to the company's advertising and marketing *at the very point at which they signal a desire to buy or not buy.* Figure 8.3 illustrates the flow of communication made possible by the intranet:

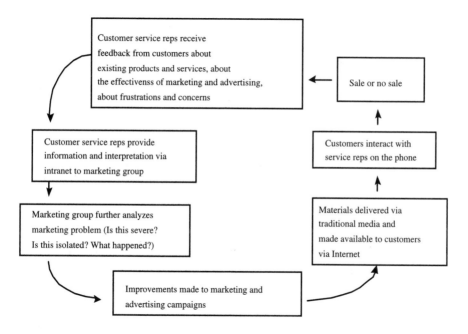

FIGURE 8.3
Feedback Loop

With this sort of dynamic process, a company is able to capture employees' and customers' ideas for improvement as representatives go about their work interacting with customers.

Automating this process so that customers simply provide their input into a voice mail box or fill out a feedback form on a page on the company's external web site would be less labor intensive and, therefore, tempting. Yet such an approach would be unfortunate since much of the meaning behind the customer's words would be lost. The value of having customers speak directly to customer service representatives is that it helps to build a relationship between the company and customers: "Somebody is listening."

Customer service representatives who are able to listen "between the lines" can gather nuances that would be lost if the customers communicated through one-way communication alone. In addition, the conversation between the customer service representative and the customer is interactive; the representative can listen and respond in real time to the feedback. Even a simple comment like, "Hmm, I understand what you are saying. We should take care of this" relieves frustration, if the words are said with genuine intent.

Such a model illustrates Fernando Flores's definition of communication as "commitment and action." Flores writes:[1]

> The IT community has been laboring under a mistaken view of communication. Distinctions of access, accuracy, and transmission miss completely for people what is at the heart of communication: commitment and action that we produce in conversation with others. When people communicate, they don't simply pass information back and forth. They *get things done*, sharing interpretations and making commitments that change the status of their work, their world, their future expectations and possibilities. In this, information plays a role, but it is a secondary, supporting role. In the end, people aren't really interested simply in transmitting information to each other. They have concerns that prompt them to reach out and build relationships with others to take care of those concerns.

Relationships are essential to the performance of a commitment; communication is the building block of relationships.

The type of coordination described here involves a series of changes in attitude and beliefs about the type of work performed by both customer service representatives and marketing specialists. Leadership from executives who can appreciate value of such a model of communication is essential. Leaders must, Flores states,[2] "put their organizations in condition to shape change in their own favor, rather than being forced to react to it." As Flores points out, coordination is more necessary today than it ever was. However, coordination is not enough to ensure the future viability and success of an organization. "Practices for the *continuous reinvention* of a company's future and for bringing meaningful change are necessary as well."

Knowledge Empowered Service

The kind of "continuous reinvention" Dr. Flores is talking about can be achieved through the creation of a "knowledge value network." If we extend the model in Figure 8.3 a bit further, we could imagine ways in which customer service representatives could communicate with more groups within the organization.

Dave Carlson, president of <u>Ontogenics Corp</u>. in Boulder, Colorado, believes that competitive advantage can be achieved relative to other firms by restructuring the traditional value chain and creating "value networks." In his paper, "<u>Harnessing the Flow of Knowledge</u>" which is available on the Ontogenics web site, Carlson lays out the new model.

A typical, traditional value chain is shown in Figure 8.4. Five primary activities define the flow from in-bound logistics through operations and outbound logistics, and on to sales and customer service. Four supporting activities are not directly in the flow of the primary value chain but provide ne necessary services for ongoing business. Customers are the final recipients of value chain activities.

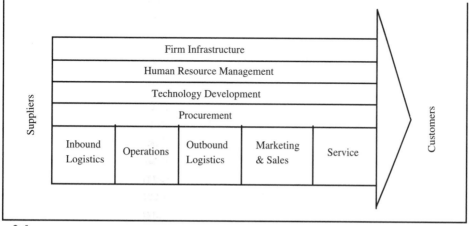

FIGURE 8.4
A Generic Value Chain

Communication among all of the different parties in this value chain is often limited, incomplete, or fractured. This means that the organization has a hard time responding quickly to changes in the marketplace and to customers' changing demands. Coordinating is difficult; each group tends to work on its own piece of the value chain and to pass tasks to the next group. This kind of value chain worked well when the marketplace was less competitive. Today, organizations need to enable knowledge to flow between product marketing, R & D, customer service, etc., to provide higher levels of customer satisfaction.

Value Networks and Knowledge

Current Practice	Future Vision
• Business processes are represented as sequences of activities in a value chain.	• Business processes are represented as knowledge flows through communities in a value network.
• Activities are process steps that consume resources and produce outputs.	• Activities are steps of the flow through both formal and informal knowledge communities.
• Activities are analyzed in terms of their costs and cost drivers.	• Activities are analyzed as knowledge-intensive tasks in terms of the knowledge that must be shared for successful collaboration.

© Dave Carlson, Ontogenics, Inc. Used by permission.

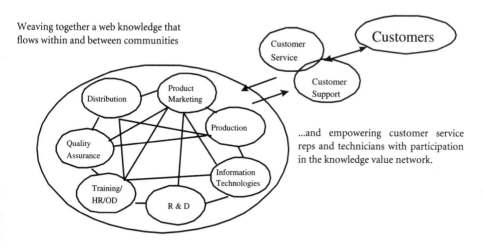

Weaving together a web knowledge that flows within and between communities

...and empowering customer service reps and technicians with participation in the knowledge value network.

FIGURE 8.5
A Knowledge Value Network.

Carlson notes that, "whereas a 'chain' implies a sequential flow, a 'network' carries a connotation of multidimensional interconnectedness. Knowledge does not come from process or activities; it comes from people and communities of people."

This model is called a *value network* because added value accrues with the flow of information through the network. For example, Carlson says, "engineering teams supply knowledge about the principles underlying product design. Product marketing shares knowledge about the rationale for marketing segmentation strategies." Armed with this knowledge, the customer service representative is able to envision the solution that fits the needs of the individual customer.

Carlson describes "Knowledge-Empowered Service." Customer support draws on the shared knowledge resulting from the collective intelligence in the organization.

The roles of customer service reps change from order-takers to consultants. They are problem-solvers supported by continuous learning opportunities.

Sharing Knowledge with Customer Service Representatives

Current Practice	Future Vision
• Customer service representatives are primarily order-takers.	• Representatives are consultants, recommending products based on customer requirements.
• Extensive training (e.g., 12 weeks) is required to teach new representatives details of current products, configuration parameters, and order processing.	• Teach representatives general problem-solving skills plus ability to search and apply shared knowledge repositories.
• Introduction of new, complex products requires significant retraining and may delay product roll-out.	• Continuous learning is enabled by shared knowledge repositories, plus electronic discussion groups for dynamic and unexpected customer situations.

© Dave Carlson, Ontogenics, Inc. Used by permission.

Carlson takes this model even further in "Harnessing the Flow of Knowledge." The knowledge value network and knowledge empowered service, he says, are the first two steps toward Electronic Consultative Commerce. In this third stage, customer service representatives cease to be the central intermediary between the customer and the sale. With Electronic Consultative Commerce, a customer would be engaged in a cooperative process in which human and computer agents both initiate communication, monitor events, and perform tasks. A software agent underlying the customer's system interface would determine when human assistance is necessary and automatically establishes a telephone connection with a service representative.

Before this type of Electronic Consultative Commerce can be achieved, however, we have a lot to learn about how people use technology, how they problem-solve with technology and how best to introduce new technologies into the workplace so to improve, not disrupt, customer service and person-to-person relationships.

■ When the Technology Cannot Flex

Most organizations are terrible at realizing how rich the workplace is with communication, commitment, action and meaningful, activity. So it is not unusual to see companies purchase new software or groupware only to find that the technology is either not flexible enough to accommodate the needs of the employees or that it does not fit with the organizational culture.

Steve G. Steinberg provides a very good example in an article he wrote for the *L.A. Times* about the myth of groupware. When Steinberg was an editor at *Wired*, the monthly magazine about culture and technology, the editors decided that they wanted to speed up the process of creating an issue. *Wired* is at the cutting edge of technology writing and magazine design, and the process of creating an issue is highly collaborative. *Wired* decided to adapt the Quark Publishing System (QPS), which is an expensive and robust software. Prior to QPS, a copy editor would finish editing an article, send it to design, and the designers would lay out the text and supporting graphics, then send it to production. There were often delays in the process and uncertainty about the status of an article. With QPS, the article flowed electronically through the system. No one ever needed to wonder where the piece had gone or what its status was. However, Steinberg relates, that after two months, "the system was junked." Steinberg writes:

> The problem was that we valued the ability to capriciously make changes at any stage too much to sacrifice it for gains in efficiency. We were willing to tolerate articles being delayed in the hope that it might result in more inspired design. The program might have made sense for a daily newspaper, where efficiency is critical, but for a monthly magazine, it was simply too structured.

Most workplace cultures, like *Wired*, are both chaotic and structured. Most blend together characteristics of both oral and written cultures. Shosana Zuboff reminds us that

> The social exchanges that surround professional work help constitute an oral culture; they vanish without a trace when the coffee break is over, when a group rises from the lunch table, when people part in the hallway, when the telephone receiver is replaced on its hook, when the meeting room empties.

Intranets and groupware are newcomers into a workplace environment that is already characterized by patterns of communication, webs of commitments, and person-to-person transactions. One of our greatest mistakes with intranet development is neglecting the context into which the technology enters.

Intranets exist within an environment. They also exist within a context of meaning. It can be challenging to understand that context of meaning but, as the next chapter and case studies show, when we take time for inquiry, we create added value.

■ References

[1] Fernado Flores, "Leaders of the Future," in Beyond Computation, eds. Peter J. Denning and Robert Metcalfe (NY: Copernicus, 1997), p. 178.

[2] Flores, p. 185.

The Value Triad

The previous chapters have suggested two governing rules for successful intranet development. First, the intranet must fulfill its "value proposition." Relative to all other options, the intranet must satisfy employees' communication and information needs, possess outstanding product features, and exhibit operational excellence. Second, pushing technology onto the employee base is not a good investment of resources. Employees must want to pull content to themselves and must want to participate in discussion areas. As internal engines of innovation, employees' own activities will suggest creative uses for the intranet.

In this chapter, the terms *Value Triad* and *Intranet Value Chain* are introduced as guideposts for intranet development. Employee attitudes and values about technologies are also discussed. The chapter concludes with the "pull" model, guaranteed to significantly increase the probability that employees will choose to use an intranet over the long term on a continuous basis.

■ Case Study 4:   Leveraging the Intranet to Fill Communication Gaps

One of the greatest challenges of running a large organization is trying to create employee commitment to a core set of management practices and principles. Often, different operating units or divisions will employ their own sets of business strategies and management methods. Senior management may not even be aware of the differences until a crisis or enterprise-wide reorganization causes the company to discover the differences. At that point, senior management has two choices: let each unit or division continue its autonomous practices or attempt to create a unified body of management principles and practices that everyone is expected to follow. This chapter begins with a case study that reveals the challenges faced by a company that took the second option and how it used an internal web site to achieve its communication objectives. The case study demonstrates how efforts to satisfy employees' communication and information needs can significantly improve the content and design of an internal web site.

In 1994, the WisdomLink Group at <u>International Learning Systems</u> was asked to help a Fortune 500 company create a web site to create awareness, understanding, acceptance, and commitment among the employee base to a core set of management principles. The principles included leadership, knowledge sharing, measurement and assessment, customer focus, and empowerment. Senior leadership believed that if all the employees integrated these principles into their daily practices, the company's chances of surviving in a hypercompetitive business environment would significantly improve. The CEO created a special office within the company to promote the principles and named a vice president to head the group. A consultant was brought in to create a set of very well-designed educational modules that taught employees how to identify, analyze, and solve problems in each of the principal areas.

The company's communications committee had tried a number of different strategies to create awareness, understanding, acceptance, and commitment to the management principles. They sponsored satellite broadcasts, awards events, training events, and seminars. Two years into the program, the committee observed that the company's intranet wasn't being used for very much and, yet, it seemed to hold potential as a powerful communication medium. A couple of committee members suggested that they leverage the intranet to provide all employees in the company all across the world with easier access to information, educational materials, knowledge, and best practices about the core principles. Tapping in-house resources, the group developed plans for a web site. A couple of months later, after the committee discovered that their in-house content development resources were limited, they brought ILS in to assist.

The Starting Point: Focus Groups

To begin the project, the team first met with employees in four focus groups in three major cities to talk about how they perceived this program overall, and what they would most like to see on a web site. One reason the team consulted these focus groups was to identify critical success factors up front, prior to making major investments in construction resources.

The focus groups included a cross-section of employees from various divisions and ranks. The team presented a colorful, graphics-rich custom-created web site "demo" to the focus group participants and found that the employees perceived great value in on-line resources. The participants gave a unanimous "yes" to the concept of on-line tools and resources, and said that, if such resources were made available, not only would they use them, they'd also enthusiastically recommend them to new employees. The participants especially liked the idea of replacing current paper-based material with a self-directed searchable on-line system that made it easy to locate and retrieve documents "just in time."

The employees also revealed that they would find value in on-line discussion areas or bulletin boards where they could "raise their hands electronically" to ask for help, where they could offer a suggestion for improvement or engage in a virtual dialog about implementing the principles. Employees occasionally felt frustrated when they had a question or needed some help and couldn't find the right person in their group to ask. The idea of being able to post something that could be seen by many other employees within the company was attractive.

Reengineering Backlash

The focus group participants confirmed the value of a web site as a communication medium. However, they also revealed why employees were not embracing the principles or integrating them into their work. The focus group participants revealed that they believed that the intent of the program was getting the program's name and logo out, rather than creating a public and shared recognition that the core set of principles summarized the most effective way to accomplish the goals of the company. Employees disclosed that they rarely heard senior management demonstrate its commitment to the principles. Many employees, therefore, regarded the entire program as "something I can do if I have time after I'm done with what I really need to do." They revealed that they approached the program as a task to do, separate from what they did on an everyday basis. The focus group participants also perceived that the company was "initiative-happy" and that it borrowed/copied/duplicated every possible best practice standard from other companies with no analysis of how it fit into the company's culture and/or industry.

The employees had revealed thoughts and feelings that echoed what other employees had reported to a different consulting group in a major research study conducted 12 months earlier. In the context of the company's history, their perceptions and attitudes were understandable. In 1994, when the company undertook a massive reengineering program, it cut 25% of the work force and reduced R & D. Rumors of more layoffs and more reengineering were in the air. In light of these circumstances, it was difficult to imagine any employee feeling committed to the program when so much was in flux.

The Challenge to Develop Meaningful Content

The focus group findings were significant. On the one hand, the news was not good news for the ILS team or for the corporate sponsors of the work. The focus group participants expressed enthusiasm for the concept of a web site, yet the discussions revealed that with so much skepticism and cynicism, it was unrealistic to believe that the web site itself could make an immediate and significant impact.

On the other hand, this information gave the team a reason to rethink the entire web site design and content requirements. The team eliminated graphics or phrases that appeared to be "mere corporate rhetoric." They asked the instructional designers to redesign the educational modules so that employees could exercise more control over the on-line materials and how they were accessed.

Then the team added a section to the site that addressed the issues that the employees had raised during the focus groups—Did the company just borrow these ideas from other companies? Was senior management truly committed? What did these terms—*leadership, empowerment, measurement* and *assessment*, etc.— really mean?

The additional section used storytelling as the primary communication form. In the book *The Change Masters* (1983), Rosabeth Moss Kanter writes:

> In conceiving a different future, change masters have to be historians as well. When innovators begin to define a project by reviewing the issues with people across areas, they are not only seeing what is possible, they may be learning more about the past; and one of the prime uses of the past is in the construction of a story that makes the future seem to grow naturally out of it in terms compatible with the organization's culture.

A shared set of understandings of the past can be used to legitimize change toward a future state. Kanter believes that the architecture of change requires an awareness of foundations—what she terms the *bases in prehistory, perhaps below the surface, that make continued construction possible.* She says that "if the foundations will not support the weight of what is about to be built, then they must be shored up before any other actions can take place."

Developing "The Story"

Accepting Kanter's premise, the team took on the *persona* of an investigative journalist and interviewed the corporation's senior management, using the focus group participants' skeptical and cynical remarks as the foundation for their line of questioning. A couple of executives were not appreciative of the questions, but the team felt that it was important to represent the voices they had heard in the focus groups.

The team then interviewed the former vice president of the program, who had been with the company for 20 years, had launched the program several years ago, and had returned, as planned, to the position of line manager. The former VP actually seemed to embody all of the principles the corporation was trying to promote. He did not flinch or buckle when the team told him about the employees' skepticism or cynicism. Instead, he offered information to counter the employees' assertions. He said, "I know that there is disbelief. We haven't been good at sharing information with employees. Let me tell you about how this whole thing got started and why we were so passionate about making it happen. Let me tell you about how we're trying to help people identify their resource needs instead of throwing money at this." His candor and honesty were inspiring. He did not argue, he explained. As he answered the team's questions, the team got the sense that being the VP of this program was not at all easy, but that this individual had the character and conviction to turn it into an opportunity of a lifetime.

"The Story," largely inspired by the team's conversation with the former VP, resulted in 40 hyperlinked web pages. The Story's central theme is that people in the corporation are struggling against the forces of change, and are doing their best to learn and to become smarter. The core principles of the program, its tools, techniques, and concepts are not "the answers" or "the truth." Rather, they are the glue that holds the conversation together so that large groups of people can go forward together. All of the tools and techniques that the company created in order to measure and make assessments, to share key learnings, to benchmark progress, etc. were created so that people within the company could learn from each other and improve. The Story communicates the idea of improvement as a design, rather than an accident.

The team also felt that, given the employees' cynicism, employees must be given a chance to respond to The Story and to tell their own stories. The Story takes them behind the scenes and provides some context for meaning. However, for knowledge sharing to be truly meaningful, employees must be given the opportunity to become "writers" to the unfolding drama as well as "readers." With that in mind, the team added discussion areas where people could post and respond, as well as forms where people could submit their stories and see them posted.

Case Study 4: Key Learnings

Most organizations will face similar corporate communication problems. Surveys sponsored by the <u>International Association of Business Communicators</u> (IABC) and the consulting firm of Towers, Perrin, Forester & Crosby reveal that employees, in general, distrust corporate communication.[1] Based on the questionnaires from 32,000 employees in 26 business organizations, the surveys show that only half of the respondents thought that company communication in their organizations was candid and accurate. Two-thirds said it was incomplete. More than half said that it appeared to be simply top-down communication without opportunity for discussion. Survey respondents indicated the greatest dissatisfaction with communication from senior executives, immediate supervisors, orientation programs, and upward communication programs. They asked for more information and more two-way communication about three topics in particular: the company's plans for the future, productivity improvement, and personnel policies and practices. So, in a sense, this was a classic case study, in that the problems that gave rise to the web site redesign could have happened almost anywhere.

There are several key learnings from this case study. First, as a result of the discussions with employees, the content changed. If the team had not understood the context in which the site was used, they would have missed an opportunity to reconsider what sort of content belonged on the site. The site could have been "flat"—just another piece of corporate rhetoric. By giving potential end users an opportunity to speak openly and honestly about the program, the team was challenged to explore how other genres of communication, like storytelling, could be folded into the site to make it more meaningful to employees.

Storytelling is a real but under-appreciated form of organizational communication. In his 1990 book, *Tell Me A Story*, Roger Schank, director of the Institute for Learning Sciences (ILS) at Northwestern University, describes the function of storytelling. Stories are an ubiquitous human experience, Schank argues, because they are efficient forms of memory storage and serve as organizational routines. Stories are important cognitive events since they encapsulate into one compact package information, knowledge, context, and emotion. In real life, people like to tell each other stories. We use stories not only to explain things to others, but to explain things to ourselves. Schank, an expert in artificial intelligence, distinguishes between story-based memory and general world memory. The former, he says, "expresses our points of view and our philosophies of life." It arises from our experiences upon telling, and gets built up by telling.

By designing The Story as a complement to the other materials, the *form* of the site was better overall. It served the needs of employees who wanted on-line educational modules and tools that answered "How" questions, as well as the needs of employees who wanted to know why they were being asked to learn all this new material.

The on-line educational modules, like most on-line training materials, required employees to engage in logical forms of analysis—to measure cost and time, to calculate cause and effect, etc. Humans do not learn through logic alone, however. As Donald Norman reminds us,[2]

> Stories have the felicitous capacity of capturing exactly those elements that formal decision methods leave out. Logic tries to generalize, to strip the decision making from the specific context, to remove it from subjective emotions. Logic generalizes, stories particularize. Logic allows one to form a detached, global judgment; storytelling allows one to take the personal point of view, to understand the particular impact the decision is apt to have on the people who will be affected by it.

> Stories aren't better than logic; logic isn't better than stories. They are distinct; they both emphasize different criteria. I think it is very appropriate that both be used in decision-making settings.

A well-designed, well-formed web site, therefore, may be one in which the on-line communication is representative of various genres and modes of "real life" human communication—from logical/analytical forms of communication to narrative and informal modes of communication.

The second key learning from the case study is that this approach challenged the team to identify what web technologies could be used to meet the employees' needs. Because employees said that they were being tired of being spoken to and wanted an opportunity to speak and be heard, threaded discussion areas were built into the site and linked to content areas. Because employees said that they needed an easy way to contribute to a database of best practices, the team built back-end scripts so that employees could submit their own stories by typing the text onto a form. Knowledge of HTML wasn't required.

Employees said that time was a real issue and that their managers wouldn't be pleased if they spent chunks of time on-line, going through the educational modules. They needed to get on, get off, and to find their bookmark when they returned. The team's instructional designers went back to the drawing boards and created an information architecture that permitted users to exercise more control over how they accessed and retrieved materials. The material was also parsed into smaller chunks.

Management's Initial Resistance to On-Line Discussions

A third point illustrated by this case study is how virtual communities can get started through web sites that provide both a great deal of valuable content *and* discussion areas. The site gave people something to react to, to chew on, to debate. Had the company decided to launch a discussion area alone, employees would be left on their own to imagine topics and issues. On this site, the content was a stimulus to discussion. Employees could react to the on-line modules, provide success stories, raise questions, or ask for clarification. They could delve deeper into The Story and discuss what it represents about the company and its operating culture. The Story is like a portal or gateway into the rest of the site, opening out to the marketplace of ideas.

Initially, the executive who sponsored the work was reluctant to add discussion areas to the site, believing that employees would use the site to say "bull shit." The team asked, "Okay, what happens when someone says that sort of thing in a meeting?"

"It becomes an opportunity to provide a counter-argument, to provide reasons," the executive answered.

"Wouldn't you rather have an employee challenge policy or practice out loud and use it as an opportunity to turn the person's thinking around than to have that person quietly subverting what you are trying to put in place?" The executive agreed, albeit reluctantly, that the "compliant yes" they had heard from employees hadn't moved the program very far up to that point. Putting the issues up in an open space—such as the discussion areas—and talking them through allowed the skepticism and reluctance to surface where it could be addressed.

The team reserved no idealistic notions about the web site becoming the catalyst for organizational change. In fact, they advocated that it be launched only as part of a larger communication strategy—one centered around person-to-person communication.

However, by listening to potential end users in a receptive environment, the team was able to identify what was and was not already working well in the environment and was then able to design a site that offered something unique and valuable.

The case studies we've looked at suggest three requirements for a successful web site. Successful intranets satisfy users' needs, possess outstanding "product features," and demonstrate operational excellence.

■ The Value Triad

To be successful—that is, to become a valued communication medium—an intranet must meet three requirements. First, it must satisfy users' needs. Those needs may be information access, archive and retrieval, two-way communication, or knowledge-sharing needs. The needs may focus primarily on employees' demands for data-based, factual information, tools, techniques, or other logical forms of communication; or they may be focused on narrative forms of communication—stories and discussion areas. When the intranet offers superior stakeholder satisfaction, people will use the technology on a continuous basis, and over time will probably adapt the technology to satisfy other needs and solve other problems as they emerge.

Second, it must possess outstanding "product features" that make it attractive as an option as compared with other options within the universe of communication opportunities. As a "product," internal web sites compare favorably to other communication options. For instance, intranets can combine graphics and text, can be updated easily and kept "fresh," and can be interactive.

However, it needs to have "operational excellence" meaning that, like a refrigerator, television, car, camera, microwave or stereo, it must function well. It shouldn't have missing pieces, broken parts, or bugs. It shouldn't stick, jam, or fail unexpectedly. Users should feel confident that it will work and that when it doesn't work, someone will be available to help troubleshoot or fix the problem.

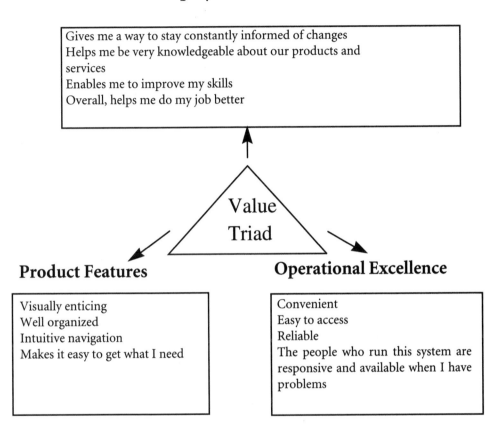

Satisfies Employees' Needs

Gives me a way to stay constantly informed of changes
Helps me be very knowledgeable about our products and
services
Enables me to improve my skills
Overall, helps me do my job better

Value
Triad

Product Features

Visually enticing
Well organized
Intuitive navigation
Makes it easy to get what I need

Operational Excellence

Convenient
Easy to access
Reliable
The people who run this system are
responsive and available when I have
problems

FIGURE 9.1
The Value Triad

Figure 9.1 is a value triad, and the three together create a value proposition. If you change any element in the triad, you change the value proposition. If, for example, employees can't log onto the network, can't access the intranet, can't get a browser loaded onto their desktop or laptop, or can't get help when they find a broken hyperlink, the product's operational dimension suffers, and the intranet's value goes down. If content is plentiful, but poor information architecture and navigation options lead to user frustration, the product exhibits poor "product features," and the value proposition cannot hold. Whereas the content may be plentiful and the information easy to navigate, if the materials are irrelevant from the employees' points of view and/ or fail to meet their needs, the value declines.

■ Case Study 5: Competitive Intelligence Web Site

The value triad is the initial basis from which to assess what would be required to create a value-added intranet. It requires a cold, hard look at the reality of the situation. In some cases, satisfying employees' needs is the hardest part. Other times, the other two areas emerge as problems.

One of ILS's best clients was a Fortune 500 company that asked the WisdomLink team to create a competitive intelligence web site. Like the Army, corporations are not immune to change. The client company was super-sensitized to the hypercompetitive environment and was ready to put a lot of resources toward a competitive intelligence web site.

Initially, things looked great. Interviews with stakeholders and discussions with employees revealed that the need for a web site to support the sharing of competitive intelligence was incontrovertible. The participants reported that they needed more and better competitive information and intelligence, and that they were very enthusiastic about the company's plans to address this need at a corporate level. Using a VisionMapping exercise (see Chapter 14), the team had uncovered employees' needs for three different *genres* of competitive intelligence: information abstracts (such as competitors' financial profiles), technical information (like competitors' product specs) and interpretive/analytical information (such as an analysis of a competitor's strategies and the company's own counter-strategies). They put together a plan to collect and/or create all of the content the employees had asked for. A "champions" group, comprised of eleven of the company's best salespeople, formed to collaborate on site design and implementation.

One looming problem, however, was IT support. During the team's discussions with members of the company's sales force, the team learned that adequate computing support had not been provided to the globally distributed sales force and, consequently, negative attitudes about computers as a productivity tool were strong. Members of the sales force reported that when laptops crash, freeze, or run out of memory, they had no resources besides themselves to get back up and running.

Therefore, the team saw it as incumbent and mandatory that the client company put in place a plan to address these IT-support issues prior to launching a competitive intelligence web site. Otherwise, some employees would decide *in advance* not to use the website, no matter how good the site was. The company would then lose some of its best potential contributors to the site, simply because the employees had stretched their own limited resources as far as they could and could not overcome technology barriers on their own. In a report to the site's sponsors, the team reluctantly wrote:

> It may be the case that the (sponsoring) group will have to champion some changes within (the company) in regards to Information Technologies budgeting, planning and so forth. But it makes no financial or strategic sense to create a web site that employees cannot use because they lack access to the network, can't get a web browser on their desktop, or because their laptops crash on a daily basis. The message the employee is sending is clear: [the company] cannot ask employees to utilize another computer-based productivity tool without additional IT support.

Case Study 5: Key Learnings

Many companies are in the same situation. In 1996, Cognitive Communications, Inc. and Xerox set out to discover barriers to implementing an intranet. Questionnaires were mailed to 731 corporate communications professionals who were selected primarily from Fortune 500 companies. A few privately held organizations were also included. In their report, titled "Employee Communications and Technology," they made a startling statement: the availability of the hardware and software were the biggest barriers to intranet development, and not the concept or its perceived value. One survey respondent stated "we are way behind technologically and money is one big reason." Only 11 percent of responding communicators cited lack of senior management support as their primary barrier, and only 21 percent cited lack of perceived value. However, communicators reported limited employee access as their number one barrier (46 percent), lack of a technology infrastructure (37 percent), lack of budget dollars (24 percent), and turf politics holding them back 21 percent of the time.

Though the situation in the client company was not unique, there obviously was some risk for the ILS team in directing its client to attend to its IT issues. If the company had decided not to address IT issues, for whatever reason, the sponsors might have canceled funding for the web site. The team's candor might have cost them a client. Fortunately, it did not. So strong was the need for a competitive intelligence web site, the team's recommendations were used to catalyze a debate at the highest levels of senior management about technology infrastructure and IT budgets. The company attended to its IT issues and provided the remote sales force with better computer and network support.

■ The Intranet Value Chain

As this example illustrates, it is impossible to accomplish the three-part value proposition alone. An intranet that (a) meets employees' needs, (b) possesses outstanding product features, and (c) has operational excellence involves many people.

IT professionals, for example, are expert at creating networks that exemplify operational excellence. They know how to engineer the network and to ensure system reliability. They are responsible for ensuring that employees have access to the network and that the network can support the increased traffic caused by web-based communication.

Programmers or web site developers are also important players. There are people who understand HTML and whatever programming interface (CGI, Java, APIs, etc.) is used to create the information architecture. Good programmers know how to add forms, search engines, and back-end scripts to make each site as useful and as valuable as possible. Good sites are visually compelling, so the team needs someone with a knowledge of tools that computer-based designers now use. That person typically is a graphics or digital designer.

Human factor specialists and instructional designers also contribute to the outstanding "product features" segment. They know how to make the technology enjoyable for people to use. Often, they are also skilled in doing usability studies and in assessing whether the technology itself seems to meet users' needs and expectations.

Others schooled in methods of inquiry such as interviews, focus groups and workplace ethnography can combine forces with IT groups and programmers to create the "value-added intranet." Somebody with the responsibility for on-going employee support is also essential.

Together, these specialists create the Intranet Value Chain (Figure 9.2).

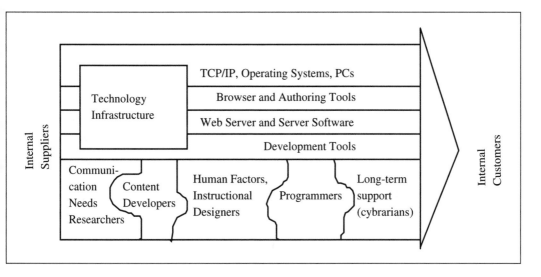

FIGURE 9.2
The Intranet Value Chain. Each activity adds value to the end product and adds value to the technology infrastructure.

The Value Chain represents a change in intranet ownership. In 1997, Jeremy Schlosberg wrote an article for the Salon web site that brought the consequences of the current politics to light. Schlosberg interviewed design expert Edward Tufte, Yale University professor and author of three books on information design, including the new *Visual Explanations,* then wrote:[3]

> Tufte bristles at the routine stupidity of screen design alone, in both multimedia software and on the Web. "You'll often find that three-fourths of the screen is devoted to non-content. What this reflects," he says, "is power. The screen is controlled first by the

programmers, secondly by the interface decorators. By the time they get done, there's not much space for the content."

Unless specialists come together to form a value chain, it will be impossible to secure employees' trust in the intranet. Paul Strassmann, president of the Information Economics consulting firm in New Canaan, Connecticut, reminds us that things we take for granted every day and come to trust have "hidden" structures of relationships and activities that exist backstage and support a decision.[4]

> If the electric supply isn't very reliable and you have intermittent failures, you're going to buy yourself a gasoline generator and keep it on standby because you don't trust those guys in the utility. Trust becomes the important unit.

> The way information flows in (organizations) right now there isn't much trust because everyone takes care of themselves. That's the way mankind has been for most of its history. The very idea of having a civilized society is being able to go to the supermarket for a quart of milk. There is a whole structure behind it. For you to walk into a supermarket and buy a quart of milk is a giant achievement of trust.

> Thousands of people had a role in that quart of milk. We'll have to earn that level of trust like all other trusts that exist everywhere.

Employees and other stakeholders will come to trust the intranet when there is a network of people who take joint responsibility for delivering the value-added intranet.

With all the hype about how the technology will revolutionize the workplace, it may seem pedestrian to think of an intranet as a product comparable to Tide, Oscar-Meyer hot dogs, or a Honda Accord. The truth, however, is that people will choose to use the intranet or not to use it at all, knowing that there are other options available. Employees will become loyal to a webbased product *not* because somebody within the company gave it to them or told them to use it, but because it fulfills its value proposition.

■ Technology Attitudes and Values

Today, understanding employees' information and communication needs is more important than it has ever been. In the late 1980s a new demographic emerged—people with opinions about hardware and software and the way they should work. This was a result of the computer-based workplace automation movement in business and the personal computer revolution in the consumer marketplace. Few people today are naïve about the impact of technology on their lives. They have seen new technologies come and go and have heard many promises about how new technologies will improve their lives and their jobs.

When people leave home to come to work, they don't lose their feelings or opinions about technology on the way to the job. In fact, many employees hold more polar opinions about workplace technologies than about technologies used in the home. As James R. Beniger points out in *The Control Revolution: Technological and Economic Origins of the Information Society,* up until recently, virtually every information technology has been an expression of business and government's efforts to control things and people. Modern bureaucracy and information technologies basically evolved together, one complementing the other.

Automation's Fallout

Over time, many employees were stripped of local decision-making power as "smart machines" automated more and more processes and as computer systems, not people, identified what were correct inputs and outputs. Shosana Zuboff tells about how employees have responded when companies automated their work processes in *In the Age of the Smart Machine.* The technology, Zuboff found, affected employees' attitudes, their work practices, and their feelings about their value to the company. The intrinsic meaning of the work was taken away from many front-line employees and, in reaction, efforts to sabotage the systems were not infrequent.

Many older employees who have experienced the effects of computer-based automation resonate with Apple's Orwellian commercial "1984," which introduced Apple's Macintosh model in a one-time-only appearance during a Super Bowl telecast. The commercial showed a young, athletic woman in white running into a shadowy room filled with pale, expressionless people who sit motionless, transfixed by a video of a dictatorial, Big-Brother-like figure. The heroine hurls a hammer forward, shattering the huge screen. Apple's message: The other companies' computers have stripped us of our vitality and humanity.

Amazingly enough, there is much suppressed enthusiasm for computers among the employee base, even among groups of employees whose jobs were profoundly affected by computer systems automating their work. Such employees actively follow technology trends and are very knowledgeable about what's happening in the high-tech market. They see their children using computers as a fully integrated part of their learning experience and feel strongly positive about it. Because the home computer market is extremely competitive, it's not unusual for employees to have better computer hardware and software at their homes than they do at work.

Generation X's Take on Technology

Shifts in the economy are being reflected in employees' expressions of attitudes about technology and the role of technology in enabling them to find satisfaction in their work. Consider "Generation X" employees. This is an excerpt from "X Nuggets" by <u>Bruce Tulgan</u>, president of <u>Rainmaker, Inc.</u>, whose work focuses on Generation X employment issues. Tulgan's essay was published on the <u>Tripod</u> web site, and it provides clear, important insight.

> First, Xers are . . . rather skeptical of institutions and cautious about investing our creative energy without any promised return. Remember, Xers entered the working world in the post-job-security, post-pension-security era. The idea of a life-long relationship with one employer is ancient history to Xers. However, Xers are capable of a new kind of loyalty which managers may earn by forging a new workplace bargain based on relationships of short-term mutual benefit.

> Second, Xers . . . think and learn differently than those of prior generations. Xers are voracious consumers of information, capable of sorting and assimilating massive quantities of information at a very fast pace, a style conditioned by our life-long immersion in the information revolution. What looks to many managers like a short

attention span is, in fact, a rapid-fire style of information consumption which goes hand in hand with our technology prowess, both of which make Xers uniquely suited to the workplace of the future.

Younger employees, therefore, may also resonate with Apple's "1984" commercial, not because they experienced the effects of computer-based automation of work processes, but because they grew up on the other side of the shattered screen. By growing up in a hypermediated society, members of this generation learned how to assemble meanings from multiple media sources and genres—from cartoons, sitcoms, game shows, radio, CDs, video tapes, books, magazines, billboard ads, film, and many forms of digitized information accessed through computers (such as video games). We are masters of bricolage, putting things and meanings together, using whatever materials happen to be available.

■ The Traditional "Push" Model

Historically, organizations have implemented new technologies and new business initiatives using a "push" model of communication and implementation. A group of specialists creates something new, and it is then brought to the employee base. The "telling" or "selling" of strategies is used to persuade employees to use the new technology.

The advantage of the push model is in its efficiency. The specialist group is responsible for design and development, and can focus exclusively on the product. However, the disadvantage of the push model is that usage over time tends to be flat. As illustrated by Figure 9.3, utilization peaks, drops, and plateaus.

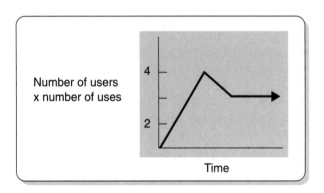

FIGURE 9.3
Usage Plateaus

According to the Gartner Group in Stamford, Connecticut, it costs a typical company $7,000 per year to own and maintain a PC on a network. According to <u>Paul Strassmann</u>, in the U.S., corporations spend nearly three times as much on information technology as they do on other basic equipment, such as transportation and production equipment and office fixtures.

Yet studies of technology utilization by employees at the desktop reveal that employees tend to use only 20 percent of the hardware and software capacity available. There may be pockets of tremendous energy, but, overall, the technology investment fails to meet initial expectations. If you anticipate a ROI at Level 4, you will find disappointment when it plateaus at Level 2.

The limits of the push model over time are illustrated through such usage diagrams. It often occurs because upper management wants to hear a "yes" from their employees. The employees want to hear that they will keep their jobs. A "compliant yes" often seems like the safest course for all. "I can go along with that," employees say. However, usage data, when collected, signal the absence of genuine commitment. This scenario is characteristic not only of technology use, but has been seen to characterize initiatives such as TQM and other organizational interventions.

The "Pull" Model

Looking to the web itself, we can see the outlines of a better model. People who use computer-mediated communication (CMC) technologies such as the Internet and the Web select the documents they want for retrieval, a model of access called *information pull*. This contrasts with *information push*, where information is sent to preconfigured lists of people, broadcast-style. The technology empowers users to pull information of value toward themselves while rejecting lower-value "noise."

For example, an on-line index of documents enables employees to pull up a web page on their computer screens, quickly scan through a list of documents, and locate the pieces of information most useful at that particular moment. Employees can read the answer on the screen or copy and paste that section into a word processing document and print it out if they wish. It saves time and money, and reduces frustrations from trying to search for paper-based information. Because it is a computer file, it is also easy to update as new data are generated. It's available at any time of the day or night.

The purpose of the technology, therefore, should be to help people get right to the heart of whatever problem they are trying to solve. Usage is driven by pressures and demands experienced by employees themselves. People pull the technology and content to themselves because it solves an immediate real-time problem.

This same model can be applied to the design and development of a new technology or a new organizational initiative. The strategy changes the environment from the kind of push process outlined above to a pull process whereby employees are requesting the tools and information they need to perform their jobs better.

The strategy begins with a question:

> *What would motivate an employee to pull the technology and the content into their daily work practices on a long-term basis?*

The next question is:

> *How can we partner with employees to (a) provide content that is significant and meaningful, and (b) leverage this particular technology investment?*

Asking these questions and paying attention to employees' answers significantly improves the likelihood of long-term success. The overall advantage of the pull model is that it creates alignment between vision and resources; between goals and objectives; between what is seen by designers as possible and what is seen by users as "real."

■ Embracing the Challenge

The old way of implementing new technologies in organizations used "telling" and "selling" strategies.

- Telling: "We've got to use this new technology. It's management's vision. Be excited about it, or reconsider your career here."

- Selling: "We've got the best technology solution. There's nothing better. We're sure that this will work for you."

Today, either strategy will raise employees' skepticism. Older employees have heard those messages for the past two decades and have seen one system replaced by another each time management's "vision" changes. Using "telling" and "selling" again probably will produce bland acceptance.

Younger employees bring a lot of energy to information technologies and get discouraged when something promoted as "new," "better," or "best" proves to be, in their minds, old, difficult, and slow, and does not enable them to expand their skill sets.

Within both those age groups—the younger and the older—as well as age groups that fall in between, there are people who feel very comfortable using a computer as a tool and people who become anxious at the thought of having to learn to use a new technology, particularly as part of their job.

Employees are people, and people have feelings and emotions about technologies. Images of computers and information technologies are part and parcel of our contemporary society. Intel, Microsoft, MCI, and IBM hire the best minds in advertising to create engaging, colorful campaigns for the consumer market. The objective is to sell products. The unintended consequence is rising expectations for how new technologies get sold. New technologies are not just appliances. They are much more meaningful than that. Like cars, clothes or cosmetics, new technologies are sold through—and carry—powerful symbolic messages.

The employee base is no longer a passive audience waiting to be told by internal "experts" or by consultants or by management that they need a new technology. Employees have opinions about technology one way or another and ought to be treated like adult consumers. If you use old models of organizational persuasion, launching an Intranet and securing employees' ongoing participation will be a challenge. Kurt Stocker, Associate Professor and Director of Graduate Public Relations at Northwestern University advocates that we do for employees what marketers do for consumers—allow employees to manage their own internal communications. "In other words," says Stocker, "address your company's employees as adult consumers rather than six-year-olds."

■ The Opportunities Lie in Dialog

Success lies in involving employees in the design, development, and implementation of the intranet. When you solicit employees' ideas and take time to understand their perspectives, you will find it easier to convince employees to use what you offer. Employees will appreciate the intranet because the product will be one that they contributed to creating, and it will speak to their needs. Your intranet will not be a maverick idea coming out of the blue. There will be ground swell seeping up from all corners of the company.

The goal is to see employees as your customers, and to make them happy in such a way that they become evangelists for your product. Guy Kawasaki's descriptions of how Apple's customers became Apple evangelists is very instructive. When Apple introduced the Macintosh in January, 1984, many experts in the computer industry thought it was doomed to failure because it did not use the MS-DOS operating system. As Kawasaki recounts[5]

> What the naysayers did not foresee was that Apple would muster a cadre of raging, thunderlizard evangelists—artists, designers, writers, students and interns who went under, around and through the folks who controlled computer purchases. Customers who become evangelists are cheaper and have much greater impact than Procter & Gamble-style marketing.

Given that group dynamics and opinion leaders are profoundly impactful in organizations, it only makes sense to pursue this same goal. Mary E. Boone, author of *Leadership and the Computer*, points out, "When you help people work better and when you eliminate some of their major frustrations with information access and organizational communication, *they* will make the business case *for* you."

A necessary first step is changing the terminology. Employees are not "users" at the end of the distribution chain, they are potential participants. In *Connections*, Professors Lee Sproull and Sara Kiesler emphasize that a first principle in developing a networked organization is "viewing people as people, not as users." With a fully distributed intranet, everyone communicates via the network; therefore, the old distinction between users and nonusers of the technology is meaningless. Sproull and Kiesler further remind us that "every employee has something to offer on a network and every employee has something to gain from it."

Set aside some of your concerns about how management thinks about intranets. Begin to think about how employees think about intranets. The case study in the following chapter illustrates how inviting employee participation can ratchet up an intranet's value proposition. The chapter also makes one final argument for engaging with employees in intranet development.

■ References

[1] As cited in Roger D'Aprix, "Employee Communications," in *Experts in Action*, Bill Cantor and Chester Burger, eds. (Longman, 1989).

[2] Donald Norman, *Things That Make Us Smart; Defending Human Attributes in the Age of the Machine* (Addison-Wesley, 1993), p. 130.

[3] Jeremy Schlosberg, "Why Multimedia Still Sucks: Too Many Buttons, Not Enough Thought," *Salon.* (03/13/97) http://www.salonmagazine.com/march97/21st/multimedia970313.html.

[4] Diane Hamblen, "Paul A. Strassmann: Turning Our Upside Down World Right Side Up," http://www.chips.navy.mil/chips/archives/92_oct/file2.htm.

[5] Guy Kawaski, "How to Drive Your Competition Crazy," *Wall Street Journal.*

The Case for Dialog as a Design Premise

All through Section Three, we've been examining the value of engaging with employees in dialog about their information and communication needs. In Case Study 4, for example, we saw how comments gathered from focus groups influenced both the content and the design of the site, improving the end product substantially. Case Study 5 revealed how dialog with employees helped the team to identify a missing part of the Value Triad. Had that set of problems not been identified early on, a portion of the sales force would have decided in advance of the site's launch not to bother.

This chapter lays out one final argument for engaging with employees as "engines of innovation." A poignant case study regarding the unmet communication needs of field technicians and supervisors is discussed first. It reveals how opportunities to use the intranet to improve an organization may lie right below the surface of our ordinary perceptions.

■ Case Study 6: A Community-Created FAQ

Throughout the past decade, organizations have used computers primarily to automate processes that in the real world appeared inefficient and time-consuming, and, therefore, costly. One of the second-order consequences of automation was the expansion of managers' "span of control." *Span of control* refers to the ratio of supervisees per supervisor. The basic premise is that workers need a certain amount of supervision if they are to perform their jobs appropriately. Until the last few decades, the ideal span of control was recognized as between six and eight supervisees per supervisor.

At a telecommunications company referred to here as *Americo*, a team from the quality group went out to the field to study groups of top-performing field technicians along with their supervisors. The purpose, initially, was to look for outstanding examples of "internal best practices" that could be shared with lower performing groups. Many of the "best practices" uncovered were related to good communication practices. For example, top-performing supervisors and their technicians kept their lines of communication open and addressed problems as they occurred instead of letting problems fester. Through word and deed, they demonstrated respect for each other as skilled craftspeople. Though this finding was not earth-shattering, the team also discovered that the computer-based automated work flow system that the company had put into place in the 1980s made it extremely difficult for people to communicate in such a fashion.

The supervisors recalled that, years ago, they were in charge of groups of eight or ten technicians. They were able to spend most of their time in the field, working alongside their techicians. The relationships resembled master-apprentice or peer-to-peer relationships. Much knowledge was exchanged—not simply about task-related issues, but also safety, personnel, and leadership issues.

When computer processes to automate work flow were put into place in the 1980s, the supervisors' span of control doubled. Some supervisors became responsible for groups as large as many as 22 technicians. The assumption was that the data on the computer screen would enable supervisors to "see" their technicians activities, requiring less face time with employees and enabling them to supervise more people. Had task demands on the job held stable or decreased, this model might have held. However, in most cases, jobs became more, not less, complex. For about a decade, technicians and their supervisors have been signaling management that the model is not working.

At Americo, one of the findings from the team's focus groups was that technicians who install and repair telephones continue to turn to their peers or to their immediate supervisors to get answers to questions. This was especially true when new equipment for use in the field, new policies, and/or new telecommunication products were issued from headquarters. One of their major frustrations in the field was getting quick answers to those questions, especially when the information was located in another division of the company or in another part of the company's territory. As a result of reengineering, technicians and engineers were no longer co-located. Most of the engineers had all been moved out of state, consolidated into one network provisioning center.

Another frustration was in attempting to share the information among the supervisor groups. None of the existing computer systems enabled supervisors to do either. With their span of control so large (from 12 to as high as 25), many supervisors felt they couldn't be as responsive to their techs' questions as they would like, as searching for answers was so time-consuming and the resulting answers contradictory. Everyone felt let down.

The Merits of On-Line Community

In an ideal world, the company would have freed the supervisors from the mind-numbing paper-pushing administrative tasks that ate their time and kept them inside, and would have encouraged the supervisors to get back to the field. In the ideal world, headquarters would modify its practice of pushing new equipment out to the field in the absence of any explanation or communication. That scenario, unfortunately, required senior management buy-in, budget changes, and so on.

In the meantime, however, it was possible to identify a few ways to use the intranet to make the supervisors' and technicians' jobs somewhat more satisfying and less frustrating. A group of technicians and supervisors got together in an "Open Space" meeting and conceived of several ways to use the intranet to get quick, timely answers to questions and to publish those questions and answers on a web site.

The basic concept of what they proposed follows the pull model of information access. Supervisors, along with experts in other parts of the company, would contribute to a frequently asked question (FAQ) section, beginning with questions that were top of mind for most technicians. Whenever technicians or supervisors needed information, they could pull up the FAQ on their web browser, quickly scan through a list of questions posted along with the answers, and locate the pieces of information most useful at that particular moment. They could read the answer on the screen or cut and paste a section into a word processing document, print it out, and distribute hard copies, if they wished. The FAQ could save time and money, and could reduce frustrations inherent in trying to search for the right person with the right answer. Because it was a computer file, it would be easy to update as new questions arose. As headquarters issued new equipment, created new policies, and offered new telecommunication products to customers – i.e., adding additional complexity to the job—technicians and supervisors would be able to integrate "just-in-time" information into their daily work practices.

Case Study 6: Key Learnings

In retrospect, creating a dynamic FAQ was an obvious solution—so obvious as to be almost meaningless to onlookers. Yet to the technicians and supervisors, it was extremely meaningful. When Americo automated its processes, much of supervisors' local decision-making power and authority was eroded. They described themselves as "like cogs in a machine" meant to carry out orders and "not think." Their relationships with their co-workers had become impersonal and more formal. The experience was more than frustrating, it was demeaning. The computers did the interpreting, assigned the work automatically, and delivered information for the supervisors to process. The technicians were instructed to respond to the requests issued from the work flow system, as illogical as they often seemed, and were discouraged from asking their supervisors or anyone else to override the systems' orders.

The FAQ could not erase that history. We cannot retrofit history to accommodate a new technology. Yet the FAQ enabled people to reconnect as a community of skilled practitioners. It provided a way for this particular group of people to contribute their ideas, thoughts, and words—not just their physical labor. In addition, the FAQ offered the participants a way to see patterns and problems for themselves, rather than being forced to passively watch the system do all the interpreting.

Much has been written about creating the "learning organization." The terms have become very trendy, and there is plenty of advice available about how to go about becoming a learning organization. Here, however, is a specific example of employees' desire for local, context-specific organizational learning. Nancy M. Dixon, an associate professor of Administrative Sciences at The George Washington University and author of *The Organizational Learning Cycle: How We Can Learn Collectively*,[1] states that

> Knowledge renewal is critical because many of the most difficult problems organizations face are ones they have never encountered before, that are unique to a given situation. Increasingly, organizational members find that they must learn their way out of problems —they must gather the available information and create meaning from it for themselves. Knowledge from experts or from other parts of the organization may inform their thinking but cannot replace it. What is required, then, are processes that allow the organization to continuously construct new meaning, to learn.

This was precisely what the supervisors and technicians wished to achieve. No one had to instruct them on the supposed value of organizational learning. The need was already there, experienced daily and weekly in countless frustrations. So determined to create such a knowledge-sharing system, a small group of technicians and supervisors spent its free time locating warehoused PCs and other supplies so that the system could be built.

Compare the meaning of a community-built, dynamic FAQ to a web site with official corporate press releases, policy statements, or training manuals. Which is more meaningful? Which is more purposeful? Which creates evangelists? The answer seems apparent. Still, it would be wrong to take this idea to your company and say, "We need community-created FAQs." It would be worse still to decide to compile an FAQ for some piece of new equipment or for a new policy or procedure without asking for contributions from the employees who will use the FAQ.

Technology is symbolic and meaningful. There are important reasons for engaging in dialog with employees from the beginning instead of creating intranet applications or web sites and then delivering them to the employee base. The dialogs are part buy-in, part reality-check, part implicit acknowledgment that *people* are the focus of the initiative, not the technology. The next chapter provides specific instructions and guidelines for involving employees in design, development, and implementation.

■ Final Argument for Engaging with Employees in Intranet Development

The esteemed <u>Donald Norman</u>, a professor emeritus, research director, and author of several books, including *Things That Make Us Smart—Defending Human Attributes in the Age of the Machine* (1993), states on his personal web page that:

> The technological problems today are sociological and organizational as much as technical. In this new age of portable, powerful, fully-communicating tools, it is ever more important to develop a humane technology, one that takes into account the needs and capabilities of people. The technical problems are relatively easy. It is the people-part that is hard: the social, psychological, cultural, and political problems are the ones that are the most difficult—and the most essential – to address.

Such a statement holds especially true for intranet development, which requires the cooperation of many to succeed. The starting point always, Norman writes in *Things That Make Us Smart*, is with the people who will be using the technology:

> Is there a way to transform the hard technology of computers. . . into a soft technology suitable for people? Yes, I think so. The correct approach. . .is to start with the needs of the human users of the system, not with the requirements of the technology.

It would seem so right to follow Donald Norman's advice. Yet, though Norman and others have been advocating this philosophy for over a decade now, we have been slow to catch on.

Organizations have not been *completely* oblivious to the needs of employees as technology users. Companies try to provide technology training, paper-based guides, and help desks, but in our failure to engage with employees in dialog, we've overcompensated and have created a log jam. Gloria Gery,[2] one of the leading practitioners in Performance Centered Design (PCD) and the author of the ground-breaking book, *Electronic Performance Support Systems* (1991), states the problem:

Developers in the consumer marketplace have long been driven by performance-oriented thinking because they can't presume that a discretionary user is going to have been trained to use their product. A discretionary user just won't buy your product if it requires training—it's only in the corporate environment, with its history of IS departments in the mainframe days thinking of their users as captive, that you get the assumption of mandatory training. . . . I think of myself as a victim's advocate, and right now it's the users who are the victims. Right now we have a situation where training is really being used as a compensatory mechanism for badly designed systems, documentation is being used as a compensatory for inadequate training, and help desks are being used to compensate for all of it.

The only way we're going to solve the problem, Gery states, is to reconceptualize how to use computers to help employees perform. Is this impossible? Part of the task ahead involves engaging with employees in dialog about their communication and information needs.

Five "Con" Arguments: Business as Usual

Let's take a careful look at the five typical reasons why intranet developers tend not to engage with employees in intranet design and development.

1. Dialog with employees is seen as expensive. The resources required to prepare, collect, analyze, and report data gathered from employees can make the cost of intranet development seem prohibitive. The cost of engaging with employees is often given as the reason for failing to undertake it.

2. Time spent with employees could be spent on something else. Instead of an initial concern for employees, there is often a concentration on other sorts of things, like dealing with internal politics, convincing management to support the intranet initiative, or evaluating intranet development tools. There is a desire to focus on immediate, visible barriers and immediate, visible results. Engagement with employees is often seen as slowing down other intranet activities.

3. Engagement with employees is seen as one of the last things to do in a linear chain of events that begins with the "vision of the future" held by a group of experts within the company and ends with selling the employees on that vision. When communication with employees is seen as a last step, it is often also handed off to another specialist group as a task item and designed as a mass-persuasion event: the selling activities are high-gloss and impersonal.

4. Management doesn't want to know what employees think about information and organizational communication and how it could be improved. Instead of seeing engagement and collaboration as a helpful activity aimed at constructing value, the dialogs are viewed as potentially threatening and negative. The fear is that given the opportunity to speak, they (the employees) will whine and complain about how bad things are or will want more than the intranet developers can deliver.

5. There are no standards or universal evaluation tools to determine whether or not it is worthwhile to involve employees.

These five reasons for failing to engage with employees in intranet development are not very persuasive. They are based on old models of technology development and on the traditional role of "specialist-as-expert." They rely on traditional forms of organizational power and control, and will not be of much use in the diverse, dynamic workplace of the 21st century.

> *This is why the much-ballyhooed multimedia revolution has so far failed so miserably in the marketplace. Everyone's waiting for the technology while what we have all along is, yes, a failure to communicate.*
>
> **Jeremy Schlosberg[3]**

Five "Pro" Reasons to Make a Systematic Effort to Change

Here are five reasons to make a systematic effort to engage with employees as partners and collaborators.

1. Meaningful dialog can save money for an organization. Intranet developers who have infrequent or limited contact with other employees or who experience very different day-to-day workplace routines often make untested assumptions about

   - what information or communication improvements employees need,
   - how those needs should be met, and
   - when the "solution" should be delivered.

   If those assumptions remain unexamined and prove to be wrong, resources will be wasted in the development process. No organization can afford to spend its human and financial resources on *the chance* that some good is being done. Engagement with employees is a way to take some of the guesswork and financial risk out of intranet development.

2. Engagement with employees functions as an ongoing feedback loop to provide information that can be used immediately or at some time in the future. Proactive dialogs help to create the conditions for the acceptance of new technologies. The dialogs foster new ways of working. When engagement with employees is viewed as part of a necessary feedback loop required for system excellence, it cannot become an "extra" to be done as time permits or as some postlaunch crisis develops with use.

3. Engagement with employees around the three dimensions of the Value Triad can reduce confusion about what is expected in a given intranet development activity. When everyone agrees that the intranet must (a) meet employees needs, (b) possess outstanding product features, and (c) exhibit operational excellence, that set of objectives clarifies planning and reduces confusion. When intranet developers know that they will be evaluated on how the internal customers (the employees) perceive the value of the system, they can plan accordingly and reduce the amount of time spent on things that drain resources unnecessarily, like soothing egos or attending to manufactured internal political crises.

4. Engagement with employees will result in more, not fewer, resources flowing toward the project. When people are treated as underlings, they tend to whine about things they perceive they cannot control, and they look to others to solve their problems. When treated as competent peers, people tend to pitch in and try to contribute to the identification of problems and to the creation of lasting solutions. They will give of themselves: their time, energy, ideas, knowledge, enthusiasm and skill. Resources then flow to—not away—from the project. Egos need not suffer as it can be very gratifying to be involved in an initiative characterized by energy, enthusiasm, and mutual positive regard.

5. Planned engagement with employees solidifies the intranet developer's position within the organization. In business today, the days of relying on hunches about what customers will buy is over. Intranet development, like all internal organizational development, must be accounted for in ways that are familiar to the organization if the activity is to be accepted as crucial to the organization. Engagement with employees removes much of the guesswork and uncertainty about the value of computer-mediated communication. When employees at all levels become evangelists for the intranet, the status of the intranet developers is enhanced.

Many times, projects are justified by trying to amass and analyze reams of data around sales, productivity measures, costs, etc. Here it is helpful to consider Karl Weick's distinction between ambiguous data and lack of data. As Weick notes, groups tend to respond to many organizational problems by citing a lack of data, believing the hoped-for solution will be found in additional information. However, most organizational problems do not require *more of the same* data for resolution. Rather, it is the problem that must be reframed. The group needs to ask different questions instead of either feigning ignorance of any available benchmarks or gathering more data about the same questions. The Value Triad encourages multiple perspectives and increases the likelihood that someone will offer a new way to reframe the problems your organization faces.

Better to begin with dialog that (a) reveals where people are experiencing the greatest needs for improved communication and information flow, (b) uncovers the consequences of not changing, and (c) points to specific, real areas where improvement is most likely.

References

[1] Nancy M. Dixon, "The Hallways of Learning," Vol. 25, *Organizational Dynamics*, February, 1997.

[2] As quoted by Ed Foster, "Enterprise Computing: Training When You Need It," Vol. 19, *InfoWorld*, February, 1997.

[3] Jeremy Schlosberg, "Why Multimedia Still Sucks; Too Many Buttons, Not Enough Thought," *Salon*, March 13, 1997.

■ Section Three Questions

In Section Two, we saw that at each stage in intranet development there are important technology issues as well as the nontechnology issues. We depicted them as activities radiating from each phase. Drawing from key learnings discussed in this chapter, here are some additional items to keep in mind.

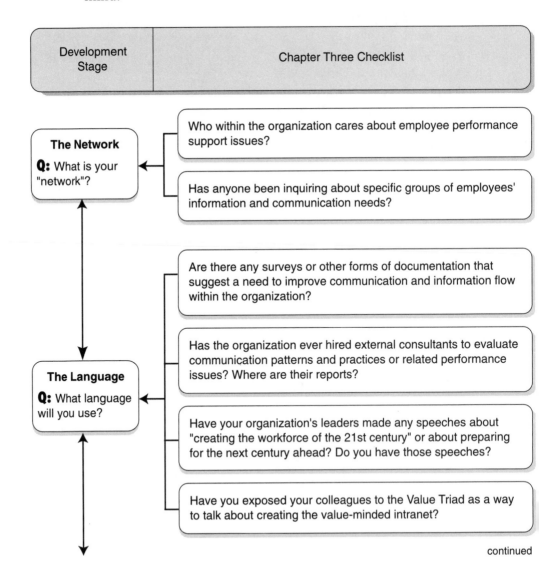

Development Stage	Chapter Three Checklist

The Network

Q: What is your "network"?

Who within the organization cares about employee performance support issues?

Has anyone been inquiring about specific groups of employees' information and communication needs?

The Language

Q: What language will you use?

Are there any surveys or other forms of documentation that suggest a need to improve communication and information flow within the organization?

Has the organization ever hired external consultants to evaluate communication patterns and practices or related performance issues? Where are their reports?

Have your organization's leaders made any speeches about "creating the workforce of the 21st century" or about preparing for the next century ahead? Do you have those speeches?

Have you exposed your colleagues to the Value Triad as a way to talk about creating the value-minded intranet?

continued

Test site and Tools

Q: What will be the test sites, and which tools will you use?

Is reengineering or any sort of organizational change providing an opportunity to evaluate communication patterns and practice? (Similar to the U S WEST MegaCenter case study?)

Are there any groups of employees who have started to address communication and information issues on their own who are in need of some assistance?

Culural Consciousness

Q: How will you enable widespread first-hand experience of the medium so that you can develop your own web culture?

How can you get the message out that you are looking for others in the organization who wish to create a value-added intranet focused on meeting employees needs? What are your communication options and opportunities? Will you use the web?

As your intranet project evolves, how will you tell or show others in the organization about what you are doing?

Gradual Transformation

Q: As the idea of "the future organization" is linked with enabling intranet technologies, how will that linkage lead to different activities and roles within your organization?

How are you going to document your engagement with employees to illustrate the value of the method to others, especially the skeptics? Will you use the web itself?

What will you do if you hear that other groups are developing web sites or other intranet applications without involving employes in the design or development? Will you share what you know?

CHAPTER 11

This Is Not Bill Gates' Playground

Computers swallow whatever they can touch, and every-thing they swallow is forced to become as unstable as they are. With the soaring and brutal progress of Moore's Law, comput-er systems have become a series of ever-faster, ever more com-plex, ever more elaborate coffins.

Bruce Sterling[1]

Engaging with employees in intranet design and development seems like a very progressive, humane thing to do. The last section provided several case studies drawn from real intranet projects demonstrating why it pays to make the internal customer the focus of intranet development.

What could possibly stand in the way of such an approach? The short an-swer: Bill Gates and the "Technology Cold War" being fought behind infor-mation technology (IT) closed doors. Today Gates is spending billions on R&D to create and market a package of Microsoft products that organiza-tions can use to create their "digital nervous systems." Is this an intranet de-veloper's dream come true or worst nightmare? This chapter opens with a look at the consequences of the Microsoft intranet campaign. We'll look at Gates' strategy to capture the intranet market and discuss the consequences for intranet champions who wish to spotlight the sorts of people issues dis-cussed in the last chapter.

There is a battle underway for the soul of the network, and it makes the skirmishes fought over Lotus Notes seem like a calm prelude to the coming storm. Having discussed employee engagement for several chapters, it is important to examine any obstacles that stand in the way. This chapter first discusses Microsoft's strategy, then outlines a counter-intelligence shaped around the strategic use of tension. The premise of this chapter is that the intranet hype is only going to get worse. It is time to arm yourself with a healthy dose of skepticism and a lot of good data.

■ Bill Gates Wants Your Intranet

A couple of years ago, Bill Gates described the advantages of networked computing in his 1995 best-seller, *The Road Ahead*, co-written with Nathan Myhrvold and Peter Rinearson.[2] Gates and his co-authors described how the information highway would revolutionize communications even more than computing. It's already happening in the workplace, they stated, since the most efficient businesses are embracing technologies to make them more productive. "The personal computer has already had a huge effect on business," they noted. "But its greatest impact won't be felt until the PCs inside the company are *intimately interconnected.* Over the next decade, businesses worldwide will be *transformed.*"

Those words foreshadowed a strategy that would emerge in full force in 1997, when Bill Gates and his leadership team decided to spotlight intranets as the most important computing phenomenon in the history of computing.

Intranet Commercials on Prime Time

The highly publicized final episode of "Roseanne" aired in the U.S. on Tuesday, May 20, 1997. One of the commercials aired during the hour was Microsoft's vibrant, exciting commercial for intranets. The intranet commercial was rich with color and displayed a variety of graphics and visual styles. The commercial began with the Microsoft icon for a cursor (the white hand) quickly floating across a desktop screen to a bright yellow icon labeled "Company Intranet." With a click, the intranet launched and we saw shot after shot of intranet applications. There were graphs and charts depicting the company's financials, a video-enhanced annual report, the cafeteria's daily lunch menu, and so on. The editing was so brisk that if you wanted to see the entire set of screen shots, you could not blink.

Imagine, a commercial for intranets on prime-time television. The intention of the commercial was not to sell a product, however. The commercial promoted a concept and created brand awareness for Microsoft's whole product solution. The same week that the commercial first ran, the business press disclosed that Microsoft had very serious intentions to capture the intranet market. As journalist David Kirkpatrick noted in *Fortune*, Microsoft, as it had done before, decided to combine its product innovation with marketing power and financial muscle to take over a market. This time, it was the corporate intranet market.

The "Digital Nervous System"

Bill Gates and Microsoft chose the month of May to tell the world that intranets were more important than anything else that had ever come along in the world of computing. Intranets were more important than the PC revolution, more important than the Internet, more important than any software.

Gates held a well publicized summit in Seattle at the Four Seasons Hotel for 100 elite business leaders from 25 countries and across 18 different industry sectors. "The Business/Technology Imperative: Corporate Transformation for Friction-Free Capitalism" featured tours of Gates' new high-tech home and keynote speeches by Gates, Vice President Al Gore, and publisher and former presidential candidate Steven Forbes.

Gates' speech[3] extolled the virtues of what he called "the digital nervous system." He explained the term:

> When I say *nervous system* of a business, what I mean is the way that a business deals with events, planned events like yearly budgeting or sales results or unplanned events—competitive activities, unhappy customers. And there's all the different systems—the meetings, the paperwork, the way information workers are organized, the way that information about customers is stored, the budgeting system, *the coordination system*. All of those are the nervous system of the company. And no matter what business you're

in, it's my claim that the excellence of that nervous system *determines your competitiveness.*

Gates' message was that companies needed to get a "digital nervous system" or their chances of competing in the 21st century would be sharply diminished.

Responding to Crisis

In his speech at the summit, Gates provided several intranet application examples from companies like Cisco, Columbia/HCA, Ernst & Young, and AIG, the insurance firm. Then Gates disclosed that Microsoft itself had actually experienced some direct benefits from its own "digital nervous system." He told his audience how the Internet phenomenon arrived as "a little bit of a surprise to us, how use was going up, and who was using it."

> The symptoms were seen by different parts of the company. Some of our sales people would *see something going on.* Some of our engineers would go to a conference and see something going on. It was only by having use of rich electronic mail and discussion groups that this came to a *fever pitch* very rapidly, and was recognized as *a crisis* that required quick change.

> Then, by using the digital nervous system, we were able to, without long meetings or anything, *quickly communicate to people* that the project plans are going to change, that the new versions of software have been scheduled. We decided we were going to put more Internet standards into key products, and the schedule was very different, *we were going to price things very differently.* All of this got compressed into about a 45-day period. That couldn't have happened if we'd had a classic nervous system.

Ironically, on the very day Gates disclosed this, *The New Yorker* hit the newstands with an article by Ken Auletta[4] analyzing a series of Nathan Myhrvold's memos to Bill Gates. A large part of Auletta's article recounts how Myhrvold, the super-smart, super-talented person who co-wrote the bestseller *The Road Ahead* with Gates, had dismissed the Internet and World Wide Web as unimportant economic and cultural phenomena. Instead, writes Auletta, Myhrvold was "deluging Gates with memos urging Microsoft to seek more alliances, and to prepare for war with consumer-electronic companies" and to outsmart its "new rivals" such as the giants AT&T and Time Warner.

Microsoft didn't begin to react to the economic opportunities presented by the Internet and the Web until one of its foot soldiers, Steven Sinofsky, Gates' technical assistant, visited Cornell on a recruiting trip. An unexpected snow storm forced an extended stay at the campus, where Sinofsky observed that students were dependent on the Internet for their e-mail and course lists. "Sinofsky reacted like Columbus setting foot in the New World—and championed the Internet when he returned to Redmond," Auletta notes.

The brains at the top of Gates' gigantic company had failed to appreciate changes in the environment that were less visible and much more subtle than the big, warlike competitive issues they had chosen to address. The Net's culture—new, undisciplined, chaotic, more egalitarian than elitist, more decentralized than hierarchical—was antithetical to the business values of Gates and Myhrvold. It was full of "opinionated people who are its self-appointed guardians," Myhrvold opined. The Net didn't fit in with Microsoft's existing plans for the Microsoft Network. Myhrvold couldn't see how Microsoft would be able to make money with it. They dismissed it as unimportant until it became clear that the phenomenon presented a market opportunity.

Fortunately for Microsoft, the emerging market opportunity was perceived by a rank-and-file member of the organization who, by fate, fortune, or circumstance, got close enough to a group of people to observe their behaviors. Sinofsky then chose to speak passionately about what he observed when he returned from the field. Thanks to e-mail and discussion groups, other people besides Sinofsky had an opportunity to report what they had also heard, seen, and experienced.

It is significant that employees throughout Microsoft were able to connect and communicate about these issues. Like most leadership at large organizations, Gates and the senior leaders were preoccupied with major battles. While the Web was emerging as a cultural phenomenon and Netscape was busy capturing the web browser market, Microsoft was occupied with the largest, most expensive consumer marketing effort in history, the launch of Windows 95. In addition, the Justice Department was aggressively investigating claims of unfair practices levied by Microsoft's competitors.

Invisible "Knowledge Workers" and "Microserfs"

Things turned out well for Microsoft for a couple of reasons: A person close to Gates with enough credibility (Sinofsky) saw something with his own eyes outside of Microsoft, came back, and kept talking about its implications. Other people in various divisions and areas of expertise across the company were having similar thoughts about this emerging phenomenon and wanted to communicate about it. They enjoyed a networked system that enabled communication. Once convinced that something of real importance was happening, senior management exploited its latent organizational capacity, added additional capacity, provided people with the resources required to succeed, created strategic partnerships, and set very clear objectives.

Let's distill that into four basic elements:

1. **People/customers outside** the company trying to solve recurrent problems in new ways.
2. **Employees inside** the company seeing the value of those changes and the inherent opportunities for the organization.
3. **Networked communication technologies** enabling cross-functional, cross-organizational communication.
4. **Management** making critical decisions on behalf of the organization, creating strategic partnerships, and taking care of resource issues.

1. Customers

2. Employees

3. Communication
Technologies

4. Management

FIGURE 11.1
The Blueprint for Success.

All four are essential. Yet in Gates' telling of his story at the summit, only the last two elements of the four are stressed. The *technology* —the "digital nervous system"—is the primary hero in Gates' story. Management, who re-acted to the crisis when the discussions reached a fever pitch and meltdown looked imminent, is the secondary hero. The employees—the knowledge workers—are sort of invisible "microserfs" that we (management) must communicate instructions *to*. Things people were doing outside the compa-ny (using the Internet and the Web to communicate) were "a surprise."

Given that his audience was comprised of 100 very elite CEOs, Gates' story could be seen as an appropriate piece of rhetoric. It matched the audience's preconceptions and didn't challenge them to do anything different than to expend more capital in the purchase new and better technology. In fact, al-though the entire summit reverberated with the theme of "empowering knowledge workers through technology," the summit contained elements of what Leo Marx has called "the rhetoric of the technological sublime"—

hymns to progress that rise "like froth on a tide of exuberant self-regard, sweeping over all misgivings, problems and contradictions."

Focusing on the Network

Why all of the interest in intranets? *Fortune* put Gates on the cover of its May 26 issue and provided greater insight into Gates' intentions in the intranet market. The cover story, "Gates' Greatest Power Grab (It's Working)" was subtitled "Forget Internet. Forget MSNBC. Windows NT, Bill Gates new software for corporate networks, is the real future of Microsoft."

David Kirkpatrick's article explained that Gates had grown tired of saying "look at this hot new *product*." He was now in the position to proclaim "look at this hot new *market*" and in a position to offer a "whole product solution," beginning with Windows NT and BackOffice—the basis of an internal corporate network.

One of the things Myhrvold believes and has helped convince Gates to see is that the network is tremendously important. However, Myhrvold never has been interested in a diffuse, extended, ephemeral, chaotic network that exists independent of clear purpose. His fascination is with the type of network that is perfectly in sync with its purpose and its ultimate *telos*; a network that performs and functions as a kind of back-end intelligence, without which there would be only chaos. So, Microsoft set its goals on creating corporate networks comprised of high-powered PCs capable of running Microsoft's robust applications yoked together by network software (Windows NT) and a central database management and groupware application (BackOffice).

Pursuing the Pragmatists

Microsoft's timing was right. The first wave of intranet development, catalyzed by innovators within corporations, did not require "whole product solutions." As Geoffrey A. Moore explains in his fantastic book, *Crossing the Chasm*, "real techies don't need whole products." Intranet visionaries took responsibility for pulling it all together. Moore notes:[5]

For *the visionaries,* there is no pleasure in pulling together a whole product on their own, but there is an acceptance that, if they are going to be the first in their industry to implement the new system —and thereby gain *a strategic advantage* over their competitors— then they are going to have to take responsibility for creating the whole product under their own steam. The *rise in interest* in systems integration is a direct response to increasing visionary interest as a source of strategic advantage.

"*Pragmatists evaluate and buy whole products,*" Moore reminds us. That is the now-maturing intranet market that Gates and Microsoft are after. Microsoft offers an attractive package. For example, Office 97 files are designed for use on an organization's intranet and integrate very tightly with Microsoft Internet Explorer. If employees are using Office 97 and Internet Explorer, they can view Office files on the intranet from right within their browser. This eliminates the need to convert everything to HTML. Using Microsoft Office 97, Microsoft FrontPage, and the free Office 97 60-Minute Intranet Kit, a developer can build a web site to support a virtual team in about an hour. These are the kinds of tools that permit people in almost any kind of organization to share their documents with each other via an intranet without needing to know a single thing about HTML.

The Implications of a Whole Product Technology Solution

However, for a lot of people in organizations, this whole product package that Microsoft is marketing to corporations is just too much weight. Nicholas Negroponte[6] states that the size and complexity of Microsoft Word and other products is outrageous. "The problem," writes Negroponte, "displays itself as featuritis and bloated software systems." We're suffering from "digital obesity," and Microsoft wants to give us more.

A series of second-order consequences follow, of course. When dealing with Microsoft, intranet developers lose control on at least three levels. First, there's the now-familiar and accelerating upgrade requirement. Each new version of Microsoft software requires a new computer, or at least another couple hundred dollars' worth of RAM upgrades. Microsoft wishes to carry its customers up-market with it, convincing them to buy far more technology than they need.

Second, there's the "buy one, buy them all" logic behind Microsoft programs. As <u>Andrew Leonard</u>[1] points out in one of his excellent *Salon* articles,

> Microsoft's choice of the image of a jigsaw puzzle as the marketing metaphor for Office is revealing, not just because of how well each piece fits together, but because of how pointless it is to attempt to jam a piece from a different puzzle into the picture. The more you use Microsoft software, the more sense makes to use more Microsoft software. In economics, this is known as the law of increasing returns—a theory that attempts to explain how certain products (the VHS cassette tape and the QWERTY keyboard leap to mind) command dominating positions in the marketplace regardless of whether or not they are technically superior to their competition. Once a technology commands enough of these "increasing returns," control and choice rests not with the purchaser, but with the seller.

Anyone who has ever watched as Netscape icons disappear from a desktop and be replaced suddenly and mysteriously with Microsoft's icons upon the installation of Microsoft's FrontPage understands this loss of control. Often it is difficult to understand why the software does certain things or even what the technology is capable of doing. Active X is perhaps the most insidious code of them all, as it does things without asking the user's permission. It has an "intelligence" of its own.

Andrew Leonard reminds us that with each new version of Microsoft software, be it an operating system or an application, the nuts and bolts of the program have become more obscure and the internal workings of the machinery further removed from users understanding.

> As a consequence, not only must we trust the interface, but we must also learn to behave as the software requires. And what the software increasingly pushes us toward is one seamless Microsoftian mind—defined by focus groups and usability testing, by interoperability and cut-and-paste ease-of-use.

This raises some important questions regarding how to train employees to use these kinds of intranet tools to publish, to share information, to link documents, and to manage their new universe of electronic communication options. Who gets equipped? Will organizations choose to provide *some* of their employees a high-powered PC with a bundle of complementary knowledge worker tools, or will *all* employees have those tools?

As we *ought* to have learned from Lotus Notes, when communication technologies become an expensive proposition, resource issues can become an ugly barrier to communication and knowledge sharing.

The organizational reality in most companies today is that not all employees are even currently equipped with "the right stuff." That is one reason the technicians and supervisors in Case Study 6, a Community-Created FAQ, had to search out warehoused PCs on their own in order to get connected to the intranet. Management did not perceive them as "knowledge workers." Within the company, summer marketing interns and administrative assistants who worked in the copy centers had better access to networked computers, browsers, and PCs than did the seasoned, highly knowledgeable technicians in the field who interacted with customers in their homes and in their businesses every working day. The technicians had a lot of technology that they lugged around in their trucks, but they did not have access to the kind of technology they needed to communicate as a community of knowledge workers.

When the cost of the technology and cost of the human support to manage the technology become barriers to intranet access, we are then talking about developing intranets for the "the knowledge elite" inside organizations, not for existing groups of "hidden" knowledge workers. The irony, therefore, is that there is a good chance that Microsoft's technology solution, "the digital nervous system," will then simply replicate existing organizational hierarchies, roles, and assumptions, impeding the organizational changes necessary to compete in the 21st century.

Technological Determinism

Microsoft is an exemplary human and financial resource manager. Creating these kinds of tools requires millions of dollars in resources. Microsoft's talented programmers wrote a lot of code to make the WYSIWYG tools easy to use. But Microsoft is not simply responding to an existing market of intranet developers who want better tools. It is putting its energies into *creating* a specific kind of intranet market—*a very expensive intranet market.*

There is an element of technological determinism here that actually has a long legacy in our culture. Reflecting about the trajectory of technological determinism in our culture, <u>John December</u>[8] remarks,

> AT&T reflected this point of view in its long-running, *"You will!"* campaign. To me, that campaign reminded me again and again how AT&T seemed to overhype a potential technology . . . while at the same time ignore the reality of the Net. So instead of focusing on the real needs of people interested in online communication . . . their strategic plans were to try to create a market for products before they were created, all with the certainty that whatever products they would create, people would adopt and use them.

Something similar is at work with Microsoft's intranet campaign. Microsoft is a $9 billion company. In 1994, it had nearly $2.5 billion in cash that grew at $100 million per month. It is hard not to get caught in the Microsoft momentum. Moreover, Microsoft's effective delivery of a series of market disruptions encompasses three key factors: vision, capabilities, and tactics. They plan to sustain their momentum over time through a series of initiatives, only one of which is the intranet initiative, rather than assuming that today's current marketing conditions will persist for a long periods of time. They anticipate change and assume that no current advantage is sustainable forever.

■ Does This Really Mean Anything?

The day Bill Gates and his advisors looked at their billion-dollar cash surplus and decided to dominate the intranet market was historical. Let's look at the up and down sides to the situation.

The up side: From a technology standpoint, this is great news for a lot of companies that have delayed or postponed enterprise-wide intranet development because of interoperability and scalability issues. The technology itself is less a the barrier to intranet development than it once was. Early majority and late majority companies that lack the resources to do full systems integration or to evaluate multiple vendors' products can purchase a competitively priced whole systems solution from Microsoft. From soup to nuts, lacking only the PCs.

The other "good" news for intranet proponents is that because of media and industry exposure, more people are becoming familiar with the concept of intranets. A commercial during the final episode of "Roseanne" is as mainstream (and as ironic) as you can get. The concept of network-based work is fast becoming part of our cultural consciousness. The term *intranet* is starting to become as normal and commonplace as *my computer* or *my Daytimer*.

That's the "good" news. Let's look at the down side.

The down side: A lot of people look to Bill Gates, the wealthiest man in the U.S., to define success. Gates and his strategic partners and allies may convince enough organizations that the *primary* reason to create a networked organization is to do it so that you are not left out. Do it so that you don't miss out on the economic opportunities on the horizon. Bill Gates says this is the wave of the future. Everyone who has a seat in this bandwagon is going to be in for *The Big Win*. Those who don't create their "digital nervous system" are not going to be able to react swiftly enough to either opportunity or crisis.

This strategy, if it works, it will create even more wealth for Bill Gates, Microsoft, its shareholders and strategic partners. Organizations that can afford to do so will buy the technologies that are required to create a robust intranet. These organizations will also have to upgrade many of their PCs. Windows 95 does much of its work in 16-bit chunks of data; NT processes information in chunks of 32 bits at a time. The most effective way to use NT will be on a 32-bit microprocessor, like Intel's Pentium Pro chip.

Whereas the bandwagon argument can be leveraged to great advantage by anyone tying to convince management to fund a fully functional intranet, it is just a Trojan horse to get through the door. By itself, it is not a good enough reason to create intranet content and applications. If it is the only argument employed, the majority of the discussion and the resources will go toward the purchase and maintenance of the technology. This would be a major mistake.

> *Is it time for a strike or a users' cartel? You bet it is. Whoever is guiding those young folks making the operating systems and applications of tomorrow should put his or her foot down. It is time to lose weight. Stop making software that options you*

*to death and start delivering simple, easy-to-use apps.   The
stuff you write is written by geeks, for geeks; why not try writing something for the rest of the world?*

Nicholas Negroponte[6]

■ Learning from Notes

The bandwagon effect was precisely one of the reasons Lotus Notes failed
in the 1990s to live up to its marketing promises to "revolutionize the workplace." In her paper, "Learning from Notes: Organizational Issues in Groupware Implementation," Wanda Orlikowski, a professor at the Sloan School
of Management at MIT, details the fallout at a large, global consulting company that implemented Notes across the *entire* enterprise, only to watch the
investment sputter and fail.[9] It's a very eye-opening and informative study.

In the late 1980s, Orlikowski reports, a few senior principals at a prestigious consulting firm realized that, relative to its competitors and client expectations, the firm was not using information technology as well as it
should. In the typical corporate fashion, the partners commissioned an internal study of the firm's technological capabilities, weaknesses, and requirements. On the basis of the study's recommendations, the firm created a new
and powerful position for a chief information officer (CIO). The CIO, responsible for the firm's internal use of information technologies, had an opportunity to review new communication software, including Notes. After a
few days of experimenting with Notes on his own, he became sold on the
product as a "breakthrough technology" and soon acquired a site license to
install Notes throughout the firm.

CIO as Lone Evangelist

The CIO became an evangelist for Notes. He marketed Notes energetically
within various arenas of the firm. He gave numerous talks to principals and
managers, both at national meetings and in local offices. He consistently
promoted his vision of how Notes could help the firm "manage our expertise
and transform our practice." As a result of the CIO's efforts, the demand for
Notes grew, and physical deployment proceeded rapidly throughout the

firm. Virtually all employees had access to Notes. Yet it was never used as anything more than a sophisticated version of electronic mail. The integration of Notes into work practices was not accomplished.

Notes arrived without a business plan, simply on the strength of the CIO's recommendation. The CIO had assumed that new technologies like Notes should be implemented as quickly as possible with no prototypes, no pilots, no evaluation. "We want to transform the way we deliver service to clients," he told Orlikowski. There was no time to waste. The CIO also believed in developing critical mass early and quickly. He assumed that if an "empowering technology" such as Notes was put in the hands of as many employees as possible, the employees "will drift into new ways of doing things." Therefore, he focused his efforts on convincing the key "opinion leaders" in the firm to see the value of the technology, and he assumed that they would spread the use of Notes throughout the firm.

What happened from there is typical of a top-down approach. Employees received only introductory, promotional communication about the groupware, so they were left to their own to make assumptions about the technology and why was being distributed. The IT group responsible for deploying the technology was overwhelmed with installation requests for Notes, could not keep up with deployment demands, and, therefore, had no time to coach or counsel employees about how to get the most from the technology. The training that was made available covered basic technology functions and features, but the "one-size-fits-all" training did not provide employees any way to see how to use the technology to think or work any differently. People in the middle of the managerial hierarchy resisted any encroachment on their time or productivity. Without a way of understanding how the technology could be used to save time or improve client satisfaction, they rejected Notes as counterproductive and antithetical to their personal and career objectives.

In the Heat of the "Revolution," No Time for Planning

In the absence of any dialog about the technology or how employees could use it to overcome their frustrations and improve work practices, employees fell back on existing shared frames of reference—assumptions and values—about doing work at the firm. Within the middle-management group, some of the assumptions and values actually ran counter to the concept of groupware and knowledge sharing. They included beliefs like: Release information carefully and only to people you can trust not to use the information out of context. Avoid situations that would cause embarrassment if information about you or your work were disclosed. Use knowledge as a source of individual power and prestige.

Ironically, the senior leaders—sponsors of the technology—never picked up on these cultural issues. Orlikowski remarks that "there is much more collegiality at the highest levels of the firm, where senior management—having attained tenure and the highest career rank—enact more of a 'fraternal culture' than the competitive individualism evident at lower levels." The guys at the top could not perceive how difficult it would be for their subordinates to break through their existing shared frames of reference—made real through firm policies and rewards—and work in a "revolutionary" new way. No substantial changes were made in business processes at the firm, despite the CIO's efforts to promote his vision of "revolution."

Who is the winner in this scenario? Apart from the people who collected revenue from selling the technology and those within the firm that got to ride the wave, it is hard to say. The CIO had a flimsy network of supporters, had no meaningful language to talk about Notes that would resonate with the employee base, never piloted the system to identify critical success factors, expected immediate "revolution," not gradual transformation, and, consequently, made little impact on the organization's cultural consciousness.

■ Intranet "Fad Surfing" and the Death Spiral

The overall problem with the bandwagon approach ("This technology will revolutionize the workplace; we need it!") is that it is as easy to jump off one technology bandwagon as it was to jump on it in the first place. How different, really, was the Lotus Notes "revolution" from the "reengineering" revolution? Art Kleiner,[10] editor of *The Fifth Discipline Handbook* and author of the incredible history of organizational change, *The Age of Heretics*, describes in *Wired* how reengineering is implemented in most companies:

> Typically, a CEO will hear a speech or read an article, decree a massive reengineering effort, and then hire an outside information-systems consulting group to implement it. Armies of young MBAs fan throughout the company, carrying clipboards and laptops,

mapping out how cycle time (the time it takes an order to be filled) should be reduced and what computers should be installed. Then the CEO approves the new designs, often wrapped around a vast new computer-networked system to be installed *tout de suite*.

Most corporate leaders, writes Kleiner, liked reengineering because they could get rid of the cumbersome, bureaucratic chain of command without giving up control. Instead of giving orders, they could "program the corporation." Technology was the solution.

We must prevent intranet implementation from replicating these types of failed scenarios over and over. Intranets could easily become the latest management fad that is first met with too much hype and then too much skepticism. In that case, it is doubtful that people inside organizations will really have an opportunity to test the tools and discover their inherent value.

Technology and management trends are always absorbing for managers and lucrative for consultants. Yet, Eileen Shapiro, in her wise and valuable book *Fad Surfing in the Boardroom: Reclaiming the Courage to Manage in the Age of Instant Answers*, points outs that the results of such fixes are often disastrous for organizations.[11] Technologies and techniques are marketed and sold as the answers to corporations' problems. Their value may lie in their efficiency. Yet they also tend to obviate the need to engage in a sufficient depth of inquiry or to improve relationships within the organization.

Eras characterized by market instability and economic disruption are the worst of times for many, yet they are the best of times for "gurus" and "prophets." Our era is no different. The business environment is replete with a seemingly endless supply of programs and techniques for accomplishing "breakthroughs" in performance and achieving "world-class" results. Shapiro reviews just a few of the options: Businesses can flatten pyramids, become horizontal organizations and eliminate hierarchies. Businesses can empower employees, listen to customers create customer-focused organizations, and commit to total customer satisfaction. Businesses can create mission statements and put together strategic plans. Another option is to engage in a process of "continual improvement," share best practices, shift paradigms and become learning organizations. Some businesses have become devoted to Deming-based Total Quality Management programs. Others have reengineered the corporation, with the intent—in the words of Michael Hammer—of creating a "business revolution."

Aggressive use of information technology has become one of the top contenders on the list of techniques: Businesses can use new technologies to enable automated work flow processes to improve productivity, to enable knowledge sharing and the "management of intellectual capital," or even to create "the digital nervous system."

Traditionally, the search for formulas for success has been disastrous to internal communications. Employees are often the first to realize that the company is in the midst of problems with its suppliers, distributors, or customers. However, most businesses have extremely poor histories of engaging with employees in dialog. Efforts to tap into the organization's collective intelligence often seem forced and unnatural. In the silence and in the absence of internal inquiry, businesses continue to search externally for solutions. The self-fulfilling prophecies of failure are often foretold in internal communication failures that occur, ironically, because companies are so stressed and pressed for quick answers.

Companies often fail to (a) fully communicate with their employees their intentions to "compete to survive" and (b) fail to engage employees in dialog. The result is that they often lose not only the hearts and minds of their best teams and best people, they lose their best opportunities to provide new value to customers. The death spiral goes on while the search for the "fix" continues.

A cluster of academic researchers including Clayton M. Christensen, Wanda Orlikowski, Shoshana Zuboff, and Tom Davenport has been able to devote time and energy to studying the deployment of technology in organizations. They are documenting IT failures with examples, case studies, and research. While web technologies and the latest IT economics are encouraging a movement away from constructing and employing rigid, mass-produced applications (like Notes) toward more customized and flexible applications, as Orlikoski points out, "it is not clear that social and cultural factors are equally as encouraging. The culture of the workplace, managerial ideology, and existing bases of expertise and power significantly influence what technologies are deployed, how they are understood, and in which ways they are used."[12]

■ A Marketplace Glutted with Conflicting Choices and Values

Adding to the complexity is that Gates et al have laid down the gauntlet and are aggressively pursuing the networked computing market. They are employing a number of strategies we could describe as "hypercompetitive." Their strategic campaign to capture the intranet market is likely to lead to very interesting and heated discussions among IT professionals. For example, if an organization decides to go with Microsoft's bundled solutions, it can enjoy a number of benefits, not just from the Microsoft technologies themselves, but also from the fact that many other supporting industries have signed on to support Microsoft products. This would include book publishers, training organizations, etc. The company also benefits from all of Microsoft's marketing efforts—even prime time commercials—which help people feel great about their technology decisions. Yet, the "cost" is flexibility.

Microsoft's competitor, Netscape, is betting on people wanting greater diversity and flexibility. Netscape's messaging client, Netscape Communicator, runs on Windows 3.1, Windows 95, Macintosh, and UNIX operating systems; Microsoft's product runs only on Windows NT. Netscape's Internet servers run on Windows NT 3.51 and UNIX; Microsoft runs on neither. Netscape offers "native" access to Informix, Oracle, Sybase, DB/2, and ODBC databases; Microsoft offers native access only for its own database running on Windows NT.

There are technical differences between Netscape and Microsoft's "push" technologies as well. Microsoft push technology is based on the channel definition format, or CDF, and Netscape's approach is based on JavaScript and HTML. Currently, content written for one company's push software will not run on the other's browser, and, since 1997, the two have been playing a high-stakes marketing game, trying to lure significant content providers to their side.

Microsoft's business model depends on customers needing and liking the convenience of one proprietary system and being willing to upgrade to the most recent version of each operating system. Microsoft is betting that people will want high-powered computers and high-powered applications that reside with the individual user right on the desktop or laptop.

Netscape's strategy depends on people needing and liking the flexibility of "crossware"—i.e., on-demand applications that run across networks, regardless of operating system. The model depends on people's willingness to assume some burden, either for application development or for the evaluation of vendors' products (such as evaluating Informix, Oracle, or Sybase data bases, or evaluating the web-based applications spotlighted in Netscape's Apps Foundry).

Netscape's model demonstrates some alignment with Sun and Oracle's Network Computer (NC) model, where all data and applications are stored on a central server and downloaded as needed. NCs run on a non-Windows operating systems, usually based on Java. It puts the job of managing the desktop in the hands of a central administrator instead of the individual user.

For people who are responsible for information technologies within organizations, these are big, important, critical issues. Debates and discussion should take place. No organization should get locked into any one vendor's whole systems solution before the issue is discussed with stakeholders who have to live with the consequences of the decision. Being a pragmatist is all right. However, being a pragmatist without a road map or vision is an open invitation for becoming a victim of exploitation.

The Standardization Argument Revisited

Historically, we know that everything brought to the market goes through the same cycle, from multiple standards to a single, common standard, the width of train tracks, the size of paper forms, the width of audio and video tape. Standardization has been essential to the growth of markets. Standardization is a control mechanism that for a century has enabled the market economy to flourish. Standardization is basically an effort to not overwhelm the system with too much information.

Some people welcome Microsoft's efforts to set the standard because it reduces the amount of information they must assimilate to make a technology decision. If everyone used Microsoft products—Windows 95, Windows NT, Explorer 4.0—developers could focus simply on taking advantage of the technology and could add features to satisfy customers without worrying about the risk of incompatibility.

On the other hand, many people want the choice. They want other vendors in this market because that means a greater variety of tools available. For example, what if an intranet development team wanted to add a feature that employees needed but that Explorer couldn't support? The Explorer standard may not permit that particular creative concept to enter the intranet marketplace and gain acceptance. The technology itself would be a barrier to satisfying employees' productivity needs

Interestingly, we stand at a historical marker. This time, we may not drive all the way toward complete standardization. The scenario is possible because of the technology itself. The web is based on the principles of open system computing. The information transmitted over the systems is digital. So long as there is consumer demand, companies will find a way to make it possible for the competing systems to work together.

A good example of how that already happened is Lotus Notes. As IBM witnessed the tremendous interest in web-based communication, they developed and marketed ways for people to get Notes-created documents and data bases onto web servers and web pages. Their customers were saying, "We have Notes, but we also plan to use intranets; give us a way to use both." From a technological perspective, it was entirely possible, and Domino was born. It is not a perfect solution because it is a recovery plan, an example of reverse engineering—so it still exhibits poor design. It did, however, enable companies who had already made the Notes investment to integrate it into their intranets without junking Notes.

Similarly, in regard to migration to the NC model of organizational computing, conversion software from Sun will offer an incentive to corporations invested heavily in PCs to make the switch to the server-centric NC architecture. By popping a disk into a machine you already own and typing in a single DOS command, the PC becomes an NC, but the user can still go back to Windows if he or she wants.

There is a very big difference between computer code and railroad tracks. Code is one thousand times more pliable.

The Media as Wild Card

In the past, consumers' voices were not represented in the debates over standardization; consumers were simply the recipients of the fallout. That, too, has changed because of internet technology.

Back when QWERTY was established as the standard for typewriting keyboards, desk telephones for offices hadn't even become popular. Mass market feedback mechanisms and opportunities didn't exist. QWERTY had enormous repercussions but did not become a public issue and it did not become part of the public discourse. There was very little anyone could do about it, primarily because few people could witness the manufacturers' activities that led to the transformation.

The standards battle between Microsoft and its competitors is being discussed widely in the popular press, in trade magazines, at professional and academic conferences, and, most importantly, over the Internet where people are joining forces to create counter-strategies. The whole thing is wild. The outcome is enormously difficult to predict. If the system cannot adapt, if there is too much information, competitors will be absorbed and we'll see widespread standardization. However, we don't know the capacity of an Internet-enabled system. That's the tremendous challenge that lies ahead.

In most organizations today, discussions about technology occur primarily among engineers, information technology specialists and senior management. It's very easy to see how intranet discussions could become entirely focused on technical debates and how those technical debates could potentially go on forever unless someone calls a halt.

> *The idea of choice is easily debased if one forgets that the aim is to have chosen successfully, not to be endlessly choosing.*
>
> **George W.S. Trow , 1981**
> *"Within the Context of No Context"*

■ A Technological "Cold War"

Make no mistake, Microsoft has introduced a great deal of instability into the industry with the motive of being the last winning player. The shakeout has begun. Today's mature intranet market is glutted with choices and competing marketing claims that render intranet developers distracted and easily open to the suggestion that the most important issues involve **technology** choices. As stated by Dan Shafer in "Desktop Warriors" (*Salon*, December 2, 1996):

> We have quietly entered the Cold War phase of the battle for your computer desktop. Just as global armed conflict gave way to subtler confrontations based on threats and propaganda, the heated battles

over operating systems and competing browsers have recently gone underground, down to the level of code. The stakes, however, are just as high.

Ultimately, you will have to live and work with whatever system prevails in this war. But you aren't likely to be asked for your opinion. The battle is being posited as too technical for you. The engineers will let you know when they've decided its outcome.

The battle is about making monstrously large things smaller and more manageable, about shattering monoliths into usable components. It's about flexibility. Ultimately, it's about freedom of choice.

During the "real" Cold War that ended about a decade ago, the values of the military–industrial complex, which President Eisenhower tried to warn us about in his farewell address, dominated public discourse for forty-odd years. The Cold War justified a technological determinism that fueled the economy and led to the creation of the current computer industry. Most of our leaders were less concerned with people's experiences with technology than with the technology itself. That computer industry today is so strong that the U.S. Department of Defense (DOD) now looks to the industry for resources. As Secretary of Defense William Perry explains, "From the end of WW II until the present, the military led R & D efforts in the computer industry. Today, a complete reversal is underway where the DOD is looking to a single, integrated computer industry to lead all R & D initiatives and to produce the technologies of the future."

The current "technology cold war" that Shafer describes in "Desktop Warriors" is being pushed forward not just by "hymns to the technological sublime" but by fear about what is going to happen to organizations during this incredible, unpredictable period of tremendous economic transformation. Our current pace of change has no precedent in human memory and it is having a fundamental, permanent effect upon the world's industries and the people who work in them.

As individuals, we have never before had a greater need for networked communication so that we can share information with each other, exchange war stories and success stories, help each other to avoid being blindsided by our own fears and anxieties, and challenge prevailing assumptions about how the world works or how it has to be.

Yet we find our cultural heroes like Bill Gates talking about "the digital nervous system" as though it is a thing separate from us: separate from the people whose words and ideas make it what it is. Gates talks about technology as possessing its own life force. It is animated by an intelligence that is created in Seattle but exists somehow apart from us. However, this time, unlike the last Cold War, we can involve ourselves in the debates and go toe-to-toe with "the experts."

The Call of Conscience

One could make the argument that we are in the midst of a historical trajectory, our destiny resembling that of a cyborg, our dependence on technology so complete there is no distinction between "the digital nervous system" and the nervous system that exists in "meat space," a term used by science fiction writer William Gibson in *Neuromancer* in 1984 and popularized by John Perry Barlow to describe the nonvirtual world. Michael J. Hyde,[13] a communication scholar and award-winning professor at Wake Forest University, writes, "There is something fundamentally 'technological' about the manner in which we exist as beings in the world. Human beings and the call of technology go hand-in-hand. It's our destiny."

Perhaps Gates and Microsoft are doing us a favor by creating technology that can be seamlessly interwoven into every aspect of our lives—from education, entertainment, cultural affairs, journalism, the arts, and the computer desktop at work. Microsoft's network and products feature component interoperability, invisible code working backstage, ease of use, and one standard set of protocols for the reproduction of information and intelligence.

Yet, Hyde also reminds us that this technological destiny does not exceed our control. "We can," Hyde states, "affirm our humanity by making responsible and conscientious decisions about how and to what extent we want to connect ourselves to our ever-growing array of technological prostheses."

Occasionally, we need to interrupt the "call" of technology to heed the sound of another call: that of "conscience." The call of conscience summons us to affirm our freedom through resolute and thoughtful choices. Hyde wisely chides us for becoming so preoccupied with technology that we become forgetful of our own "being in the world." One of the things that makes us uniquely human beings is the call of conscience. According to Michael Zimmerman, the call of conscience "testifies that human existence has the power of self-correction. In Aristotelian terms, human beings have their own *telos* and move towards its full manifestation. Our *telos* is to become open to our possibilities; existence yearns to be truthful . . .Conscience is the sign that our temporal openness is dissatisfied with functioning deficiently."[14]

Who is not dissatisfied with organizational communication? If sales of Scott Adam's enormously popular Dilbert books are a measure of anything, it is clear evidence that we are functioning deficiently within our organizations. So it is not the call of technology or the even the call of Bill Gates that moves us to create intranets; it is the call of conscience.

The call has been seeping through our consciousness for at least 40 years, during which "management by numbers" has come to dominate management theory and practice. We have not always managed by numbers, Art Kleiner points out. Before WWII, there really were no well-publicized formulas or techniques. However, by the mid-1950s, nearly every large company had begun to emulate management formulas pioneered by Alfred Sloan, Henry Ford, and Frederick Taylor. Philosophically, they represented nothing less than a breakthrough in human capability. Kleiner[15] writes,

> Like incantations, the numbers gave names to elements of the world which had previously been vague, abstract entities; the value of human effort and the way that value might change over time could now be translated into "break-even points," "market sensitivities," "net present values," and the all-purpose measuring tool of "earnings per share." A manager, through the numbers, could keep track of hundreds of people spending millions of dollars on dozens of thoroughly different projects. The marketer, through the numbers, could set a product's distribution and advertising patterns with the determination and strategic overview of a general plotting a war. The financier, through the numbers, could build an explicit model of the forces of the future, forces which people from more traditional cultures could only comprehend through concepts like "karma," "hubris," and "destiny."

Management by numbers and the postwar economy grew up together, intimately entwined by structures and practices that characterized the industrial and postindustrial culture. It is hard to break from the formulas and from the belief that the numbers provide the best and most accurate depiction of reality.

Luminaries like Tom Peters, Peter Senge, Warren Bennis, Chris Argyris, Dee Hock, Margaret Wheatley, Steven Covey, Alan Webber, and many others have shifted attention from the numbers toward other elements. There is more to talk about now: the learning organization, the Fast Company, chaordic principles, team building, etc.—which challenges management to think about the importance of people. Writes Kleiner:[16]

> Where once a few people within the company had dared to say, "The emperor has no clothes," now the corridors of many large organizations are thronged with people shouting that message, each with a different set of garments to promote.

The "call of conscience" is represented in such efforts. The challenge now for intranet development will be involving people from all levels of the organization, not just professional management—in discussions about technology and organizational change. Intranet development will be distinguished by the fact that organizational change was not accomplished by senior members of the organization but by a cross-section of technology-savvy employees themselves, many of them very young.

■ The Role of Technology: A Doppelganger Reflecting Our Own Performance

Technology is neither hero nor demon. Rather, it acts as a *doppelganger*. The word means "ghostly double of a living person, especially one that haunts its own fleshly counterpart." It comes from the German, *double-goer*.

ACM is the largest, oldest professional organization for people interested in computers, and counts among its membership the very best and brightest minds in the computer industry. The ACM '97 conference held in San Jose the first week of March, 1997 celebrated the 50th anniversary of ACM. The three-day program was designed to be a watershed event to provoke the membership to think seriously and critically about what our world, our cultures and our societies will look like in the next 50 years, and the pivotal role computers will play. It was entitled "The Next Fifty Years of Computing" and featured keynotes from luminaries from the computing world.

One of the best moments of the conference was during a dialog between James Burke, BBC television host and author, and Carver Mead, who pioneered virtual reality design. Their exchange at the conclusion of Mead's presentation went something like this:

> **Burke:** What happens when it's not just us knowing things, but computers knowing things as well?
>
> **Mead:** It's forcing us to think about what *thinking* is. What is it that makes us uniquely human?
>
> **Burke:** We're worried, though, what happens when computers really do our thinking? Will there be room for us?
>
> **Mead:** Yes, there'll be room for us. But perhaps not room for us to be *stupid*.

A little bit of laughter came up from the audience. Mead paused for a long, reflective moment. He then concluded:

> There was a book about Einstein that came out recently. It asked the question, What makes scientists want to think about problems, to generate questions? This is interesting. I expect *that* never to change. That gets at what makes us human.

No one rustled or moved for several minutes. This emblematic moment captured one of the underlying conference themes: Use this particular time in history to become smarter about *ourselves*.

Our use of computers is a window to the reality we ourselves are in the midst of constructing. How we use computers and how we think about them tells us *a lot* about ourselves, our organizations, how smart and future-oriented we want to be, and what we're afraid to face or wish to ignore.

■ Revisiting the Value Triad

To conclude, Gates, Microsoft, and its competitors are directing the discussion of intranets toward only two parts of the Value Triad. First, toward "Operational Excellence." The issues there are things like system integration, scalability, manageability, and security. The industry is also very focused on "Product Features." People who like the Web have become focused on issues like push versus pull technologies, using JavaScript to enhance web sites' functionality, etc.

> *I see the best minds of my generation strung out on HTML, Shockwave, Java, and screaming for a fix of technologies to keep them at the crest of some 'cutting edge.' Unfortunately, being conversant with the latest technological buzzwords doesn't necessarily lead to a better ability to shape meaning.*
>
> **John December,**[17]
> author of books on web development and the publisher
> of *Computer-Mediated Communication Magazine*

When technology is the primary focus, the IT solutions are bound to fail. We need to focus harder on the other dimension of the Value Triad, "Satisfying Employees' Needs."

The point is that if you want your intranet to be more than a technology – that is, if you want it to become a virtual place where people can share information and communicate with each other—*you must make sure that organizational resources are not directed at technology acquisition and maintenance alone.* Organizational resources include not only money but also *what* gets discussed.

Therefore, intranet development requires a larger arsenal of argumentation strategies than, "If we don't do this, we will have missed an opportunity and will lag behind." It requires tactics to open up the discussion to people issues as well as technology issues. Yet how do you open up that discussion when technology is the current obsession, and the public debate is being led by one of the richest—and some would say most powerful—men on the planet?

■ The Upside Revisited: Strategic Use of Tension

Harriet Rubin, publisher of one of the most cutting-edge books in print today, is a successful and an extremely savvy person. Rubin[18] advises us to review challenging sorts of situations and dig out the ways in which they can be turned to our advantage. Let's heed Rubin's worldly advice and revisit the situation.

The advantage is this: Intranets used to be described as technology that was inexpensive to create and implement. That has changed. For example, _Webmaster_ magazine, an excellent source of intranet information, told how executives at Work/Family Directions, Inc., a 14-year-old consulting firm, wanted to provide its clients, the employees of Fortune 500 and smaller companies, intranet access to Work/Family's services. Work/Family constantly surveys the people it serves in order to identify ways to improve its services. One of their surveys revealed that a large majority—71 percent—of the employees in the client companies surveyed wanted technology-based access. Work/Family identified intranet development as a strategic objective, realized that they needed to do it quickly, and decided it was important to provide superior stakeholder satisfaction.

Work/Family teamed up with Cambridge Technology Partners, Inc. (CTP), which helped it sort through difficult technology decisions. One of the services CTP provided was the assessment of various technology alternatives, which helped Work/Family transcend some of the infighting and politics that often come with systems development. CTP assumed the burden of decision-making on behalf of the client. CTP also presented options that extended Work/Family's initial concept of how the intranet services ought to be designed. They recommended that Work/Family deliver their services two ways: into their client companies' intranets and via the Internet. CTP helped Work/Family to see that a major advantage of using the Internet as a communications platform is that future changes can be made to a single source code. To build the intranet/extranet, CTP put four full-time and two part-time people on the project. The price tag for their services and deliverables was "not inconsiderable."[19]

As intranets evolve from basic publication _platforms_ toward mission-critical, transaction-based and collaboration-supporting _strategic tools_, companies are finding themselves having to reach into deeper pockets. "To put this basic infrastructure together is a very serious investment," Gates told his summit guests. Building and supporting web-based transaction applications is more complex than creating and posting HTML files. When customer relationships are on the line, there is even more put at risk. The price tags are getting steeper and steeper, and because of the instability in the marketplace catalyzed by Microsoft, technology investment is serious.

Large, well-known consulting firms <u>BDM Technologies</u>, <u>Cambridge Technology Partners</u> and <u>Systems Resources Consulting</u>, as well as smaller firms, are rushing to fill the enormous demand for intranet technology advice and services. *Webmaster* magazine reported that one market research firm, Input, predicts that internet and intranet outsourcing business *alone* will grow from about $300 million in 1996 to $1.4 billion in 2001.

Harriet Rubin reminds us that one of our greatest allies is the "strategic use of tension." In the next few years, there is going to be a lot of tension, particularly around issues regarding how big an investment to make in an intranet, what brand(s) of technology to choose, whether or not to outsource some or all of the work, and so on. *However, if an organization is going to invest in intranet technologies, satisfying obvious or assumed information and communication needs is not enough.* Who can afford to invest resources today in technology that is exciting and full of outstanding product features but barely used and undervalued by its users? Who can afford to connect only the workers currently perceived by management as "knowledge workers" and leave all other employees unconnected? The answer is, no one can afford this. No organization, no corporation should become Bill Gates' playground.

The key to leveraging a technology investment and gaining real competitive advantage through a technology investment lies in shaping the future and creating self-fulfilling prophecies. This involves:

- Identifying employee communication needs that even the employees may have trouble articulating for themselves.
- Finding new, previously unserved internal customers to serve.
- Creating new communication and information opportunities that never existed before.
- Predicting changes in internal communication patterns and practices before they happen.

This is, in effect, "strategic soothsaying." It is exactly what Microsoft and other successful companies do in regard to external customers. You can do it for internal customers and create your own competitive advantage. As illustrated by the case studies in the previous chapter, the process begins with dialog and getting close to employees as customers. The next chapter introduces some more tension, just to make this a little more interesting.

■ References

1 Bruce Sterling, "Digital Revolution In Retrospect," *Communication of the ACM*, February 1997, p. 79.

[2] Bill Gates, *The Road Ahead* (NY: Viking, 1995), p. 135.

[3] Remarks by Bill Gates, Microsoft CEO Summit, May 8, 1997, Seattle, Washington,http://www.microsoft.com/BillGates/speeches/CEOSummit/CEO-Bill.htm.

[4] Ken Auletta, "The Microsoft Provocateur," *The New Yorker*, May 12, 1997, pp. 66–77.

[5] Geoffrey A. Moore, *Crossing the Chasm; Marketing and Selling High-Tech Products to Mainstream Customers* (NY: HarperBusiness), 1991.

[6] Nicholas Negroponte, "Digital Obesity," *Wired*, July, 1997, p. 188.

[7] Andrew Leonard, "Office97—or Office 1984?" *Salon 1999*, May 1, 1997, http://www.salonmagazine.com/may97/21st/office970501.html.

[8] John December, "Blinded by Science?" http://www.december.com/cmc/mag/1996/feb/ed.html.

[9] Wanda J. Orlikowski, "Learning From Notes: Organizational Issues in Groupware Implementation," CSCW '92 Proceedings, November, 1992, pp. 356–363.

[10] Art Kleiner, "The Battle for the Soul of Corporate America," *Wired*, August, 1995, p. 169.

[11] Eileen Shapiro, *Fad Surfing in the Boardroom: Reclaiming the Courage to Manage in the Age of the Instant Answers* (Addison-Wesley, 1995).

[12] Wanda J. Orlikowski, "The Duality of Technology: Rethinking the Concept of Technology in Organizations," *Organizational Science*, Vol. 3, No. 3, August, 1992, p. 422.

[13] Michael J. Hyde, "Human Beings and the Call of Technology," in *Toward the 21st Century*, Julia T. Wood and Richard B. Gregg, eds. (Hampton Press, 1995), p. 70.

[14] p. 58.

[15] Art Kleiner, *The Age of Heretics; Heroes, Outlaws, and the Forerunners of Corporate Change* (NY: Currency-Doubleday), 1996, p. 11.

[16] p. 335.

[17] John December, "Where Has All the Hypertext Gone?" *Computer-Mediated Communication Magazine*, December 1996, http://www.december.com/cmc/mag/1996/dec/last.html.

[18] Harriet Rubin, *The Princessa: Machiavelli for Women* (NY: Currency-Doubleday), 1997.

[19] Peter Fabris, "Takeout Technologies," *Webmaster*, May, 1997, pp. 27–31.

Intranet Development Road Map

Given all of the turbulence on the technology side of intranet development involving choices between Microsoft's whole product solution versus an open system intranet based on Netscape and other vendors' products, relinquishing intranet development during this "technology Cold War" to an information technology (IT) group or a management information systems (MIS) group may seem very attractive. That would not be the right approach, however, as those technology specialists are not in the *human* communication business.

Essentially, intranets are communication technologies. Our goal is to find ways to put those technologies at our service to improve communication within and among organizations.

This chapter lays out a road map for intranet development. The model begins with thinking about how people use information and how they communicate—not with how people use computers. The model is fluid and dynamic; it takes into account the unpredictable growth in information and changes in human behavior. This chapter also lays out some reasons why communication is the forgotten step-sibling of all other organizational change initiatives, and why it should be recovered as the pivotal issue in organizational change.

We begin with a review of Thomas Davenport's findings on failed IT initiatives. Davenport's key learnings help to set the compass for the road map.

■ Davenport Sets the Compass

Harvard Business Review published an article by Tom Davenport after Professor Orlikowski's paper that ought to have rocked the IT world. It documented not just one but a string of failures with information technology deployment. At one large pharmaceutical company, for example, IT managers tried to implement a shared database to speed up R & D, only to learn that the researchers were either hostile or apathetic. Something went very wrong. Davenport recounted that the IT group failed to understand the rules of scientific exploration that govern how scientists think about information. The scientists were trained to be competitive and to follow the scientific method of research; they did not want to share early or incomplete results of clinical trials with other groups within the organization. The technology did not fit their communication norms and their research culture.

At another company, IT managers set up a system to provide bankers with access to financial data. The bankers could use a search engine to specify in general terms the information they wanted and the system would search the databases and send news items and financial reports to the bankers' desktops automatically. The IT group expected that the bankers' information demands would initially rise and then taper off, as the information could be reused and shared within the organization. They were wrong. Demands increased, as did costs to maintain the system. What happened? Davenport reported that the IT managers planned a low level of human support. No one helped the bankers learn how the new technology could be used to create better deals and working relationships with colleagues and clients. The technology made no improvement on work practices; it simply added another layer of complexity to the organization and added another set of tasks to the bankers' workloads.

Davenport concluded that:[1]

> Some managers have always been distrustful of information system approaches of their companies, largely because they didn't understand them. In many cases, they were right to feel uneasy. As the diverse company experiences [in the article] suggests, *grand IT schemes that don't match what rank-and-file workers want simply won't work.*

Davenport argues that one of the critical success factors for IT system implementation is switching from a machine-centered view to a people-centered view. Davenport's rules of thumb include the following:

From: The Computer-Based Approach With a Focus on Information Architecture	To: The Human-Centered Approach With a Focus on People and Communication
Focus on computerized data	Focus on broad information types
Emphasize information provision	Emphasize information use and sharing
Assume permanence of solutions	Assume transience of solutions
Assume single meaning of terms	Assume multiple meaning of terms
Stop when design is done or when system is built	Continue until desired behavior is achieved enterprise-wide
Build enterprise-wide structures	Build point-specific structures
Assume compliance with policies	Assume compliance is gained over time through influence
Control users' information environments	Let individuals design their own information environments

One of Davenport's most significant statements in the article is that *"the willingness of individuals to use a specified information format is directly proportional to how much they have participated in defining it or trust others who did."*

It makes no strategic or financial sense to deploy communication technologies using the traditional push model. It is dead, and its continued use only contributes to organizational rot and decay.

■ A Road Map for Success

Learning from all of the academic literature available about why IT projects either fail or succeed, we can see that successful communication technologies often seem to involve four distinct processes:

1. Exploring the potentials inherent in some technological phenomenon.
2. Identifying and describing problems in existing business processes.
3. A problem-scanning or intelligence function through which problems identified in the organization can be relieved through the deployment of communication technologies.
4. A top-down/bottom-up deployment process, which helps people adjust their shared frames of reference. (Top-down through training, coaching, internal marketing, leadership evangelism, and reward. Bottom-up through discussion, dialog, experimentation, prototyping, and piloting.)

This, overall, is a process of matching the right technology to the right people for the right purposes. It requires highly developed self-knowledge of organizational capabilities and problems.

Most organizations have trouble with this model because one group of specialists (the IT group) possesses legitimate authority for step #1 while other specialists possess legitimate authority for step #2. Rarely do they comment on each other's work or work collaboratively. The current techniques and methods for "identifying and describing problems in existing business processes" typically focus on macro issues (e.g., cost, productivity, customer churn), and the discussions fail to tap employees' local and resident knowledge. Steps #3 is often accomplished through an internal "white paper" rather than through intraorganizational stakeholder discussions. Step #4 rarely occurs because so much of the focus has been placed on technology issues alone.

To reverse our trajectory of failure and actually put this kind of approach into practice, this model lays out an effective road map for intranet development. Here are the basic components:

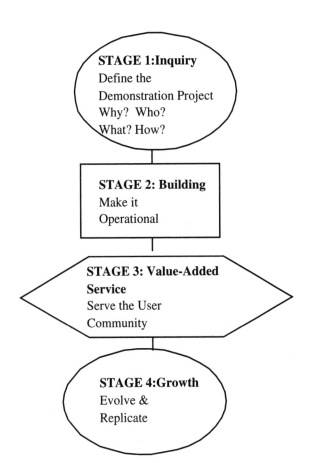

A more detailed version of the model looks like this:

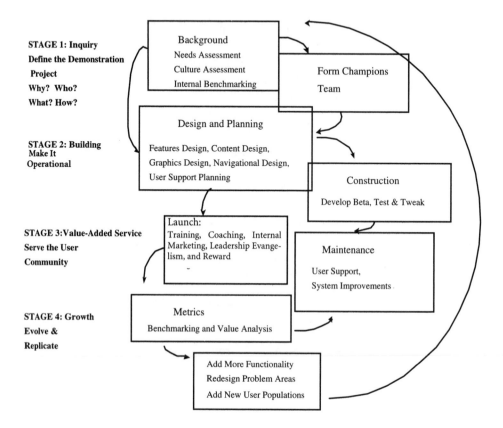

STAGE 1: Inquiry
Define the Demonstration
Project
Why? Who?
What? How?

STAGE 2: Building
Make It
Operational

STAGE 3: Value-Added Service
Serve the User
Community

STAGE 4: Growth
Evolve &
Replicate

Background
Needs Assessment
Culture Assessment
Internal Benchmarking

Form Champions
Team

Design and Planning
Features Design, Content Design,
Graphics Design, Navigational Design,
User Support Planning

Construction
Develop Beta, Test & Tweak

Launch:
Training, Coaching, Internal
Marketing, Leadership Evange-
lism, and Reward

Maintenance
User Support,
System Improvements

Metrics
Benchmarking and Value Analysis

Add More Functionality
Redesign Problem Areas
Add New User Populations

There is a substage between Stage 1 and Stage 2 that involves the "make or buy decision." Do you create the technology that fits employees' needs in-house or do you outsource and/or purchase it? That question will be addressed in detail in Chapter 17. Right now, let's focus on the overall advantages of the road map.

Advantages to the Road Map

The model begins with thinking about how people use information and how they communicate—not with how people use computers. It accounts for the unpredictable growth of information and changes in human behavior. Roger Schank, director of the Institute for the Learning Sciences (ILS) at Northwestern University, says that we must begin to design systems that actually anticipate this uncertainty:

> We are in an age of change. The volume of knowledge that our culture claims to be significant is exploding. Information systems are revamping our administrative organizations. It is impossible to predict what and how people will do things in the future. This "age of change" means we cannot predict all the knowledge and abilities people will need to have.

Intranet development using this model is achieved in stages, beginning with one or more demonstration projects. Demonstration projects are typically more complex than are "pilot projects." They involve system-wide changes introduced at a single web site and are undertaken with the goal of developing new organizational capacity. All of the case studies discussed in the last chapter were demonstration projects.

■ Demonstration Projects

Demonstration projects serve as a proving ground for change. Successful implementation of communication technology requires changes in organizational culture, reward, roles, responsibilities, and activities. Employees must feel that the benefits of their participation exceed the cost; otherwise, they will not participate. Demonstration projects enable intranet developers to gather information about critical success factors for enterprise-wide deployment.

Such demonstration projects reveal what sorts of informal "social contracts" employees expect from intranet developers. How much initial human support will be available? How much future support is planned? When the web site is not working right, when employees' computers are not working right, who will take responsibility? Who will populate the sites with content? How will the employees be recognized for their contributions? In the event that management becomes concerned about "inappropriate" uses of the Internet or intranet, who will be involved with helping to manage those issues? Who will moderate discussions?

The demonstration projects basically employ principles and approaches (such as knowledge sharing) that the organization hopes to adopt later on a larger scale. As Professor David A. Garvin writes, they are "transitional" efforts rather than end points and involve considerable "learning by doing."[2] Midcourse corrections are common. The idea is to keep novel ideas flowing. During their life cycle, however, demonstration projects also implicitly establish policy guidelines and precedents for later projects. Intranet developers, therefore, need to be sensitive to the precedents they are setting and must send strong signals if they expect to set new norms.

Demonstration projects are developed by strong, multifunctional, interdisciplinary teams that report directly to the client or to senior management. Intranet demonstration projects can become a showcase for teams of technical and nontechnical specialists working together to achieve objectives that enhance the organization's capacity and positively affect productivity and profitability.

In most companies, the IT department is developing the intranet while other groups, such as the training department, human resources (HR) department, or corporate communications department, are trying to find the money to support electronic delivery of materials. Internal organizational development groups may be interested in leveraging the intranet to create learning organizations or knowledge-sharing communities of practice. When these groups recognize how they can help each other, employee services (like HR, public relations [PR] or organizational development [OD]) *become the vehicles to leverage the money already being spent on the technology.* IT directs its resources toward intranet construction, growth, and maintenance (i.e., the "Operational Excellence" part of the Value Triad). The nontechnology groups direct their resources toward content development and satisfying employees' information and communication needs (i.e., the parts of the Value Triad labeled *Satisfying Employees' Needs.*) Together, they combine resources and take joint responsibility for ensuring that resources are also directed toward the third area, "Outstanding Product Features," which involves the work of digital designers, information architects, human factors specialists, instructional designers, web site designers, content developers and application developers.

This sort of road map turns roadblocks into opportunities. Typical roadblocks to intranet development include:

1. Inability to convince employees to use the intranet and its applications consistently to improve performance.
2. Lack of middle management buy-in and support.
3. Cultural barriers.
4. Pressure to demonstrate short-term success.

We could tackle each roadblock one by one as they emerge. The more successful route is to plan on these issues emerging, to create a proactive strategy and to address these issues together in a unified fashion. That way, we avoid wasting resources.

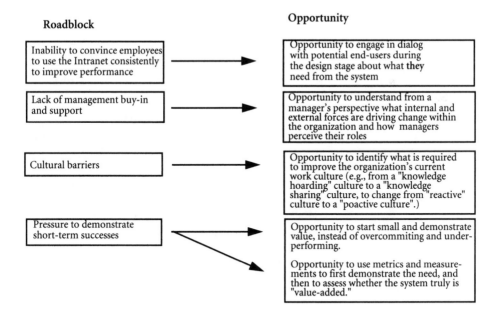

The very first step is engaging in a process of inquiry and gathering data to support design and development. Establish an engagement philosophy that will allow you to let the intranet design structure grow directly from employees' needs.

- Who would be the *best* customers for the enhanced intranet?
- What are *their* needs?
- What are our *best options* for satisfying those needs?
- How can we *partner and collaborate* with employees to ensure that our product (the intranet) is truly "value-added"?

■ Why Look at "Work"?

We begin intranet development with inquiry into the kind of work that people in the organization actually do. With so much literature on the market about "business" and about "managerial strategies," we have a sense that we already understand how people work. The truth is, we don't. Because of the specialization of occupations, the growth of the managerial sector and the focus on things like operations, management philosophy, and strategy, "work" has become an abstraction, a generalized input into a production function. Stephen R. Barley, editor of the Cornell University Press series on Technology and Work puts it eloquently. His words are worth quoting at length because they capture the essence of the problem so clearly.[3]

> How can a firm effectively reorganize or re-engineer its operations without *understanding the work* that its employees do? The answer is, it can't. Yet lack of knowledge does not appear to stop organizations from trying. How can computers and microelectronics change the economy or restructure the way organizations do business without *changing the nature of work?* The obvious answer is, they can't. Yet this fact is hard to detect in the burgeoning literature on information systems.
>
> From the pages of *MIS Quarterly* to *PC Magazine*, the computer revolution is typically fought in a black box where we never learn *what people do*, only that they should now be able to do whatever they do faster and more easily by computing. What meaning can the

"service economy," the "information economy," the "knowledge economy," and similar terms have unless they denote substantive changes in either what people do for a living or how they do it? The obvious answer is, very little.

Yet journalists, futurists, and even sociologists routinely employ such epithets without explaining precisely *what kinds of work they have in mind.* In fact, if one looks carefully at how these terms are used, one discovers that they seem to cover just about any kind of work except for blue-collar work and farming. They seem to be little more than trendy synonyms for "white-collar." The upshot is that millions of people go to work each day to do things *that almost no one but themselves understands* but which large numbers of people believe they know enough about to set policy, offer advice, or redesign. Work has become invisible.

The world of work is so taken for granted, employees' activities are not explored unless something problematic occurs—i.e., productivity falls, absenteeism increases, customers complain. In general, we do not really pay attention to how people work; we attempt to control work through exhortations, measurement, punishment, and reward.

◼ Communication: Invisible Particles of Change

Communication is the key to unlocking the mystery of what people *do.* Communication is the foundation of all work, just as it is the foundation of all human relationships. Strangely, we don't pay enough attention to communication. In an age where we talk at length about "the information economy" and "the knowledge economy," human communication is overlooked and underappreciated. Why? What's going on? There are a couple of things happening.

First, communication is so ubiquitous and "second nature," we tend not to see communication as quite as important as concrete *techniques* like total quality managment (TQM) or other management strategies, even though communication underlies every one of them. People assume that they already know how to communicate, that no special attention is required.

Second, a cynic might say that another reason why we don't pay attention to communication patterns and practices is because communication has been made perverse. The practice of communication is, for the most part, degenerate. "This is a world," journalist Jonathan Alter[4] notes, "where 'communicating' is more important than what you communicate, where words are mistaken for deeds and images are magically transformed into accomplishments." Most of the officially sanctioned, well-funded communication "events" in organizations are devoid of honesty and are only superficially meaningful. Only in <u>Dilbert</u> cartoons can the truth of organizational communication be permitted to become public knowledge. Michael Schrage, in *Shared Minds; The New Technologies of Collaboration*, a significant and important book, notes that organizational communication is characterized primarily by deception. He writes:[5]

> When it comes to human communication, there's a factor more influential in everyday life than most people care to admit. . . . It's our *ability to deceive ourselves*. . . .In his book *Groupthink*, Irving Janis warns that most elite groups—the well-educated, hardworking sorts who run organizations—end up mutually reinforcing their biases all the way to self-destruction. Janis cites the Bay of Pigs fiasco as one example. These victims of *groupthink* have various flavors of self-deception in common. They think they're communicating when they're not. They think they're exploring the interesting aspects of a question when they're not. They think they're talking a collective innovative approach to the challenges that confront them – and they're not. This *self-deception* runs through most organizational communications. It's why people think meetings are a waste of time, and it helps explain the frustrations most people feel when they try to collaborate. Most people kid themselves into thinking that they're collaborating with someone when, in reality, they're *just saying words*.

Benevolent censorship; face-saving efforts; socially "upbeat" behavior; the avoidance of risk, vulnerability, or embarrassment; these forms of "good organizational communication," writes Chris Argyris,[6] are prevalent and endemic in organizational life. What we accept as "good communication," Argyris warns, actually blocks organizational learning and discourages us from correcting the course. Unfortunately, in an age where what is accepted as good communication is actually "bad" communication, it makes it hard to argue that we should pay more, not less, attention to organizational communication.

One last problem is that whenever we wish to explore communication, we face a problem with representation. Human communication is a symbolic activity. We use symbols, such as words and images, to represent thought. To communicate about communicating requires a method, as Clifford Geertz says, for rescuing discourse from its "perishing occasions" and "fixing" it in perusable terms. We face two challenges: to gain an understanding about how people communicate and what they communicate about, and to use that understanding to look at the relationship between work as it is being done and work as it might be improved. Not all work shows itself through talking, however. John Seely Brown and Estee Solomon Gray[7] remind us in their article, "The People Are the Company"

> The more you explore real work, the more you appreciate the power of a different kind of knowledge: tacit knowledge. With individuals, tacit knowledge means intuition, judgment, common sense—the capacity to do something without necessarily being able to explain it.

Tacit knowledge exists in the distinct practices and relationships that emerge when people work together over time. "Work," therefore, shows itself not simply through the ways in which we talk about work, but through the social fabric that connects communities of workers. We need ways to express the inexpressible.

Management theorist Peter Drucker notes that "In no other area have intelligent men and women worked harder or with greater dedication than psychologists, human relations experts, managers, and management students have worked on improving communication in our major institutions. Yet communication remains as elusive as the unicorn." True. However, while it can be somewhat tricky, the study of how employees work and communicate can be one of the most valuable activities afforded corporate sponsorship.

To understand employee communication is to understand the way work gets done. To understand work is to understand the production of value. Making work "visible" by focusing on communication is essential today. "Too often, what is unofficial remains invisible—perhaps to members of our own trusted community," notes Seely Brown and Solomon Gray.[7]"In the Knowledge Era, invisible is often what's most valuable."

The information gathered through dialog and field research is like a database of code; it can be used and reused for a number of different purposes: in the business plan, in white papers, for development of internal marketing materials and employee training, for charting the impact ofz the intranet over time, and for identifying critical success factors that must be met if it is to become a valued, integrated organizational tool.

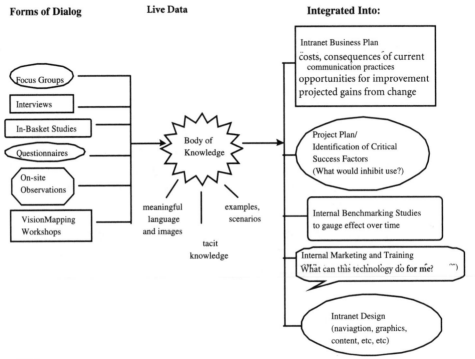

FIGURE 12.1
Using Dialog as the Foundation.

■ Reclaiming "Communication" and "Work" as Valid Issues

To begin to explore communication and work practices within your organization, consider using these five steps of issue management as a template.

1. Avoidance—avoiding the issue completely
2. Exploration—exploring the issue

3. Organization—organizing thoughts and data on the issue
4. Integration—putting these thoughts and data together to form an understanding
5. Conceptualization—an understanding of the issue and how to resolve it

One of the rules is that you can't move on to the next step without completely getting through the one you are currently addressing. In other words, how can you explore the issue of internal communication if you are avoiding it, and how can you organize thoughts on the topic if you have not really explored it? How can you conceptualize a solution before you've understood contradictory data?

Assuming that you've decided it's no longer smart to avoid issues relating to work and communication, exploration is your first action item. The next chapter takes us through the first two steps of inquiry: setting objectives and creating a research protocol.

■ References

[1] Thomas H. Davenport, "Saving IT's Soul: Human-Centered Information Management," *Harvard Business Review*, March–April, 1994.

[2] David A. Garvin, "Building a Learning Organization," *Business Credit*, January, 1994, p. 22.

[3] Stephen R. Barley, "Foreword," in Julian E. Orr, *Talking About Machines: An Ethnography of a Modern Job*, ILR Press, 1966, pp. x-xi.

[4] Jonathan Alter, "Lost in the Big Blur," *Newsweek*, June 9, 1997, p. 43.

[5] Michael Schrage, Shared Minds: *The New Technologies of Collaboration*, Random House, 1990, p. 29.

[6] Chris Argyris, "Good Communication That Blocks Learning," *Harvard Business Review*, July–August, 1994, pp. 77–85.

[7] John Seely Brown and Estee Solomon Gray, "The People Are the Company," *Fast Company* premier issue, p. 78.

A Protocol Is a Handshake

> *Seek constant communication, risk it without reserve, renounce the defiant self-assertion which forces itself upon you in ever new disguises, live in the hope that in your very renunciation you will in some incalculable way be given back to yourself.*
>
> ***Karl Jaspers***

The road map proposed in the last chapter outlined a model for web site development. It began with "Inquiry," the very first stage in any web development project. Going forward, this chapter provides guidelines for the inquiry stage. How do you set objectives for the inquiry stage? We'll revisit the five case studies presented throughout the book thus far and extract project goals and objectives.

Next, we'll look at questions such as, Who should be involved with the discussions with employees? What should the relationships between the "researchers" and the employees be like? What sort of ethical issues emerge when you begin to get close to people and their daily work practices? How can we gain employees' trust and avoid being perceived as being like all other consultants who have come before us?

275

This chapter answers these important questions and warns intranet developers to take *proactive* measures to ensure that the sins of previous waves of consultants are not repeated.

■ The First Step of Inquiry: What Are Your Objectives?

The first step in any process of inquiry is to list your objectives. What do you want to understand? Let's use the case studies from the last chapters to illustrate.

Case Study 2: In the case study involving the U S WEST MegaCenters, the overall task was to develop a communications process to deliver a variety of different types of messages to and from the customer service representatives.

Project Goal

To develop a communication process that was easy to use, fast, enabled employee choice, incorporated a mix of communication tools, was measureable, easy to replicate and would allow two-way communication.

Employee Engagement Objectives

1. Understand what types of information were utilized in the environment.
2. Understand how customer service reps used information in their daily work.
3. Identify oppurtunities to improve commmunication within the MegaCenters.
4. Identify existing and potential communication media that could be used to improve communication.

Because the objectives were essentially to "map" the current information flow for all employees in the MegaCenters and to improve the communication process, the interdisciplinary team chose to use a variety of methods of inquiry: in-basket studies (a form of ethnography), interviews, and focus groups. They had high-level sponsorship and the freedom to experiment with several different inquiry methods.

Case Study 3: In the case of the web site the WisdomLink group created to promote a core set of management principles for the Fortune 500 company, the project was focused not on communication broadly defined, but on communicating a specific body of information.

Project Goal

To leverage the intranet to provide all employees within the company, all across the world, with easier access to information, educational materials, knowledge, and best practices about the core principles.

Employee Engagement Objectives

1. Review the approach and reasoning for the site with employees in order to check assumptions.
2. Determine the current levels of awareness, understanding, acceptance and commitment among employees to the core set of management principles.
3. Assess employees' current use of the company's intranet and identify any technology barriers.
4. Uncover critical success factors for design, development and implementation.

Because the client was already persuaded that the need for a web site existed, they did not want to fund extensive field research. Yet they did agree to fund a series of focus groups in several locations with employees representative of various divisions, titles, and rank. The client also provided the team with the results of another consulting firm's prior research on how the employees perceived the core principle project.

Case Study 4. A project that illustrates how multiple, multilayered objectives come into play is the competitive intelligence web site case study. Because the company did not already possess a robust information technology infrastructure or a fully functional intranet, the objectives of the field research went beyond the examples above, in that the team wished to get data not only from the employees themselves, but from management and other stakeholders who would have an active role in constructing policies to support the use of the site.

Project Goal

To create a web site that provided current information about competitors and their products, allowed for updates to be input by employees, enable the employees to share best practices about how to win against various competitors, was perceived as valuable and fun to use.

Employee Engagement Objectives

1. Understand organizational supports and barriers.
2. Understand management perspective of computer-based performance support.

The executive who sponsored this work agreed that it was important to do a thorough situation and stakeholder analysis as the first step. He agreed to invest ample resources in the inquiry phase, and to communicate the importance of the inquiry to other stakeholders.

To gather the data, the team first interviewed key stakeholders including senior management, members of the IT group, marketing experts who supported the sales force through the creation of competitive strategies, and members of the R & D group that evaluated competitors' products. Some interviews were individual interviews, others involved groups of 3–4 stakeholders. Then, after the interviews were completed, the team designed a day-long off-site workshop for a representative group of employees who volunteered to participate. The workshop focused on group discussion and a VisionMapping exercise.

Case Study 5. The field work objectives for Case Study 5, a community-created FAQ, were completely different from all the rest of the other case studies, as the initial goal of the field work had nothing to do with intranet development. The group's goal was to uncover internal best practices and to identify opportunities for the transfer of best practices from qualified sources to potential recipients. The group created methodologies to identify sources of best practices, to understand those best practices, and to evaluate various communication options for transferring best practices. The methods included surveys, "ride-alongs" with techs in their trucks, group interviews, and one-on-one interviews with supervisors.

The data the group received about the need for a community-generated FAQ was an "emergent" finding: it emerged in the course of the study without being based on explicit hypotheses or research objectives. In fact, one could argue that this case study represents the most real and genuine example of using technology to satisfy employees' communication needs. It was free of what researchers call *design causality*, i.e., the design of an objective in order to realize a specific outcome or intention. Here, the need was first articulated; identifying the appropriate technology to satisfy the need came second.

Setting Your Own Objectives

These examples are all specific to individual projects and may or may not be applicable to your unique situation. To generate a set of objectives for your intranet initiative, you might begin by asking yourself these questions:

---

1. What do we know about how employees currently use information in their day-to-day activities?

   What is their "information diet"?

   Are employees getting too much of the wrong kind of communication, information, or training and not enough of the right kind?

2. What do we know about how employees communicate
   a) with their peers,
   b) with their supervisors,
   c) with senior management,
   d) with other "upstream" and "downstream" groups that affect the work?

   Where are there examples of communication that works well?

   Where are there examples of communication that is failing?

   Who do employees consider "trusted" sources?

3. What do we know about employees' current experiences with the organization's information technologies?

   What are employees' attitudes about technology?

   What is the history of technology deployment here?

   When things go wrong, who takes responsibility?

These are simply some questions to help kick-start the process. From here, you can customize a set of objectives that are right for the type of project on which you are working.

■ The Second Step: The Protocol

The second step is creating a protocol. A *protocol* is a procedure for adding order to the exchange of data from one source to another. It comes from the Greek term *protokollon*, the first sheet of a volume : Greek *proto-* + Greek *kollêma*, sheets of a papyrus glued together (from *kollan*, "to glue together," from *kolla*, "glue"). *Technology protocols* are standard procedures for regulating data transmission between computers. In Chapter 1, we saw how the developers of the Internet wrestled with the question of how to create the "handshake" to permit data to be transfered seamlessly from one kind of computer to another. The protocols they created (i.e., TCP/IP) created "the handshake."

Professional protocols are codes of correct conduct. They are often articulated as sets of rules or procedures. Machinists and construction workers, for example, follow safety protocols. Graduate students in the sciences and social sciences are trained to follow research protocols for their experiments. Physicians and nurses follow medical protocols in the treatment of patients. The professional asks, How do I approach this sort of situation? The protocol responds, "Within this profession, taking these sorts of things into conderation, this is the correct way to do it." These protocols are far more than cold, impersonal rules; they are actually implicit moral and ethical codes of conduct.

All protocols are, in essence, designed to protect the *integrity* of something. Integrity is a "state of being unimpaired; soundness." It is a "quality or condition of being whole or undivided; completeness."* In the case of computers, technology protocols like TCP/IP protect the integrity of data, so that the data does not get corrupted. The data stays whole and error-free through the course of the transmission. Safety protocols, research protocols, and medical protocols also help to ensure the integrity of data and information as it is transferred from person to person to person. Imagine the tremendous potential for injury if physicians failed to follow correct protocols when administering drugs or preparing patients for surgery. The protocol protects the integrity or wholeness of the data; it also protects the integrity or wholeness of the human beings involved.

*The American Heritage Dictionary of the English Language, Third Edition, is licensed from Houghton Mifflin Company. Copyright © 1992 by Houghton Mifflin Company. All rights reserved.

Here, we speak of protocols as the "handshake" between two or more people, and as one of the most important steps in intranet development. Protocols are our starting point, our glue, our way of ordering the exchange of information and knowledge. They reveal our moral and ethical beliefs. One of the most important questions to ask is, How do we create a "handshake" that keeps us whole, that guards integrity?

Part of the process of developing a protocol is developing your attitude toward the whole employee engagement endeavor, and then setting down your ethical principles for engagement with employees.

We live in a culture and society that is strongly influenced by the "scientific attitude" and by values such as *measurement* and *rationality* for the purposes of *problem-solving* and *strategy*. People who are seen by researchers as *subjects* or *survey respondents* are then perceived as serving an instrumental function —a prescribed means to an end. The problem with going into a focus group or into the field or onto the shop floor with that sort of attitude is that it makes it hard to listen to what people have to say. When you approach people in the "scientific attitude," they tend to respond in a guarded fashion, disclosing only that which is safest to disclose and guarding the truth by giving you what they think you want to know and/or can accept.

Chris Argyris, distinguished author and Professor of Education and Organizational Behavior at Harvard University, and Donald Schon, distinguished author and Professor Emeritus at MIT, remind us that people are always looking for the meanings inherent in any human interaction. The effect of engaging with people in "the scientific attitude" complicates and often subverts one's quest for valid information. Argyris and Schon have watched a lot of research go south because of the researcher/experts' tendency to treat people as "subjects."

Argyris and Schon remind us that people being interviewed always bring their entire selves and their intelligence to the situation. The person being interviewed may answer questions in light of what he or she believes the inquirer expects. The interviewee may construe the situation as one that calls for putting the best possible face on prior actions. The interviewee may design the interaction, more or less consciously, as a form of image management. To the extent that the interviewee feels threatened or distrustful, the interviewee may deliberately withhold information. Then, like mining without a head lamp, the interviewer leaves with only coal on his or her hands, the diamonds still "in the rough." Unfortunately, too many people think they see diamonds when all they've really got is coal. "People spoke to me, so it mus be good data," they think. However, as any programmer knows, there is a difference between corrupt and noncorrupt data.

To engage with employees, we need a stance that is both ethical and objective. In their outstanding book, *Organizational Learning II*, Argyris and Schon note that organizations need people who can help the extended organization learn more about itself. They write that "normal" organizational life tends to constrain inquiry. Argyris and Schon recommend that "practitioners"—people who work inside organizations—take a more active role in the process of inquiry.

One starting point is the acknowledgment that, as "practitioners," we've been really interested all along in understanding things so that we can change them or adapt to them. Here is how Argyris and Schon describe "practitioners":[1]

> Organizational practitioners may be curious about the process through which they carry out the day-to-day business of organizational inquiry. Often they are capable of reflection on organizational practice, which researchers tend to see as their special prerogative. Practitioners are sometimes *curious about how success and failure are defined* in organizational terms, how goals and priorities are set, and how ends of action are chosen as desirable. Practitioners, as well as researchers, may be interested in *threats to the validity of organizational learning*, that is, the kinds of reasoning and the forms of behavior that lead them to draw distorted lessons from past experience. Often they see that by focusing on immediate issues of local importance they may become blind to the larger significance of their actions. Increasingly they suspect that *existing structures and incentive systems* may undermine their ability to function well in a changing environment. Many of them want to learn how to create new structures and incentives and how to acquire new skills, enabling them to increase the learning capacity of their own organizations.

There are two very important thoughts here. The first is that the concept of inquiry is not new or foreign to most working people. We do it naturally, informally, all of the time. Experts are not the only people who are interested in why things happen the way they do or why they aren't working very well. People who work are interested and thoughtful about organizational problems. William Foote Whyte has been sending this message for a long while.

Whyte has a remarkable record of scholarly work that he has sustained for four decades, culminated in his book, *Social Theory for Action: How Individuals and Organizations Learn to Change.* Arguing against the orthodox concept of rigor in social research, with its reliance on professional control of the research process, Whyte advocates an approach, "participatory action research" (PAR), in which professional social researchers treat their "subjects" as active collaborators.

Employees posses the kind of insight, intelligence, and knowledge that is *required* to correct the course rather than just to make a short-term "fix." If we see employees as people interested in communication issues as much we are and as full of wisdom and insight, our frame of reference will change. Modifying a schema suggested by James E. Spradley, it might look like this:

From: Research with "Subjects"	To: Dialog with "Informants"
1. What do I know about a business problem that will allow me to formulate and test a hypothesis about its solution?	1. What do the people working here, my "informants", know about their organization that I can discover?
2. What concepts can I use to develop this hypothesis?	2. What concepts and terms do employees use to talk about their experience?
3. How can I define these concepts?	3. How do employees define their concepts and terms?
4. What scientific theory can explain the data?	4. What practical "theories" do employees use to explain their experiences?
5. How can I interpret the results and report them in the language of management?	5. How can I *translate* the knowledge of employees into a description that management will understand?

Adopting this kind of stance toward people with whom we engage in dialog is a radical departure from treating people as "survey respondents" or "research subjects." Spradley writes:[2]

> By word and action, in subtle ways and direct statements, [it] says, "I want to understand the world from your point of view. I want to

know what you know in the way you know it. I want to understand the meaning of your experience, to walk in your shoes, to feel things as you feel them, to explain things as you explain them. Will you become my teacher and help me understand?"

External versus Internal Consultants: A Real Issue?

We cannot assume that the only people in the world who can engage in organizational inquiry are external consultants or academics. External consultants and academics have an advantage: they are perceived as having a particular competence, as being credible experts, able to transcend a lot (but not all) of the organizational politics, and as being impartial and free from bias. They also have the advantage, therefore, of having an easier time being heard by management.

However, not every organization can afford consultants, nor has every organization easy access to academic researchers. Being able to cross a financial threshold should not determine whether or not an organization begins its intranet development with an inquiry phase or even whether intranet development involves employees in design, development, and deployment.

Internal Consultants

Many times, "internal consultants" are already on the payroll. In large organizations, people within the company serve as "internal consultants" providing services to the rest of the organization. Julian Orr, for example, works as an internal consultant at Xerox, using his skills and training as an ethnographer to help the company understand how its own employees work. While a member of the research staff in the Work Practice and Technology Area of the Systems and Practices Laboratory at Xerox's Palo Alto Research Center, Orr studied the work of Xerox field service technicians who repair copiers. Not only did Orr help Xerox to better understand its employees' work, his boss, John Seeley Brown, relied on Orr's findings in several essays written for *Fast Company* and other publications. Julian Orr also wrote up his research findings in his own instructive, insightful book, _Talking About Machines: An Ethnography of a Modern Job_.

The Work-Systems Design group at NYNEX is composed of managers and employees from various parts of the business, anthropologists, expert system designers, even filmmakers. "Together," writes Art Kleiner, "they're trying to understand, as ethnographers would, the organizational culture that drives the flow of work, including the attitudes, situations, and frustrations that go unspoken in the average workday."[3] Their leader, Patricia Sachs, has published some of their findings in publications such as *Communications of the ACM*. Sachs' excellent article, "Transforming Work: Collaboration, Learning and Design," discusses how her group came to appreciate the need to take "the human system" into account in redesigning business.[4]

Deone Zell's book, *Changing by Design: Organizational Innovation at Hewlett-Packard,* provides a fascinating account of Hewlett-Packard's socio-technical systems (STS) redesign, involving front-line employees in analysis and redesign of the entire organization and in explicit examination of an organization's culture. The goal of STS is to integrate the social requirements of people doing the work with the technical requirements needed to keep the work systems productive and alive with regard to their environments. STS is not new, however. It was developed by Eric Trist over 50 years ago when he observed how miners had "rediscovered" a successful, small-group approach that had been used before the advent of mechanization. Trist introduced his ideas to the British Psychological Society in 1950 in a paper entitled "The Relations of Social and Technical Systems in Coal-Mining." Today, research on the adaptation and further development of STS concepts and practices is being pursued by various organizations and research centers. Among the organizations in North America are Alcan, the American Productivity Center in Houston, AT&T, Best Foods, Clark Equipment, Cummins Engine, Digital Equipment Company, Exxon, and Ford.[5]

Smaller organizations have a tougher time developing an official position of "internal consultant" because their budgets don't permit many staffed services positions. Because they don't have internal resources for a separate staffed position, small organizations often have an even greater need for temporary consulting assistance.

Whether the people engaging with employees in inquiry and dialog are external consultants or members of the organization is the least of our worries, as long as the person or groups doing this type of work possess two things.

Two Main Requirements for Consulting: Legitimacy and Ethics

The first requirement is legitimacy. Legitimacy is important because without it, the findings from the field, no matter how good, are too easily dismissed by management as irrelevant. If you, the intranet developer, don't have it, develop it. External consultants and academics actually work very hard to establish their legitimacy and credibility. It's not bestowed by the Fates. Chapter 15 provides some more suggestions about how to gain legitimacy within the organization if you do this work as an internal employee.

The second requirement is ethics. Although consulting is a growth industry, there are no qualifying exams or required courses for consultants. Among the ranks are former business people who decided to be self-employed. Apart from MBA graduates hired by the major consulting firms, few people train to be consultants. As one consequence, consultants engage with employees without sitting down and thinking about what sort of ethical code should guide their interactions. That, unfortunately, leads to abuses large and small that damage the workplace environment even further.

There is no better time than now to emphasize the importance of ethics when engaging with employees. One reason is that external consultants who swept through many organizations in the 1980s and 90s left buried mines.

Buried Land Mines in the Organizational Environment

If you are a business, it may not seem contradictory to spend thousands of dollars on external consulting fees *and* to look to your own employees for ideas and solutions. Intelligence, after all, can be found in many places—often in unexpected places. In the current economic model of consulting, however, it is against consultants' best interests to promote and spotlight the intelligence offered by employees. Consultants have become expert at tapping that intelligence, especially while engaged in their "research" or "discovery" phase. Yet they tend not to credit employees for their participation or contributions. To do so would appear to some as contrary to their sales and marketing efforts, which position consultants as having better solutions than *anyone else*.

The worst offenders have been the reengineering consultants who were brought in to extinguish old business practices and procedures and rebuild the organization's work flow around new capabilities of advanced computer systems. This description of the process, written by Art Kleiner in 1995,[6] will hit home for many people:

> A typical Hammer-style reengineering project will bring in 15 to 20 young experts from high-priced consulting firms, like the Boston Consulting Group or Andersen Consulting, to redesign the workflow "with a blank sheet of paper," as Hammer puts it. They descend on a company, draw up maps of process flows, propose discarding old billing and accounting procedures, suggest that people from finance and engineering work together on one team (reducing the head count by a third), and insist that everyone communicate by Lotus Notes instead of memo. Often they build computer simulations of corporate workflows to see how work speeds up when they snip a particular bureaucratic task or unnecessary form.

We have never before witnessed a more complete version of "the scientific attitude" or instrumental rationality." Michael Hammer, a former computer science professor at MIT, developed his idea of reengineering as an extension of technology management consulting. The reengineering wave that hit corporate America in the early 1990s was one great big "organizational hack," as Kleiner puts it. "The algorithm for programming real life. . . the bits are the people."

Fernando Flores, in an address to the Association for Computing Machinery, stated:[7]

> Working with banks, engineering companies, manufacturing companies, everyone has the same problem: how do we organize, coordinate, and use this new technology? My opinion is that the explosion of business reengineering happened in the hope of an answer. But they got it wrong: they began to reengineer the flows of paper, and failed to see that the central issue is people.

Employee Attitudes About Consultants and the Implications for Inquiry

For most employees actually doing the work, the "reengineering" experience was disruptive, both in the professional sphere and in the personal sphere. As a consequence, today many employees have become skeptical and cynical about the presence of consultants in the workplace. Just as companies like IBM and Microsoft attempted to forestall moves by competitors with their misleading information, it is not unusual for employees to strategically manage their communication with consultants to forestall change, even to the extent of attempting to sabotage the consultants' efforts. The street runs both ways.

Many employees have felt used and abused over the years by consultants. Employees have disclosed their problems and frustrations, only to feel abandoned. They have provided an insight into organizational problems and have offered compelling, practical solutions, only to receive no name recognition or public thanks. They have suffered silently while consultants were paid to tell the employees things they already knew. These are all symptoms of "the scientific attitude" and the kind of "instrumental rationality" discussed earlier. They are also symptoms of the economics of consulting, and collusion with management, and these activities are contributing factors to "groupthink."

Employees who serve as internal consultants may or may not be as instrumental as external consultants. Sometimes they do not have the luxury of being able to use their informants as means to an end and then vanish from sight. Internal consultants remain part of the same organization that their own actions affected and may experience direct or indirect consequences of their words and deeds.

Being an internal consultant can be a more difficult role, however. An external consultant's "for-hire" status helps external consultants avoid role confusion. The external consultant is a professional hired by a person of authority in the organization to carry out a specific task. The internal consultant, on the other hand, may have preexisting or potential relationships with employees or management and may feel torn between "serving two masters." The crossover may prove to be a disadvantage within the particular politics of an organization.

■ A Transfer of Best Practices from the Field of Anthropology

To guide us through this thorny ethical terrain, we can take a lesson from a group that knows a lot about how to tap people's knowledge without exploiting them: the anthropologists.

In 1971, the Council of the American Anthropological Association (AAA) adopted a set of principles to guide researchers when faced with conflicting values and choices. These ethical principles are very helpful to anyone engaging with employees in dialog.

At first glance, intranet developers and professional anthropologists may seem like creatures from two distant planets. One group is driven by business realities and "the bottom line," the other by an entirely different set of professional pressures, such as publishing in academic journals or becoming known within the field for contributing to a particular knowledge domain. Yet anthropologists have two things in common with people doing inquiry in organizations.

First, both groups are interested primarily in *how people work and live.*

Second, both face *uniquely varied and complex situations.* Anthropologists are involved with their discipline, their colleagues in their research institutions and throughout the world, their students, their sponsors, their own and their host governments, the particular individuals and groups with whom they do their field work, *and* other interest groups in the nations in which they work.

Anthropologists are also very *aware of the link between power and knowledge.* In 1995, the <u>Commission to Review the AAA Statements on Ethics</u> wrote, "For the most part, study in isolated sites and of isolated people are opportunities of the past. Information causes change and creates power. The people studied often want to study themselves, protect their histories, plan their own futures, use the information and results of anthropological studies." Precisely because of information flow, this group of professionals has rightly perceived the need for ever greater accountability to the people they study.

The <u>Principles of Professional Responsibility</u> were approved in 1971 and still stand today—almost three decades later—as AAA's ethical code. The code's preamble warns researchers that it is *their responsibility* to anticipate complex involvements, misunderstandings, and conflicts, and to plan to resolve them in such a way as to do damage neither to those whom they study nor, insofar as possible, to their professional community.

To help researchers chart an ethical course, the AAA laid out a group of ethical principles which, with some slight modification, are very useful for intranet developers who plan to engage with employees in dialog about their work.

Consider informants first.

> In research, an anthropologist's paramount responsibility is to those he or she studies. When there is a conflict of interest, these individuals must come first. The anthropologist must do everything within his or her power to protect their physical, social and psychological welfare and to honor their dignity and privacy.
>
> **Principles of Professional Responsibility, 1971**

Management may provide funds for the work, gatekeepers like supervisors may have the power to give or withhold permission to conduct interviews or focus groups, data analysts may be involved with providing quantitative analyses of productivity, peers may be anxious about anyone within their groups betraying a confidence. Organizations are like complex societies in which employees' lives are frequently intertwined with other people.

Employees' interests are not always the same as those of other people in different positions of power, authority, or prestige. During dialog with employees, one often learns things of which management is unaware. Conversely, during dialog with management, one often learns things of which employees are unaware. When choices about disclosure are made, they should be made with care as to whose interests may be damaged and whose protected. The rule of thumb is that the welfare of the source of information comes first.

Safeguard employees' rights, interests and sensitivities.

> Where research involves the acquisition of material and information transferred on the assumption of trust between persons, it is axiomatic that the rights, interests, and sensitivities of those studied must be safeguarded.
>
> **Principles of Professional Responsibility, 1971**

This principle suggests that when engaging with employees, we must go beyond merely considering the interests of informants. We have to *safeguard* their rights, their interests, and even their sensitivities. No matter how short or how unobtrusive, field-based inquiry always pries into the lives of informants. Employee engagement and dialog represents a powerful tool for intruding on other people's privacy.

In a tense business climate, the smallest piece of information can be turned the wrong way. This principle reminds us that information can be used to affirm people's rights, interests, and sensitivities, or to violate them. Because our work lives and personal lives are so closely intertwined these days, we occasionally say things "off the record," assuming confidentiality. Everyone deserves to have their personal privacy safeguarded from disclosure. To betray a confidence is to reveal one's own insecurities about one's own organizational power and authority. To safeguard a confidence is to stand for community and communication, rather than self-interest.

Communicate research objectives.

> *The aims of the investigation should be communicated as well as possible to the informant.*
>
> **Principles of Professional Responsibility, 1971**

Employees have a right to know why we are looking into the ways in which they work, communicate, and share information. Managers and supervisors have a right to know why the project is going forward, who is sponsoring the work, and what the objectives are.

Communicating the purpose of the inquiry is rarely a one-shot declaration of intent. As Spradley notes, it's more a "process of unfolding" as the process of inquiry continues on. Often, knowing more about other people's own interests will help one explain the purpose of the inquiry.

Because intranets and the concept of computer-based communication are still very new in most organizations, people ask a lot of questions like, Why are you asking us these questions about how we work? and, Why are you interested in how we learn or how we communicate? or, What is this web site project supposed to do? The questions come up again and again.

Not everyone is at the same point in the learning curve; you may have to explain the purpose of the work a number of times before it sticks. Rarely is the intent behind people's questions to challenge your authority. People just want to know, and the common language is not quite there yet. Be patient. Everyone has a right to ask and to get a straight answer. We are all learning. One benefit of explanation is that people's reactions to our words helps us to get clearer about the central purpose of the work.

Protect the privacy of informants.

> *Informants have a right to remain anonymous. This right should be respected both where it has been promised explicitly and where no clear understanding to the contrary has been reached.*
>
> Principles of Professional Responsibility, 1971

Inquiry into the nature of work and communication can involve sensitive information about relationships among supervisors and employees, about performance measures, and so on. If informants have not explicitly volunteered that they would like comments attributed to them, their anonymity must be protected.

Informants' identities typically are not disclosed deliberately, with malice or ill will. They get disclosed "innocently" through conversation. Revealing informants' identities compromises the integrity of the inquiry. Such disclosure also permits people to turn the focus away from the situation toward the personalities. The only people who should make the choice to disclose the source of any information should be the informants themselves.

Don't exploit the situation for personal gain.

> *There is an obligation to reflect on the foreseeable repercussions of research and publication on the general population being studied.*
>
> Principles of Professional Responsibility, 1971

Leave a place better than you found it, not worse. The act of inquiry itself affects what people in the workplace talk about and what they believe will happen to improve their situations. It is unwise to build up hopes that may be dashed; don't make promises about the future outcome of the work, no matter how probable it may seem to you.

Some workplaces should be circumvented because they are already too toxic. If a workplace situation is already too tense, too filled with emotion, or undergoing too many changes at once, engagement with employees about communication and information issues during such turmoil may make the situation worse. If management is already feeling attacked and under pressure, don't add gas to the bonfire because the bad energy will flow toward subordinates. Crisis is not an opportunity to expose the inner working of the workplace. As Fernando Flores reminds us, "We can get so addicted to novelty and quick response that we forget that people need also a certain stability, a certain form of well-being." Be patient and wait until emotions are not so high.

Make reports available to informants.

> *Fair return should be given them for all services. . . . In accordance with the Association's general position on clandestine and secret research, no reports should be provided to sponsors that are not also available to the general public and, where practicable, to the population studied.*

Principles of Professional Responsibility, 1971

"Fair exchange" for the informants' time and contributions in the organizational context has typically meant a breakfast or lunch during a long working session. Feeding the body is not enough these days. If long-term employee participation and continuous use are the goals of intranet development, we have to feed the mind. Anyone who participates in discussions regarding intranet development should be given easy and free access to copies of "white papers" or final reports that result from the discussions. Such materials can be published on a web site. If participants have an interest in reading the report, they can do so at their convenience.

There is no particular "truth" to be known, but knowing that the participants or informants may read the report will certainly influence the way in which it is written. Open access is a safeguard on the "truth."

■ Generating "Moral Intelligence"

Today, in this computer age, ethics are somewhat like pens or pieces of paper. Often we really don't miss not having them until we realize that we really need them. The need often has to be experienced somewhat before the concept of ethics is appreciated. Yet, ethics are not things that can be dictated or declared. Even Mary Warnock, the esteemed Cambridge philosopher, wrote, "I have not, I hope [in writing this book], had any preconceived idea of what ethics *is*."[8] Ethics are our modalities of conversation not only with other people but also with ourselves. Just as one learns to use a pen and a piece of paper to construct meaning, one learns to employ ethics to construct meaningful ways of working with other people in organizations, helping to find opportunities to improve the organization.

To do intranet development successfully, we often just stumble on to situations in which we find ourselves collecting a lot of information about an organization in order to improve it. As much as we want to guide our actions by thoughts like, "Do unto others as you would have them do unto you" in many organizations, counter forces are pushing *hard* against that idea. Unless we make a point to ask questions like, What is "good" consulting? or, What is the "good" use of data? or, What is "good" partnership with employees in intranet development? such questions tend not to get asked or answered.

The AAA's *Handbook on Ethics* warns its members: Know who you are and what you represent before going into the field and intruding on a natural setting. The wise, experienced anthropologists make that warning as our ethical style is the most difficult thing for us to see because it is closest to us. However, it is more essential today, in this age of hypercompetition and information overload. Fernando Flores puts it this way:[7]

> Committing ourselves to a "path of care" means finding some concern that you are going to serve, that means something to other people. That is what gives us focus, captures and guides our attention. Without that, we feel scattered, too many equally important things to deal with. That's when people talk about information overload. I believe information overload is a consequence of lack of clarity about who we are. To get this focus, we need certain social skills. What is the first thing we need to do to develop a strong identity? A strong identity needs to be developed with others.

Ethics might be the wrong word, then. Intranet developers require "moral intelligence." Moral intelligence means how we behave. It's moral behavior tested by life, lived out in the course of our everyday experience. Often, it is learned through example and through storytelling. The protocol in the Tool Kit at the end of this book illustrates how some moral intelligence can be hard-coded into our engagement with employees.

This chapter has provided some guidelines for organizing the very first phases within the inquiry stage. We've looked at setting objectives and creating ethical protocols. We've talked about "participant action research" (PAR) as a method to engage with employees in dialog. Having set the stage, the next chapter offers several scripts for going forward. We'll look at a variety of methods from focus groups to something called *The VisionMapping Exercise.*

■ References

[1] Chris Argyris and Donald A. Schon, *Organizational Learning II: Theory, Method and Practice* (Addison-Wesley Publishing, 1996), p. 36.

[2] James P. Spradley, *The Ethnographic Interview* (Holt, Rinehart and Winston, Inc., 1979), p. 34.

[3] Art Kleiner, "The Battle for the Soul of Corporate America," *Wired*, August, 1995, p. 170.

[4] Patricia Sachs, "The Transforming Work: Collaboration, Learning and Design," *Communications of the ACM*, September, 1995, Vol. 38, No. 9, pp. 36–45.

[5] William Fox, "Sociotechnical Systems Principles and Guidelines: Past and Present," Vol. 31, *Journal of Applied Behavioral Science*, March 1, 1995, p. 91.

[6] Art Kleiner, "The Battle for the Soul of Corporate America," *Wired*, August, 1995, p. 125.

[7] Fernando Flores, "The Impact of Information Technology on Business," Address to the 50th Anniversary Conference of the Association for Computing Machinery, San Jose, CA, March, 1997.

[8] Mary Warnock, *Ethics Since 1900* (NY: Oxford University Press), 1978, preface.

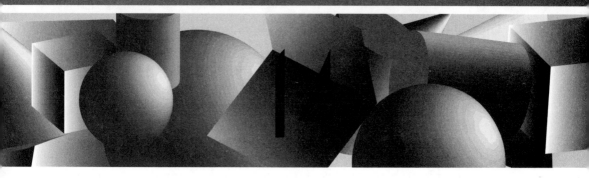

Methods of Engagement

Inquiry is the bedrock of intranet development. Well-planned, well-designed inquiry will result in valuable data that can be used in a number of different ways: in the business plan, in white papers, in site design and content development, etc. The last chapter discussed the first two phases in the process of inquiry: setting objectives and creating the protocol. This chapter now looks at five different methods for dialog with employees. We'll outline who needs to be involved, materials and resources required, and critical success factors for each method. We'll also talk about why combining qualitative research such as focus groups and quantitative research such as surveys can provide a double punch.

Sometimes intranet developers wish to engage with employees in dialog but back away because they don't know how to get going or where to begin. This chapter is designed to be very practical and straightforward so that the methods of inquiry can be easily integrated into an intranet or web site project plan.

■ The Value of Qualitative Research

This chapter discuss various interpretive methods then presents a sixth method—surveying. The five interpretive methods are: In-Basket Studies, Focus Groups, VisionMapping Exercises, On-Site Observations, and Interviews.

These five methods share similar characteristics. They emphasize the *subjectivity* of organizational realities and downplay their objectivity. Things like hierarchies, technologies, or the impact of training programs on behavior are not the focus. Rather, the focus is on *how employees interpret* these things. The approaches here in this chapter emphasize the *meaning* of organizational phenomena to employees.

The methods help us to appreciate the dynamics of organizational realities and deemphasize their stability. Morgan and Smircich[1] said, over a decade ago, with their call for qualitative research in organizations: "Order in the social world, however real in surface appearance, rests on precarious, socially constructed webs of symbolic relationships that are continually negotiated, renegotiated, affirmed, or changed." In other words, these methods invite us to appreciate how *organizational activities are constantly in flux* because people engage in actions that constantly shape and reshape their view of the organization.

Third, we are offered an opportunity to understand a particular organizational context. The unique dimensions of a situation come to light through inquiry. No generalizable global laws govern organizational behavior throughout the company. Organizations are collections of different individuals, groups, and constituencies who have different and often competing interests. These methods give us a way to emphasize the pluralism of organizational realities—to understand that organizations have as many organizational "realities" as individuals.

Last, these methods permit us to take advantage of something that comes to us almost as a gift. That is the fact that most people enjoy genuine human communication. People really like to talk about things that matter to them and, if we ask the right questions, people will always tell us more than we ever expected to learn.

The sixth method, surveys, can be used to complement the other methods. Taken alone, surveys are necessary but not sufficient. They are necessary in that the survey results provide "hard" statistical data that can be crunched and analyzed. They are good complements to qualitative methods. However, for our purposes they are not sufficient alone because they are useless in uncovering valid disagreement and/or agreement about meanings. A survey, for example, would never have uncovered some of the findings from our case studies in the last chapter: why a community-generated FAQ would prove to be so valuable to field technicians and supervisors, why a background "story" was an essential element in the corporate site developed by WisdomLink, or why sales people would decide *in advance* not to use a competitive intelligence web site if the company did not provide additional IT support.

■ In-Basket Studies

The purpose of an in-basket study is to (a) distinguish between information and noninformation, and to (b) identify areas for improvement in organizational communication. Participatory action researchers (PARS) shadow employees, recording all communication media used, purposes of the use, frequency of use, and value. Afterward, the PARS notes are summarized with taxonomies or flowcharts.

The In-Basket Study

Who is involved?	1. Management that gives permission for its employees' communication activities to be studied. 2. Employees who volunteer to participate in the study. 3. The PARS.
Materials and resources?	• A memo to the employees explaining the purpose of the study. • Preprinted forms so that the PARS can record their data. • A notebook to collect the PARS notes. • A place where the PARS can discuss their findings.
Critical success factors?	1. Communicating the purposes of the study. 2. Being humble, not acting like a threat to management or to employees. 3. Being unobtrusive. 4. Preparing good questions in advance. 5. Allowing enough time to observe employees engaged in a variety of activities. 6. Capturing information quickly.

■ Focus Groups

Focus groups are a form of group interviewing. They're frequently used as a research strategy to understand audience/consumer attitudes and behavior. From four to eight people are interviewed simultaneously with a moderator or facilitator leading the participants in a fairly free discussion about the topic at hand. Before the focus group is convened, the moderator creates a list of broad questions relating to the topic. During the course of the focus group, listening to the participants, the moderator can ask more probing questions or can follow up on particular comments to elicit more detailed responses.

With a topic like intranets and communication technologies, which are somewhat unfamiliar territories, you can design the focus group to begin with a written questionnaire. The prediscussion questionnaire basically covers the material that will be discussed during the group session. It serves as a way to stimulate people's thinking on the topic. Some participants may assume that they don't know anything about communication technologies or intranets and therefore are not "qualified" to speak among the group. By writing something on paper, people are less likely to disqualify themselves. Examples of questionnaires that can be used in the context of focus groups are provided in the Tool Kit at the end of the book.

Focus Groups

Who is involved?	1. Management that gives permission for its employees to participate in focus groups. 2. Employees who volunteer to participate in the focus groups. 3. The PARS who facilitate the focus group discussion.
Materials and resources?	• Focus group protocol and facilitators. • Agenda to distribute to the participants that states the purpose of the discussion and outlines how the time will be spent. • A notebook to collect the PARS notes. • A place where the PARS can discuss their findings.
Critical success factors?	1. Communicating the purposes of the study. 2. Being humble, not acting like a threat to management or to employees. 3. Being unobtrusive. 4. Preparing good questions in advance. 5. Allowing enough time to observe employees engaged in a variety of activities. 6. Capturing information quickly.

■ The VisionMapping Exercise

Often, when we are trying to implement something new in an organization, verbal speech alone is not sufficient. In our efforts to describe problems and to create innovative solutions, we get stuck in old terms, models, and metaphors that slow us down and become sources of frustration. Part of the problem is with the limits of language itself.

The VisionMapping Exercise (VME) is a technique to represent ideas, thoughts, observations and activities in a visual form. The exercise requires only "soft" media, things like construction paper, markers, tape, scissors, glue, and magazines. The process is very much like the one used in the film industry, where story conferences are held to discuss an idea for a new film. The process, like the story itself, is dynamic and organic. When the story takes a living shape, it becomes vivid and memorable. Much like producers, we come to the exercise with some pre-formed ideas. However, during the exercise, as we give visual representation to our ideas, more detail, depth, and color comes to life. The VME helps us:

- to become clear about why change needs to occur (whether the introduction of a new technology or a new management model);

- to identify and capture end users' needs; and

- to find new words, new terms, new models, and new metaphors to be used in the road map for going forward.

Theoretical Background

The VME is based on three central tenets drawn from research in the field of communication.

1. *Every medium of communication has its own language, its own "code."* Each communication medium represents "reality" in somewhat different ways. Verbal and written speech are only two of the many ways we can represent our thoughts, ideas, and observations.

2. *Visual elements of communication are as powerful, if not more powerful, as speech.* Combinations of speech and visual images enable people to communicate more content and more emotion than does speech alone.

3. *People are active participants in mediated communication events.* People bring themselves to the communication experience. They bring their ideas, opinions, preconceptions, and expectations. They bring a background of knowledge and sources of energy. People do not passively "consume" communication or media; they actively engage with media and other participants in the communication event.

Procedure

The exercise has five parts:

1. Open discussion of the current situation.
2. Presentation or review of a set of questions developed to guide the exercise.
3. Creation of individual "maps" or "story boards."
4. Presentation of each participant's creation.
5. Discussion of the data (looking for patterns, themes, and insights).

There are two VisionMapping protocols included in the Tool Kit in Chapter 19. In addition, the Communications Questionnaire also included in the Tool Kit can be used as a protocol for the exercise.

This exercise is very valuable because it helps people get right to the questions: How do people in this group or this organization think about the role of information and communication as related to their day-to-day jobs? Where do frustrations with broken communication lie? Where are the greatest opportunities for improvement? The exercise is a storytelling method that helps us to get at what is buried, what is often not discussable.

The VME has been proven very effective in a variety of corporate situations. The method has been used:

- To develop the rationale and design for a Total Quality Community's web site.

- To identify breakdowns in communication patterns and practices among technicians and engineers, and to map an improved communication flow.

- To help an interdisciplinary team create a communications strategy for the roll-out of a corporate-wide educational initiative.

- To determine what sales people will need on a competitive intelligence web site and how the site should be designed.
- To identify critical success factors in transitioning from classroom-based training to desktop training at a Fortune 500 company.

One of the best reasons to use the VME in intranet development is that it brings out metaphors and meanings that are especially powerful to a particular group.

For example, in one VME designed to identify critical success factors in transitioning from classroom-based training to desktop training, the participants were asked to visually represent how learning takes place within the organization. They were asked to think about questions such as, What are the various learning opportunities inside the company? Where does the best learning take place? With whom? What are the outcomes? How can learning be improved? Three members of the training department decided to collaborate on their VisionMaps instead of creating individual maps. Together, they drew a "House of Learning" with several different levels and rooms. Their metaphor "House of Learning" resonated so strongly within the group that the participants adapted the term to help them shape the transitional plan. They began to say things like, "If we want this change to occur, we'll need a strong foundation. What should the foundation look like?"

The power of this particular image may have been related to the fact that people in this company were extremely proud of their campuslike setting. Part of the corporate lore was how senior management chose to invest in the creation of an attractive, comfortable, healthy physical environment . The metaphor, "House of Learning," communicated a set of unspoken values and principles that distinguished this particular company—i.e., values such as the benefits of good planning and using quality materials.

Visual metaphors carry a tremendous amount of meaning and symbolism. To understand a group or organization's metaphors is to understand emotions and ideas that guide choices and behaviors.

Visual Storytelling

Increasingly, visual storytelling methods, such as the VME, are being used to gather valuable information from external consumers. Gerald Zaltman, a

Harvard Business School professor, uses a similar but different method to help companies identify the need to develop new products or to change their marketing strategies. He asks a representative group of consumers to cut pictures from magazines and create a collage that somehow conveys their experiences with certain products. Then the consumers meet with Zaltman in his lab to tell stories about the images they selected and the connections between them. Du Pont used this method to help the marketing group understand women's emotions about panty hose, which resulted in a significant change in marketing strategy.[2]

PsiPhi Communications in Colorado, founded by Todd Siler,[3] has patented its method of visual storytelling, "Think Like a Genius" (formerly called the *ArtScience method*). Siler, author of several books, including *Metaphorming Worlds, Metaphorming Minds, Breaking the Mind Barrier,* and *Think Like A Genius,* has been exploring the power of metaphors to transform our thinking for over a decade. In *Think Like a Genius*, Dr. Siler writes that one can achieve breakthrough thinking by using a process he calls *metaphorming*.

> The term *metaphorming* is derived from the Greek words *meta* (transcending) and *phora* (transference). It refers to the act of changing something from one state of matter and meaning to another. It begins with transferring new meanings and associations from one object or idea to another. . . . Think of [metaphorming] as a word with real purpose and usefulness. It may be a word you'll use for the rest of your life, once you understand how essential it is to everything you do. Actually, it's a process that is as much a part of you as your organs are. It's something you know intuitively without being aware.

The Silers have used their method with a wide variety of groups—in schools, corporations, with street gang members and police, and civic organizations. They have helped people to become clearer about their interdependencies and have enabled people who were once strangers to each other to chart a collective course toward the future.

Critical Success Factors

The keys to making a VisionMapping session successful is good facilitation and a clear sense of direction. A good facilitator will listen carefully to the participants' stories, ask questions, draw out details, and make connections from one story to the next. If the facilitator takes a genuine interest in the stories people are telling and provides positive, encouraging feedback, the participants will unleash their creativity and courage.

The facilitator also needs to help the group to use the data they've provided in order to answer the "What now?" question. "We've told our stories, we've identified recurrent themes and problems . . . what now?" VisionMapping Exercises that end with a clear sense of purpose and direction leave participants feeling energized and responsible. So, for example, if you use a VME to help a group of people identify an area for organizational improvement and to create a rationale for intranet or web site development, the session should end with a list of action items or an agreed-upon road map.

The VisionMaps usually turn out to be surprisingly colorful, vivid, and visually compelling. Because they are the size of poster board, they are difficult to save and store. One idea is to capture the images with a digital camera and post the VisionMaps on a web site. For one group, this turned out to be extremely valuable several months later when they needed to recapture some of the spirit that had dissipated over time. By being able to refer to their VisionMaps and to the transcripts of their stories, the group was able to share their experience with other people in the company and were able to create a kind of living memory of the event.

VisionMapping Exercise

Who is involved?	1. Anyone who potentially would be involved in any kind of change initiative such as intranet development. 2. The PARS.
Materials and resources?	• A memo to the employees explaining the purpose of the VME distributed in advance of the workshop. • "Vision Boxes" containing soft media (pens, markers, crayons, construction paper, glue, scissors, tape, business magazines like *Fortune, Forbes, Working Woman, Inc., Money, Fast Company.*) • One white poster board for each participant. • A flip chart to capture some key themes and ideas. • A sign-in sheet where participants can provide contact information for follow-up. • Tables with large enough working surfaces. • One person to facilitate the exercise and discussion. A second person to transcribe the stories and deal with any logistics issues.
Critical success factors?	1. A clear sense of the kinds of information you intend to uncover. 2. Encouragement of the participants to let go of their fears of not being good artists. 3. Sufficient time for the creation of the VisionMaps. (20 minutes minimum if using markers and paper. 40 minutes minimum if magazines are included in the VisionBoxes.) 4. Sufficient time for each participant to tell his or her story and for the facilitator to summarize recurrent themes and issues. 5. Conclusion of the exercise with an action plan or road map.

■ Advantages and Disadvantages of Qualitative Methods

So far in this chapter, we've looked at various qualitative methods of inquiry. Each one, in its own way, allows the participant-action researcher to "get close to the data." Qualitative methods have certain advantages. They permit us to view employees' activities in natural settings without the artificiality that sometimes surrounds survey research. They enable us to increase our depth of understanding about the workplace, how people communicate, and what people's needs are. Finally, they are flexible. We can pursue new lines of dialog with participants as those lines emerge through interaction. A questionnaire or survey is unlikely to provide information about questions that were not asked, but a person conducting a focus group or VME might discover things that were not even considered before the interaction began.

There are a few disadvantages, however. One is that qualitative methods tend to be time- and labor-intensive. Not everyone can take time from tasks to participate. Second, critics may question the reliability of the data. How representative are the thoughts and feelings expressed by the participants? Are the stories merely anecdotal evidence? How valid are deductive claims drawn from the stories? To open participation to more people and to collect "hard" data that can be put to a statistical analysis, it's a good idea to use quantitative methods, such as surveys, to round out the inquiry.

■ Quantitative Methods: Surveys

Basically, survey research is concerned with how often a variable is present. Numbers are used to communicate the amounts. One advantage is that numbers allow greater precision in reporting data. Another advantage is that the same survey can be administered over the course of weeks or months and used to detect changes that may occur through time. Three surveys are included in the Tool Kit in Chapter 19. We'll describe them briefly here.

Work Environment Profile

This questionnaire was developed by Peggy Holman and Kim Bishop in 1994 as a way to access a work environment. It incorporates a number of environmental factors, including:

> Autonomy/Personal Responsibility
> Respect
> Communication
> Organizational Direction
> Team Cohesion
> Team Support
> Innovation/Risk
> Conflict Management
> Personal Growth
> Individual Contribution

Holman and Bishop designed the survey so that individual items within each scale may be distinguished based on the perceptions of the work environment at the individual, team, or organizational levels. Intranet developers can use this questionnaire

- to get a baseline reading of the organizational environment,
- to identify specific areas in need of improvement that may affect employees' use of new communication technologies; and
- if administered periodically, as a means to gauge the impact of an intranet over time, specifically in the area of communication, but in other areas as well.

Communication Questionnaire

This is another effective way to collect quantitative data about opportunities to improve communication within the organization. Like the other questionnaires in the Tool Kit, it can be used first to benchmark employees' current satisfaction with communication in the organization, then as data to prioritize intranet applications, and as a follow-up study to access change.

Communication and Knowledge-Sharing Survey

The purpose of this questionnaire is to gather information about opportunities to improve communication within the organization. It can be reformatted, printed, and distributed for employees to fill out. The survey can also be used to lead a focus group.

■ iVALS: Measuring Experiences with and Attitudes Toward the Net

Would you like to find out where you, your colleagues, or management fit in regard to internet values and attitudes? SRI International created a survey, available on their web site, that enables people to understand themselves relative to other internet users. iVALS segments the population according to internet values, attitudes, and life styles. The iVALS segments include the following categories: Immigrant, Seeker, Surfer, Mainstreamer, Sociable, Worker, Pioneer, Upstreamer, Socialite, and Wizard. iVALS suggests that people within these different categories use the Net for very different purposes and that they perceive its value in vastly different ways. IVALS also helps us to understand how people's experiences in real life influence their perceptions of the on-line world.

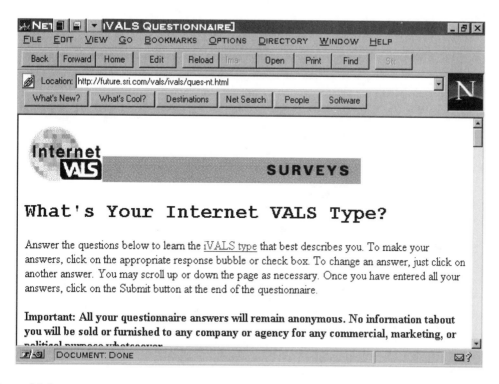

FIGURE 14.1

http://future.sri.com/vals/ivals/ques-nt.html. Copyright SRI International. Used by permission.

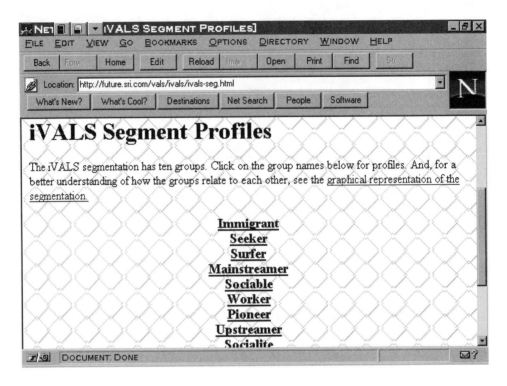

FIGURE 14.2
http://future.sri.com/vals/ivals/ivals-seg.html. Copyright SRI International. Used by permission.

■ Required Core Competencies and Skill Sets

The intranet development road map begins with inquiry. What we learn during the inquiry phase helps us to avoid making bad assumptions about why people in the company would want new technologies or why they would use it consistently over time. The inquiry phase also sends a powerful message to people who will eventually use the new technology. The message is that the intranet is being designed specifically with real business issues and real communication needs at the forefront.

The kinds of skills and competencies required to do this sort of work generally are not found among groups of people who have chosen to work primarily with computer hardware or computer code for a career. To engage with people in dialog requires a desire to communicate with people and an enjoyment and affinity for listening to their points of view. Some programmers and web developers do enjoy those activities. However, many have chosen to work with inanimate objects precisely because they would rather not have to listen to others. So this sort of work shouldn't be pushed off on people who don't enjoy it simply because they have the title "Intranet Developer."

This points to an important requirement of intranet development for the 21st century: the need to create of networks of people who share an enthusiasm for intranet technologies but who bring different skill sets, competencies, and perspectives to the table. In the next section, Section Five, we look at several different techniques for forming networks of intranet developers who can help and support each other. Chapters 15 and 16 discuss network development. Chapter 17 turns to a discussion of leadership buy-in and support, which are other essential aspects of intranet development. Taken together, the next three chapters will help intranet champions create a stable, long-lasting foundation for success.

■ References

[1] G. Morgan and L. Smircich (1980), "The Case for Qualitative Research," *Academy of Management Review*, 1980, No. 5, pp. 491–500.

[2] Ronald B. Lieber, "Storytelling: A New Way to Get Close to Your Customer," *Fortune*, February 3, 1997, p. 102.

[3] Todd Siler, *Think Like a Genius* (Englewood, CO: ArtScience Publications, 1996), p. 7.

15

CHAPTER

The Power of the Network

Developing and implementing an intranet brings a unique set of challenges. There are a host of technology issues on one side, and a host of "people issues" on the other. It would be impossible for any one group within an organization to assume the entire responsibility for achieving the Value Triad and for managing the intranet over the long run. It takes a community.

This chapter discusses the benefits of creating a network of intranet champions—both technical and nontechnical professionals—who can combine resources and talent to accelerate intranet development within the organization. The chapter includes the book's final case study: the creation of a web developers' coalition at a Fortune 500 company. The case study illuminates how the need for a network emerged through trial and error, how it took shape, and how it influenced the actions of information technology (IT) executives within the company. By exploring this case study, we'll develop some key learnings that can help people avoid typical internal intranet politics and turf battles.

First, let's review five myths of intranet development. They summarize many of the key learnings outlined in the previous 14 chapters.

■ A Review of the Five Myths of Intranet Development

The five myths of intranet development are:

■ Intranets are easy and cheap: resources don't matter

■ Hard work and ingenuity will result in eventual reward

■ The battle over site and page design standards isn't important

■ Developing content is a no-brainer

■ It's obvious why your organization needs an intranet

Intranets Are Easy and Cheap: Resources Don't Matter

There is a great deal of press about how easy and cheap intranets are to create. Carried along by this myth, a few people in the organization will spend some portion of their time working on internal web sites and use whatever development tools they can easily obtain. They produce some short-term gains and are, for the short-term, delighted about their ability to do so much with so little.

Intranets that are relatively simple platforms for publishing information face low performance, security, consistency, and manageability requirements. However, as people begin to use intranets for collaborative applications such as electronic mail, discussion groups, work flow, and document management, there is a higher risk and longer development time frames.

To stay in for the long term, you need labor resources and capital resources. Both are required if you wish to (a) produce content, (b) support users, and (c) maintain site as it evolves. Intranets are "easy and cheap" relative only to fat technologies.

Hard Work + Ingenuity + Technology = Reward

Stories about people reaping huge rewards from web development abound. We've read about entrepreneurial folks staying up all night, working with the technology for the sheer love of it, and becoming millionaires. It would be wonderful if that happened in all organizations. Most people would like to make something and get noticed and rewarded.

The reality is that the group whose support is essential to an Intranet's long-term success—senior management—isn't monitoring your organization's intranet, trolling for examples of great work. They are busy doing "work as usual." To succeed, you need to cultivate patrons who will derive direct and indirect benefits from your efforts. (The other alternative is to leave your organization and sell your skills on the open market.)

Financial reward and official recognition obviously do not motivate everyone. Some intranet champions are motivated primarily by opportunities to stretch their skill sets and deliver results. They want another assignment that gives them an opportunity to do it again.[1] If you are among this group, your ability to secure the confidence of management is essential.

The Battle Over Site and Page Design Standards Isn't Important

Many organizations have taken taking a grassroots approach to intranet development. Web site development is distributed across the organization, with no central "web authority" to oversee what's going on. That approach capitalizes on employees' enthusiasm and desire to use the medium for communication. However, as a consequence, some sites look fantastic. Others don't. Among the sites, there may be little consistency in design. Poor communication practices (grammar, syntax, punctuation) make the content difficult to read. Some sites are like mazes, difficult to navigate. Some web sites feature the corporate logo, others don't.

Information on the intranet will compete with other forms of organizational communication for employees' attention. When the pages are poorly executed, it's difficult to persuade employees to migrate to the intranet as a preferred communication medium. Intranets don't have to be incredibly beautiful or sophisticated However, without some standards, they send the wrong message about the value of the intranet to employees. Marshal McLuhan said, "the medium is the message." In other words, the *medium itself* carries information. A well-designed and managed intranet sends a message about how the organization values this particular form of communication. If we want others to take our intranets seriously, we must establish common standards and develop some consistency in design and presentation.

Developing Content is a No-Brainer

Some people assume that it's fine to use existing printed materials when developing web sites. Their focus is directed primarily on using the technology for on-line publishing or transactions. However, how valuable were those materials in the first place? What added value do you really gain by putting them on a web site? How much revision do the materials require so that people can read them on a computer screen rather than a printed page? What do employees really need in terms of content?

The two main requirements for content development are (a) knowing what employees need and (b) having the right tools to develop content. Finding the right tools requires brain power. There are dozens of authoring tools, and more people within organizations want to put material up on their intranets. Given all of the various choices and tools, content creation can get lost in a sea of options.

It's Obvious to Management Why Your Organization Needs an Intranet

It's the wave of the future. Everyone is doing it. It will result in better communication, collaboration, and knowledge sharing. Really? Canned phrases become meaningless when you think about intranets in terms of the resources required to create it, maintain them, and support their evolution.

Your organization probably does need an intranet, but perhaps not for the reasons that, at first, seem most obvious.

■ How Can You Win If You Play Alone?

Chapter 9 explained the Value Triad and suggested how it could be used as a model for intranet development. Satisfying employees and stakeholder needs, creating outstanding product features, and achieving operation excellence are solid, straightforward goals. No one group within the organization, however, can be responsible for all three parts of the Value Triad. Each segment involves a different set of core competencies; each segment represents different roles and responsibilities. Gathering together all of the different people who can help achieve this vision can be difficult, especially in large organizations where distance and position limits people's opportunity to learn about each other's work and passions.

If your immediate work community is basically limited to people within your own specialty, how would you even begin to start to look for other people in the organization with different specialties who might be interested in contributing to intranet development? Visiting people in their offices or cubicles to gauge their interest in participation is one way to approach the problem. Yet that assumes you know who to visit and that you have a lot of time on your hands. This chapter presents three more effective different methods for creating a self-organized network or coalition of people who can together own the enormous task of developing a future-proof intranet. The methods are the Request for Comments (RFC), the Open-Space Meeting, and Electronic Meetings.

The methods can be used to create a network or coalition of intranet champions – both technical and nontechnical professionals—who together can deal with issues that affect everyone involved with intranet development within the organization.

■ Case Study 7: Web Developers Network Creation at U S WEST

For years, web development at U S WEST happened behind the scenes while more and more employees "discovered" the intranet and developed their own sites. Web developers who knew about each other turned to each other for help, and as they did it became clear that resources were one of the biggest barriers to intranet development. Tired of fighting the same battles again and again, a small group brainstormed the idea of a web developers' group. Their invitation to the first meeting went out via e-mail, fliers and posters, and over 400 people responded via e-mail, signaling an interest in joining. When the first U S West Web Developer's Coalition meeting was held, over 100 people attended.

At that first meeting, the founders passed out a survey in an effort to discover what the people at the meeting saw as the purpose and mission of the

Coalition. Through the survey, people responded with a long list of issues they saw as critical to successful intranet development within the company. Among the list were these 27 issues:

1. Web page development that isn't browser-dependent
2. Minimizing duplication of effort; internal reuse of templates, code, graphics
3. Server utilization
4. Cataloging of information
5. Legal and regulatory issues regarding internal information exchange
6. Standards for page design
7. Use of corporate logo
8. Security, encryption and secure transactions
9. Network scalability
10. Time/date stamping pages
11. Directory or map of all internal sites
12. Ownership of a central search engine
13. Selection and distribution of drag-and-drop content-authoring tools
14. Purchasing new tools for digital designers (upgrade Photoshop, etc.)
15. Official support, executive buy-in, and funding
16. Corporate licensing of web software and tools
17. Development of an FAQ re: pitfalls of web development
18. Education and training opportunities for people who want to upgrade skills
19. Strategic rather than accidental software upgrades
20. How to share the vision of web-enabled work
21. FAQs for developing newsgroups (discussion groups)
22. Getting intranet access to employees in the field
23. Sharing success stories
24. A web site to support communication among the Coalition members
25. Increasing network speed
26. Increasing bandwidth for audio and video capacity
27. E-mail migration from proprietary systems (cc:mail, Profs, etc.) to web-based STMP

When the list was distributed to the members the next week, one of the people who happened to receive a copy was Barbara Bauer, a senior executive in the information technology (IT) group. Patricia Hursh, a communications specialists responsible for the IT group's outstanding web site, attended the meeting, came back and told Bauer about the energy being unleashed through the Coalition. Previously, Bauer had provided IT support for Sherman Woo's legacy systems web projects, and over the months she had many conversations with Sherman, Patricia and others about the potential of the web to significantly improve information flow in the company. Bauer was one of the few executives at the company who really "got it." So, when the list came out, Bauer felt strongly that some of the issues on the list ought to be owned by IT. Consequently, IT began to craft a plan to address the issues that are starred in the list above (server utilization, security, encryption and secure transactions, ownership of a central search engine, increasing network speed, and increasing bandwidth for audio and video capacity.)

The IT Group Assumes Ownership for Network-Related Issues

Within the constraints of their charter and their budget, the IT group could dedicate resources to network-related issues and relieve some of the frustrations with web site development. Bauer revealed that IT had a sense that the demand for improvements in these areas existed. When the members of the Coalition came together and articulated the need as a group, she was delighted to assume leadership.

Many of the other issues did not belong to any existing department or group, however. Issues such as "standards for page design" and "how to share the vision of web-enabled work" were not network architecture or infrastructure issues. In fact, the vast majority of the issues did not relate to IT's organizational function. Rather, these remaining issues related to how the organizational context should be modified to assimilate the technology into standard work routines and practices. They involved the processes of transferring technology and knowledge to and from different parts of the organization. They involved soliciting feedback, discussing ideas, and obtaining approval from management for specific uses and functions of the intranet.

From the beginning, there was a strong sense that the remaining issues should not be farmed out to other departments, but that the Coalition membership should deal with them together. Everyone arrived at the Coalition as equals; no one wanted PR or Advanced Technologies or any other group to dictate what people in other divisions of the company ought to do. That approach would not have worked anyway. Everyone knew that if one group had tried to dictate to the other groups, people would have simply returned to their home offices and cubicles and would ignore the mandates. Once outside of the Coalition, they would be back to being invisible to each other. The rules would be as valuable as the two-cent piece of paper they were photocopied on.

A New Model for Organization

Mike Vaughan, one of the founders of the Coalition, proposed a model for organizing members of the Coalition so that the group could introduce some structure to a chaotic situation. He proposed the creation of three overlapping entities:

1. Special interest groups whose volunteer members would each be responsible for particular issues, like evaluating and recommending authoring tools.
2. A Web Forum comprised of representatives of different divisions of the company who would take responsibility for organizing the monthly meetings, making decisions on behalf of the Coalition when necessary, and who would represent the Coalition to upper management. The forum members would serve as nodes in the network, helping to keep the membership informed of changes.
3. The Coalition membership, which would be open to anyone who wished to join.

They weren't tiers, Mike explained. The entities would be formed around the purposes the group was trying to achieve. The intention was to break down organizational walls and to create a network that could sustain itself through constant communication and the creation of shared goals. Figure 15.1 illustrates the concept.

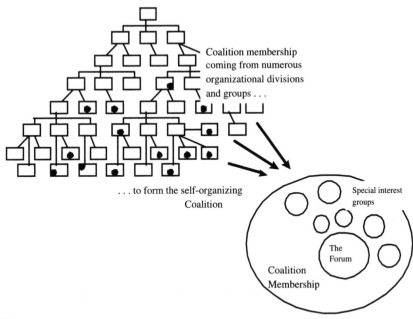

FIGURE 15.1
The Evolution of the Coalition.

When this organizing principle was introduced at the first meeting, the Coalition members were very responsive. For some people, this felt like a sea of change in the company: Finally, no one was going to try to impose rules or dictate an action plan. The group would decide for itself what its goals were and how to achieve them.

One interesting result was that new leaders emerged. For example, when discussing the value of special interest groups, one member asked who would determine which issues would be addressed. Because the answer was "any issue you think is important," the member volunteered to lead a special interest group for web developers who used Apple hardware. "Apple versus PC" wasn't even on the initial list of issues submitted by the membership, but it emerged as important when people began thinking about the sorts of issues they personally would like to become involved with.

Another special interest group formed to create and manage web-based communications for the Coalition. They created a listserve for the members for sending announcements via e-mail and developed a web site which included a searchable "mentoring database" so that people could list their competencies and willingness to mentor other members.

Case Study 7: Key Learnings

1. *The obvious.* Some key learnings are obvious, such as the fact that you can do more together as a group than you can do alone. Gathering people together for a common purpose unleashes tremendous energy when people see themselves as part of something larger than their own concerns. These are the sorts of things that are very difficult to capture in words. Making the case for self-organizing without sounding pedantic is not easy. In some form or another, most people have an immediate grasp of and appreciation for purposeful, self-organized groups.

2. *The role of IT.* IT groups are responsible for some, but not all, of the issues that emerge from intranet development. Most organizations have an existing technology infrastructure. Few organizations or companies are network virgins. Intranet development places an added layer of complexity onto the IT group's existing set of responsibilities. Intranet development often strains bandwidth capacity and makes it necessary for IT groups to purchase additional equipment and hire additional staff.

If a group of intranet developers within an organization can come together as a group to articulate a collective need, IT has an easier time projecting network requirements and making the case that more resources are required. Also, if the group shows that it will assume responsibility for other issues relating to intranet development, an IT group will be better able to anticipate the fruit of its labor.

3. *There is no such thing as "universal" value for web development.* For those who wanted to benefit from shared resources and shared authority, the concept of the Coalition was very attractive. However, for people who wanted to protect their resource base and their authority, the Coalition was initially somewhat of an irritant.

Following a stock split, a new business unit was created at U S West for web-based commerce. Within the new Media Group, several young, highly paid executive directors and directors were formulating plans to launch several company-supported web sites on the Internet for services such as entertainment and travel. The sites they planned were intended to be very different than the company's external web site, which told about the company, its product and services. The Media Group intended to produce sites that were stand-alone, revenue-generating "products." When the Coalition emerged, declaring its purpose as "guiding web development within the company," folks from the Media Group were very concerned. In their minds, *they* were "leading web development within the company"! They had the salaries, budgets, programmers, and authoring tools to prove it.

The founders of the Coalition had hoped that the Media Group would become involved in sharing knowledge about things like authoring tools or outstanding web design concepts. Members of the Coalition could become outstanding sounding boards for external site design – after all, the Coalition members were web innovators and had a sense of why the medium was so unique and so potentially powerful. One of the founders, Kristina Jonell Yarrington, at that time a member of the PR group, had recently assumed responsibility for the company's external web site, and she perceived a lot of crossover between internal and external site development.

In regard to the Media Group, however, ideas for sharing knowledge and perhaps some resources were entirely too idealistic. The pressures and rules for developing external web sites for electronic commerce and the pressures and rules for developing internal web sites for internal communication were entirely different. The stakeholders were different. The anticipated outcomes were different. The salaries and titles were different. Even the cultures of the two groups were different. The Media Group recruited cutting-edge executives from ad agencies in New York and San Francisco who conceived of their roles as similar to movie producers. Web-based commerce was cutting edge; it was cool. The Coalition members, on the other hand, were basically motivated by a desire to correct defects in the organizational environment by utilizing new communication technologies. Their efforts were indirectly—not directly—related to revenue generation. The differences between the two groups were insurmountable. After the first meeting, members of the Media Group expressed sincere good will for the Coalition and bade it goodbye.

The Break Reveals the Need for the Network

The break cast into sharp relief the need for a Coalition. Web-based commerce is perceived in many organizations as more worthy of huge amounts of resources because most senior management perceive that expanding mar-

ket share through electric commerce will result in a positive return on investment (ROI). That is still a debated question but, nonetheless, more senior
executives seem to grasp the value of web-based commerce than the concept
of web-based internal knowledge sharing and communication. The point is
that the mass media and business press are doing plenty to make the case for
web-based commerce, but the value of intranet development is not quite as
appreciated at this particular moment in history, although it's getting there.
In the interim, until the value is clear and well-established, intranet developers need to find ways to share their collective resources and to gain legitimacy
together as a group.

The net gain from the formation of an intranet network is.

1. Heightened visibility for intranet work.
2. Collective voice and, thus, bargaining power.
3. A shared, distributed knowledge base (of technology requirements, costs,
   applications and business problem solutions), which enables people to
   maximize, not waste, whatever resources they have.

Legitimacy is not conferred externally, as it is with web-based commerce.
It is created organically, from the source itself. It is, therefore, a much more
solid form of legitimacy.

■ The Network versus Business as Usual

The third point above raises an interesting question: Which would you
rather be, a highly paid "web producer" in the Media Group, or a member
of the Coalition? Honestly? If you had data that showed who was still employed two years later, would that make a difference in your answer? What
if the network helped to keep you immune from political back-biting?

Internal politics have become one of the greatest stumbling blocks for intranet development. Networks or coalitions like these cannot completely
prevent in-fighting, but they can change the ways in which people perceive
success.

The Situation

Webmaster is the hot new job title of the decade. It even made it into *Working Women* magazine's "Top 25 Careers for Women." As more and more people talk about and write about intranets, the term gathers an increasing amount of currency. *Currency* means general acceptance or use; prevalence. It also means "a medium of exchange." One anxiety in many organizations where intranet development is already underway is that someone else is going to "ride the intranet ticket" to boost their own careers at the expense of others.

Intranet proponents often talk about how intranets can be used to break down communication silos, enable cross-boundary management, and facilitate organization-wide learning. One of the major selling points is that intranets can be used to punch through organizational hierarchy so that people can coordinate their efforts and work more cooperatively. Yet, ironically, often intranet developers' own actions are completely contrary to that way of thinking. In Christine Comaford's survey, "turf conflicts" were identified by 42 percent of the intranet developers as a major issue.[2]

A lot of intranet development in its initial stages begins as grassroots, home-based initiatives. Whereas you would never expect dozens of individual units or departments to begin publishing their own four-color printed newsletters, web technology makes it possible for groups to put up their own web sites. No one really "asks permission." So each group may have its own webmaster, its own ways of doing things, and its own opinions about what intranets are all about.

The groups often work independently, unaware of the others' existence. As intranets enter later stages in their evolution, the individual groups either discover each other by chance or are asked to work together. Often, their interaction is colored by rivalry, contention, competitiveness and even jealousy. Sometimes, hostility is displayed in very subtle ways, other times it's overt. This kind of behavior is often labeled *politics*.

The term *envy* might be a better label. It conveys the feeling of discontent, stress, or tension. It hints at how people are reacting emotionally to changes in the economy and the growing expectation that employees are now entirely responsible for managing their own careers. Although the term *envy* has a negative connotation, it can, at the same time, be a kind of praise—for getting there first, for getting resources, for asserting oneself. Many intranets, like the U S WEST "Global Village," were created by techies who were gutsy and who liked being somewhat like heretics. Now, more people appear to be rushing to join the bandwagon, including managerial types.

■ Who Is the Intranet Champion?

The American Heritage Dictionary defines a *champion* as "one who is clearly superior or has the attributes of a winner; an ardent defender or supporter of a cause or other person." To *champion* means "to fight for, defend, or support." The academic literature tells us that championing is the process by which an individual employs various strategies to get members of an organization to support a new idea that other members of the organization do not initially support. Champions have and use strategies that turn *ideas* into *realities*.

Champion is an appropriate name to give to people who develop intranets, especially as such individuals tend to defy traditional job descriptions. Intranet champions are knowledgeable about technology. They see the potential of leveraging technology to improve the way their organization works. They often help others learn how to use the technology, or they take charge of finding learning resources. They tend to bridge two worlds (the technical and nontechnical) and act as boundary spanners, translating meanings so that different groups can come to agreement. Intranet champions have a zeal, a passion, and a drive. They herald the coming of a new way of thinking about technology and communication in organizations. Intranet champions can be found in many different places within an organization.

Technical Professionals

Often, intranet champions come from management information systems (MIS) or IT departments. People with MIS or IT backgrounds typically know how to program, set up servers, create networks, and manage a local area network (LAN). Many MIS and IT professionals embody the characteristics of intranet champions. Technical people are likely to adopt championing roles because innovation is an important part of many technical jobs.

People with science and engineering backgrounds also tend to be more supportive of innovation and strategic change.[3]

For the past several years, MIS and IT professionals have been at the forefront of web site and internet development. One 1995 survey, for example, found that a significant portion of corporate sites on the Web were initiated by MIS departments. Of the companies studied in 1995, 44 percent of corporate web sites were started by MIS departments. (This surprised the researchers, who had expected to find that marketing departments had initiated the work.)[4]

Many intranets are started by MIS and IT professionals. Intranet and web development is an opportunity to delve into new and forward-looking technologies. Some MIS and IT professionals are moving into this area of their own accord; others are prompted by opportunities created by their companies. For example, to build in-house intranet expertise, companies such as BMW are now retraining some of their mainframe developers. They are providing employees with UNIX training and are encouraging employees to become more knowledgeable about intranet servers and network maintenance.

Christine Comaford reports that the greatest staff transition issues are retraining programmers, establishing transition teams to identify new skill sets, monitoring or managing performance measurement and workload indicators, and hiring management consultants to evaluate existing skill sets.[2]

Nontechnical Professionals

Intranet champions also come from the nontechnical side. Some have backgrounds in organizational development and come from fields such as Human Resources or Planning. They are especially interested in improving the way an organization functions. They are specialists in aligning resources with the organization's needs. Their interest in intranets often comes from their ability to perceive the potential of the new technology to improve the way organizations work and the way that resources (such as people, information, capital) are distributed and used.

Other nontechnical intranet proponents have communications backgrounds and come from fields such as Public Relations and Corporate Communications. They are specialists in effective communication and have a keen awareness of the importance of good message design, presentation, and delivery. Graphic artists, writers, editors, and media production managers are included in this group.

Librarians, records managers, and information specialists often emerge as advocates of intranet development. As specialists in information cataloging, indexing, and dissemination, many information professionals are adapting intranet technologies as their preferred storage, retrieval and distribution medium. In fact, John Draper reports that the first intranet created for Microsoft was championed by the Corporate Library.[5] Individuals in this group possess skills such as information analysis, strategic information services, environmental scanning, competitor intelligence, research support, and information repackaging.

Members of corporate training departments are also becoming increasingly interested in intranets. They see how the Web can be used to automate registration processes, distribute learning resources, access learning preferences, and create virtual on-line learning environments and dynamic learning communities.

Typically, individuals from organizational development, communications, and information sciences are highly attuned to the importance of knowledge in organizations. They see the intranet as a powerful tool to improve information flow and to facilitate two-way and multidirectional communication. Many such nontechnical managers are beginning to establish themselves as strategic counselors to their organizations about media transformation.

One of the major findings of "Employee Communications and Technology," a report by Cognitive Communications, Inc. and Xerox, was that 95 percent of 165 professional communicators polled want to play a key role in their company's technology upgrades. The Internet and intranets are areas of special interest.

A Convergence Of Roles

MIS professionals who see computers and data management as their domain may be uncomfortable about these developments on the nontechnical side of the organization. Back in the days of mainframes, MIS and IT professionals were the high priests of computers, revered for their ability to speak a technical language and to solve technological problems. They had almost absolute authority to decide technical matters as they chose.[6]

Today, MIS managers still have the primary responsibility for supporting hardware and software, and for fixing things when they break. Technical professionals provide the backbone of intranet development. Without MIS, IT, and information systems (IS) professionals, there would be no intranet system to implement.

Now, however, other types of employees are migrating into technical professionals' knowledge domain. Nontechnical employees are reading computer magazines, attending trade conferences, and participating in Usenet groups. The Internet has made it possible for people to extend their knowledge base, and many nontechnical managers are taking advantage of the free flow of information about intranet products and applications.

Why are so many nontechnical managers becoming interested in intranet technologies? It is, in part, a reaction to changes in the economy. Many nontechnical managers are becoming more knowledgeable about new technologies so that they can provide greater value to their organizations. Numerous professional associations are working hard to support their members in that effort. For example, the Public Relations Society of America (PRSA) has a Technology Section that hosts its own web site to keep members current on web technology. The PRSA National Conference now includes a Technology College, an opportunity for PR practitioners to learn about today's new enabling technologies for communications.

Increasingly, nontechnical mangers are being courted by intranet vendors as potentially resource-rich intranet developers. At PRSA's National Conference, for instance, several workshop presentations were made by vendors of specific technologies. These included virtual reality, the Internet, automated measurement and tracking of audience response, multimedia, and electronic web-based publishing. Nontechnical managers do not necessarily need to go to technology conferences to be introduced to the latest intranet products. Increasingly, vendors, who see lucrative markets within the professional groups, are coming to them.

■ Among the Professions, Differences in Preferences

Between different expert groups, preference is expressed for:
- technology rather than marketing (or vice versa);

  ▦ product design rather than sales or research (or vice versa),

  ▦ management roles rather than specialist roles (or vice versa),

  ▦ scientific qualifications rather than other specialist or managemen qualifications (or vice versa), and

  ▦ commercial attitude rather than technological interest.

Because of specialization of job functions, members of an organization often are not even aware of the others' existence. If they are aware, they often have difficulty seeing the type of contribution the other individuals or groups can make, because they don't know what it is, exactly, that the other people do.

■ The Value of an Interdisciplinary Group

Intranet development creates both a need and an opportunity for people from many different departments to come together. Researchers have found that employees from different functional areas view the same work issues in significantly different ways. In fact, employees tended to define problems largely in terms of the activities and goals of their own areas. Functional interpretation may result from "groupthink," which encourages individuals working closely together to think the same way about issues.

Kristina Jonell Yarrington relates that one of the interesting aspects of The Link project (Chapter 8, Case Study 3: "Redesigning Communication at U S WEST's MegaCenters") was teaming with IT Director Sherman Woo on the demo as they each brought different perspectives about the importance of the web as a communication medium. Kristina recalls:

> Sherman was key to helping us develop a vision of what the technology itself could do. For example, Sherman talked a lot about how the web could be used to provide personalized, customized information to the service reps. While Sherman was interested in the technology's capabilities, I was concerned about the look and feel of the site, graphics, and how the information was categorized. Sherman really didn't care about those things. I was very interested in using the web as a repository for mass-distributed information, a

virtual library. Sherman wasn't really opposed, but he really didn't care.

■ Cultural Distance and Competition

There are many advantages of interdisciplinary teams and networks. When they work well together, the synergy is apparent. When there is difficulty, however, the causes may be hard to determine. Part of the problem can be described as "cultural distance" between groups. Many web innovators are very much like the "hackers" of the 1960s and 70s described by Steven Levy. Among the beliefs that hackers held sacred:

- Information should flow to whomever can use it.
- No one should need to be authorized to use the tools that get things done.
- No system or program is ever completed—you can always make it better.
- People should always work incrementally on improvements.
- What matters is improving programs, not who owns them.
- Mistrust authority, promote decentralization.
- Hackers should be judged by their hacking, not by criteria such as degrees, age, race, or position.
- Mistakes are a tool for learning, not evidence of failure.
- Above all, honor the "hands-on imperative"—whatever you imagine, you must also try to produce.

"Manager types" are often seen to represent the exact polar opposite set of values. They are perceived to have succeeded within a system that emphasizes hierarchy, competition, power, control, and reward. They don't actually "do" the work and they don't really understand it. Nontechnical managers, therefore, are often automatically seen as somehow disingenuous about why they want to create an intranet for their organization. As one bitter information specialist and intranet expert at a Fortune 500 company explained, "they came to us and said 'let's all collaborate on this,' but what I think they really wanted to do was colonize us." She was bitter because she felt extremely used and had resolved in her own mind not to get "sucked in again."

Those who are ahead of the rest sometimes prefer to remain envied by others than to risk working collaboratively. For web developers who see themselves as mavericks or heretics, that's somewhat ironic. As John Berger puts it, "The envied are like bureaucrats; the more impersonal they are, the greater the illusion (for themselves and for others) of their power."[7] Yet it makes some intuitive sense. When people or groups are afraid of losing their power, they have a hard time sharing information and working collaboratively.

Another part of the problem is that some managers still enter into relationships with the expectation of competition. Fred Kofman writes:[8]

> Fascinated by competition, we often find ourselves competing with the very people with whom we need to collaborate. Members of a management team compete with one another to show who is right, who knows more, or who is more articulate or persuasive. Divisions compete with one another when they ought to cooperate to share knowledge. Team project leaders compete to show who is the best manager, even if it means covering up problems for which, ultimately, everyone will pay.

Competition seems to be an enormous problem for intranet proponents. At the same time, competition is endemic and highly valued in many organizations.

The Challenge

Competition and envy over resources, authority, or decision-making power can sharply diminish the chances of developing a successful intranet. First, it leads to the waste of a lot of resources. No company can afford to lose resources and compete in the marketplace today. Second, it makes learning difficult. To learn, we have to acknowledge that there is something we don't know, and the ability to learn is essential to solid intranet development. Intranet technologies are always changing, their potential applications are evolving, and managers are struggling with decisions about which technologies will solve business problems.

If internal politics, competition, and envy consume too much energy, it is almost impossible to tackle the Value Triad. Intranet proponents will have trouble coordinating their efforts to solicit opinions and ideas from the employee base. Intranet proponents will find it difficult to come together as a group to sell the concept to senior management because without cohesion it is hard to produce a coherent and eloquent story about the gains that will result from a fully functional intranet. At that point, intranet proponents are back to square one, frustrated because the intranet isn't having a significant impact.

■ Identifying Personal Values and Increasing Shareholder Value

In a *Harvard Business Review* article, Alan M. Webber, the founder of *Fast Company* magazine, pointed out that as the economy is changing, so is the meaning and purpose of work. Webber writes:[9]

> If the [new management] books are right, work in the twenty-first century will be as much about the spirit as about the dollar, as much about identifying and fulfilling personal values as about increasing shareholder value. Work in the New Economy is about making sense. It is about expressing authenticity and creating meaning. It is more and more about making art—a form of self-expression that touches others—and thus giving meaning to life.

Perhaps that is precisely why so many people are gravitating to intranets as the next stage in their careers. Developing great web sites for internal purposes *is* an art form. Moreover, the medium itself permits tremendous creativity to be unleashed. People are discovering new ways to combine words, illustrations and photographs, and to use layout and hyperlinks to communicate facts, tell stories, and create history. The Web enables profoundly meaningful, creative, and intriguing forms of self-expression, as psychologist Sherry Turkle's studies and MUD designer Amy Bruckman's studies continue to point out.

However, the new economy is not only about personal satisfaction. Webber also directs our attention to the importance of networks. "We are all struggling to get to the future, and no one can get there alone," Webber writes. "All work emerges through relationships."[9]

Yes, Webber is right, yet we're struggling to appreciate that portrait of reality. What does it really mean? What would it feel like? In an age where *down-sized* is a verb, as in "I've been down-sized," and full-time, loyal employees are turned into temporary "contractors" overnight at the discretion of senior management who want to cut costs by cutting payroll, what does that mean? It certainly does not mean "privilege your relationship with senior management over other relationships." Perhaps a better signpost on this new highway of work would be, "All work emerges through *networks* of relationships." What would that feel like?

■ What Kind of Party Is This, Anyway?

At a Mecklermedia Internet conference in Dallas in 1995, one of the sessions focused on how to get a web developer team together. The presenter, a systems designer, talked only about the kinds of technical skills that belonged on the team.

During the question and answer session that followed, a member of the audience stood up. He said, "The problem with trying to build a web team is that it's like a cool party that everyone wants to get invited to." To him, it was a big problem. There is a more positive way to look at the party metaphor, though.

A party is an interesting and useful metaphor for intranet development. Not because parties are always so much fun, but, rather, because parties are meaningful communication events in the same way that developing intranets can be.

If you examine a party the way a sociologist would, you'd find that the people in attendance are there for many different reasons. People go to parties out of a sense of obligation to show up, or because they have an expectation that it's all right to step outside the norms of every day and "let loose" a little bit (or a lot). They may attend because they need to perform a particular role (such as being the host, or being the person who helps the host). Some people even go to parties out of a desire to collect information about other people in a casual way (often by inconspicuously observing their behavior). While some people observe others, some people show off—they like parties because the situation permits them to attract attention to themselves or to have an audience. There are even times when people go to a party because they need to have a group of people acknowledge a new social role (like the newly married couple or the graduate). When people are dating, parties serve a different function; they permit people to be visible to each other person or in close physical proximity to them.

People actually have a lot of different motives for coming to the event. It's the same with intranet development. There are probably no two people with the same exact reasons for wanting to participate. Their official job title or role may provide some clues, but probably not enough. Wanting to advance their career or to step outside of what is usually expected from them may be just the tip of the iceberg.

Another similarity between parties and intranet development is that there is no predefined outcome. The stated purpose for a party may be to launch a new product, to celebrate a birthday or holiday, or to mark the end of a work week. Yet, once you get a group of people together, they use the event to achieve all sorts of outcomes. People use parties to make new acquaintances and to grow their circle of friends, to reinforce or change their position in the social hierarchy, to help others meet and learn about each other. People use parties to connect with others who are like themselves and to exchange information about common interests. It's the same with intranet development. There are a lot of different "take aways" besides implementing a new technology.

Appreciating Difference

Some people really like parties; others prefer different kinds of social interaction. Some people, particularly extroverts, will leave the party feeling very "jazzed" by the whole experience. They get very energized by being around other people. Others, however, leave feeling drained, even though they may have enjoyed themselves tremendously. Most introverts are like that. People bring their own predispositions to parties, their own feelings about group interaction. It's the same with intranet development. That means that some people will feel great about opening the doors wide and inviting lots of people to join. Others are less comfortable having to deal with the large group dynamics, and feel that if they can keep the circle small, they'll be less stressed by the situation. It may or may not have anything to do with how much power or authority they seek. There will always be some people who would prefer to keep the circle small, manageable, and predictable, and others who can't wait to see who else would like to come.

Opening the Door

The last way parties are like intranet development has to do with the question of "who gets to come." Is it "our cool party and no one comes but us," or "we're going to do something interesting here, who wants to come?" Parties with a vague purpose constituted of the same group of people over and over tend to get stale. They may be very comfortable, and people may know just what to do and say, but sociologists have observed that people are always looking for some purpose for being together, some meaning to their interaction. When purposes are ambiguous or difficult to define or have an inherent contradiction, people manufacture something stimulating to create meaning, and start doing weird and sometimes stupid things, although it seems perfectly "normal" and sensible to them. It happens the same way in organizations. The work of theorists Watzlawick, Bevin and Jackson, Chris Argyris, Irving Janis, as well as writer Stanley Bing's columns in *Fortune* magazine make that point exquisitely.

On the other hand, when the party includes people who bring different backgrounds and different perspectives, there is energy and light because not everyone shares the same assumptions about how the world works or how things should be or even how people at the party are going to act. Some conversations at parties are just amazing. People you'd never expect to have much to say will tell the most incredible story or offer a poignant insight about something, or will have found the perfect solution to one of your biggest problems.

Intranet development does not have to *be* a party. Development teams can shoot themselves in the foot by acting like intranet development is their chance to cut loose from the rest of their organization's norms and culture. But intranet development can be *like* a party. It can be both serious and fun. It can be an opportunity to bring together people from diverse points of view. It can be an occasion for self-expression and for strengthening relationships. Some people are going to find it very energizing and will want to move at the speed of light. They will be excellent at driving the team toward project milestones. Other people are going to need a break in the action for periods of reflection so that they can sort out what's been happening. These team members will be very important as well, because they will help others to see where things could be improved. Everyone who participates in the project will come with some preformed motives and expectations.

The purpose and meaning of the project will be constructed from the kinds of conversations that take place among the group. From those conversations, you'll create a *party* in the second dictionary definition of the term: "*an alliance, a unit, a force, a coalition, organized to promote and support a set of principles.*"

Intranet as "Meaning Attractor"

Success lies in the conversations. It begins with finding allies who want to contribute to the development/evolution of a purposeful intranet. The first step is talking about what a vision of that might look like, who it might benefit, and what sorts of hurdles you think you might face.

The vision of the intranet's purpose that results from the conversations can serve as a point of reference, or a "meaning attractor." Taken from scientific observations about the role of "strange attractors," Meg Wheatley writes that when a "meaning attractor" is in place in an organization, people are able to wander through the realms of chaos and emerge with a discernible shape to their activities. The meaning or purpose of an intranet does not need to be carved in stone before you embark on the endeavor. In fact, both the technology and the vision of what can be achieved with the technology *should* evolve.

"In chaos theory it is axiomatic that you can never tell where the system is headed until you've observed it over time," Wheatley reminds us. The idea is to see the intranet project as a point of reference, a "meaning attractor," and to continually strive to create meanings for it that will resonate powerfully with employees.

Envy is often displayed in the most trivial and frivolous ways, and intranet development can easily become the field on which people attempt to exercise control, compete for reward and recognition and attempt to claim the role of "most knowledgeable expert." On the other hand, intranet development can serve as a model for system-wide communication via a new medium where what you *actually do with your knowledge* is more important than official titles or claims to expertise.

Intranets pose fundamentally new choices for our organizational futures. As Shosana Zuboff puts it, the ways in which employees and managers respond to these choices will "determine whether our era becomes a time for radical change or a return to the familiar patterns and pitfalls of the traditional workplace."[10]

Keeping your eyes trained on the team's overall vision and purpose allows you to focus on what is truly important. Focus can be better maintained, and weird and stupid behavior can be avoided, when you've involved others in the creation of the plan.

This chapter argued that networks are essential to successful intranet development. There is no way to achieve the Value Triad without them. How do you actually create the network? What are some specific techniques? The next chapter answers those questions.

■ References

[1] Stratford Sherman, "Wanted: Company Change Agents," *Fortune*, Dec., 1995.

[2] Christine Comaford, "What % of Your Sanity Do Intranets Take?" *PC Week*, 13, no. 20 (May 20, 1996), p. 63.

[3] Scott Shane, "Uncertainty Avoidance and the Preference for Innovation Championing Roles." Vol. 26, *Journal of International Business Studies,* Jan. 1, 1995, p. 47.

[4] Bob Woods, "77% of U.S. Firms in Cyberspace By 1997—Study," *Newsbytes News Network*, Oct. 19, 1995.

[5] John Draper, "Intranets: The Untold Story," http://www.iabc.com/.

[6] Michael Antonoff, "Technology's Growth Challenges Systems Managers," *N.Y. Times,* July 15, 1996.

[7] John Berger, *Ways of Seeing*, Ch. 7 (1972).

[8] Fred Kofman, "Communities of Commitment; The Heart of Learning Organizations," *Organizational Dynamics*, September, 1993, p. 4.

[9] Alan M. Webber, "Surviving the New Economy," *Harvard Business Review*, September–October 1994, p. 91.

[10] Shosana Zuboff, *In the Age of the Smart Machine; The Future of Work and Power* (New York: Basic Books, 1988).

Designing the Open Network

A vast number of books on shelves and racks of the business sections in major bookstores offers advice about how to create teams and organize networks. There is no shortage of advice in this area. In the last chapter, we looked at the major benefits of creating an internal network of intranet champions. The benefits included heightened visibility for intranet-related work, collective voice and, thus, collective bargaining power, and a shared, distributed knowledge base that enables network members to maximize their resources. How do you put together such a network? Does somebody have to take responsibility for managing the network?

Most advice in this area offers a technique or set of rule-governed steps for organizing teams and networks. This chapter offers something different. Not a technique but an attitude. It is the same attitude that permeated the creation of the intranet that was discussed in the very first chapters of the book. It can be summed up in four words: minimum ego, maximum vision. Here are three tried-and-true methods for creating networks that won't implode.

■ Request for Comments

Back in Chapter 2, we talked about how, in the 1970s, an ad hoc group comprised primarily of graduate students in California was working on the problem of how to develop the basic "handshake" between two computers. One of the graduate students who helped to lead the initiative, Steve Crocker, captured the problem in a note he sent out to other groups of graduate students. He labeled it *Request for Comments,* which came to be known as an RFC. Crocker's invitation reflected the graduate student ethos of everybody learning together, and Crocker's RFC helped to set the tone for the work of creating the Internet. As his colleagues recounted to Katie Hafner and Matthew Lyon for their wonderful book *Where Wizards Stay Up Late: The Origins of the Internet,* Crocker wrote the RFC in a tone that was welcoming and free of ego. Hafner and Lyon write:[1]

> The fact that Crocker kept his ego out of the first RFC set the style and inspired others to follow suit in the hundreds of friendly and cooperative RFCs that followed. "It is impossible to underestimate the importance of that," Reid asserted. "I did not feel excluded by a little core of protocol kings. I felt included by a friendly group of people who recognized that the purpose of networking was to bring everybody in." For years afterward (and to this day) RFCs have been the principal means of open expression in the computer networking community, the accepted way of recommending, reviewing, and adopting new technical standards.

An RFC for intranet development does not have to be technical in nature. In fact, it shouldn't be focused primarily on technology issues. The objective would be to solve the problem of creating the "handshake"—not between computers but between people.

The procedure would be straightforward. Someone or some group in the organization with a burning desire to improve an existing intranet or to develop a new intranet would draft an RFC explaining why it was important for the organization to create an intranet and why doing so has proved to be challenging thus far. The RFC would outline the sorts of issues that the authors felt needed to be addressed (e.g., lack of standards on internal web sites, lack of funding to improve bandwidth, lack of senior management support or confusion about who really "owns" the intranet). It would then briefly propose a tentative solution and invite comment on the proposal. The next step would be a round of discussions, meetings, or e-mail to discover whether anyone else had any ideas and to discuss next steps.

As the starting place for discussion among self-interested parties, the RFC can stimulate the creation of a loose federation of independent groups organized to achieve a common goal. It is more like the Preamble to the Constitution than a memo.

Because RFCs are sent to a wide range of people, it really shouldn't be written in a vacuum. At U S WEST, the RFC that kickstarted the creation of the Web Developers Coalition was co-written by four people, each with a different competence (a programmer, a public relations specialist, an organizational development specialist, and a technical consultant).

The Basic Outline for an Intranet RFC

I. Statement of Problem
What is the situation?
What are the big issues?

II. Actions Taken So Far and By Whom

III. Proposal for Next Step
A proposed course of action
What we should do, who would be responsible, time frame

IV. Expected Outcomes

V. Invitation to Comment
" We believe that others may be interested in the issues. There probably are more issues to address that we haven't thought about. We invite your response."

VI/ Instructions for Comment
Names of authors, e-mail addresses, URL for web site

What next? From that point, there are several options: (a) summarize people's responses and distribute another document, (b) convene a meeting, inviting everyone who received the RFC, not just those who responded, or (c) issue a broader invitation to an Open-Space Meeting.

■ Open-Space Meetings

Open Space Technology (OST) is a powerful way to catalyze change and it can be a very good way to stimulate intranet development. It is one of the rare change techniques that thrives in areas of conflict and confusion. An RFC in advance is not necessary, though it could be helpful.

Most people who are familiar with OST associate it with its founder, Harrison Owen, an Episcopal priest and former photojournalist, who first developed Open Space in 1984 and authored the quirky, useful book, *Open Space Technology: A User's Guide.*

Owen writes in his book that he was motivated to create OST after organizing an international conference for 250 participants in 1983. Although the event was a success, the truly useful part had been the coffee breaks. After months and months of preparation and planning, dealing with egos, and working out logistics, the participants enjoyed and valued the coffee breaks more than any other part of the conference.

Reflecting on the pain of the experience, Owen wondered, would it be possible to combine the level of synergy and excitement present in a good coffee break with substantial activity and results characteristic of a good meeting?

> The line of inquiry I choose to follow took some interesting turns, but essentially it started with the notion that if I could identify certain basic mechanisms of meeting, or human gathering, it might be possible to build them into an approach that would be so simple that it could not fail and so elemental that it might possess the natural power of a good coffee break.

The technique, or "technology" that Owen developed is based on four principles:

1. Whoever comes are the right people.

2. Whatever happens is the only thing that could have.
3. Whenever it starts is the right time.
4. When it's over, it's over.

A fifth principles guides the interaction: "The Law of Two Feet," which illustrates the voluntary nature of participation. If anyone is bored, not learning anything, or felt that they had nothing to contribute, they are honor-bound to walk away.

A Legacy of Success

Despite the mystical-sounding ideas, Open Space Technology has been used successfully all over the world with corporations (such as Rockport, AC-COR, the world's largest hotel company, Owens Corning, Honeywell, and U S WEST), international organizations such as the World Bank, governments large and small, and nonprofit organizations. It has even been used to design new technologies. Harrison Owen notes, "Open Space is used so much all over the world, I've now lost track of all the places it has been used. But [in regard to technology development] it has been used very successfully for software development and system design."

Open Space meetings are based on the principle that the people most equipped to make changes and solve problems are those who are most affected. The group gathers together in a seated circle. A facilitator introduces the group to the process principles.

There are two mechanisms for the creation of Open Space: The Camp Sign-Up Board and the Village Market Place. Each participant is invited to identify any issue or opportunity around the given theme that they would like to take personal responsibility for developing. They give it a short title on a small piece of paper, indicating time and place, and post it on the wall. After every person has posted whatever they have in mind, the Village Market Place opens, and all participants are invited to sign up for whatever appeals to them. When conflicts of space or schedule arise, the interested parties negotiate solutions while the rest of the group goes about its business. As Owens says, "Nobody is in charge. Everybody is."

Participants who post issues become responsible for convening the groups, facilitating the discussions, and recording minutes of the proceedings. Often computers are set up to make it easier for people to record and print the minutes. Participants leave the meeting with copies of all the groups' notes and action plans.

Leveraging Uncertainty and Ambiguity

Open-Space Meetings may be a very good way to gather people within the organization together to chart a collective course for intranet development. Open-Space Meetings seem to work best in situations characterized by uncertainty, ambiguity and dead ends, which is typically the case when new technologies are being discussed or when people within organizations compete to "own" the intranet but find other groups resisting. Open-Space Meetings permit people to break out of their roles and routines to create new knowledge needed to solve problems. Open-Space Meetings help make assumptions explicit and bring out into the open issues about communication, information access and knowledge sharing. They are a great way to leverage diversity. In Open-Space Meetings, everyone has an equal chance to talk about topics about which they are passionate.

Research into OTS reports[3] that participants

- Emerge feeling energized with a sense of the larger mission of the organization
- Act with courage, take psychological risks
- Act with respect toward other participants
- Share information freely/network
- Assume personal responsibility
- Experience a sense of interconnectedness
- Have a sense of optimism about the organization

There are two direct paybacks to Open-Space Meetings. First, the creation of shared understanding of different people's viewpoints of what is really important. Second, the creation of cross-functional teams capable of solving problems. Third, the development of action plans that include persons responsible, the time frame, and expected output.

Steps:

1. Identify sponsor, someone who feels that they can call an Open-Space Meeting.
2. Select a time and place for the meeting; a half-day is the minimum for a large group.
3. Issue invitations via e-mail, internal mail, hand-to-hand.
4. Logistics; food, equipment, supplies.
5. Hold event.
6. Postevent, debrief via a web site set up for follow-up communication.

Open-Space Meetings

Who is involved?	1. Sponsor
	2. Anyone who wishes to attend
Materials and resources?	• An invitation explaining the purpose of the Open-Space Meeting
	• Supplies (masking tape, flip charts, magic markers, paper to post issues, Post-it notes)
	• One main meeting room
	• Name tags

Optional

- Breakout rooms
- Computers (about 10 per 100 people)
- Laser printer
- Food

Critical success factors?	1. A clear theme
	2. A sponsor
	3. Diverse population of invitees
	4. Understanding that this will "let the genie out of the bottle"

The Basic Outline for an Open Space Invitation

I.   Statement that clarifies this as an invitation (there is a choice of attending)

II. Purpose of the session and desired outcomes

III. The host(s)

IV. Times; start and end times

V.   Logistics; where, appropriate dress

VI. Who received the invitation

VII. Idea that people should come for the whole event, not drop in for part

VIII. How to contact someone for more information.

An example of an Open-Space invitation is included in the Tool Kit at the end of the book.

Responsibility for Action Items

One of the very interesting questions about the use of Open-Space Meetings in organizations is the question of responsibility for resolving the issues the participants have raised. To what extent does management own any of the issues? To what extent do the employees? At an Open-Space Meeting around the theme "Discovering Our Priorities," a group of field technicians identified "communication" as one of their passionate issues and created an ad hoc group called "The Information Co-Op." They were frustrated with their attempts to communicate with engineers and product support technicians in Denver whose decisions impacted the technicians' ability to perform.

Their plan was to create a BBS to link field technicians and supervisors with engineering and technical groups in other parts of the organization and other parts of the company. The concept was well conceived and the Info Co-Op team went forward with a great deal of enthusiasm. Believing that they needed to solve the problem they identified during Open Space, the group attempted to secure the resources required for the BBS. Though the Info Co-Op group received praise and support from their own managers for taking such initiative on behalf of the other technicians, they had a miniscule budget and had to scrounge for hardware and technical help in getting connected to the company network.

One could argue at this point that this was an issue that management really ought to have solved as they had better contacts within the company and, thus, greater ability to secure the required buy-in from the engineering and technical groups. The problem with that answer is that management couldn't articulate the problem. They recognized the problem as somehow related to reegineering, but they lacked a coherent story to tell about why this was such a burning issue from the technicians' point of view.

Perhaps we head in the wrong direction when we ask, "to what extent does management own any of the issues? To what extent do the employees? Unbeknownst to the Info Co-Op group or to their assistant managers, there were ample resources within the company—both people and technology—that could have been tapped. The problem was lack of information. The technicians simply did not know that the resources existed, and few people with the ability to help caught wind of their problem. Thus, the people who could have helped had little opportunity to help. By themselves, the technicians were trying to reinvent the wheel. They struggled and struggled to turn their dream into reality.

Extending the Parameters of the Network

This is a situation where an RFC could have been useful. Instead of trying to solve the *technology problems* associated with the creation of the Info Co-Op (securing hardware and network connectivity), the technicians might have approached this as a *communication problem*. The problem might have been framed this way, How do we tell the story of our problem to other groups in such a way that they will see the problem as theirs, as well as ours, as one we all share? The action item at the end of the Open-Space Meeting would not be a technology plan, but a communication plan.

There are some situations where the people who attend an Open-Space Meeting have all the resources they need to resolve their open issues. The entire resource pool is represented among the participants. Yet there are other times when the resources exist not within the network of immediate participants, but someplace in the larger network.

When organizations and companies develop their intranets and allow their employees to communicate, these sorts of situations will become remnants of the past. We will look back and wonder how we could have been so blind to think we had to solve problems on our own. We will shake our heads to think that we divided a line between "management" responsibilities and "employee" responsibilities.

Until then, in this interim period when we are trying to get connected electronically, we need to focus less of our attention on technology and more attention on storytelling and communication. It's a big deal, a hard task to create an infrastructure that will support the electronic exchange of communication across organizational divisions and geographies. Creating technology that people will want to use and getting their buy-in about why it's important to use that technology is challenging. No one group should have to shoulder the entire burden on its own.

Because many organizations and companies have nascent intranets running, used primarily for on-line publishing or asymmetrical communication (work-flow automation), one option is to hold an Open Space event to be followed by ongoing communication in cyberspace. In itself, this is not a novel idea. For example, Vice President Al Gore's task force on reinventing government used follow-up discussions on the MetaNetwork, an electronic conferencing and e-mail network in Arlington, Virginia. Gore's National Performance Review (NPR) staff was drawn from dozens of federal agencies to produce the report "From Red Tape to Results: Government That Works Better and Costs Less." After the report was finalized, the participants returned to their respective homes and agencies but stayed connected through an on-line network called *Net Results*. Despite busy calendars, complex travel, and multiple work locations, they maintained a high quality of communication. As Srikumar Rao reported in *Training* magazine in April, 1994, the group used the space to do real work. They met in "cyberspace to brainstorm possibilities, make decisions, develop plans and manage projects. In doing so . . . they spread the culture of open space throughout their organizations."[4]

This is one way to use an intranet or other form of electronic conferencing: follow-up conversation. These kinds of conversations are tremendously effective, partly because, through their work together in real life, people got to know each other. They established relationships with each other in the real world and carried those forward via a communication platform that extended time and space.

Another way is to use cyberspace is to blow out the parameters of participation. Instead of limiting the cyberspace conversation to those who are already part of "the network," the intranet can be used to invite participation from others.

■ The Benefits of Self-Reliance

If we do intranet development the old way, looking to a CEO or CIO to set the agenda, clarify roles and responsibilities, determine outputs, and create definitions of success, we rely too much on that one person (or his/her staff) to know everything there is to know. Today, leaders just can't know everything. The perfect CEO or CIO for the 21st century would have as much feel and knowledge about computers as a member of "Generation X." He or she would see computers as an essential part of who we are, how we live, and how we achieve our goals. The perfect CEO or CIO would also know a lot about the business world and how to "do deals." He or she would have be exposed to linguistics, the philosophy of science, or theories of communication and would look at human speech and at numbers as two imperfect representations of reality, not reality itself.

Combine a Generation Xer, a seasoned executive, and a philosopher and we have our CEO or CIO for the 21st century. Such individuals exist, and some have risen so fast in this new economy that they are already VPs at age 30. However, they are not CEOs or CIOs at the moment. Our current CEOs and CIOs are still basically Newtonians at heart. Most still believe in the numbers, in cause and effect, in changing organizations by changing people's behaviors.

Which leaves us in a position of needing to be more self-reliant and more involved in networks of like-minded colleagues. It is hard to be posed at the brink of a "paradigm" shift, talking about the emergence of the organization of the 21st century, when the people with the resources, power, and authority are still being rewarded so well for playing the old paradigm game.

   If what we want to do is to create a robust technology network of value to employees, our single recourse is not more internal politicking and trying to enter the game by playing someone else's rules. Our recourse is to model excellence in networking ourselves.

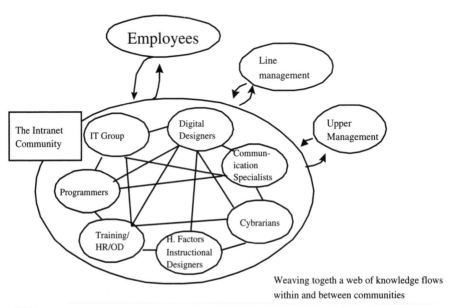

Weaving togeth a web of knowledge flows
within and between communities

FIGURE 16.1
The Intranet Developer's Network as a Mediator.

   Through your organizing and your conversations, you'll help to bring into being a vision of the future of the organization defined by people and technologies. Peter Schwartz and Peter Leyden write:[5]

> Today, without the old visions, it's easy enough to see how the world might unravel into chaos. It's much more difficult to see how it could all weave together into something better. But without an expansive vision of the future, people tend to get short-sighted and mean-spirited, looking out only for themselves. A positive scenario can inspire us through what will inevitably be traumatic times ahead.[5]

The network is the source of that position scenario.

■ Document the Birth

Tell your story of how the network was born and how it grew and how it arrived at its compelling vision. We are visual creatures who have a tendency to believe in the visual representation of reality. Like politicans, we can use images to bring into focus the future we want to see. Using things like digital cameras, meeting minutes, quotes, clips from ads, sound bytes, etc., the group's web site can come alive with the story of change.

Modeling Good Communication

Any of the methods discussed in this chapter can be used to expand networks or coalitions of intranet champions. By modeling good communication, members of the network can strengthen their relationships and create a compelling example. Good communication is simple in principle:

- Listen with the intent of understanding
- Appreciate the role of emotions
- Work at being clear and direct
- Play fair; don't use subterfuge and don't ambush
- Have some fun and realize that it's going to be difficult, but rise to the challenge.

As cultural critic Kenneth Burke argues, the rest is just drama we create to keep ourselves within the space of some role we wish to play or wish others to perceive.

If in developing our intranets we could relax in the knowledge that there really are no clear-cut roles to play because the demands on us are changing so rapidly, we would have an easier time inviting the participation of others. With intranet development, we are all either learning or teaching each other, sometimes simultaneously. Being open, curious, and purposeful goes a long way.

■ The Salary Factor

Always in human society, we find tension between the material and ideal realms. Something that complicates this network scenario is money. Some people in this area are being compensated very generously, while others are making even less than they were a few years ago doing something else. The problem is that salary benchmarks simply do not exist. A 25-year-old programmer may make as much money as a 35-year-old manager. Age, education, and salary don't correlate the same way any more.

■ Your Intranet Portfolio

Here are three rules of thumb. First, don't get mad at or resent other individuals who make more money than you do unless their wealth increased directly at your expense. Don't make this a personal thing. Second, be smart about it. Learn to ask and to negotiate. *Fast Company* magazine's November 1996 article, "How to Get a Piece of the Action," is a must read. The article is on their web site at *www.fastcompany.com.* One of the best quotes in the article is from Leigh Steinberg, a top agent and expert negotiator. He said, "You need to get comfortable with the concept of irreplaceability—the proposition that an organization can't function without you. The more you make yourself instrumental to the company's success, the more bargaining power you have."

Know what you want and learn to ask. Start to create an intranet portfolio or dossier for yourself—a kind of career biography that brings results forward. Keep track of your core competencies; keep an inventory of your strengths and skills and how you're using them to improve the company. "This is what I brought to the party, this is what we did, and it resulted in this." Don't view any current advantage as sustainable. Use your dossier help you see a clear picture of your contributions and as a catalyst to keep learning and improving. Once, it was possible to link financial security to the organization that employed you. All you needed to know was the organization's story. No longer. Don't wait until there is a need to sit down with your boss to explain what you've been doing or until you decide you want to work someplace else. Start writing your story now.

There have been instances where people who worked very hard to implement an intranet could not show a direct return on the investment in terms of money saved or costs eliminated. However, they were able to demonstrate that employee job satisfaction increased, that turnover was decreasing, and, moreover, that the organization was able to attract customers from a different market sector because the customers saw the intranet in action and perceived the organization very favorably. The point is that if the intranet is valued and used by employees, there will be many, many ripple effects across the organization. Stay attuned to them, partly so that they can be captured in your story. The more people in your network who help create the value-added intranet and the more people who alert the group to the effects, the more data you'll have and the more confident you'll feel about the credit you deserve.

■ Providing Value

The network is essential, but equally as important today is the support and buy-in of people in positions of influence and power. Management sets the business strategy, controls resources, and strongly influences the organization's culture. The next chapter is focused on securing upper and middle-management support. How do you win support without bending over backward? We'll take a sympathetic look at management's current dilemma and suggest specific ways intranet champions can demonstrate the value of their vision and their net worth.

■ References

[1] Kate Hafner and Mathew Lyon, *Where Wizards Stay Up Late: The Origins of the Internet* (NY: Simon & Schuster, 1996), pp. 144–145.

[2] Harrison Owen, *Open Space Technology; A User's Guide* (Potomac, MD: Abbott Publishing), 1992.

[3] Peggy Holman, "Open Space Research Design," unpublished paper, Febuary, 1995.

[4] Srikumar S. Rao, "Welcome to Open Space," *Training*, April 1994, p. 53.

[5] Peter Schwartz and Peter Leyden, "The Long Boom," *Wired*, July, 1997, p. 118.

Communicating with Management

The hallmark of responsible comment is not to sit in judgment on events as an idle spectator, but to enter imaginatively into the role of a participant in the action. Responsibility consists in sharing the burden of people directing what is to be done, or the burden of offering some other course of action in the mood of one who has realized what it would mean to undertake it.

Walter Lippman

Persuading management to fund and support an intranet is not a tremendous challenge if the challenge is approached from several directions simultaneously. There are three basic steps. First, know your company's business and where the greatest needs exist for improved information and communication. Second, spend time with front-line employees and line managers to better understand their problems and needs. The third step is to get top management support. An effective intranet strategy begins by including top management in the decision-making process.

Section Four focused exclusively on the first two areas. We looked at several methods to find the best opportunities to use the intranet to make improvements. This chapter focuses on communicating with top management. There is no one way to get buy-in from senior management, so this chapter will offer several different routes: conversation and demos, the business plan, and the "Warning Signs" Argument. In addition to the material in this chapter, there are valuable materials in the Tool Kit in Chapter 19. There you will find (a) an outline of a speech to persuade senior management to invest in an intranet, (b) an outline of an intranet business plan, and (c) a reprint of Tom Stewart's article, "Why Dumb Things Happen to Smart Companies." The article was originally publishing in *Fortune* magazine, June 23, 1997. Stewart makes a compelling case; the article belongs on managers' desktops everywhere.

Because it's always good to know critical success factors in advance, let's begin by discussing why intranet champions might sense some push-back from management around intranet and communication issues. Why wouldn't management be thrilled about the idea of creating a "digital nervous system" like Bill Gates? Let's explore the situation.

■ Instabilities within the Hypercompetitive Environment

In 1995, Netscape published a white paper[1] that laid out three philosophical underpinnings for the move to internal web servers:

1. Open systems are better than closed,
2. Open companies are better than closed, and
3. Saving money is always important.

A few years later, it's clear that the third premise has been widely accepted. If there is one primary driver behind the intranet phenomenon, it is savings. The other two premises have become sticking points. Even though the current management movements include learning organizations, knowledge management and knowledge sharing, the "flattening" of the organization, shared learnings, and the identification of "intellectual capital," managers are still the guardians of the organization's knowledge base. Their legitimate authority, writes Shoshana Zuboff, comes from being credited as "someone fit to receive, interpret and communicate orders based on the command of information."[2] Although change is in the wind, most organizations struggle with the degree of openness they will admit.

Entropy, a characteristic of closed systems, is a problem for many organizations. *The American Heritage Dictionary* defines *entropy* as the hypothetical tendency for all matter and energy in the universe to evolve toward a state of inert uniformity. Meg Wheatley writes that it is an inverse measure of a system's capacity to change.[3] The more entropy there is, the less a system is capable of changing. In information theory, entropy represents the "noise," or random errors, occurring in the transmission of signals or messages.

Entropy occurs in organizations when management becomes overly anxious about what will happen when information and communication flow improve, and then revert to control. To this point, managers have been the official gatekeepers of information and communication. Those gatekeeping actions have created equilibrium in organizational systems. What new role is in store for gatekeepers when the gates are opened? What unexpected disturbances will result?

There is a lot of fear about potential disequilibrium caused by improved communication. As Meg Wheatley puts it,[4]

> Some organizations have rigid chains of command to keep people from talking to anyone outside their department; and in most companies, protocols define who can be consulted, advised or criticized. We are afraid of what would happen if we let those elements of the organization recombine, reconfigure, or speak truthfully to one another. We are afraid that things will fall apart.

New communication technology can amplify those fears. Lee Sproull and Sara Keisler point out that communication technology "leads people to pay attention to different things, have contact with different people, and depend on one another differently." Sproull and Keisler[5] describe the ripple effects this way:

> Change in attention means a change in how people spend their time and what they think is important. Change in social contract patterns means change in who people know and how they feel about them. Change in interdependence means change in what people do with and for each other and how those coupled functions are organized in norms, roles, procedures, jobs, and departments.

Mary Holland and Janell Picard came up against management resistance when they championed an intranet at National Semiconductor in the mid-1990s.[6]

> NSC has always had a traditional hierarchical command structure. Information here belongs to departments or divisions and has rarely been shared beyond the vertical boundaries of the silo. . . . Free-form information sharing, an ideal held by much of the Internet and UNIX communities, was a foreign concept to managers, who preferred their systems highly structured and carefully controlled. . . . We had to convince those at the top of the hierarchy that no corporate secrets were being disclosed, that desktop access was a good thing, and that information sharing would be a boon to the company.

In the old managerial paradigm, management controlled the organizational system and focused on its stability. Today, intranet technologies complement a paradigm shift in which information and decision-making power is being distributed more widely. What happens when those "empowered" employees start to use the intranet to report that the situation is not stable, or that senior management's strategy is flawed or is backfiring? In the new paradigm, the free flow of information through communication technologies can create feedback loops that amplify into troubling messages. Meg Wheatley writes that, on one hand, those disturbances can lead to growth. Systems with the capacity to react can reconfigure themselves so that they can deal with new information. However, on the other hand, "for those interested in system stability," Wheatley notes, "amplification is very threatening, and there is a need to quell it before eardrums burst."[7]

Entropy and the quest for equilibrium are among the strongest counter-forces to developing an open systems intranet that permits fluid, cross-functional communication. Often, a group may have the potential to develop a highly useful intranet, but never gets the chance because the organization as a whole proves too resistant or because management cannot envision how information technologies can help the organization grow.

Mary E. Boone, consultant and noted author, advises intranet champions to be careful about managing expectations.

> There is a big problem with managing expectations about intranets. We have developed assumptions that the technologies can

be applied to enable a company to grow, and to reach new markets. But, the reality is that intranets are really another means to address fundamental business problems. We must be careful not to blow expectations out of proportion.

It would be tempting to see your organization's intranet as *the* way to transform the organization. It would also be tempting to try to "coach" management about why its knowledge-hoarding habits are leading to disaster. There is ample literature from ever-expanding knowledge management and knowledge-sharing fields available that could be used for support.

■ Seeking Alignment

Eileen Shapiro, author of *Fad Surfing in the Boardroom,* would probably counsel us to take a different approach. Proselytizing about intranets or knowledge-sharing will not galvanize people to work differently and more effectively. Even if you have enough power or authority in your organization to get people to listen, the "intervention" could have a counter-effect and wreak organizational havoc. The impressive short-term gains will not balance out the longer-term problems.

In contrast to implementing a management "fad," creating positive, long-lasting change requires courage to manage the situation "consciously and actively." "Demonstrating this courage," Shapiro writes, "requires the willingness to assess situations, think through available options, decide on the tools to be used and how to adopt them as needed, and then to accept the accountability for the decisions made and the results achieved." Success lies in understanding your organization's technological and cultural readiness and in aligning proposed technology changes with opportunities where success is most likely.

Intranet technologies came onto the market during an interesting time in history. The rules of business success have changed dramatically. The economy is in the process of reinventing itself, and most companies are watching their finances very closely. Mergers, acquisitions, business process reengineering, down-sizing, outsourcing, and broad-banding of salaries are among the related trends. Restructuring and layoffs are facts of corporate life.

The future feels uncertain, and convincing people of the value of innovative activities or ideas, like intranets, is significantly harder during uncertain times. When organizations innovate, managers in those organizations must make decisions about how to combine resources without knowing whether or not those innovations will pay off. During high levels of uncertainty, management typically demands a lot of documentary evidence before making decisions. They rely on formal mechanisms such as business plans and projections before they'll agree to try things that come without a guarantee of success.[8] To those who see a lot of urgency around the need for developing an intranet, this may seem like backward thinking. To others, it's prudent management of resources.

If you work for an organization that has an "uncertainty-accepting" culture, if the senior management style is oriented toward innovation and risk-taking, you will probably find it easier to implement an intranet. However, the majority of organizations have "uncertainty-avoiding" cultures and have risk-adverse management styles. So selling the concept of an intranet and getting it funded for the long-term is harder and more time-consuming than expected. It doesn't have to be so hard, however.

■ Speak the Language

By learning to speak the management's language and in demonstrating that your business case is sound, an intranet champion can secure buy-in and support. As Scott Stratton advises, "Put yourself in managements' shoes. Do everything you can to ease their fears that the money may be ill-spent."[9]

Overcome potential objections as the first building block. A common objection comes from managements' fear that employees are going to be "surfing" when they should be on task. Answer that objection and help them see further than their immediate reservations. Some guidelines are provided in the Tool Kit in Chapter 19.

In the new economy, it's imperative to be able to cut costs, to be responsive to customers, to eliminate unnecessary redundancies, and to give employees tools to think faster and smarter. Show management how the intranet specifically can help the organization achieve those goals. Finding the right tone and the right language is very important. No one likes to hear that things they put into place are having negative secondary consequences or that their employees feel terrible. One key learning at U S WEST was that it was much more effective to expose senior management to potential savings that would result from the system than to disclose why employees would find the intranet so meaningful. Upper management isn't uncaring or insensitive, but management, a particular group of individuals performing an organizational role, is feeling their own set of pressures and their own form of pain. The substance of that pain—the fundamental root causes—may be very similar to the pain experienced at lower levels of the hierarchy. The form is different, as is the language used to analyze the symptoms and solutions.

If the story told to management about why your organization needs an intranet is based on an analysis of management's weaknesses or the failure of a senior level strategy, chances are strong that the story will simply reinforce already present feelings of anxiety and uncertainty. Management will question whether the intranet is a genuine solution to a business problem or whether the proposal signals something that needs to be brought back into line.

Pushed too far along the anxiety curve, upper management may react and do things like monitoring e-mail or obsessing about security breaches. Particularly if there is a feeling that management is on one side of a divide and the employees are on another side, the technology will be used strategically to exert control. Try not to be one of the pressures or forces that produces a counter-action.

Solicit ideas and opinions from management. Use a business plan and an implementation plan to signal that you have taken time and energy to understand the challenges management faces, that you recognize that there is risk involved, and that you have applied your resources wisely to the construction of the proposal. When you speak to employees about how they would like to use the intranet and where they see value, the type of data you collect will be highly qualitative. Some may reveal years of frustration and be emotionally charged. One critical success factor is translating qualitative data into quantitative data—parsing them into a form of speech that management can hear.

■ The Business Plan

The importance of a business plan for intranet development cannot be underestimated. The creation of the business plan is an opportunity to thoroughly examine the potential of intranet technologies, to explore the best opportunities to use them within the organization, and to identify critical success factors in advance. Creation of the business plan is an opportunity to engage in dialog with key stakeholders about their burning issues and business drivers. The best business plans represent the thinking of many people; the worst are created in a vacuum and are, therefore, either too self-referential or too theoretical. Good business plans are loaded with data and evidence to back up claims. An outline of a business plan is included in the Tool Kit in Chapter 19.

■ The Power of Conversations

In addition to a formal document such as a business plan, intranet champions can leverage opportunities for informal conversation with upper management. The story of how a conversation between Marc Andreessen and Jim Clark resulted in Netscape Communications Corporation illustrates why conversations can be so important.

The Path to Dialog: Andreessen's Journey

In November, 1992, Marc Andreessen, a undergraduate earning $4.50 an hour writing code for the National Center for Supercomputing Applications (NCSA) at the University of Illinois, approached his colleague, Eric Bina, with a proposal. Andreessen observed that the Internet was difficult for ordinary people to use. The software was 10 years behind the hardware. To use the Internet, a person had to learn several sets of commands to get anything accomplished. Although Tim Berners-Lee and his network of colleagues had created the World Wide Web, at that point, people still had to learn FTP to download documents from other computers; learn to "gopher" to help locate documents; and learn to telnet to log onto someone else's computer for things like interrelay chat. Figuring out the commands for getting into a directory or changing a directory, using *get* and *put* to upload and download, searching a database, etc. were not impossible. For most people, however, the command scripts were not second nature. Ordinary people who were not familiar with computer languages relied on handbooks like *Zen and the Art of the Internet: A Beginner's Guide,* which contained sets of instructions for doing things with the Internet. Andreessen wondered, How can we improve this situation? He proposed to Bina that they set out to bring the technology forward by hiding all those different functions behind an attractive user interface.

Bina, who had a BS and an MA in computer science, had been developing a program called *Collage.* Working out of small offices in the basement of the school's Oil Chemistry building, the two wrote Mosaic, the first web browser that made the World Wide Web accessible to anyone with an Internet connection. They wrote code at night and on the weekends, and completed the first version in six weeks.

They did not continue alone, however. Andreessen acted as a team leader, bringing in other programmers to write versions of Mosaic for PCs and Macs to complement the version they had written for UNIX-based work stations. As legend goes, two months after Andreessen's proposal, in January 1993, the first version of Mosaic was released for free on the Net, and people all over the world began downloading it by the thousands.

Andreessen had another idea. Could he make a business of the browser? As Rick Tetzeli [10] reports, Andreessen approached Larry Smarr, the director of NCSA, with the idea. NCSA and the University of Illinois, like most organizations, owns the "intellectual capital" created by their employees, and this included the code behind Mosaic. Smarr explained that while the university was glad to license code its employees had written, it did not have a system in place to incubate commercial companies. Andreessen was on his own.

After graduating from Illinois, Andreessen packed up and headed for the Silicon Valley, where he went to work for a small software company called Enterprise Integration Technologies, which had recruited Andreessen because of his work on Mosaic. How ironic: The person largely responsible for creating this breakthrough technology was, at that point, working in relative obscurity.

Then, one day, he received e-mail from Jim Clark, former founder and CEO of Silicon Graphics, who had decided to leave the company after losing a fight over the direction of the company he had helped to create. Silicon

Graphics' technology had become instrumental in the creation of graphics-rich digital content for including in film and for television. Clark was looking to the future of interactive television and the software required to create it. He contacted Andreessen with the idea of using the Mosaic browser as the interface for interactive television subscribers. The millionaire and the 22-year-old college graduate met at Clark's home to talk informally and, as they talked, Andreessen sold Clark not only on the concept of the World Wide Web, but also on the brilliance of his own mind. With a blue sky and sparkling water as a backdrop, Andreessen continued sharing his ideas with Clark on Clark's yacht. Shortly after that, Clark proposed that he and Andreessen go into business together.

It is almost possible to imagine what those conversations must have been like. Here was Clark, with all his years of business experience and accumen, his wealth and energy, his house and yacht, looking toward the future with an intent to make another significant mark on the world beyond what he'd already accomplished at Silicon Graphics. Here was Andreessen, a very gifted and talented young person from New Lisbon, Wisconsin, who was open to learning about a lot in life—from computers to philosophy and classical music, contemporary history, and Ford Mustangs—who had an eye toward the potential inherent in the new web technologies. Here were two people who felt that they could and should make a difference, conversing with one another.

The Gift of Dialog

David Bohm has argued that people and groups like to think of themselves as separate. However, if we could engage with each other in conversation at a meaningful level, we would find ways to relate to each other that would dissolve the perception of separateness. Moreover, Bohm says, it is through conversation that we recognize how we're fundamentally connected and how our futures are interwoven. Somehow, that is what transpired when Clark and Andreessen met to talk. In 1994, Clark's ambitions to create software for interactive television were aligned with 1994 technology trends. HDTV was being touted as one of the most exciting and promising new breakthroughs in consumer electronics technology. Backed by Sony and the other giants, HDTV and the associated concept of interactive television was receiving a steady stream of press. The Web, on the other hand, was just emerging as an underground phenomenon and it was backed only by pockets of enthusiastic, idealistic "gearheads." Yet the conversation between Clark and Andreessen opened up a new horizon of possibilities for both men.

Conversations and Demos

Sometimes we become so preoccupied with winning the battle to capture someone's attention and their buy-in that we neglect the opportunities for more subtle persuasion, such as the conversations that took place between Andreessen and Clark.

Sherman Woo, the IT visionary at US WEST, whose projects are discussed several times throughout this book, has mastered the art of subtle persuasion. Woo enjoys telling the story of how a group of senior-level managers came to visit the Global Village simply to learn about the Internet and ended up asking Woo if it was possible to use a web browser as the GUI to the company's legacy systems. Woo's internet tour illustrated how multiple forms of digital information could be linked together on the Web. The senior managers immediately perceived the value to the company and commissioned Woo right on the spot to begin working on the project.

The power of a demo and a conversation can be enormous. Tom Smith, general manager of the Network Organization in Arizona, saw the Netscape At Work demos on the laptop of one of U S WEST's internal consultants during a lunch break. Immediately, Smith perceived the potential of a web-based system to improve communication among technicians and customer service representatives. Within a week, Tom made a visit to the Global Village to discuss with Sherman Woo how to make such a project a reality.

One of the reasons that a CD-ROM was packaged with this book was to make it easier for intranet champions to show senior management what an intranet would look like and what it can do. An intranet is fundamentally a visual medium; to attempt to describe it in words alone short-changes its uniqueness. The demos can be used to give presentations to small and large groups. If you have a CD-ROM drive and a laptop, you can carry the demo with you. When the right moment presents itself, you'll be armed with a visual argument.

■ The "Warning Signs" Argument

For several years, journalist Thomas A. Stewart has tracked the evolution of knowledge management for *Fortune* magazine. Starting in 1991, long before anyone else was interested in the topic, Stewart began exploring how companies were managing their "intellectual assets." His work resulted in cover stories on the topic, a series of articles for *Fortune* entitled "Brainpower," and a book, *Intellectual Capital: The New Wealth of Organizations*, published in 1997. The book is highly relevant to intranet development, as it contains case studies of how companies used information technology to improve information flow and communication. Shortly after Stewart's book was on the shelves, *Fortune* published what is perhaps Stewart's best article of all, "Why Dumb Things Happen to Smart Companies."

Stewart's questions were, How does one make the case for managing intellectual capital to CEOs and CFOs? And where do we start? Stewart writes:[11]

> The two questions are cousins, since the best way to build support for any management effort is to start where you'll get early results. Mind you, the forgotten key to succeeding in management is not to stop there; quitting too soon condemns you to the hummingbird style of management, forever flitting and sipping from one blooming idea to another. But you've got to start somewhere, and here's a way to figure out where: a list of nine symptoms of a "knowledge problem"—something wrong with how your company manages its brainpower.

The original list of nine comes from David H. Smith, head of knowledge development for Unilever. Stewart added examples and antidotes to add punch and realism.

> **The Warning Signs**
> *Nine symptoms of bad brainpower management.*
> 1. You repeat mistakes.
> 2. Work gets duplicated.
> 3. Customer relations are strained.
> 4. Good ideas don't get shared.
> 5. You have to compete on price.
> 6. You can't keep up with market leaders.
> 7. You're dependent on key individuals.
> 8. You're slow to launch new products.
> 9. You don't know how to price for service.

This is a "cut-and-run" article. Cut (or copy) it and offer it to your organization's management with a brief cover letter explaining how Stewart's article relates to your organization's unique situation, then suggest a follow-up. The article can serve as a portal to conversation about how to use the intranet to improve this situation.

■ Armed and Ready

This chapter offered a variety of approaches for communicating with senior management about the need to invest resources in intranet development. They include conversation and demos, the business plan, and the "Warning Signs" argument. In addition, the speech outline, business plan outline, and reprint of Stewart's article can all become part of the persuasion campaign. Here are a few more tips for dealing with management:

1. *Check unsupported claims.* Although it would be great to see the same degree of evidence from management in regard to claims about technology development that management expects from us, we often find situations when senior people make unsupported claims. If an executive says, "We can't use the technologies you propose because the whole company is going to be using Notes," either ask for more explanation or check into it yourself.

What is said with the tone of authority may be a rumor picked up at the last corporate outing. Don't base an action plan on rumors.

2. *Help management build and communicate a vision of how technology can further the organization's goals.* Upper management needs to communicate a clear, strong vision about the possibilities the technology offers to the organization in the pursuit of specific objectives. Often, top management sends two messages out simultaneously: (a) the fact that the organization is going to make aggressive use of new technologies and (b) a message about the future of the organization.

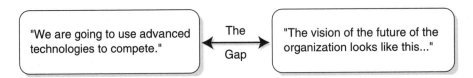

However, there is a gap between the two: Specifically, how are people expected to use the new technologies to achieve the company's future vision?

Intranet champions can help top management create a vision and a message that bridges the "disconnection":

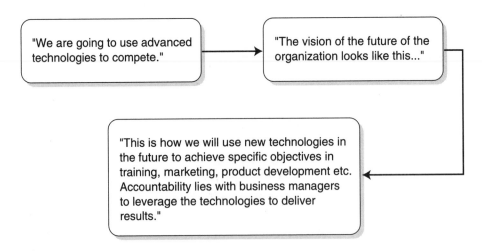

3. *Request active participation.* After top management has agreed to fund and support intranet development, request active participation. Try to involve senior people in all aspects of the project—from sending pilot project participants a memo to acknowledging their participation to posting in discussion areas. The more involved they are, the greater the perception of legitimacy, and the more they can experience the value of the technology for themselves.

■ Who Are the Leaders of Tomorrow?

This chapter concludes with a passage from Shoshana Zuboff's classic, *In the Age of the Smart Machine.* These words, first published in 1988, ring as true today as they did 10 years ago. This eloquent call to arms unites all intranet champions going forward to use new technologies to create better, more humane forms of communications.[12]

> The questions that we face today are finally about leadership. Will there be leaders who are able to recognize the historical moment and the choices it presents? Will they find ways to create the organizational conditions in which new visions, new concepts, and new language of workplace relations can emerge? Will they be able to create organizational innovations that can exploit the unique capabilities of the new technology and thus mobilize their organization's productive and potential to meet heightened rigors of global competition? Will there be leaders who understand the crucial role that human beings from each organizational stratum can play in adding value to the production of goods and services?

> If not, we will be stranded in a new world with old solutions. We will suffer through the unintended consequences of change, because we have failed to understand this technology and how it differs from what came before. By neglecting the unique informatting capacity of advanced computer-based technology and ignoring the need for a new vision of work and organization, we will have forfeited the dramatic business benefits it can provide. Instead, we will find ways

to absorb the dysfunctions, putting out brush fires and patching wounds in a slow-burning bewilderment.

■ References

[1] "Enter the Interplasm," *ComputerLetter*, Vol. 11, Number 28 (August 21, 1995), p. 2.

[2] Shoshana Zuboff, "The Emperor's New Workplace," *Scientific American*, September 1995, p. 204.

[3] Margaret J. Wheatley, *Leadership and the New Science: Learning About Organization from an Orderly Universe* (Berrett-Koehler, 1994), p. 76.

[4] Wheatley, p. 17.

[5] Sproull and Keisler, p. 5.

[6] Mary Holland and Janell Picard, "Librarians at the Gate," *Webmaster*, September 1996.

[7] Wheatley, p. 87.

[8] Scott Shane, "Uncertainty Avoidance and the Preference for Innovation Championing Roles," *Journal of International Business Studies*, Vol. 26, January 1995, p. 47.

[9] Scott Straton, "How to Sell an Information System to Your Boss," *American Demographics*, Vol. 16, February 1994, p. 54.

[10] Rick Tetzeli, "What It's Really Like to Be Marc Andreessen," *Fortune*, December 9, 1996.

[11] Thomas A. Stewart, "Why Dumb Things Happen to Smart Companies," *Fortune*, June 23, 1997, pp. 159–160.

[12] Shoshana Zuboff, *In the Age of the Smart Machine: The Future of Work and Power* (NY: Basic Books, 1988), p. 12.

C H A P T E R

Cybrarians and Other Secrets of Cyberspace

There are few secrets for intranet success, so this is the shortest chapter in the book. It contains three very valuable "secrets," however: the role of "cybrarians," a way to create "virtual training," and Chris Locke's Seven-Step method to effective on-line networking.

Cybrarians

One of the critical success factors in technology-enabled knowledge-sharing systems in organizations is human presence. When McKinsey, Coopers & Lybrand, and Buckman Labs developed their electronic knowledge-sharing systems, each saw a need to identify a person who could work behind the scenes. They appointed "cybrarians," who became responsible for creating virtual libraries, or knowledge repositories, and for connecting people with ideas and with each other.

The involvement of cybrarians is one of the critical success factors behind intranet development. They:

- encourage participation in discussion areas by "seeding" questions
- alert people to particular posts that they should see
- solicit participation from reluctant contributors
- find SMEs who can add insight or provide answers
- spend time "playing" or searching the network for new information
- keep discussions fresh, and
- act as knowledge-sharing coaches.

A good cybrarian is a good knowledge broker always on the lookout for an opportunity to foster a connection. Making sure that people get answers to their questions quickly is an important way that knowledge brokers help to ensure that user participation stabilizes and continues after an initial novelty period. When someone needs an answer to a question, the knowledge broker or cybrarian helps to find the right person who can provide help "just in time." That's essential, as the moment someone asks a question is the moment they are most ready to learn.

Cybrarians serve as guides to ensure that conversations stay on track, arguments are not repeated, and harsh personal attacks (known as *flames*) are rapidly quelled. If the group is getting stuck on a question that was resolved months before, for example, the cybrarian might post a message that explains the answer arrived at by the group. If someone is posting insulting or offensive messages, the cybrarian might send private e-mail reminding the guilty party of the rules of civility that prevail in the discussion.

■ The Virtual Classroom

One advantage of intranets as compared to "fat-client" groupware such as Lotus Notes or Microsoft BackOffice is that the entire employee base doesn't have to be trained to use the system. In situations where training becomes necessary, one option is to create a "virtual classroom."

All of the participants and the teacher are linked together via a conference call. This eliminates the need to travel, and the people learn the new skills while sitting at their own computers, where they are comfortable. The participants actually experience what it would feel like to integrate the new activity into their day-to-day work practices. As the instructor guides the students through a series of activities, everyone can listen to each other and learn from each others' questions.

Performing a technology check a few days before the session is very important. Students need to be equipped with everything they might need in terms of hardware, software, and network connections prior to the beginning of the class.

■ Rules of Conduct

An entire book could be written about how one should conduct oneself in cyberspace. The best guidelines ever published were created by Chris Locke, long-time net expert and communicator extraordinaire. This article first appeared in *Information Week*, June 24, 1994. It is reprinted here with the permission of the author and publisher.

> *"Networking On and Off-Line—The True Value of Networks: They Support the Sharing of Information Key to Your Business."*
>
> **by Christopher Locke**

The real advantage of networks is that they support networking. This is obvious both to those who understand the power of the Internet and those who haven't a clue as to what the fuss is all about. Technical issues, however, too often shape corporate policy concerning the Internet. While these issues are important, they shouldn't be the primary factors driving decisions fundamental to your organization's future identity and strategies.

Networking is primarily social. If it doesn't enable people to work together more effectively, it isn't worth the investment—no matter how fast, secure, or efficient the physical infrastructure.

Seven-Step Method

What follows are my seven principles of effective networking, most of which pose radical challenges to conventional wisdom:

1. Talk to anyone about anything. Participate in other people's thinking whenever possible. Being too important or too busy is a thin excuse when your more attentive competitor snags a chunk of your market share. Aloof one-liners such as "Ms. Webster will be addressing your concerns on our behalf" are a curt invitation to take a flying leap. Valuable colleagues and customers are likely to take you up on the offer.

2. Develop a high tolerance for ambiguity. Being too attached to "the right answer" is a serious character flaw. In an environment of continual and dynamic upheavals, yesterday's right answer can easily precipitate tomorrow's fatal misstep. Listen to everybody's point of view without deciding too quickly which is correct. This can be difficult for managers schooled in the value of crisp precision and unwavering certainty. Like beauty, chaos is in the eye of the beholder—learn to surf it. Consider, ponder, delay judgment. When you do decide, notice how much smarter you've suddenly become.

3. Be willing to look stupid. People in management positions seldom ask questions that might belie their ignorance. Where knowledge is power and nothing more, the desire to understand is regarded as a dangerous indicator of weakness. Expose this attitude for what it is: counterproductive to your organization's mental and financial health. The more senior you are, the more you should be asking for help. Nobody believes you know it all anyway—starting with yourself. A lot of smart folks together probably know more than you do alone. Remember: Appearing slightly stupid always beats true ignorance.

4. Give more than you take. Reserving knowledge for personal advantage runs counter to the real demands on businesses. Offering useful information builds robust relationships and powerful work teams across long distances. "What can I do for you?" can be a truly unfriendly question. Don't ask; just do it. Then watch how your professional life changes.

5. Cultivate fearlessness. Get comfortable with risk. The "not invented here" syndrome has buried a lot of companies. If you're afraid of losing your job because you took action, be prepared to move on. If you're in a company geared for survival and success, you probably won't have to. A company that would fire you for taking an intelligent initiative doesn't have much of a half-life anyway. In the words of W. Edward Deming, "Drive out fear!"

6. Go on gut instinct. Hone your intuition and learn to trust it. Quantitative analysis works wonders when all the assumptions are accurate and the variables selected are the right ones. This happens approximately once every million years. You need to move faster than that. Genuine insight is seldom reflected in spreadsheets. Rather, it grows organically out of experience and imagination, neither of which can be applied as context-free rule sets.

7. Expand your sense of humor. Delusions of self-importance are usually harbingers of early senility. Ditto nagging doubts. A prominent cardiologist once proposed a simple formula guaranteed to prevent heart failure: a. Don't sweat the small stuff and b(s). It's all small stuff. Work less, play more, dream always. You'll be far more effective.

None of these principles work in isolation from the rest. Taken together, they constitute the social bedrock on which high-performance organizations are built. Networking is not some isolated phenomenon that arrived with the advent of high technology. But networking technology may very well encourage and promote these invaluable human qualities at a critical moment in your company's evolution.

CHAPTER

Tool Kit

Contents of the Tool Kit:

VisionMapping Exercise Protocol 1

In thinking about how you do your job every day,

- Where do you get information you need to help you answer customers' questions?

- How do you become more knowledgeable while on the job?   What tools do you use? What people do you consult?

- In your opinion, where does the best learning at work take place?

- How do you signal that you need more information, more knowledge or more training? Who do you tell?

- What kind of information is at the "periphery" of your mind, i.e., things you are attuned to without attending to explicitly? What sort of information is at the center?

During the meeting, we'll be asking you to visually represent your answers to these questions. If it is helpful to you, you may wish to sketch or doodle some of your thoughts beforehand.

VisionMapping Exercise Protocol 2

Generally,

What are you seeing from your perspective about why we need to introduce change?

More specifically,

How are we working with our customers?
How are we working with our suppliers?
How do we get feedback from these two groups?
What do we do with that information today?

Where are our employees in this loop? *Are* they actually in the loop?
Where are our managers in this loop? *Are* they actually in the loop?
How do we get feedback from these two groups?
What do we do with that information today?

What external forces are affecting our business?
How do those forces affect our ability to bring satisfaction and added value to the customer?

Work Environment Profile

Instructions

This survey is designed to collect information about employees' perceptions of different aspects of their work environment. For each statement, please circle the response that best describes your perception of your work environment. When a statement contains the words *organization* or (*our company name*) choose an answer that reflects your opinion about the entire organization. When the term *department* is used, choose an answer describing the group or team that you feel closest to. Your first thoughts are usually the most accurate, so try not to think too long about the response to any one statement.

We would like to emphasize that you may be assured of complete confidentiality. Your individual responses will not in any way be attached to your name. All of the information we obtain will be grouped with that from other respondents and summarized.

	Definitely Disagree	Disagree	Slightly Disagree	Slightly Agree	Agree	Definitely Agree
I make most of the decisions that affect the way my job is performed	DD	D	SD	SA	A	DA
I determine my own work procedures	DD	D	SD	SA	A	DA
I schedule my own work activities	DD	D	SD	SA	A	DA
I set the performance standards for my job	DD	D	SD	SA	A	DA
I organize my work as I see best	DD	D	SD	SA	A	DA
I feel valued by my colleagues in my department	DD	D	SD	SA	A	DA

I value my colleagues in my department	DD	D	SD	SA	A	DA
I feel valued by my colleagues in the organization as a whole	DD	D	SD	SA	A	DA
I value my colleagues in the organization as a whole	DD	D	SD	SA	A	DA
My department respects the other departments	DD	D	SD	SA	A	DA
My department is respected by other departments	DD	D	SD	SA	A	DA
I receive all the information I need to carry out my work	DD	D	SD	SA	A	DA
I am kept adequately informed about significant issues in the organization as a whole	DD	D	SD	SA	A	DA
In general, communication is effective in the organization	DD	D	SD	SA	A	DA
My department receives all the information it needs to carry out its function well	DD	D	SD	SA	A	DA

My department is kept adequately informed about significant issues in the organization as a whole	DD	D	SD	SA	A	DA
My co-workers and I communicate clearly and effectively	DD	D	SD	SA	A	DA
I am clear about the part I can play in helping (the organization) achieve its goals	DD	D	SD	SA	A	DA
The future of (the organization) has been communicated to us all	DD	D	SD	SA	A	DA
The future objectives of (the organization) are consistent with my personal objectives	DD	D	SD	SA	A	DA
The future of (the organization) will be brighter than its past	DD	D	SD	SA	A	DA
The vast majority of the employees share a clear understanding of where the organization is going and what it is trying to achieve	DD	D	SD	SA	A	DA
Employees of (the organization) pitch in to help each other out.	DD	D	SD	SA	A	DA
Employees of (the organization) take an interest in one another	DD	D	SD	SA	A	DA

There is a lot of "team spirit" among employees	DD	D	SD	SA	A	DA
My department collaborates well with other departments	DD	D	SD	SA	A	DA
I am rarely put under undue work pressure by my colleagues	DD	D	SD	SA	A	DA
Work rarely piles up faster than I can complete it	DD	D	SD	SA	A	DA
People at (the organization) generally support each other well	DD	D	SD	SA	A	DA
I have to put in long hours to complete my work	DD	D	SD	SA	A	DA
I often feel the pressure of work is excessive	DD	D	SD	SA	A	DA
In general, this is a caring and cooperative organization	DD	D	SD	SA	A	DA
I am encouraged to innovate in my work	DD	D	SD	SA	A	DA
My department is encouraged to innovate	DD	D	SD	SA	A	DA
The philosophy of our management is that in the long run we get ahead by playing it slow, safe, and sure	DD	D	SD	SA	A	DA

Decision-making in this organization is too cautious for maximum effectiveness	DD	D	SD	SA	A	DA
I am encouraged to try new ways of doing my job	DD	D	SD	SA	A	DA
Change comes slowly at (the organization); people would rather do things the old way	DD	D	SD	SA	A	DA
Conflicts are constructively/positively solved	DD	D	SD	SA	A	DA
We are generally encouraged to resolve our conflicts quickly, rather than let them simmer	DD	D	SD	SA	A	DA
There are helpful ways of preventing conflict at (the organization)	DD	D	SD	SA	A	DA
There is little conflict between departments	DD	D	SD	SA	A	DA
In general, conflict is managed well at (The organization)	DD	D	SD	SA	A	DA
Ample opportunities for promotion are available within the organization	DD	D	SD	SA	A	DA
My job presents a significant challenge to me	DD	D	SD	SA	A	DA
(the organization) is successful in developing its people for bigger jobs	DD	D	SD	SA	A	DA

(The organization) provides ample opportunities for individual growth and development	DD	D	SD	SA	A	DA
I feel my contribution at (the organization) is helping to make us more competitive in the future	DD	D	SD	SA	A	DA
I feel that I have a significant impact on my work team	DD	D	SD	SA	A	DA
I feel that I have a significant impact on the organization as a whole	DD	D	SD	SA	A	DA
Overall, I am satisfied with my work environment	DD	D	SD	SA	A	DA

Communication and Knowledge-
Sharing Survey

A. Group Description
Describe your group's

    1) mission
    2) clients and suppliers
    3) number of employees and geographic dispersion
    4) daily activities
    5) recent trends
    6) management structure

B. Communication
Describe how your group communicates

    1) internally and externally (e.g. telephone, written notes, voice mail, e-mail, conference call, personally)
    2) percentage estimate for each medium
    3) what types of information do you communicate/ in what form (e.g. client concerns communicated via a team meeting; project updates communicated via a memo)

Describe how *you personally* communicate. Do you use any communication media that members of your group do not use? What is your preferred way to communicate?

Describe how your group uses, maintains, and disseminates information

Describe how you personally use, maintain, and disseminate information

What are the major communication problems for the group?

    1) how are these problems being manifested?
    2) what appears to be causing these problems?
    3) whom do these problems affect (primarily and secondarily)?
    4) what are the problems costing?

5) what actions have been taken to solve these problems in the past?
6) what outcomes are sought by the group?

C. Collaboration

What type of work collaboration occurs

1) within your group?
2) among other groups in the organization?
3) with groups that are not part of this organization?

D. Culture

How would you describe the work culture of your group

1) in terms of communication?
2) in terms of sharing?
3) in terms of teamwork?

E. Vision

What is your ideal vision for this group

1) in terms of communication?
2) in terms of information access and dissemination?
3) in terms of work flow?

Communication Questionnaire

When responding to the questions below, please think about the kinds of communication that apply to your job. On a scale of 1 to 5, how satisfied are you with these communication processes? Please circle the number that best represents your response.

	Not satisfied				Very satisfied
A. Sharing key learnings or accomplishments with others	1	2	3	4	5
B. Sharing techniques and strategies for problem-solving	1	2	3	4	5
C. Methods available at (the organization) for accessing relevant industry information	1	2	3	4	5
D. Sharing relevant industry information within (the organization)	1	2	3	4	5
E. Quickly identifying people who have experience and expertise and can help	1	2	3	4	5
F. Alerting management to existing and potential problems	1	2	3	4	5
G. Sharing downward communication coming from top-level management	1	2	3	4	5
H. Seeing resolution to problems identified by employees	1	2	3	4	5
I. Being heard	1	2	3	4	5
J. Openness of communication among project teams	1	2	3	4	5
K. Honesty of communication among project teams	1	2	3	4	5

Focus Group Protocol

The protocol illustrates how several research methodologies can be used in the course of one focus group—in this case, discussions, surveys, reactions to a demo, and anonymous comments. The protocol is a modified version of one actually used by the WisdomLink team at International Learning Systems. The team created it with the intention of understanding employees' needs for a web site to support corporate training and learning. The term *Zeus* is used to represent both the name of the organization and the name of its intranet.

Part I: Introduction of Facilitators

Greeting	Good morning. My name is (name) and my name is (name). We're here from (home organization), and we thank you for joining us today.
Statement of Purpose	The purpose of this focus group is to identify how a web site on the company's intranet can be used to improve the ways in which "Zeus" provides training and learning opportunities to its employees.
Who We Are	We are from (home organization), and "Zeus" has asked us to help design and develop the web site. Our specialty is creating web sites that support the organizational learning. We want to make the "Zeus" site as effective as possible. To do that, we'd like to gather your thoughts and opinions about the learning and training opportunities available at "Zeus" in general, and more specifically, your thoughts about the nature of the content of the web site.
Why Their Participation Is Important	Your participation helps to ensure that we create a web site that actually helps "Zeus" employees, instead of becoming a frustration or headache. We want to design a site that meets your needs, and we can't do that without hearing from you about your needs in this area.
Confidentiality	Everything you say here and everything we talk about will be kept in confidence. We will be writing up our findings from all of our (X number) of focus groups and interviews in a report that we'll deliver to the sponsor of this work, (Mr. or Mrs. Sponsor). No names will be attached to any comments. Unless you tell us otherwise, we will keep you anonymous.

Opportunity to Review the Findings	We've arranged in advance to provide each of you with a copy of the report. We do our very best to interpret and translate the focus group discussions, but we know that sometimes misunderstanding or misinterpretation can occur. So, we're interested not only in giving you an opportunity to review the report, but also to comment on it. We've created a link off of our web site where you can access the report and provide comments directly to us on-line. The URL will be written in the "thank you" note that we'll be sending to you next week. We hope that you'll take a few minutes to take a look at it when it comes on-line.
Logistics	We're going to be (talking) together for X hours. We will take a break midpoint at 00:00 o'clock. We would appreciate it if you would turn off pagers or cell phones. Bathrooms are (location).
Group Introductions (Write Down People's Names as They Introduce Themselves)	Let's start with some introductions. Let's go around the table and introduce ourselves. Please tell us your • name, • division, • how long you've been with "Zeus"
Remark on Results	(It's good to have such a variety. It's good to have so many long-time "Zeus" employees, as well as some new people, etc.)

Part II: Employees' Perceptions of "Zeus" Training and Learning Opportunities

Introduce Segment	We want to begin with your familiarity with "Zeus" training and learning opportunities. What do you know about training and learning opportunities "Zeus" provides for its employees? How accessible they are to you? What is the extent to which you've been involved since you became an employee?
Introduce Questionnaire	We have a brief survey for you to fill out. It's designed to help us understand what you already know about how "Zeus" provides training and learning opportunities and what you think about the current approach. Please spend about 10 minutes answering the questions. We'll resume discussion when everyone is finished. (Note: A version of the questionnaire is included in the ToolKit)
Pass Out Survey	(Give participants enough time to fill out survey.)

Collect Survey	Thanks very much. You'll be able to see the collective results in the report we put on-line in a couple of weeks.
Round-Table Discussion with Answers Captured on White Board	We'd like to spend just a few minutes talking with you about the benefits "Zeus" provides in training and learning opportunities, as you perceive it. Give prompts. • What benefits have you seen? • How has this been positive for the company overall? • How has it been positive for your business unit? (Note: Be sure that every participant gets a chance to say something.)
Introduce Discussion of Limitations of How "Zeus" Provides Training and Learning Opportunities	We'd like to spend just a few minutes talking with you about the limitations of how "Zeus" provides training and learning opportunities, as you perceive them.
Roundtable Discussion with Answers Captured on White Board	Give prompts. • What hasn't worked so well? • What do you think about how the overall message about continuous training and learning has been communicated to you? • Where do you see shortcomings? (Note: Be sure that every participant gets a chance to say something.)
Remark on Results	An example might be: While you have seen the company begin to change as a result of recent training and learning initiatives provided by "Zeus," the messages are not always clear about resources or time, and your needs are not always being met. Thank you for your candor.
Restate Purpose of Focus Group and Conclude Segment	Again, the purpose of the focus group is to understand what would motivate "Zeus" employees to actively use the web site as a platform for increasing their knowledge and skills. Let's turn to a discussion about the Web.

Part III: The Web Site

Establish Understanding of Technical Terms	To begin with, let's talk about your familiarity with the "Zeus" Intranet. We want to make sure that everyone knows what we mean by *web site* and *web page*.
Show of Hands Poll	• How many of you have used the "Zeus" Intranet? • How many of you have used it on a weekly basis?
Recap Results	An example might be: "It looks like everyone here has used it. About half of the people here use it on a weekly basis."
Define "Web Site"	The "Zeus" web site is going to be a portion of the "Zeus" Intranet. It will be accessible from the Intranet Hom Page; anyone in the company will be able to use it. The site will contain a number of pages that will be linked together. By clicking onto a hypertext link, you'll be able to move to another section within a document, or to another document altogether. You, as a user, won't need to know how those documents are linked. It all happens "backstage."
Define "Web Page"	Each file or document is called a *web page*, and as you know, web pages can include graphics, text, and even audio and video clips.
Clarify Advantages of the Medium	Some of the advantages of using the Web as a communication medium are: 1. Time/Space: Unlike printed material, unlimited copies of materials are available to anyone at any time or place. 2. Dynamic: It's easy to eliminate outdated material or to update material. Changes can happen in "real time": example of stock market ticker, or policy updates. 3. Interactivity: The Web allows *you* to contribute information—you become a participant, not just an observer. You can comment on the cotent, offer your ideas and suggestions and "see" other people's comments. It's dynamic, like a conversation. 4. Linked Content: Hypertext links can help you see how information fits together—how documents are related.
Establish Clarity of Terms	Is everyone comfortable with these concepts and the terms *web site* and *web page*?

Introduce Demo Segment	We'd like to show you a demo of the "Zeus Learning" web site, and gather your reactions to it. A few caveats: 1. The graphics will change. These are just sketches. 2. The demo is just a skeleton, the actual content is in development. In fact, what we hear from you today will help us to create content that is valuable.
Show Demo Page By Page	(Show demo. Ideally, each participant should be encouraged to explore the demo on their own or with a partner at an assigned computer in the room. If logistics are too difficult, the facilitator can provide a "tour," but this is not the best approach.)
Gather Reactions. **Generally Positive or** **Negative**	Would this: • Be something you'd use as a resource? • Be something you would recommend to a new employee as a resource?
Specifically, Which Part **Did They Favor?**	• Which parts appeared most useful? • Least useful?
Gather Content Ideas for **Home Page**	• What information would you like to see on the first page? • What might distinguish that information on the web page from everything else you've ever seen/heard about the origins and the importance of training and learning "Zeus"?
On-Line Tools—Value? **Ideas to Improve?**	• What is your reaction to the On-Line Tools section? • Would you use it as a resource? • What would be helpful to you?
Discussion Areas	• Would you see advantages to providing feedback through the web site? • If you posted a question on a discussion area, what would be your expectation for seeing a reply?
Current Use of Lotus **Notes**	• Right now, "Zeus Shared Learnings and Best Practices" is being published on a Lotus Notes database.
Show Hands Poll	• How many people have access to the database? • How many people have used the database?

Discussion of the Lotus Notes Database and Possible Link to the Web Site	• Could you give us your reactions? • Could you tell us what is like to search the database for shared learnings that are useful to you? • What do you think would make the Lotus Notes database more attractive to you? • What would make you use it more? • Would there be value in creating links from the web site into the Lotus Notes database?
Introduce Final Segment	You've shared a lot of valuable thoughts and ideas with us today. Thank you very much. To bring some closure to the session, we'd like to go have everyone give three reasons why they would use the web site as a learning resource. Then, we'd like you to give three reasons they would not use it. To get the most candid responses, we ask that you fill out your answers on these 3" x 5" cards. After you have written your responses on the cards, we'll collect them and shuffle them. We will list your answers responses on the white board. They'll be anonymous.
Why/Why Not? Exercise	The "why" responses are read out loud and listed on a white board. After the "why" list is complete, the "why not" responses are read and listed.
Rank Ordering of Responses	We're going to ask you to rate these reasons in order of their salience, or strength.
Review Results	Looks like your top three reasons why you would use a "Zeus Learning" web site are (X,Y,Z). Your top three reasons why you would not are (A,B,C).
Invite Comment	I wonder if you have any reaction to this list or comments that you'd like to make.
Invite Involvement	This list represents a lot of work down the pike as well as the involvement of many people. If you have any interest in becoming involved with these critical success factors, we would welcome and appreciate your involvement.
Conclusion	End session. Thank participants. Pass out business cards. Provide contact information to be used if the participants wish to follow-up with additional thoughts.

Improving Learning Questionnaire

Please circle your answers

	Definitely Disagree	Disagree	Slightly Disagree	Slightly Agree	Agree	Definitely Agree
1. "Zeus Learning" is more than a set of new "buzz" words for the same principles we used previously. It's a significantly improved way of doing business.	DD	D	SD	SA	A	DA
2. I can see connections between "Zeus Learning" and other business practices I have been asked to do. For example, ISO certification.	DD	D	SD	SA	A	DA
3. I can see evi3dence of how employees are using "Zeus Learning" to improve the business.	DD	D	SD	SA	A	DA
4. I am confident that senior management is fully committed to the "Zeus Learning" initiative.	DD	D	SD	SA	A	DA
5. I regard continuous training as "something I really need to do."	DD	D	SD	SA	A	DA

6. Zeus has demonstrated
   that there are "smart" rea-
   sons for adopting "Best   DD   D   SD   SA   A   DA
   Practices" from other
   companies.

7. How have you received information about "Zeus Learning"? Please check all that apply.

   ___ printed materials I've received at my workplace

   ___ classroom instruction

   ___ discussions with my peers at my workplace

   ___ conversations with my supervisor

   ___ conversations with a Learning Consultant

8. How useful has the information about "Zeus Learning" been to you? Please rate these sources from 1 to 5, with 5 being very valuable.

   ___ printed materials I've received at my workplace

   ___ classroom instruction

   ___ discussions with my peers at my workplace

   ___ conversations with my supervisor

   ___ conversations with a Learning Consultant

9. How often do you use the "Zeus" Intranet? Please circle your answer.

A. More than once a day
B. Daily
C. Weekly
D. Monthly
E. Never

10. Why do you use the "Zeus" Intranet? Please check all that apply.

___ to gather information

___ to do collaborative work

___ to provide information to others

___ to find new problem-solving strategies

___ to find others who are interested in the same business issues that interest me

11. Are there other reasons why you use the intranet?

12. Please list two strengths of the "Zeus" Intranet.

1.
2.

13. Please list two weaknesses.

1.
2.
14. In your opinion, is "Zeus" ahead, behind or equal to other Fortune 500 companies in use of the Intranet? Why?

Guidelines for E-mail Surveys

Typical Problems With E-Mail as a Medium for Surveys and Questionnaires

1. E-mail addresses are assumed to be correct when they are not. So a percentage of the sample never receives the message.

2. Employees disregard or discard the message because they do not recognize the sender's name as important.

3. Employees do not understand how to complete the questionnaire. A portion of the returned responses must be disqualified because of completion errors.

4. Employees do not understand how to return the questionnaire or to whom it should be sent. They may inadvertently "spam" all other recipients, or not return it at all.

1. Employees often are concerned about who will have access to the responses and whether they will remain anonymous participants. To preserve anonymity, they may choose not to reply.

Recommendations

1. Verify e-mail addresses.

2. Use other media such as a company newsletter to announce the questionnaire. Lead time should be no longer than one month, no shorter than one week.

3. Send an e-mail message from the president of the company about a week prior to the day the questionnaire is to be sent. That message should inform the employee that the questionnaire will be arriving on a set date, it should explain the questionnaire's objective, and it should set expectations for employees' participation.
4. Develop clear instructions for how to respond to the questionnaire. The

instructions must be designed with the specific e-mail system in mind. For example, if the system allows an employee to chose "Reply to All" or "Reply," be sure to point out that they should select "Reply."

5. Develop a clear statement about anonymity. Provide a contact name and number that employees can use if they want to speak with a person about the questionnaire.

2. Set up the format so that there is only one employee's name in the recipient's line of text. (e.g., To: David Smith). Do not use the formatting option that allows all recipients to see the list of other recipients.

Preliminary Questions to Ask the Information Technologies (IT) or Information Systems (IS) Group

1. When was the last time the e-mail addresses were verified?

2. Are all employees using the same e-mail software? If no, what types of e-mail software are being used? (Are there any differences, e.g., Attachments, Reply/Reply to All, formatting, graphics?)

3. How frequently do employees receive broadcast e-mail messages? Who is the primary originator of those messages?

4. Do all employees access their e-mail at their own terminals, or do they use shared terminals?

Example of an Open-Space Meeting Invitation

Open-Space Meeting
on
"Developing Our Intranet: Exploring Opportunities
for Change"
July 16, 199X
Sagan Conference Center
8:30a.m–4:30p.m

You are invited to voluntarily participate in discovering ways to create an intranet that will enable our company's employees to get easier access to information, to improve communication, to learn and to share knowledge. This meeting is for anybody who is interested in our company's intranet and/or improving communication. It is not for people who expect a tightly structured, carefully controlled event. We will begin *without* a prepared agenda or clear-cut knowledge as to where our journey will end.

Our Theme—"Developing Our Intranet: Exploring Opportunities for Change"

We face many challenges and opportunities in 199X. As our company transforms itself and as we struggle to transform in response, the need to prioritize our intranet strategies becomes increasingly critical. Equally critical is the broader engagement of the total organization in the use of communication technologies. The theme of the meeting "Developing our Intranet: Exploring Opportunities for Change," suggests that intranet development is not simply a technology project; rather it is an opportunity to identify areas for organizational improvement and change.

What's Going to Happen?

There are no predetermined outcomes. We propose simply to create an environment in which good thinking, creating, and problem-solving can occur.

We will give everyone who wishes to speak an opportunity to express their "passionate issues." We will then allow people to "vote with their feet" to join others, if they wish, in conversation about those issues. This will involve some chaos, but it can become a seed bed of opportunity, if we choose to make it so.

Who Has Been Invited?

This invitation is being sent across the entire organization to all divisions and departments, to all employees, regardless of rank or title. Because information and knowledge are the lifeblood of our company, our intranet can be used in many, many ways to improve the ways in which we work. No issue, no opportunity, no concern around this subject is "off limits." We only ask that the people who attend feel passionately about intranet and internal web site development, and that they are willing to work on the issues they feel strongly about.

Full Voluntary Participation
The meeting simply won't work with drop-ins. So if you choose to attend, please plan to join us at the beginning of the meeting. This is your opportunity to participate in setting the direction for our intranet for 199X. If you cannot attend or choose not to, please give your support to the priorities developed at the meeting. Dress is business casual.

The Place and Time
The meeting will take place at . . .

RSVP Required
Please RSVP to (name name) at (e-mail) or (telephone) by (date). We look forward to sharing this experience with you.

Thanks.

Sincerely,

name of sponsor
e-mail of sponsor

Policy on Employee Use of the Internet

Avoid executive paranoia on employee use of the Internet by recommending a policy that everyone can live with. Most of the time, executives' fears of widespread internet abuse are unfounded. However, if employees are abusing internet access, the problem is larger than personal use of the Net. The problems lie with managers, not computers.

The goal of intranet development is to foster wide use of communication technologies, not to provide management with a reason to be suspicious of how employees spend their time. Here is a simple policy statement Jim Seymour proposed several years ago. It's good because it doesn't sound like Big Brother watching.

> Access to the Internet can be an important business tool, and we're pleased to provide it to those employees who will find it useful. Please remember that, as with other corporate facilities and assets provided for your use, Internet accounts are for business, not personal use, which violates your employment agreement.

Education is a wonderful antidote to ignorance. There are a few more things organizations can do in respect to employee use of the Internet.

1. Guide employees toward sites and information related to your industry and business by creating an area of the intranet dedicated to links.

2. In that section, provide a list of summaries or overviews of valuable sites. Let employees review the list and decide whether visiting the site is worth their time.

3. Immunize your organization from viruses by creating a web page that describes what viruses are, how they get transferred onto the organizational network via the Internet, and what to do if you suspect you have accidentally transferred a virus.

4. Help your employees understand the amount of information about the organization communicated in the part of an e-mail message people rarely see. Help people to understand how easy it is to pass along confidential information (such as employees' private e-mail addresses) when they use listserves or forward e-mail.

Speech to Persuade Management to Fund Intranet Development

Introduction

Thanks for the opportunity to meet with you today.

As you probably have heard, intranets are "hot." Forrester Research reported that most companies either have an intranet, plan to get one, or are studying it.

Our company has had an informal intranet since (199X) but we are here today to ask you to fund the development of an enterprise-wide intranet that can support the exchange of more information, that is secure from external tampering, and that meet employees' needs to improved communication, collaboration, and knowledge-sharing.

We're going to talk first about why the need for an intranet is so great at (our organization), then outline our funding request.

Five Arguments in Favor of Intranet Development

1. Although this represents an additional expenditure, we believe that the intranet provides an opportunity to leverage our current investment in technology.

    A. Forrester Research reports that companies spend between $5,000 and $10,000 per employee to provide information technologies and support.

    B. Our company has spent X, or an average of X per employee.

    C. By themselves, PCs support only individual work. But networked together through an intranet, employees can use their PC's to communicate with each other and to access information. The potential return on the technology investment is, therefore, much higher, because people can use their computers to do more things.

    D. Our intranet could become a platform for publishing internal corporate communications, for team-based collaboration, for performance support and continuous learning, and for developing our competitive intelligence.

2. Our employees are saying very clearly that they need better information and better communication in order to perform at their highest capacity. Right now, there is much wasted effort, duplication, redundancy, and missed opportunity

because we have poor internal communication. Here are two examples.
  A. Example #1
  B. Example #2
  C. These are not isolated incidents. They are representative of what is happening enterprise-wide.

3. If we do not improve this situation, we will continue to waste human and material resources, our costs will continue to be high, and we won't be providing the level of service our customers are demanding.

4. The savings from making information available on-line instead of printing and distributing it will justify much of the initial intranet investment.
  A. n dollars on Federal Express packages to our own employees.
  B. n dollars to print and distribute the corporate newsletter and internal communications.
  C. n dollars to print and distribute HR benefit information.
  D. incalculable amount of money for time wasted through telephone tag, from providing the wrong information to a lot of people, and from processing mundane information requests and transactions.

5. Beyond cutting waste and saving money, the intranet will help us to build capacity. In fact, the best reason for building a robust intranet is that it will enable this organization to do things it never was able to do before. This includes building capacity through
  A. Rapid identification of problems and creation of appropriate solutions.
  B. Identification of people with experience or knowledge on particular topics, issues or problems.
  C. Documenting key learnings so that people and groups can use them to avoid making the same mistakes twice.
  D. Sharing more information about what we know about our customers and our competitors: being able to predict the future before it happens.

Address Reservations
6. You may be wondering, will our employees use the intranet? After studying why other companies' intranets have succeeded and failed, we've learned that one critical success factor is employee involvement in the design and development of the intranet. We want to make sure that the intranet applications meet real, not assumed, needs. Our plan is to engage with employees in every step along the way. Part of our proposal, therefore, will include a needs analysis and some in-

ternal benchmarking analyses.

7. You also may be wondering, Aren't we already doing intranet development? You
   have probably seen (home page example) or (home page example). Well, so far,
   development has been ad hoc, with little planning, no standards, pockets of activity but with many employees left out. Many of the employees who could benefit the most from an intranet aren't able to develop their own web sites on their
   own because they don't have local resources or staff. This should be a company-
   wide, coordinated initiative support from the top. It doesn't make sense to
   make a lot of web development in several different directions at once. That's a
   waste of energy.

Outline the Proposal

8. What kind of investment are we talking about?
   A. As you can see on your handout, we are requesting n dollars for this first
      quarter, n dollars for the second, and n dollars for the third and fourth
      quarters.
   B. Summary of expenses.

Offer a Comparison of Value

9. This compares favorably to other investments the organization has made in per-
   formance support areas.
   A. We spent n dollars last year per employee for corporate communication.
   B. n dollars last year per employee for training, development and continu-
      ous education.
   C. n dollars per employee to help employees manage work and family issues.
   D. n dollars per employee on providing each person with a place to work.

10. All of these current activities are valuable. To put the intranet investment in
    perspective, we are actually asking for less per employee than any of these others.
    The initial investment breaks down to n dollars per employee, with a much
    higher probability of making a direct contribution to improved performance
    and customer satisfaction.

Explain the Benefits of Open Systems Architecture

11. In addition, we don't have to build the intranet and our intranet applications all
    at once. The beauty of open systems architecture is that we can take a modular ap-
    proach. We will begin application development and deployment where the needs

are the greatest, then we'll add more features over time.

Describe the Proposal in Greater Detail
12. The three areas we'd like to target first are
     A. area #1
     B. area #2
     B. area #3

13. These are our "demonstration projects" that will help us to develop some key learnings about the best ways to use intranet technologies within our own company.

14 One of the issues we will be addressing in our demonstration project is the best way to provide training to employees about how to use the intranet. One thing we've learned from other companies is that it's important to tie training to real business issues so that we can answer the employees' questions, What's in it for me? and, Why should I use this new technology? We know that generic, sweeping generalizations don't work. So we plan to work closely with line managers and supervisors to understand where the real productivity gains can be made.

15 One issue we've thought a lot about is whether to do all of the intranet development in-house or to bring in outside consultants.
     A. Successful intranet development requires the talents and skill sets from four different groups of specialists: (1) IT professionals to develop and maintain the network and the hardware, (2) a work group to engage with employees and managers to understand what would motivate employees to use the intranet consistently over time, (3) a developers group to create web applications or evaluate applications on the market, and (4) a support group who is responsible for long-term maintenance and growth of the intranet, to which employees can turn for assistance.

     B. In our organization, we have enough staffing resources to cover areas (x) and (y). We will need to outsource or hire on a temporary basis staff for the (first, second, third, forth) area. We will need to outsource or hire on a permanent basis staff for the (first, second, third, forth) area.

     C. There is a line item in our budget on the handout that represents staffing or consulting requirements.
     D. We've spoken with (this) consultant and (that) consultant to get a sense

of what they can provide and how much it would cost. Both consultants have already worked on a number of intranet projects including projects for (company) and (company).

Restate Sales Objective

16. We are asking for a commitment of n dollars and the permission to outsource or hire people who can fill in some of the competencies we don't possess in-house.

Demonstrate Competence

17. We have put together an Intranet Developers Team, which represents a cross-section of the entire organization. Review key team players.

Q & A

18. We would be happy to answer any questions for you.

Propose Next Step

19. As a next step, we would propose that (person) and (person) meet with you to-morrow to discuss your decision.

"Why Dumb Things Happen to Smart Companies"
by Thomas A. Stewart
Fortune, June 23, 1997
Used by permission.

Few people quarrel with the notion that companies must learn to invest in and manage knowledge if they hope to compete in an economy where, more than ever, knowledge is what we buy and sell. But how, they wonder, does one make the case for managing intellectual capital to CEOs and CFOs? And where do we start?

The two questions are cousins, since the best way to build support for any management effort is to start where you'll get early results. Mind you, the forgotten key to succeeding in management is not to stop there; quitting too soon condemns you to the hummingbird style of management, forever flitting and sipping from one blooming idea to another.

But you've got to start somewhere, and here's a way to figure out where: a list of nine symptoms of a "knowledge problem"—something wrong with how your company manages its brainpower. The list comes from David H. Smith, head of knowledge development for Unilever, the giant (1996 sales: $52 billion) maker of ice cream, soaps and detergents, frozen foods, and personal products. Smith, a witty Englishman who works in the Netherlands, has a background in both information technology and business. Nine months ago he was given the task of "helping Unilever act more intelligently"—that is, learn faster and leverage what it knows. You can reconstruct the conversation, since you've had the same one: "The solution to our problem isn't to work harder. We got to work smarter. . ." That, as Smith says, "is obviously true but also extremely trite." Besides, when your boss says, "Work smarter, Charlie," how exactly are you supposed to do that come Monday?

Like Lyme disease, knowledge problems have symptoms that sometimes mimic other problems, more benign or even more malign. But each of the following, says Smith, is a symptom that suggests that you don't manage knowledge well: People aren't finding it, moving it around, keeping it refreshed and up to date, sharing it, or using it.

The list is Smith's, the bells and whistles mine.

> **The Warning Signs**
> *Nine symptoms of bad brainpower management.*
> 1. You repeat mistakes.
> 2. Work gets duplicated.
> 3. Customer relations are strained.
> 4. Good ideas don't get shared.
> 5. You have to compete on price.
> 6. You can't keep up with market leaders.
> 7. You're dependent on key individuals.
> 8. You're slow to launch new products.
> 9. You don't know how to price for service.

•**You repeat mistakes.** "Your best teacher is your last mistake," Ralph Nader once told me. He, of course, has made a career out of publicizing companies that display this knowledge problem. It's rampant. Negligence lawyers don't wear Gucci loafers because companies make mistakes; they wear them because companies make the same mistake twice. The nature of icebergs being what it is, for every million-dollar lawsuit there must be tens of millions lost or wasted from repeated mistakes that are dumb but not tortious.

Why does it happen? Fear, I'd guess, is the No. 1 reason: fear of being embarrassed, chewed out, or worse. Many people and companies are so busy trying to hide boners (from the boss, from stock analysts, from customers and competitors) that they tuck away the learning along with the evidence.

You don't, obviously, want to encourage goofs just to learn from them. But the best way to avoid repeated errors is to study failure as assiduously as success. The history of medicine shows that you can learn as much from autopsies as you can from cures.

• **You duplicate work.** "Reinventing the wheel" is the inevitable phrase, and most companies spend so much time doing it you would think they were suppliers to Schwinn. A classic example: You inspect the goods before you ship them, and your customer inspects them again after they arrive. Worse, you do the same thing in-house. Usually the underlying cause is a knowledge problem: Customer and supplier don't know what each expects of the other, or they don't trust each other because they haven't shared processes or results.

People fail to copy success for the same reason that they succeed in copying mistakes: They're afraid or embarrassed to ask. Sometimes the problem is in systems and structures: They don't know where to look or looking takes too much time or they have no place to store corporate memory. Sometimes the problem is what one might call an overdeveloped engineer's mind: I know Eddie already did this, but I can do it better.

•**You have poor customer relations**. If you're not selling schlock, why does a customer get peevish? Probably one of three reasons, all knowledge problems. First, communication at the point of sale: Either he didn't understand what you were selling or you didn't understand what she was buying. Second, service: If I get the runaround when I have a problem, chances are the people who answer your 800 number are little more than switchboard operators, who don't know what they should.

The third reason is subtler and more interesting. Knowledge work tends to be custom work, or at least customized. That changes the nature of the transaction. You don't just sell janitorial services the same way you sell mops. Too often salespeople are in a hurry to hear a "yes" so they can write up the order. (Too often the incentives encourage that practice.) Result: You talked about the sale but not the deal.

• **Good ideas don't transfer between departments, units, or countries**. This is the most common knowledge problem of all: How do we get people to share ideas rather than hoard them, to accept ideas rather than reject them? There's no easy answer. Says Hewlett-Packard's CEO, Lewis Platt: "Knowledge transfer is a problem that yields ten different initiatives, not one." Here's a starter kit:

Set an example. Great bosses love teaching; great teachers produce great students. Once, interviewing Allied Signal CEO Larry Bossidy, I confessed to not knowing what working capital was. Bossidy positively lit up, grabbed a sheet of paper, scooted around the table, and taught me; his pleasure in teaching turned an interview into a sharing of minds.

Nudge: Nothing will get the troops to use the Lotus Notes database faster than a leader who asks at a staff meeting, "I'd like to hear everyone's thoughts on Kay's posting about the situation in Germany. Bill, let's start with you: What do you think we should do?"

Create incentives: Says Robert Buckman, CEO of specialty-chemical maker Buckman Laboratories: "The most powerful incentives you have are salaries and promotions." Buckman makes sure—and makes it known—that he hands them out based substantially on how well people share and borrow ideas.

Benchmark: Be sure Phoenix knows it has twice as much bad debt as Dayton—and reward both if they close the gap.

Make it fun: When you return from a convention, which do you write up first, your convention expense account or your trip report? Which contains more creative thinking? Which is read more attentively? One group at Monsanto makes knowledge sharing fun by arming people with digital cameras when they go on trip; when they get back, they show their pictures at the next staff meeting.

•**You're competing on price**. No company wants to find itself in a commodity business. What makes the difference? Why could an executive in General Electric's lighting business—light bulbs, for Pete's sake –tell me, in a mock-serious tone, "Cutting prices is not a core value of the General Electric Co.," while some companies are making computers—computers, for Pete's sake—are forced to do just that?

The answer is almost always knowledge, or lack of it. Whatever you sell, you can get out of the price game if you and your customer ride the learning curve together. Everything you learn about a customer—from how he likes pallets stacked to what his plans are—is an opportunity to make it harder for competitors to horn in. The results: margin.

•**You can't compete with market leaders.** Sometimes the big guys win because they've got something you ain't got, like prime-rate loans or Super Bowl-size ad budgets. But don't blame your problems on scale until you have explored this question: What do they know that we don't know? Toyota, Wal-Mart, and Southwest Airlines are just three examples of formerly small companies that outwitted bigger competitors.

•You're dependent on key individuals. Remember the old Allan Sherman song?

> *Oh, salesmen come and salesmen go*
> *And my best one is gone I know*
> *And if he don't come back to me*
> *I'll have to close the factory . . .*

Nothing's more dangerous than depending on a few key people. Usually this signals too little teamwork or an absence of ways to encourage star performers to reveal the secrets of their success.

Note, though: The fault may not lie in your stars. Sometimes people have greatness thrust upon them because others are unwilling to achieve it themselves. HP's Lew Platt says, "You've got a knowledge problem when decisions are being made too high in the organization." When things come to Platt's desk that shouldn't, he takes it as a sign that people lack knowledge that would let them think for themselves.

•**You're slow to launch new products or enter new markets**. It's obvious that being slow to market is a knowledge problem. But diagnosing its cause can be tricky; as with referred pain, the source may be far from the symptom. It could be a weak lab, a sludge-slowed commercialization process, a rigid budget bureaucracy, failure of competitor and market intelligence, or something else.

•**You don't know how to price for service**. Do you build the cost of service into your price? Sell a service contract? Bill by the hour, the day, the job? Let someone in the distribution channel handle it? Can you clearly explain why you do what you do, or are you just following industry practice?
Of all the symptoms on Smith's list, this intrigues me the most because the underlying knowledge problem is least self-evident. Here it is: IF you don't know how to price for service or why to charge one way vs. Another, it's a sign that you don't fully understand what your customers do with whatever you sell them. Some customers just buy on price. More often, however, they are buying the solution to a problem. They don't want drills; they want holes. One adhesive company, Smith says, knew a way to help customers speed up assembly lines with the added benefit (for customers) of using less glue. But its sales force had no ideas how to value and price this knowledge; worse, the reps were paid by the pound. If you know what customers are really paying for, you'd know better who should pay what.

Smith's list is diagnostic, not prescriptive. But each item on it is a knowledge problem with real business consequences that even a skeptical boss will want to fix. It's a start.

Intranet Business Plan Outline

Organization Name
Intranet
Request for Funding for System Implementation

by the Intranet Team

ABSTRACT

This document outlines the cost benefit analysis of implementing (organization's) intranet, an enabler of enhanced communication and information sharing, and requests funding for 1998 and 1999 implementation.

I. CUSTOMER BENEFIT

The implementation of a fully functional intranet within (organization) will provide direct customer benefits and will facilitate the adoption and lower the cost of deployment of similar systems throughout (organization).

Benefits to (Organization)

II. TRANSFORMATION BENEFITS FOR (ORGANIZATION)

** One-paragraph description of current situation and how it will be transformed **

Meeting Current Requirements

Preparing for Future Needs
III. CURRENT SITUATION
IV. PROJECT DESCRIPTION
V.   PROJECT PLAN OVERVIEW
VI. QUANTIFICATION/COST INFORMATION
VII. RECOMMENDATIONS

Appendix : Resources on the Web for Intranet Champions

There are literally hundreds of on-line resources available, and the list grows daily. The following pages list some of the most useful, sorted by topic.

Computer-Mediated Communication

Resource	Type	URL
CMC Magazine, a publication of December Communications	Archive of CMC articles about all areas related to computer-mediated communication including articles on cyberculture, the use of new technologies for learning, the creation of identity on-line and more.	http://www.december.com/cmc/mag/archive/author.html
CMC Magazine	Lists of courses at universities about cyberspace, technologies in the workplace, and the web.	http://www.december.com/cmc/st courses.html

Human Factors

Resource	Type	URL
Human Factors and Ergonomics Society	Web site to support the HFES; includes lists of links to other human factors sites.	http://hfes.org/

Intranets, Analysis and Commentary

Resource	Type	URL
Strassman, Inc	Recent articles by or about Paul A. Strassmann regarding corporate use of information technologies	http://www.strassmann.com/
CMP Net Techweb	A virtual library. Nearly 100 articles about intranets from CMP publications such as *Information Week*, *Computer Reseller News*, *Communications Week*, Electronic Engineering Times and NetGuide. On the home page, look for "Search the Archives," type "intranets" in the search box, and select the button "All CMP publications."	http://www.techweb.com/
Intranet Partners	Several valuable position papers and project worksheets authored by the members of Intranet Partners, a consulting firm.	http://www.ip.com/
PC Week	Essays by first-rate commentators like Jesse Berst and Christine Comaford on the use of intranets and information technologies in organizations.	http://www8.zdnet.com/pcweek/builder/ibpast.html#opinion

Intranets, Books

Resource	Type	URL
Amazon.com	Comprehensive list of all intranet books on the market. Use the Search feature with the keyword "intranet" to generate an up-to-date list of books related to intranets.	http://www.amazon.com

Intranets, case studies

Resource	Type	URL
WebMaster	Well-written case studies originally published in *WebMaster*.	http://www.cio.com/ WebMaster/wm_cases.html
PC Week	Literally dozens of interesting intranet case studies with good summaries and lists of tools used.	http://www8.zdnet.com/ pcweek/builder/ibpast.html#case
Ragan Communications	Case studies originally published in Ragan's *Intranet Report* newsletter.	http://www.ragan.com/ intranets/

Intranets, conferences

Resource	Type	URL
CMC Magazine, a publication of December Communications	List of links to forums, meetings and activities	http://www.december.com/cmc/info/forums-meetings.html
WebMaster	List of links of intranet-related conferences	http://www.cio.com/WebMaster/wm_calendar.html
EduCom	List of links to national and international conferences, seminars and workshops related to information technology and higher education.	http://www.educom.edu/web/calendar/calendar.html
The Association for Computers and the Humanities	List with links to conferences related to the use of computers in the humanities.	http://www.ach.org/ACH_Conference/
International Quality & Productivity Center	Internet and intranet conferences sponsored by the IQPC.	http://www.iqpc.com/upevent.html
BES Inc.'s *The Intranet Journal*	List with links to conferences of interest to intranet developers.	http://www.intranetjournal.com/calendar.html

Complete Intranet Resource	List with links to conferences of interest to intranet developers.	http://www.intrack.com/intranet/events.shtml
Intranet Design Magazine Published biweekly by Innergy, Inc.	Complete, well organized calendar of events and conferences of interest to intranet developers.	http://www.innergy.com/ievents.html

Intranets, comprehensive, multi-functional sites

Resource	*Type*	*URL*
Intranet Design Magazine	Intranet FAQ, very active discussion group focused on the technical side of intranet development, product reviews, and a well organized calendar of events.	http://www.innergy.com/
WebMaster Intranet Resource Center	News, product reviews, case studies, commentary.	http://www.cio.com/WebMaster/wm_irc.html
Ragan Communications *All About Intranets*	Includes excerpts from Ragan's *Intranet Report* newsletter.	http://www.ragan.com/intranets/

IntraNut	Articles and discussion group sponsored by Just In Time Solutions.	http://www.intranut.com
BES Inc.'s *The Intranet Journal*	Very active discussion group along with intranet news, information about new technologies, and book reviews.	http://www.intranetjournal.com/
Smart Infotech LTD's Complete Intranet Resource	Somewhat similar to *The Intranet Journal.* Features news, products, trends, case studies, and many links to additional sites. Has a good "intro to intranets" set of links.	http://www.intrack.com/intranet/
Netscape Communication Corp's Enterprise Solutions	A subsection of the Netscape web site devoted exclusively to intranet development. Includes demos, white papers, customer profiles and testimonials, descriptions of Netscape's products for intranets, an events calendar and links to the AppsFoundary (showcase of intranet application software).	http://www.netscape.com/ comprod/at_work/index.html

Microsoft's Intranet Solutions Center	Super-promotional web site dedicated to Microsoft's products for the intranet. Includes press releases, product information, case studies, demos and promotions for Microsoft Press's intranet books.	http://www.microsoft.com/intranet/
Yahoo's intranet links	Hundreds of links under the category Computers and Internet: Communications and Networking: intranet.	http://www.yahoo.com/Computers_and_Internet/Communications_and_Networking/Intranet/
The Mining Company	Mining Company guide Teresa Bettenhauser's "Best of the Net" selections for intranets.	http://intranets.miningco.com/mbest.htm
The National Center for Employee Ownership	A brief list of links to intranet-related materials. A good starting point.	http://www.nceo.org/resource/intranet.html

Intranets, project management worksheets by other authors

Resource	Type	URL
Intranet Partners	Project Definition Heuristic.	http://www.ip.com/html_docs/info/projinfoform.html
Just In Time Solutions	A set of practical templates for intranet deployment created by Kevin Han, Chief Information Architect.	http://www.justin-time.com/resources/kevin1/template.htm

Intranets, white papers

Resource	Type	URL
Intranets and Adaptive Innovation: The move from control to coordination in today's organizations	White paper by Steven L. Telleen, Ph.D.	http://amdahl.com/doc/products/bsg/intra/adapt.html

| Netscape's Enterprise Solutions white papers | A number of very useful white papers on a variety of subjects including Netscape's intranet strategies, intranet business applications, and information exchange and collaboration. Among the papers is THE INTRANET: SLASHING THE COST OF BUSINESS by International Data Corporation (IDC). An in-depth ROI case studies for Netscape intranet customers Booz-Allen & Hamilton, Cadence Design Systems, Lockheed Martin, Amdahl, and Silicon Graphics. Reports that "typical implementations are achieving ROIs well over 1000%." | http://www.net-scape.com/comprod/at_work/white_paper/ |

Knowledge Sharing

Resource	*Type*	*URL*
Yogesh Malhotra's A Business Researcher's Interests©	Links to every conceivable type of information about Knowledge Management & Organizational Learning.	http://www.brint.com/gLrng.htm

Community Intelligence Labs	Discussion group and white papers on the topics of workplace communities, knowledge sharing, knowledge ecology and communities of practice.	http://www.co-i-l.com
The Ernst & Young Center for Business Innovation	Research papers, interviews, case studies and a list of events relating to knowledge management.	http://www.businessinnovation.ey.com/journal/features/toc/loader.html
Electric Minds	Open discussions on a variety of topics relating to knowledge sharing, the design of online communities, the use of "A Pattern Language" as a model for online design, new tools and technologies and more.	http://www.minds.com

Questionnaires

Resource	Type	URL
SRI International	Surveys developed by SRI as part of their "internet values and lifestyles" program.	http://future.sri.com/ survey.html
Personality Tests on the WWW	Lists of links to all sorts of personality tests, including the "Techno Personality" test.	http://www.2h.com/T personality.phtml

Web-Based Training and Technology-Enabled Learning

Resource	Type	URL
Association for the Advancement of Computing in Education (AACE).	Descriptions of seven AACE scholarly journals including the Journal of Interactive Learning Research (JILR) and descriptions of over a dozen AACE conferences and seminars per year, including the prestigious WebNet conference.	http://www.aace.org

The American Society for Training and Development	Training and Performance links.	http://www.astd.org/ t&pinfo/t&pindex/tpindex.htm
The Masie Center, a Technology & Learning Think Tank	Training and Development links.	http://www.masie.com/ trlinks.htm
Educom, a nonprofit consortium of higher education institutions that facilitates the introduction, use, and access to and management of information resources in teaching, learning, scholarship, and research	Papers, interviews and publications on issues related to teaching and learning and publishing.	http://www.educom.edu/
University of Colorado at Denver, School of Education	"Instructional Technology Connections," a hugely comprehensive, award-winning list of links.	http://www.cudenver.edu/ ~mryder/itcon.html
Web-Based Training Information Center, the creation of Tim Kilby	A primer about on-line learning, design guidelines, and lists of other online resources.	http://www.filename.com/ wbt/index.html

Web-Site Makeovers

Resource	Type	URL
ZD Internet Magazine	Web site makeovers originally published in Internet magazine. Each month features business site makeover with the help of a leading designer. This is an incredible resource for learning how to implement new technologies, improve organization, establishing new presentation styles and develop value-added content.	http://www8.zdnet.com/zdimag/makeover/

Hyperlinks

Acknowledgments

Prentice Hall
http://www.prenhall.com

Charles Goldfarb
http://www.sgmlsource.com

IntraNetics
http://www.intranetics.com

RadNet
http://www.radnet.com

Netscape
http://www.netscape.com

Tom Stewart
http://fortune.com

Chris Locke
http://www.panix.com/~clocke/
Business Design Associates
http://www.bdaus.com

Excel, Inc
http://www.excelcorp.com

Ontogenics
http://www.ontogenics.com

U S WEST
http://www.uswest.com

The Trip.com
http://www.thetrip.com

International Learning Systems
http://www.ilsinc.com

Howard Rhinegold
http://www.well.com/user/hlr/index.htm

Electric Minds
http://www.minds.com

Cambridge Technology Partners
http://www.ctp.com

Chris Stone
http://home.earthlink.net/~seestone/

Figure One, Inc
http://www.figureone.com

Psi Phi Communications
http://www.metaphorming.com

Terra Firma Design
http:// www.terraplex.com

Boone & Associates
http://www.maryboone.com/

Open Space Technologies
http://www.tmn.com/openspace

Colorado Advanced Technology Institute
http://www.cati.com

Electric Library
http://www.elibrary.com

Epix
http://www.epix.net

Amazon.com
http://www.amazon.com

Executive Summary Hyperlinks

Intranet Design magazine's Intranet FAQ
http://www.innergy.com/ifaq.html
This online FAQ is good place to begin to learn about technical issues such as server configuration, firewalls, HTML, JAVA, etc.

David Siegel's *Creating Killer Web Sites*
http://www.killersites.com
Using digital design to communicate information and engage audiences.
This is a beautiful site that includes links to other well designed award-winning sites.

Chapter One Hyperlinks

Fernando Flores, "The Impact of Information Technology on Business, address

to the 50th Anniversary Conference of the Association for Computing Machinery, San Jose, CA, March 5, 1997.
http://www.bdaus.com/html/speech.html

Vinton Cerf's essay "Computer Networking: Global Infrastructure for the 21st Century."
http://cra.org/research.impact
Cerf explains from a technical perspective how the Internet was created, and directs our attention toward important technical issues which the telecommunications and computer industries will need to address as we go forward.

Katie Hafner and Matthew Lyon's *Where Wizards Stay Up Late: The Origins of the Internet*. This book, and any other book referenced in the text or listed in the bibliography, can be ordered online through Amazon.com, the world's largest bookstore.

http://www.Amazon.com
At Amazon.com, you'll find an interesting interview with Katie Hafner about why she and her husband Matt wrote this book. You'll also find links to other books they've written such as *Cyberpunk: Outlaws and Hackers on the Computer Frontier*.

Vannevar Bush's 1944 report to President Roosevelt, "Science, The Endless Frontier."
http://www.physics.uiuc.edu/ysn/docs/html_articles/VBush1945.html

Charles F. Goldfarb's SGML SOURCE HOME PAGE
http://www.sgmlsource.com/

Vannevar Bush's 1945 essay "As We May Think."
http://www.theAtlantic.com/atlantic/atlweb/flashbks/computer/tech.htm

Chapter Two Hyperlinks

Robert Cailliau's speech "A Short History of the Web," delivered at the launching of the European Branch of the W3 Consortium in Paris, November 2, 1995.
http://www.inria.fr/Actualites/Cailliau-fra.html

"Information Management: A Proposal" by Tim Berners-Lee.
http://www.w3.org/pub/WWW/History/1989/proposal.html

Tim Berners-Lee's speech "The World Wide Web—Past , Present and Future,"
delivered to the British Computer Society, July 17, 1996 explains the vision he
had for an internal web at CERN.
http://bcs.org.uk/news/timbl.htm

Netscape.
http://www.netscape.com

Donna Hoffman and Thomas Novak's Project 2000, Research Program on Marketing in Computer-Mediated Environments.
http://www2000.ogsm.vanderbilt.edu/

Howard Rhinegold's web site.
http://www.well.com/user/hlr/index.html

Howard Rhinegold's The Virtual Community: Homesteading on the Electronic
Frontier.
http://www.well.com/user/hlr/vcbook/index.html

The Parentsplace.com site for parents with young children .
http://www.parentsplace.com

The Intranet Journal for Intranet developers.
http://www.brill.com/intranet

The Tripod site for members of Generation X.
http://www.tripod.com

Salon 1999 for people interested in ideas and culture.
http://www.salon1999.com

Electric Minds, a meeting place on the Web for discussion about communication, community, technology, history and the future.
http://www.minds.com

Public Broadcasting Service (PBS) series "Life on the Internet" Web Site.

http://www.pbs.org/internet
Jim Pitkow and colleagues GVU's WWW User Surveys.
http://www.cc.gatech.edu/gvu/user_surveys

Women's Wire.
http://www.women.com
A Web resource with information on fitness, work and women in the news.

Cybergrrl.
http://www.cybergrrl.com
A women's guide to the Internet, including business tips, chats, entertainment
and more.

WWWomen.
http://www.wwwomen.com
This site is a search directory for women online. Categories include science and
technology, women in sports, and women throughout history.

A Woman's Space.
http://www.yoyoweb.com/wospace
A collection of articles for mothers. Highlighted topics include health, work and
consumer issues.

Voices of Women Online.
http://www.voiceofwomen.com
This journal and resource guide contains a directory of women-friendly businesses, a calendar of events, featured sites and more.

Herspace.
http://www.herspace.com
A wide collection of links dealing with women's issues.

Women@Work.
http://www.nafe.com
Maintained by the National Association for Female Executives, this site contains
a magazine for women, job resources and recent news for working women.

Expect the Best From a Girl.
http://www.academic.org

This site emphasizes parental involvement in educating daughters.
Women Online Worldwide.
http://www.wowwomen.com/TOC.html
Live chats and message boards for women are a focus at this site.

Femina.
http://www.femina.com
Offers a comprehensive, searchable directory of links to female-friendly sites
and information on the World Wide Web.

Mothers Who Think.
http://www.salonmagazine.com/mothers/
A daily section on the Salon site that offers moms a chance to exercise their
brains. In the first week, Mothers Who Think featured a profile of "Republican
chick" Mary Matalin.

On "Democracy and the New Information Highway" debates hosted by the Boston Review.
http://www-polisci.mit.edu/BostonReview/BR18.6/debatemitch.html

Chapter Three Hyperlinks

Art Kleiner's home page for *The Age of Heretics.*
http://www.well.com/user/art/

The Knowledge Management Forum.
http://revolution.3-cities.com/~bonewman/

The Community Intelligence Labs' Discussion Area.
http://www.co-i-l.com/coil/iacenter/index.shtml

Yogesh Malhotra's "A Business Researcher's Interest's" Links.
http://www.brint.com/interest.html
Malhotra's links for Organizational Knowledge Management & Organizational
Learning.
http://www.brint.com/OrgLrng.htm

US WEST Home Page.
http://www.uswest.com/

RadNet's WebShare intranet suite.
http://www.radnet.com
Intranetics intranet suite.
http://www.intranetics.com

PFN, Inc.
http://www.pfn.com

Computerworld.
http://www.computerworld.com

PCWeek's Intranet Builder.
http://www8.zdnet.com/pcweek/builder/builder.html

Webmaster.
http://www.web-master.com/

Netscape Intranet Solutions.
http://www.netscape.com/comprod/at_work/index.html

Netscape Intranet Application Demos.
http://www.netscape.com/comprod/at_work/application_demo/index.html
Netscape-enhanced intranet demos from Hewlett-Packard, 3M, Cushman &
Wakefield, and National Semiconductor.

Netscape Intranet Customer Profiles – over 30 Case Studies and "Intranets in
Progress."
http://www.netscape.com/comprod/at_work/customer_profiles/index.html

Netscape Intranet White Papers.
http://www.netscape.com/comprod/at_work/white_paper/index.html
White papers on ROI, collaboration, Intranets as groupware, and Intranet application design. Most are targeted at the IT and IS professionals.

Lists of Upcoming Seminars for IT Professionals Sponsored by Netscape.
http://www.netscape.com/comprod/at_work/seminars.html
Netscape's Intranet Press Clippings.
http://www.netscape.com/comprod/at_work/press_clippings/index.html
From Computerworld, Fortune, Inter@ctive, PC Week and the San Jose Mercu-

ry News.
Netscape Intranet Developers Forum.
http://www.netscape.com/one_stop/intranet_apps/index.html

Chapter Four Hyperlinks

FireWall/Plus firewall software.
http://www.network-1.com/products/firewall/

SmartWall firewall software.
http://www.v-one.com/html/products.html

Chris Stone's Home Page.
http://home.earthlink.net/~seestone/

RadNet's WebShare intranet suite.
http://www.radnet.com

Intranetics intranet suite.
http://www.intranetics.com

WisdomLink learning suite.
http://www.ilsinc.com/Capabilities/WisdomLink/wisdom.htm

International Learning Systems.
http://www.ilsinc.com

Watson Wyatt Worldwide.
http://www.watsonwyatt.com

The Masie Center.
http://www.masie.com
Netscape's to intranet demos.
http://www.netscape.com/comprod/at_work/linklist.html

A detailed description of what Sun has achieved with their Intranet is available
at **http://www.sun.com/sun-on-net/moneystories.html.** There, you'll find a
narrative tour of Sun's Intranet, (dubbed SunWeb).

Zdnet University (ZDU).
http://www.zdu.com/

A demo of National Semiconductor's Intranet illustrating "Communities of Practice.
http://www.netscape.com/comprod/at_work/application_demo/national/index.html

Apple Computer.
http://www.apple.com

"Designing Calm Technology" by Mark Weiser and John Seely Brown.
http://powergrid.electriciti.com/1.01/calmtech-wp.html

John Seely Brown.
http://www.startribune.com/digage/seelybro.htm

Mark Weiser.
http://www.ubiq.com/weiser

World Wide Web Consortium (W3C).
http://www.w3.org/

XML
Extensible Markup Language (XML) W3C Working Draft 14-Nov-96.
http://www.w3.org/pub/WWW/TR/WD-xml-961114.html
Latest version:
http://www.textuality.com/sgml-erb/WD-xml.html

Wired magazine's experts predicted in 1996 that the number of telecommuters will triple in the next fifteen years to 20 percent of the US work force.
http://www.hotwired.com/wired/3.10/departments/reality.check.html

Chapter Five Hyperlinks

Chris Stone's Home Page.
http://home.earthlink.net/~seestone/
International Learning Systems.

http://www.ilsinc.com

Bernice McCarthy and Excel Corp.
http://www.excelcorp.com

John Perry Barlow, "@Home on the Range," Doors of Perception 2 @HOME
Conference, November 4-6 1994, Amsterdam, sponsored by the Netherlands
Design Institute and the Institute and Mediamatic.
http://www.mediamatic.nl/Doors/Doors2/Barlow/Barlow-Doors2-E.html

Chapter Six Hyperlinks

Lotus Notes.
http://www2.lotus.com/home.nsf

RadNet's WebShare intranet suite.
http://www.radnet.com

Intranetics intranet suite.
http://www.intranetics.com

International Learning Systems.
http://www.ilsinc.com

Ontogenics Corp.
http://www.ontogenics.com

Some notes on Christopher Alexander by Nikos A. Salingaros.
http://www.math.utsa.edu/sphere/salingar/Chris.text.html

Christopher Alexander, "Domestic Architecture," Doors of Perception 2
@HOME Conference, November 4-6 1994, Amsterdam, sponsored by the
Netherlands Design Institute and the Institute and Mediamatic.
http://www.mediamatic.nl/Doors/Doors2/Alexander/Alexander-Doors2-
E1.html
The Patterns Home Page is a useful repository of information about the
application of Pattern Languages in Computer Science. Here, one can find a
comprehensive bibliography on the subject, which is constantly being updated.
http://st-www.cs.uiuc.edu/users/patterns/

Chapter Seven Hyperlinks

Elizabeth Weil, "The Future is Younger Than You Think," Fast Company magazine, Issue 8.
http://www.fastcompany.com/08/kids.html

Ft. Hood.
http://www.hood-pao.army.mil/

William Perry, U.S. Secretary of Defense, speech at ACM '97, March 4, 1997
The speech has also been published to the web in streaming video by VX-TREME. Note that you must download their viewer Web Theater to be able to view the speeches from ACM97.
http://www.vxtreme.com/live/acm97/live.html

Bruce Sterling's *Wired* cover story "War is Virtual Hell," Premier Issue, 1993.
http://wwww.wired.com/wired/1.1/features/virthell.html

Force XXI.
 http://204.7.227.75:443/force21/f21book/vision/vision.html

"The Army in the Information Age," by General Gordon R. Sullivan and Lieutenant Colonel Anthony M. Coroalles.
http://204.7.227.75:443/force21/articles/sull-1-1.html

Regis McKenna.
http://www.mckenna-group.com/profile/partners/r_mckenna.html

Regis McKenna Group.
http://www.mckenna-group.com/index.html

InContext Enterprises.
http://www.incent.com/
Computer Professionals for Social Responsibility.
http://www.cpsr.org

ACM's Special Interest Group for Computer-Human Interaction (SIGCHI).
http://www.acm.org/sigchi/

Carol Hildebrand, "Face Facts," WebMaster, February 1997.
http://www.cio.com/WebMaster/020197_facts.html

Chapter Eight Hyperlinks

U S WEST.
http://www.uswest.com

Uses and Gratification Research
To learn more about Uses and Gratification, visit the Electronic Library at **http://www3.elibrary.com**, register as a temporary user and search for "gratification theory."

Fernando Flores.
http://www.bdaus.com/html/pg2.fernando.html

Terry Winograd.
http://pcd.Stanford.EDU/hci/people/winograd.html

Ontogenics, Inc.
http://www.ontogenics.com

Dave Carlson, "Harnessing the Flow of Knowledge"
http://www.dimensional.com/~dcarlson/papers/KnowFlow.htm

Chapter Nine Hyperlinks

International Learning Systems.
http://www.ilsinc.com
Rosabeth Moss Kanter.
http://www.goodmeasure.com/author.html

International Association of Business Communicators.
http://www.iabc.com

Roger C. Schank, director of the Institute for the Learning Sciences (ILS) at Northwestern University.
http://www.ils.nwu.edu/~e_for_e/people/RCS.html

"Employee Communications and Technology," by Cognitive Communications, Inc and Xerox **http://www.iabc.com/products/ectwebsi/index.htm**

Paul Strassmann.
http://www.strassmann.com

Bruce Tulgan, President of Rainmaker, Inc.
http://members.aol.com/rainworld/rainmake.htm

Bruce Tulgan, "Beyond the Slacker Myth, " Tripod, September 19,1996.
http://www.tripod.com/work/columns/tulgan/960919.html

Donald Norman's Home Page.
http://cogsci.ucsd.edu:80/~norman/

Chapter Ten Hyperlinks

Donald Norman's Home Page
http://cogsci.ucsd.edu:80/~norman/

Jeremy Schlosberg, "Why Multimedia Still Sucks: Too Many Buttons, Not Enough Thought," *Salon,* February 13, 1997.
http://www.salonmagazine.com/march97/21st/multimedia970313.html

Chapter Eleven Hyperlinks

The Business/Technology Imperative; Corporate Transformation for Friction-Free Capitalism as reported by *Wired News.*
http://www.wired.com/news/culture/story/3708.html
Bill Gates speech at the CEO Summit.
http://www.microsoft.com/billGates/speeches/ceosummit/ceobill.htm

Nathan Myhrvold's bio.
http://www.microsoft.com/corpinfo/staff/nathanm.htm

List of attendees as reported by Wired News.
http://www.wired.com/news/business/story/3747.html

Gates' Greatest Power Grab (It's Working).

http://www.pathfinder.com/@@w0YcQAQATsLa4XWv/fortune/1997/
970526/mic.html

Andrew Leonard, "Office97—or Office 1984?," *Salon* magazine.
http://www.salonmagazine.com/may97/21st/office970501.html

John December, "Blinded by Science?"
http://www.december.com/cmc/mag/1996/feb/ed.html

"Learning from Notes: Organizational Issues in Groupware Implementation,"
by Prof. Wanda Orlikowski.
http://ccs.mit.edu/CCSWP134.html

Professor Wanda J. Orlikowski.
http://ccs.mit.edu/Wanda.html

Dan Shafer, "Desktop Warriors", *Salon*, 12/2/96.
http://www.salonmagazine.com/dec96/deskwars961202.html

Wake Forest University Department of Communication.
http://wwwp.wfu.edu/Academic-departments/Speech-Communication/

Association for Computing Machinery.
http://www.acm.org

Webmaster Magazine.
http://www.web-master.com
Work/Family Directions, Inc.
http://www.wfd.com
Cambridge Technology Partners.
http://www.ctp.com

BDM Technologies.
http://www.bdm.com

Systems Resources Consulting.
http://www.srcinc.com/

Chapter Twelve Hyperlinks

John December, "Where HAS All the Hypertext Gone?"
http://december.com/cmc/mag/1996/dec/last.html

Roger C. Schank, director of the Institute for the Learning Sciences (ILS) at
Northwestern University.
http://www.ils.nwu.edu/~e_for_e/people/RCS.html

The Dilbert Zone.
http://www.unitedmedia.com/comics/dilbert/

John Seely Brown & Estee Solomon Gray, "The People Are the Company." *Fast
Company* magazine.
http://www.fastcompany.com/01/people.html

Chapter Thirteen Hyperlinks

Julian Orr, *Talking about Machines; An Ethnography of a Modern Job.*
http://www.ilr.cornell.edu/depts/ILRPress/97cat/

Deone Zell, "Changing by Design; Organizational Innovation at Hewlett-Packard."
http://www.ilr.cornell.edu/depts/ILRPress/97cat/

Fernando Flores, "The Impact of Information Technology on Business," address
to the 50th Anniversary Conference of the Association for Computing Machinery, San Jose, CA, March 5, 1997.
http://www.bdaus.com/html/speech.html
Final Report of the Commission to Review the AAA Statements on Ethics, 1995.
http://www.ameranthassn.org/ethrpt.htm

STATEMENTS ON ETHICS Principles of Professional Responsibility Adopted
by the Council of the American Anthropological Association May 1971.
http://www.ameranthassn.org/ethstmnt.htm

Principles of Professional Responsibility Adopted by the Council of the American Anthropological Association May 1971.
http://www.ameranthassn.org/ethstmnt.htm

Handbook on Ethical Issues in Anthropology.
http://www.ameranthassn.org/sp23.htm#cands

Chapter Fifteen Hyperlinks

Public Relations Society of America (PRSA) Technology Section.
http://www.tech.prsa.org/

Chapter Sixteen Hyperlinks

Open Space Technology and Harrison Owen.
http://www.tmn.com/openspace/

About the Software

The CD-ROM includes intranet demos from four different vendors: IntraNetics, RadNet's WebShare, Netscape's intranet demos, and MindWare by Durand Communications. The vendor demos were included with the book for several different reasons:

1. To introduce readers to some first-rate intranet products, each a good value for the money. These products are all showcased on the vendor's own web sites, but, by putting them on a CD-ROM, we've made it convenient for you to evaluate several products at once.

2. To provide a way for readers to create a *visual* argument for intranet development. The demos can be used to answer the question, "What would a fully functional intranet look like?" Often, words alone are insufficient. You can use the CD-ROM to demonstrate to your audiences—from the CEO to line managers to employees—what intranets can look like and how they can be designed to achieve specific business objectives.

3. To assist with the question, "Should we create our intranet applications in-house or purchase them from a vendor?" Oftentimes, people assume that since intranet development tools are so readily available, all intranet development must occur in-house. However, the cost of creating *and* maintaining intranet applications so that they are state of the art is beyond the economic reach of most companies. Companies that are able to move the fastest buy some intranet application packages to gain a competitive advantage.

The intranet demos on the CD-ROM are described below.

IntraNetics Intranet Suite

Developed to cost-effectively meet the intranet needs of small- to medium-sized businesses and departments of larger organizations, IntraNetics is a complete intranet-in-a-box. The CD-ROM provides narrated multimedia presentation about how IntraNetics works for the fictional company "Urban Motors." Then, you'll also find an IntraNetics demo of the product, "The Urban Motors Intranet," that you can walk though.

IntraNetics 97 includes 17 fully featured intranet applications, and each application can be customized. All of the IntraNetics applications share a common database. This means that once data is entered in one application, such as the employee directory, it will automatically appear in other connected applications, such as the organization chart. IntraNetics uses an industry-standard database to ensure compatibility with data that may already exist in your organization.

IntraNetics suite of intranet applications is well-conceived and designed. They include an applications for an employee directory, contact manager, organizational chart, company handbook, new employee orientation guide, expense reporting, internal job openings, presentation library, software library, corporate calendar of events, internal newsletter, and discussion areas. IntraNetics 97 also accommodates newsfeeds which can be made available broadcast-style, or directed at specific groups of employees. IntraNetics is committed to meeting the evolving and varied needs of different groups for intranet applications. New applications will be available for downloading from the IntraNetics web site as they are developed by IntraNetics and third-party developers.

The IntraNetics suite can be added to existing intranets, or can be used as the starting point of intranet development. IntraNetics has been designed with industry standards in mind. With a few exceptions, IntraNetics can be used with most existing servers, databases, and messaging systems an organization already has in place. The product currently runs on Windows NT, but IntraNetics plans to offer a Unix Solaris version as well. Employees access the IntraNetics applications through their standard Web browsers.

RadNet's WebShare

RadNet's WebShare is an intranet application development platform. On the CD-ROM, you will find a 30-day evaluation version of WebShare Server (which is software, not hardware), Web Share Designer (a development environment), and a set of eight starter applications—Calendar, Contacts, Discussion, Document Management, Employee Director, Job Posting, Moderated Discussion, and Problem Tracking.

RadNet was founded by a group of experts in the groupware and collaborative applications field, and many were in the core of the original Lotus Notes team. Several of the Lotus Notes selling points are matched and exceeded with the RadNet WebShare products. WebShare Designer is an object-oriented development environment that enables intranet designers to create customized intranet applications quickly and easily. Unlike Lotus Domino, which provides a similar architecture for building custom applications, WebShare stores its information in any ODBC-compliant database instead of a proprietary format.

RadNet also offers roles-based security. Precise access control lets a webmaster define who can see specific fields per selected document. Permissions can be set down to the field level.

RadNet also offers a replication option for mobile or remote users. When an employee presses the "replicate" button, WebShare copies the application and its data to the employee's computer hard drive. Employees can then run the application in a totally disconnected state. When reconnected to the server, the replicate button synchronizes data on both the server and stand-alone machine.

Netscape's "Airius Intranet"

One of the best intranet demos ever created is Netscape's "Airius Intranet." On the CD-ROM, you will find an HTML page which will link you to Netscape's web site where you can run the demo live, as though you are an employee of the fictional company. By linking you to a live intranet demo, Netscape is providing a way for you to fully experience a live, dynamic intranet. Besides the Netscape page with the active hyperlink, the CD-ROM also includes several of the Netscape applications used to build the demo. You'll be able to actually unzip and play with the applications.

Development Decision Heuristic

One of the strongest arguments to be made for purchasing intranet products from qualified vendors is that the people costs of writing code in-house is not going down. If it is not possible to spread the cost of writing sophisticated code over a large, growing user base, then it is extremely difficult to get desirable economies of scale. Vendors oftentimes have the large user base and economies of scale necessary to provide solid applications *and* ongoing enhancements at the lower cost.

How to View the Demos

To view the intranet demos on the CD-ROM packaged with this book, you'll need a Macintosh or a Windows PC with a minimum of 8 megabytes of RAM and an 8-bit color monitor. You'll also need a web browser such as Netscape Navigator 3.0 or Intranet Explorer.

Launching the Intranet Demos

Each product has its own set of instructions for installing or launching the demo. The Read-Me documents in each folder are the key because they provide the instruction you need.

For example, inside the IntraNetics folder, you'll find Read Me First!

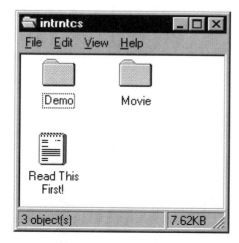

Inside the Appfound folder (inside the Netscape folder), you'll look for "Readme."

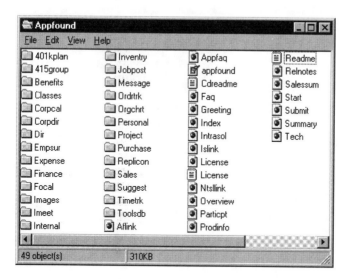

Look for the Read-Me files in each folder and have fun!

CD Previews

What is on the CD-ROM that might interest you? The following pages preview what you'll find.

IntraNetics Demo and Multimedia Presentation

The CD-ROM includes a demo of the "Urban Motors Intranet" created by IntraNetics. The demo on the CD-ROM allows you to envision what your intranet might look like if you used IntraNetics to build an intranet. IntraNetics has an easy to use interface and colorful graphic design. When you launch the IntraNetics demo through your browser (E:\intrntcs\Demo\index.html), this is the first screen you will see:

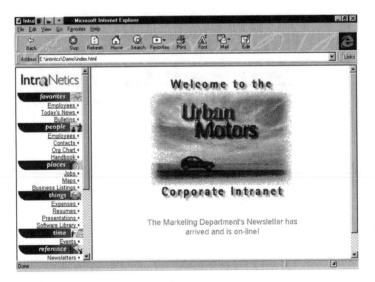

All of the hyperlinks on the left column are active.

You'll be able to see what each feature would look like if it were actually populated with information from a real company. For example, this is what is in the Presentations Library:

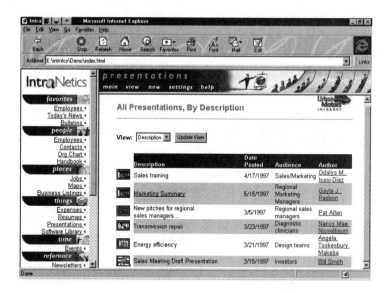

From here, you can click onto the active hyperlinks to see examples of real presentations, or see information about the employees who created them. One of the interesting things illustrated in the demo is how information can be integrated from one IntraNetics application to the next.

The CD-ROM also includes IntraNetics' lively, colorful multimedia presentation about how intranetics can be used to improve business communications, information flow, and operations. It's fun, educational, and motivating.

Netscape Intranet Application Demos

Netscape offers a full spectrum of software tools for intranet development. The materials on the CD-ROM spotlight Netscape AppFoundry.

The entry point in the demos is an HTML page on the CD-ROM. It will link you to Netscape's web site where you can run Netscape's "Airius Intranet" demo live, as though you were a real employee of the company. The "Airius Intranet" demo is best viewed with Netscape Navigator 3.0 or higher.

The HTML page on the CD-ROM then lists Netscape applications used to build the demo. You will be able to unzip and play with the applications.

The CD-ROM provides all of the applications available at production time, as well as general and technical information to help you use the applications for your intranet:

- Netscape AppFoundry Overview
- Executive Summary
- Overview of all applications
- Getting Started: Setting Up Your Environment
- AppFoundry End User License Agreement
- Fequently Asked Questions
- How Developers Can Participate in the AppFoundry Program

The following Intranet starter applications are provided on the CD-ROM:

- The 415 Group, Inc.—Partner Communication System
- Acclaim Technology—Travel and Expense Reporting
- Austin-Hayne—Job Posting and Applicant Processing
- Booz-Allen & Hamilton—Purchasing Analysis Tool
- CSG Interactive—Employee Survery Designer
- Data Systems West—Class Catalog and Registration
- DTAI—Interactive Organizational Chart
- I.Consulting—Internal Purchasing
- Informix Software—Corporate Directory
- Ingenia Communications Corporation—Meeting Room Database
- Internet Media Services—Time Tracking
- Lante Corporation—Sales Trend Analyzer
- Manual 3—Finance Forms
- Netscape Communications Corporation—Focal Salary Review Tool
- Netscape Communications Corporation—Personal Start Page Builder
- Netscape Communications Corporation—Suggestions Box
- Oblix—Corporate Directory/Org Chart
- Prologic Management Systems—Inventory Tracking
- Prologic Management Systems—Order Status Tracking
- Replicon—Customer Service/Help Desk
- Sage Solutions—Sales and Marketing Knowledge Manager

- Sapient Corporation—Corporate Events Calendar
- Stonebridge Technologies—Benefits Enrollment
- Transaction Information Systems—401(k) Asset Allocation and Savings Model
- USWeb WorldPort—Project Information Manager

When you launch the Netscape demo on the CD-ROM through your brower (e:\netscape\APPFOUND\Index.htm), this is the screen you'll see:

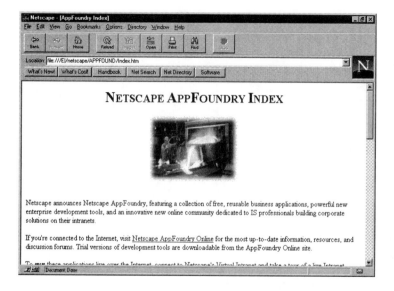

Scrolling, you'll be able to choose the application you'd like to preview.

For example, you can take a look at a Travel and Expense reporting application like this one:

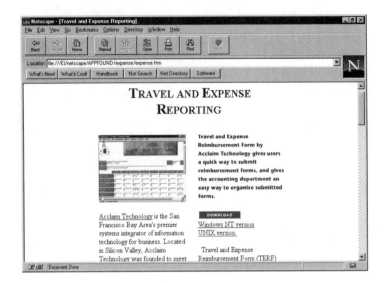

You'll find additional screen shots of each Netscape application, information about the companies that developed them, and instructions for using the applications on your own intranet.

MindWare Software Client

MindWare is an end-to-end, real-time community server that can be used to build a robust intranet with features like live chat, video, and audio conferencing and multi-user games. The MindWare client is on the CD-ROM. When you install the software and connect to the MindWare server at Durand Communications, you'll be able to see a live, real-time demo of how MindWare works.

After you install the client and estabish your Internet connection, this is the first screen you'll see:

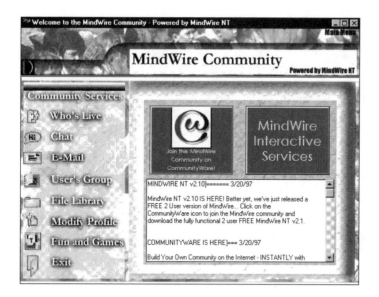

Click onto Interactive Services to get the next screen:

From here, you can take a look at various features built into the MindWare server that people are using every day to accomplish specific business objectives.

For example, businesses are using MindWare to create and manage on-line catalogs. Clicking "Business Service Center" brings up an overview of features designed to facilitate electronic commerce.

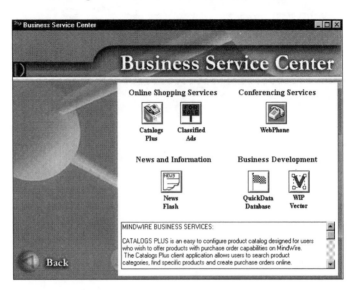

The live demo provides an opportunity for you to get a feel for the MindWare server capabilities and to experience its benefits first-hand.

RadNet WebShare Software 30-Day Evaluation Version

RadNet WebShare is an intranet application development environment. The 30-day evaluation version of WebShare server and WebShare Designer on the CD-ROM will probably be of greatest interest to intranet application developers who already know how to run a web server.

The RadNet demo on the CD-ROM is only for Windows NT computers. It will not run on anything else and will only run if a web server is already installed.

How can you take a look at this product and the eight starter applications if you are not already running a Windows NT web server? The best way is to visit RadNet's web site at **Error! Bookmark not defined**. After you register as a new user, you will be able to connect to a live demo of WebShare.

For example, you can take a look at the Employee Directory application and see how you might enter personnel into on-line forms. Then you can see how the data can be viewed a number of different ways, and then integrated into the other intranet applications.

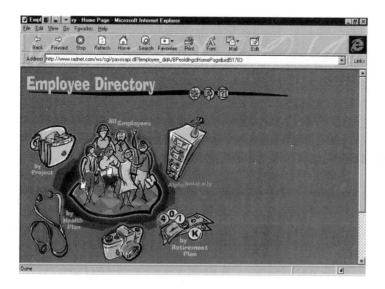

The RadNet WebShare demo at **Error! Bookmark not defined** provides a clear picture of how the product works and how the applications can benefit an organization. The 30-day evaluation version of the software provides intranet developers with an opportunity to test the product and evaluate it before making a purchase.

Contact Information

IntraNetics	www.intranetics.com
Netscape	www.netscape.com
MindWare	www.durand.com
RadNet WebShare	www.radnet.com

Index

O

Q

R

P

Out-of-the-Box
Ready-to-Go

Take advantage of the intranet explosion with IntraNetics 97, the world's first complete intranet-in-a-box! Just open the box and install the software, and your corporate intranet is complete.

IntraNetics 97 includes 17 powerful yet easy-to-use business applications, as well as all the software necessary to deploy an intranet!

IntraNetics 97 will help you maintain up-to-date employee records with the Employees application, call up customized and point-to-point driving instructions with the Maps application, access the latest company files in Documents. And more!

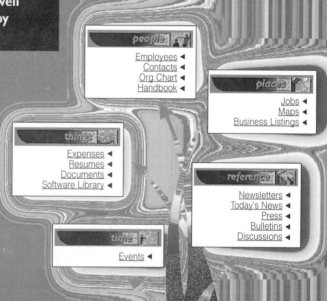

people
Employees ◄
Contacts ◄
Org Chart ◄
Handbook ◄

places
Jobs ◄
Maps ◄
Business Listings ◄

things
Expenses ◄
Resumes ◄
Documents ◄
Software Library ◄

reference
Newsletters ◄
Today's News ◄
Press ◄
Bulletins ◄
Discussions ◄

time
Events ◄

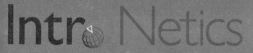

For more information contact your preferred reseller. Or call IntraNetics at
800-730-0960

Intr⬤Netics

The Complete Intranet-in-a-Box

www.intranetics.com

LICENSE AGREEMENT AND LIMITED WARRANTY

READ THE FOLLOWING TERMS AND CONDITIONS CAREFULLY BEFORE OPENING THIS CD PACKAGE. THIS LEGAL DOCUMENT IS AN AGREEMENT BETWEEN YOU AND PRENTICE-HALL, INC. (THE "COMPANY"). BY OPENING THIS SEALED CD PACKAGE, YOU ARE AGREEING TO BE BOUND BY THESE TERMS AND CONDITIONS. IF YOU DO NOT AGREE WITH THESE TERMS AND CONDITIONS, DO NOT OPEN THE CD PACKAGE. PROMPTLY RETURN THE UNOPENED CD PACKAGE AND ALL ACCOMPANYING ITEMS TO THE PLACE YOU OBTAINED THEM FOR A FULL REFUND OF ANY SUMS YOU HAVE PAID.

1.   **GRANT OF LICENSE:** In consideration of your purchase of this book, and your agreement to abide by the terms and conditions of this Agreement, the Company grants to you a nonexclusive right to use and display the copy of the enclosed software program (hereinafter the "SOFTWARE") on a single computer (i.e., with a single CPU) at a single location so long as you comply with the terms of this Agreement. The Company reserves all rights not expressly granted to you under this Agreement.

2.   **OWNERSHIP OF SOFTWARE:** You own only the magnetic or physical media (the enclosed CD) on which the SOFTWARE is recorded or fixed, but the Company and the software developers retain all the rights, title, and ownership to the SOFTWARE recorded on the original CD copy(ies) and all subsequent copies of the SOFTWARE, regardless of the form or media on which the original or other copies may exist. This license is not a sale of the original SOFTWARE or any copy to you.

3.   **COPY RESTRICTIONS:** This SOFTWARE and the accompanying printed materials and user manual (the "Documentation") are the subject of copyright. The individual programs on the CD are copyrighted by the authors of each program. You may not copy the Documentation or the SOFTWARE, except that you may make a single copy of the SOFTWARE for backup or archival purposes only. You may be held legally responsible for any copying or copyright infringement which is caused or encouraged by your failure to abide by the terms of this restriction.

4.   **USE RESTRICTIONS:** You may not network the SOFTWARE or otherwise use it on more than one computer or computer terminal at the same time. You may physically transfer the SOFTWARE from one computer to another provided that the SOFTWARE is used on only one computer at a time. You may not distribute copies of the SOFTWARE or Documentation to others. You may not reverse engineer, disassemble, decompile, modify, adapt, translate, or create derivative works based on the SOFTWARE or the Documentation without the prior written consent of the Company.

5.   **TRANSFER RESTRICTIONS:** The enclosed SOFTWARE is licensed only to you and may not be transferred to any one else without the prior written consent of the Company. Any unauthorized transfer of the SOFTWARE shall result in the immediate termination of this Agreement.

6.   **TERMINATION:** This license is effective until terminated. This license will terminate automatically without notice from the Company and become null and void if you fail to comply with any provisions or limitations of this license. Upon termination, you shall destroy the Documentation and all copies of the SOFTWARE. All provisions of this Agreement as to warranties, limitation of liability, remedies or damages, and our ownership rights shall survive termination.

7.   **MISCELLANEOUS:** This Agreement shall be construed in accordance with the laws of the United States of America and the State of New York and shall benefit the Company, its affiliates, and assignees.

8.   **LIMITED WARRANTY AND DISCLAIMER OF WARRANTY:** The Company warrants that the SOFTWARE, when properly used in accordance with the Documentation, will operate in substantial conformity with the description of the SOFTWARE set forth in the Documentation. The Company does not warrant that the SOFTWARE will meet your requirements or that the operation of the SOFTWARE will be uninterrupted or error-free. The Company warrants that the media on which the SOFTWARE is delivered shall be free from defects in materials and workmanship under

normal use for a period of thirty (30) days from the date of your purchase. Your only remedy and the Company's only obligation under these limited warranties is, at the Company's option, return of the warranted item for a refund of any amounts paid by you or replacement of the item. Any replacement of SOFTWARE or media under the warranties shall not extend the original warranty period. The limited warranty set forth above shall not apply to any SOFTWARE which the Company determines in good faith has been subject to misuse, neglect, improper installation, repair, alteration, or damage by you. EXCEPT FOR THE EXPRESSED WARRANTIES SET FORTH ABOVE, THE COMPANY DISCLAIMS ALL WARRANTIES, EXPRESS OR IMPLIED, INCLUDING WITHOUT LIMITATION, THE IMPLIED WARRANTIES OF MERCHANTABILITY AND FITNESS FOR A PARTICULAR PURPOSE. EXCEPT FOR THE EXPRESS WARRANTY SET FORTH ABOVE, THE COMPANY DOES NOT WARRANT, GUARANTEE, OR MAKE ANY REPRESENTATION REGARDING THE USE OR THE RESULTS OF THE USE OF THE SOFTWARE IN TERMS OF ITS CORRECTNESS, ACCURACY, RELIABILITY, CURRENTNESS, OR OTHERWISE.

IN NO EVENT, SHALL THE COMPANY OR ITS EMPLOYEES, AGENTS, SUPPLIERS, OR CONTRACTORS BE LIABLE FOR ANY INCIDENTAL, INDIRECT, SPECIAL, OR CONSEQUENTIAL DAMAGES ARISING OUT OF OR IN CONNECTION WITH THE LICENSE GRANTED UNDER THIS AGREEMENT, OR FOR LOSS OF USE, LOSS OF DATA, LOSS OF INCOME OR PROFIT, OR OTHER LOSSES, SUSTAINED AS A RESULT OF INJURY TO ANY PERSON, OR LOSS OF OR DAMAGE TO PROPERTY, OR CLAIMS OF THIRD PARTIES, EVEN IF THE COMPANY OR AN AUTHORIZED REPRESENTATIVE OF THE COMPANY HAS BEEN ADVISED OF THE POSSIBILITY OF SUCH DAMAGES. IN NO EVENT SHALL LIABILITY OF THE COMPANY FOR DAMAGES WITH RESPECT TO THE SOFTWARE EXCEED THE AMOUNTS ACTUALLY PAID BY YOU, IF ANY, FOR THE SOFTWARE.

SOME JURISDICTIONS DO NOT ALLOW THE LIMITATION OF IMPLIED WARRANTIES OR LIABILITY FOR INCIDENTAL, INDIRECT, SPECIAL, OR CONSEQUENTIAL DAMAGES, SO THE ABOVE LIMITATIONS MAY NOT ALWAYS APPLY. THE WARRANTIES IN THIS AGREEMENT GIVE YOU SPECIFIC LEGAL RIGHTS AND YOU MAY ALSO HAVE OTHER RIGHTS WHICH VARY IN ACCORDANCE WITH LOCAL LAW.

ACKNOWLEDGMENT

YOU ACKNOWLEDGE THAT YOU HAVE READ THIS AGREEMENT, UNDERSTAND IT, AND AGREE TO BE BOUND BY ITS TERMS AND CONDITIONS. YOU ALSO AGREE THAT THIS AGREEMENT IS THE COMPLETE AND EXCLUSIVE STATEMENT OF THE AGREEMENT BETWEEN YOU AND THE COMPANY AND SUPERSEDES ALL PROPOSALS OR PRIOR AGREEMENTS, ORAL, OR WRITTEN, AND ANY OTHER COMMUNICATIONS BETWEEN YOU AND THE COMPANY OR ANY REPRESENTATIVE OF THE COMPANY RELATING TO THE SUBJECT MATTER OF THIS AGREEMENT.

Should you have any questions concerning this Agreement or if you wish to contact the Company for any reason, please contact in writing at the address below.

Robin Short
Prentice Hall PTR
One Lake Street
Upper Saddle River, New Jersey 07458